THE AMERICAN COLONIES

IN THE

SEVENTEENTH CENTURY

THE AMERICAN COLONIES

IN THE

SEVENTEENTH CENTURY

BY

HERBERT L. OSGOOD, Ph.D.

PROFESSOR OF HISTORY IN COLUMBIA UNIVERSITY

VOLUME II

THE CHARTERED COLONIES. BEGINNINGS OF
SELF-GOVERNMENT

GLOUCESTER, MASS.

PETER SMITH

1957

CONTENTS

PART THIRD

THE PROPRIETARY PROVINCE IN ITS LATER FORMS

CHAPTER I

GENERAL CHARACTERISTICS OF THE LATER PROPRIETARY PROVINCES

CHAPTER II

THE LAND SYSTEM OF THE LATER PROPRIETARY PROVINCES

v

CHAPTER III

The Official System in Maryland

CHAPTER IV

The Legislature in Maryland and its Relations with the Executive

CHAPTER V

THE OFFICIAL SYSTEM IN PROPRIETARY NEW NETHERLAND

CHAPTER VI

THE TRANSITION FROM DUTCH TO ENGLISH GOVERNMENT. THE EXECUTIVE IN PROPRIETARY NEW YORK

CHAPTER VIII

The Governmental System of New Jersey

CHAPTER IX

CAROLINA AS A PROPRIETARY PROVINCE. THE CAPE FEAR AND ASHLEY RIVER SETTLEMENTS, SOUTH CAROLINA

CHAPTER X

CAROLINA AS A PROPRIETARY PROVINCE. THE ALBEMARLE SETTLEMENT, NORTH CAROLINA

CHAPTER XI

PROPRIETARY GOVERNMENT IN PENNSYLVANIA

CHAPTER XII

THE JUDICIARY IN THE LATER PROPRIETARY PROVINCES

CHAPTER XIII

ECCLESIASTICAL RELATIONS IN THE LATER PROPRIETARY
PROVINCES

CHAPTER XIV

THE FINANCIAL SYSTEM OF THE LATER PROPRIETARY PROVINCES

CHAPTER XV

The System of Defence in the Later Proprietary
Provinces

CHAPTER XVI

INDIAN RELATIONS AMONG THE LATER PROPRIETARY PROVINCES

CONCLUSION

PART THIRD

THE PROPRIETARY PROVINCE IN ITS LATER FORMS

PART THIRD

THE PROPRIETARY PRINCIPLES

CHAPTER I

GENERAL CHARACTERISTICS OF THE LATER PROPRIETARY PROVINCES

OUR review of the provinces which were founded by trading companies at the beginning of English colonization revealed the fact that they originated in a joint-stock system. That system in the colonies themselves gave rise, for a time and in varying degrees, to joint management both of land and trade. It was in that way that the incorporators or adventurers sought to overcome the great difficulties of settling a new continent and to insure, so far as it was possible, a return to themselves. Joint management of land and trade, so far as it existed and was characteristic of the provinces as such, was the reflection of the joint-stock system under which they were created. More than that cannot be safely affirmed respecting it. It developed among a people whose ancestors for centuries had lived under a system of private property, though they were acquainted with various survivals of a time when a considerable part of the soil of England was subject to joint cultivation or lay waste and unimproved. Though under the stress of a new migration they resorted to common agriculture and trade, this was but a temporary device. They remained true to their instincts as individualists. That the device was temporary has already been shown by the history of its abandonment in Virginia and also in New England, except as a phase of agrarian policy in towns whose settlement was in a way a reproduction of the original form of colonization by groups. Trade, even in New England, passed wholly into private hands. The limits of the phenomenon will be further defined by a review of the methods under which land and trade were managed in the later proprietary provinces. It

3

will be seen that they began at the point which Virginia had reached at the close of her proprietary period.

British colonization on the American continent was successfully begun by corporations, but it was not continued by them. Only four corporations resident in England were founded for this purpose, and these, with one exception, — the Georgia trustees, — came into existence prior to 1630. That this indicates a preference of the government for the proprietor or proprietary board over the corporation resident in England, as an agent for colonizing purposes, it would be rash to affirm. In that age of dawning industrialism it was easier to found a proprietorship than to establish a corporation. The initiative of a single individual, be he courtier or idealist in government and religion, would suffice for the former, while the members of a corporation, with the capital they contributed, could be brought together only as the result of a prolonged effort. Oftener than otherwise the proprietary grant was an expression of royal favor which implied nothing except reward for political or personal services rendered by the patentee. On the American continent six more or less permanent proprietorships were established directly under grants from the king — Nova Scotia, Maryland, Maine, New York, Carolina, and Pennsylvania. Of these all that proved of lasting importance, except Maryland, were founded during the period of the Restoration. Many sub-fiefs — chief among which was New Jersey — were granted by the corporations and the proprietors, but these had a brief and always a very imperfect existence. But in the multiplication of grants under this form, we discern no permanent tendency of the proprietorship to supplant the corporation as an agency in colonization.

In the corporate colonies, and indeed in the provinces which were founded by corporations, it is difficult to see any vestiges of the fief. They were dependencies of the modern industrial and political type. The obligations under which their grantees stood to the king were not distinctively personal, territorial, or military, but political in the broad sense of the term. The relations, moreover, between the grantees and their tenants or colonists were industrial and

political, not feudal. In the corporate colonies no effort
even was made to develop a system of quitrents. But in
the later proprietary provinces more of the forms of the
fief appear. In the charters of Maryland, Maine, and Carolina it is distinctly stated that the rights of the grantees
should be as great as those enjoyed by the bishops of
Durham.[1] In Penn's charter no reference is made to the
bishop of Durham, but otherwise, with the exception of
certain limitations introduced with the purpose of uphold-
ing British sovereignty, its provisions were the same as
those of the others. Tenure by free and common socage
and nominal payments to the king these grantees enjoyed,
as did the corporations which preceded them.

The reference in these charters to the bishops of Durham
indicates a certain general fact, which, indeed, would have
been true had the expression been altogether omitted. It
means that it was the intention of the crown to bestow on
these grantees rights and privileges which, in a general way,
should be the equivalent of those enjoyed in the later middle
age by a count palatine.[2] These were regalities, or powers in
their essential nature regal, and they were possessed in larger
variety and higher degree by the count palatine than by any
other English subject. In the cases of Chester and Durham
they originated in prescription, and were confirmed by royal
allowance and judicial decision. In nature they were territorial and governmental, and their combination made of the
county palatine a great fief, an *imperium in imperio*. In
Durham the bishop was the feudal superior; all land was
held directly or indirectly of him, and he possessed full seigniorial rights. Land escheated to him; he was entitled to forfeitures for felony, and even for treason. Special royal rights,
as those over forests, those to mines, wrecks, treasure-trove,

[1] The charters of Maryland and Carolina refer to the rights as coextensive with those of " any " bishop of Durham, while the language in Gorges's
charter implies that comparison was intended only with the bishopric as it
was in the seventeenth century. As the rights of the bishops had been seriously curtailed in the reign of Henry VIII, this, had it proved to be more
than legal verbiage, might have involved differences of some moment.

[2] Lapsley, The County Palatine of Durham, Harvard Historical Studies,
VIII. ; Surtees, History of Durham, I. ; Coke, Fourth Institute.

and the like, attached to him.   Baronies developed within
the palatinate, and those who held them were the tenants in
chief of the earl or bishop, served him in council, and held
toward him a relation analogous to that sustained by the
barons of England toward the king.   The lord bishop and
his county were also served by a body of officials, not so
large or so perfectly differentiated as that of the kingdom,
but still analogous to it.   Among them were a sheriff of
varied functions, a steward, coroner, constable, chamberlain,
escheators, and above all a chancellor.   Officers of the house-
hold also appear as distinct from the officers of state.   A
judicial system existed, with a *curia episcopi* at its head, and
before these courts all varieties of pleas, including pleas of
the crown, were held.   In the fourteenth century, a court of
chancery developed.   Full right of pardon belonged to the
count.   Councils in the nature of parliaments were held,
aids and subsidies were levied, tenants called out in military
array.   Money was coined ; ports, markets, and fairs established ; writs, precepts, and commissions issued ; letters of
incorporation and charters of privileges were granted.   The
counties palatine being situated on the borders and being
remote from the residence of the king, their lords had a
certain status in foreign relations.

Until the legislation of Henry VIII, by which the independence of the counties palatine was seriously curtailed, all
royal writs, except that of error, were excluded, and government was conducted with only occasional recognition of the
king.   Transitory actions, by virtue of the general principle
covering them, might be tried in an adjacent county, but all
other civil suits in which both parties were tenants of the
count must be tried in the palatinate.   But by the act of
1535 [1] it was provided that thenceforth all writs, original as
well as judicial, should run into these liberties, as they did
elsewhere in the kingdom; that indictments should be in the
name of the king; that the king should appoint civil and
criminal justices and justices of the peace in the liberties,
and that all statutes made concerning sheriffs and under-
sheriffs should be in force against the stewards and other

[1] 27 Henry VIII, c. 24.

similar officers of the counts palatine. Thus the king became the keeper of the peace in the palatinate. In the same
reign representatives were first summoned from Chester to
attend the House of Commons, though Durham remained
legally free from that obligation until 1675.[1] When the
counties palatine came to be represented in parliament, the
system of taxation existing in the realm was extended into
these liberties, and all except the shadow of former independence disappeared. Thus the growth of national unity
proved in this case an irresistible foe to the continuance of
special jurisdictions, with large and somewhat exclusive
powers, existing as they did where neither location, race, nor
culture made their survival a necessity.

It is evident that neither the London company nor the
Plymouth merchants were guided by such a model or ideal
as this. The corporate colonies exhibit none of its characteristics. The London merchants, though they founded a proprietary province, departed widely in most respects from the
forms which the palatinate suggested. It would be too
much to say that Gilbert and Raleigh had it distinctly in
mind. But Gorges, at least during his later career, was an
advocate of the feudal type of colony, and, could he have
had his way, would have firmly established it in New England. Lord Baltimore and the Carolina proprietors followed
in much the same line, though with abundant variation in
detail. In some respects also they showed greater liberality
of spirit than did Gorges. The development in New York
was strongly aristocratic and feudal, though Dutch feudalism
and wealth gained largely by trade furnished the bases on
which it rested. In New Jersey and Pennsylvania, tendencies were operative which to a large extent democratized the
province and obscured the original type. In the case of
none of these provinces did the English palatinate serve as
more than a general type, a background, a sketch, an outline.
The picture in each case was filled in with a free hand. The
province was the result of a development upon lines broadly
suggested by the palatinate, rather than an exact reproduction

[1] Durham was represented in the three parliaments of the Protectorate.
Surtees, 1, 106.

or copy of the original.   The offspring, if a filial relation
in any true sense could be affirmed, grew to maturity under
physical and social conditions which were very different from
those to which the parent was subjected.   Corresponding
variations of type were the result.   These appear in the
land system, in the official system, in local subdivisions and
government, in the administration of affairs in all departments.

The object of the study of these provinces as institutions
is to show how, while they were fundamentally of the same
type, they exhibit many variations and divergences from it.
The general outcome from the whole, and the contribution
brought through each province to the total result, will appear
only after such a comparison.   Social and political forces of
different kinds, and combined in various ways, operating
both upon the proprietors and the people of the provinces,
produced the final result.   In order to show exhaustively
what the result was and why it was, all the sources of the
history of the period, so far as they relate to the provinces
in question, might well be brought into requisition.   All,
however, that can now be done is to indicate some of the
leading phases of the process.

By the Maryland charter, which reveals as distinctly as
any the characteristics of this form of grant, the patentee,
his heirs and assigns, were given all and as ample rights,
jurisdictions, and immunities within the limits of the province, as were or had been enjoyed by any bishop of Durham
within his bishopric or county palatine.   This also is the
meaning of the statement that Lord Baltimore and his heirs
were made the " true and absolute lords and proprietaries "
of the region.   The territory granted was, moreover, expressly
made a province, a name was given to it, and it was declared
that it should be independent of all other provinces.[1]   The
fact that the grant was made to Lord Baltimore, his heirs
and assigns, shows that it was heritable with power of alienation in the grantee.   It could be leased, sold, or otherwise
disposed of, like any estate of land; and in the case of other
proprietary grants such transfers were common.   It was pro-

[1] This separated it from Virginia.

vided that the proprietor, though tenant in chief, should
hold by socage, paying annually a nominal rent to the king.
The province was made subject to the king's sovereign control, and all its inhabitants were his liegemen. They retained
the right to buy, receive, and hold lands, and corresponding
to this the proprietor was empowered to grant or lease the
lands of the province to settlers in fee simple or fee tail.
The operation of the statute *quia emptores* within the province was suspended, so as to admit of subinfeudation, and in
addition it was expressly provided that grants should be held
of the proprietor and not of the king. Upon the estates thus
bestowed, power was given the proprietor to erect manors
with manorial courts and view of frank-pledge. These were
the seigniorial or territorial rights and powers, so far as they
were expressed in the charter. Few of them, and those not
the most characteristic, appear in the patents issued to corporations. Connected with them more or less closely was
the right to transport colonists and their goods to the province, and to carry on trade with the settlers. In the exercise
of this power harbors were to be erected, where exclusively
the business of import and export should be carried on,
while taxes and subsidies imposed at the ports were reserved
to the proprietor.

But governmental powers, or the minor regalities, were
also bestowed on the proprietor in full measure. He was
authorized to legislate through an assembly of the freemen
concerning all matters of public interest and private utility
within the province. The laws thus passed should be published under the proprietor's seal, and executed by him on
all inhabitants of the province, and on all going to and proceeding from it, either to England or to foreign countries.
The right to issue ordinances was bestowed in such a way as
to supplement the legislative power, and, under the general limitations specified in the act 31 Henry VIII, c. 8,
concerning proclamations, it was to be used for the preservation of the peace, and the better government of the people,
when there was not time to call the deputies together. The
proprietor was given authority to inflict all punishments,
even to the death penalty (*haute justice*), and to pardon

every crime which he could punish.   As the statute of
Henry VIII limiting the independence of the counts palatine
did not extend to plantations, Baltimore was empowered to
establish courts and appoint all officers, judicial and others,
who were necessary for the execution of the laws.   He was
also given the right to bestow titles of honor, erect towns
and boroughs, and incorporate cities.   The powers of a
captain general were given him, with authority by proper
means to arm and train the inhabitants, and lead them in
defensive war.   Closely connected with this was the right
to execute martial law for the suppression of rebellion.   The
advowson of churches and chapels, the right to found these
and to cause them to be consecrated according to the ecclesiastical laws of England, was also bestowed.   The language
used apparently excluded the consecrating of other than
Anglican churches.   The organization of the government
was left wholly to the proprietor.   The only limitation on
the legislative and ordinance powers was, that the enactments and orders issued should be consonant to reason, and
as agreeable as might be to the laws and rights of England.
No provision was made for the submission of the acts of the
legislature to the king, or for appeal to the English courts,
though cases could probably be removed into those courts
under the forms and conditions which of old had applied to
the palatinates.   Moreover, the right to hear appeals existed
by virtue of the sovereign power of the crown, and the right
to claim its advantages belonged to the subject by common
law.   Finally, following in the strictest manner the principle
of immunity, the king expressly renounced the right to levy
taxes upon the province.   He declared that he would not
levy any tax or contribution on the persons, lands, or goods
of its inhabitants, either in the province or in the ports of
the same.   So far as American charters are concerned, this
feature of the grant is unique.   In general it is true that the
provisions of this charter concerning government are much
more full and precise than those of the earlier charters to
corporations, those documents being mainly concerned with
the internal organization of the companies, and containing
nothing specific concerning the relations between the com-

panies and their colonists.   The existence of colonial assem-

In their provisions the charter of Maine and that of Carolina, except in the point last mentioned, differ only in slight
details from the Maryland patent.   The Carolina charter
provided for a board of eight proprietors, but as they were
not incorporated, no regulations as to the way in which
they should hold their meetings appear.   In the grant of
Maine to Sir Ferdinando Gorges the way was left open for
the proper exercise of royal control by the provision that in
matters of government the province should be subject to the
regulations issued by the board of commissioners of plantations, which had been created in 1634.   By implication in
the Carolina charter the right of the colonists to appeal to
the English courts was guarantied in the clause providing that they should not answer in any courts outside the
province, except those of England.   Each charter had special
provisions concerning religion, and to an extent also concerning trade.   The charter of New York was brief, but it
outlined the salient features of the palatinate.   It made
express provision for appeals, but included no reference to a
legislature.

The charter of Pennsylvania was granted late, after some
of the defects in the proprietary system had begun to appear.
These arose from the difficulty of enforcing royal control, so
as to secure the trade interests of the mother country and the
defence of the empire.   Hence the points in which Penn's
charter differs from the earlier patents have reference mainly
to relations with the home government.   The right of the
inhabitants of the province to appeal to the king was
expressly guarantied.   It was provided that, within five
years after their passage, all acts of the general assembly
should be submitted to the king for his acceptance or rejection, and that, if they were not rejected within six months
after presentation, they should stand.   The reasons, so far
as mentioned, which should justify rejection, were incon-
sistency with the lawful and sovereign prerogatives of the
king and with the faith and allegiance due to the government of the realm.   The proprietor was also required to

keep an agent resident in or near London, so that he might
appear at courts to answer any complaints against the proprietor and pay damages.   If for one year there should be
no such agent, or if for a year he should neglect to answer
for penalties, it was declared lawful for the crown to resume
the government of the province and keep it till payment
should be made.   The king also agreed to levy no tax on
the province without the consent of the proprietor or chief
governor, the consent of the assembly, or by act of parliament.   Thus the possibility that parliament might tax the
colony was clearly recognized.   This group of provisions
gives a completeness to the Pennsylvania grant, so far as
relations to the home government are concerned, which
appears in no other charter.   Such being the case, there
was no need of specifically guarantying to colonists the
rights of English subjects.   Finally, the absence of any
clause authorizing the bestowment of titles of nobility is
suggestive of the political views of the Quaker proprietor.

The difference between the institution sketched in these
charters and the corporate colony is very clear.   When a
proprietary province of this type was created the governmental machinery of the palatinate was not removed into
America, as was done in the case of the corporation of
Massachusetts.   That would have been useless, to say nothing of its impracticability, for, in the case of the proprietorship, the grantee was a natural person, and the form of the
province could not be affected by the place of his residence.
Its organization would be the same, whether he resided in
England or in the territory which had been granted to him.
The spirit also in which the powers of the proprietor were
administered would not necessarily be modified to a great
degree by his residence in the province.   As a matter of
fact, the American proprietors often spent a part of
their time in their provinces, and part in England.   When
in their provinces, it would be less easy to reach them by
writ than if they were in England ; but power was transmitted, held, and exercised in the same way, whatever might
be the place of residence chosen by the proprietor.   As the
proprietor was the grantee of power, and all was derived

through him, however intimate might be his relation to the
province, he could never lose his identity and become merged
in it, as was the case with the corporation, when it was removed into the colony or created on the place. Whether
resident in England or in America, he always remained distinct from the province, in the same sense as that in which
the king is distinct from the kingdom. He held strictly by
hereditary right, and the powers to which he was entitled
were not derived from the province or its inhabitants.
They were not the grantees, as might be true in the case
of the corporation, and therefore could neither hold land
nor exercise political rights except as the result of concessions made by or through the proprietor. The proprietor,
and not a general court, or general assembly, was the origin
and centre of the provincial organism. Authority proceeded
originally from above downward, though its exercise was
greatly modified and limited by influences which came from
below upward. The province in this form was a miniature
kingdom, and the proprietor, if he chose to exercise his
powers, was a petty king. To be sure, the powers which he
exercised were not sovereign, but, as Coke said, they were
kinglike, and they were used under the same forms as if
they had been sovereign. In all of the later proprietary
provinces where a serious effort was made to uphold the
power of the executive, we find on a small scale and with
modifications a reproduction of the governmental forms and
usages of the kingdom of England.

The province, therefore, was not democratic, and, if it remained true to its essential nature, it could not become so.
But its nature could be obscured and changed. As an institution it could be changed by the development within it of elements of a popular character, and by their encroachment upon
the powers of the proprietor. The legislature might gradually
limit or draw to itself the powers of the executive, and thus
come to exercise a controlling influence. English institutions in their growth since the Norman period have passed
through a development of that nature ; and in the American
provinces an analogous process may be seen at work, though
in them the time required for its unfolding was much shorter

than in the parent kingdom. The history of the American provinces is emphatically the history of the adaptation of English institutions to the conditions of life on a newly settled continent. There the tendencies favorable to the democratic element in the constitution of the province were stronger than they were in England prior to the close of the eighteenth century, while the obstacles to its development were less powerful than in the mother country. Through migration to the New World the bonds of custom were relaxed, and freer scope was given to innovation. Those who became colonists came largely from the classes which were least wedded to the aristocratic and monarchical institutions of the Old World. The political and social privileges which were attached to land-holding in England could never be reproduced in a new country, and under an exclusively socage tenure. There was necessarily far less social inequality in the colonies than in the old countries, and the proprietor could scarcely hope that an aristocracy would develop and become a support for his power. So sparsely were the colonies settled, that large estates, even where they existed, had relatively few tenants, and hence yielded only a small income. The proprietor, with his hundreds of thousands of acres, might be and often was land poor. He, moreover, possessed none of the dignity which belongs to the office and title of king. He himself was a subject, and, whether peer or commoner, inviolability attached to his person in no higher degree than it did to any of his class among the population of England. The church could awaken for him only the respect which attaches to magistracy. The proprietor also, in any struggle upon which he was forced to enter for the maintenance of his claims, could command only the resources of a single family or group of families. Sometimes these resources were pitifully small, and were even the subject of litigation in the bankruptcy court. In any event they were likely to be too limited to admit of great displays of political energy, to say nothing of military power. These all are causes and tendencies which facilitated the democratizing of the American province, which made the process shorter and more certain of ultimate success than in the European king-

dom.   But it took the entire colonial period of our history
and a revolution at its close to complete this course of development, and thus to transform the province into the
democratic commonwealth.   A transformation which in the
case of the corporate colony was virtually effected by a single
act, required for its completion in the province a century and
a half.   This of itself is adequate proof of the radical difference between the two forms of colonial government which
we are studying.   The province could not be democratized
until the proprietor was gotten rid of, and that object was
not attained until independence of England was declared.

CHAPTER II

THE LAND SYSTEM OF THE LATER PROPRIETARY
PROVINCES

THE most prominent feature of the New England land system was the town grant, which in every case became the territorial basis of a group settlement. Though grants were made by the general court to individuals, they were the exception rather than the rule. The result was that the landed estate of nearly every individual in New England was located in one or more towns, and was subject to the regulations which were made by towns for the management of land. The territorial affairs of the colony were largely administered through the towns as agencies. Land passed from joint control to individual ownership chiefly by means of town allotments. The towns came nearer to performing the function of proprietors than did any other administrative bodies in New England.

In the corporate colonies, moreover, the characteristic elements of the fief were lacking. The quitrent does not appear as a distinct form of income, and land was not extensively leased. The result was that the tenement or holding, which was so characteristic of English land law, was practically obliterated, and an allodial system was substituted. Had the New England governments sought revenue from the land in the form of rents, this result could not have followed. A system of tenure would have been perpetuated, and the general court would have acted as a proprietor. As it was, the court avoided the private legal attitude toward land, and kept itself well within the range of public law. The only revenue which it sought from land was in the form of taxes. This is one of the most notable consequences which resulted from the founding of the corporate colonies of New England.

The territorial relations within the provinces were quite unlike this. Though the provinces, in this as in all other matters, exhibit much variety of practice, the distinction between them and the corporate colonies, when considered territorially, is clear and indisputable. The proprietary grant was an estate of inheritance, descending to heirs. The attitude of the proprietors toward their provinces, both legally and actually, was that of landlords toward a private estate. They were investors, speculators if you please, in land. They advertised for settlers, and, in doing so, an ever present motive with them was the desire to secure more private income from their land. Like the Duke of York, they might watch carefully the trade of their provinces, in order that revenue from that source might be increased. Like William Penn, they might be idealists. But investors in land they must be by virtue of their proprietary relation. This, when combined with powers of government, made them territorial lords, and in order to collect their quitrents and fines on alienation, they had to institute a system of territorial administration.

Such a system of administration Virginia had while the London company was its proprietor. Had the company continued to exist until individual property had become firmly established within the province, a land system like that of the other proprietary provinces would doubtless have developed in Virginia. But in one respect Virginia under the company would have differed from the provinces with individual proprietors or proprietary boards; and in this respect its position would have resembled that of the corporate colonies of New England. As a province, whose proprietor was a corporation, it would have passed to successors, and would not have been liable to the conditions of natural inheritance. As long as the corporation continued, the province was not likely to have been divided or the continuity of its existence broken by a sudden change of owners or rulers. In Virginia, as well as in the corporate colonies, these conditions have furnished a suggestion of the territorial, as well as the political, unity of the modern state.

Provinces whose proprietors were natural persons did not

enjoy this guaranty. Not only might the entire province
be sold, mortgaged, leased, devised, or conveyed in trust, like
a farm or homestead, but simply by the process of inheritance
it might be divided among any number of heirs.

The Duke of York, in 1664, sold New Jersey to Lord
Berkeley and Sir George Carteret, and the sale was effected
by deeds of lease and release.[1] By that act the province
which the duke had just received from the crown was
divided, and his territorial rights over a part of it went to
the purchasers. But this was only the beginning of the process of subdivision. By subsequent agreements and conveyances not only was New Jersey itself divided, but the number
of proprietors of each share was very largely increased. In
the case of West Jersey this was effected by the creation of
trusteeships, and by the admission of settlers to the position
of proprietors. The proprietors of East Jersey were increased from one to twenty-four by successive sales of individual shares of the province. So large became the number
of proprietors that it was necessary in each of these provinces to choose a council or committee for the management
of their affairs. The history of New Jersey suggests the
process by which the fiefs of continental Europe were subdivided.

In 1708 William Penn, for £6600, mortgaged Pennsylvania
to Henry Gouldey, Joshua Gee, and seven other individuals
in England. When, in 1718, Penn died, the mortgage had
not been entirely paid off. In his will he devised the government of the province and territories to the Earls of
Oxford, Mortimer, and Powlett and their heirs in trust, to
dispose thereof to the queen or any other person, as advantage should dictate. To his widow and eleven others, part
resident in England and part in America, he devised all his
lands, rents, and other profits in Pennsylvania, the territories,
or elsewhere on the continent, in trust with instruction to
sell or otherwise dispose of enough to pay his debts. Of
that which remained, all except thirty thousand acres should
be bestowed by the trustees on the three sons of the founder

---

[1] Leaming and Spicer, Grants and Concessions, 8 ; N. J. Archives, I. 8,
10.

by his second wife — John, Thomas, and Richard Penn. All
the personal estate and arrears of rent he gave to his wife
for the equal benefit of herself and her children, and her he
made sole executrix. As, after his father's death, William
Penn, Jr., the heir-at-law, claimed the government of the
province, some delay arose, resulting in a suit in chancery.
It was, however, finally decided that the sons by the second
marriage should inherit both the territorial and governmental
rights as designated in the will.[1]

By transfers and the process of natural inheritance the
personnel of the board of Carolina proprietors had been
changed, and in the case of some seats repeatedly so, when
in 1729 the act of parliament was passed establishing an
agreement with seven of their number for the surrender of
their title and interest in the province to the crown.[2] Here,
as in the case of other provinces with multiple proprietors,
the colony might upon agreement have been divided. The
undivided shares might at any time have become divided
shares. That the single proprietor could do the same has
been shown by reference to the origin of New Jersey.
That this did not occur in the history of Maryland is due
to good fortune and good management. In the American
proprietary provinces there was the same possibility of the
indefinite subdivision of territory which in the middle age
we find working itself out in the states of continental Europe.
These general observations will open the way to the more
specific discussion of the proprietary land system.

In all the later proprietary charters, except that of New
York, the operation of the statute *quia emptores* was expressly
suspended, so far as relations between the proprietor and his
immediate grantees were concerned. By virtue of this provision each proprietor, or board of proprietors, as mesne lord,
became the centre from which originated an indefinite number of grants. These were held directly of the proprietor,
and through him of the crown. In practice the same was
true also in New York, although no reference was made to
the statute *quia emptores* in its charter. In the provinces of

[1] Proud, History of Pennsylvania, II. 115–124.
[2] N. C. Col. Recs. III. 34 *et seq.*

this class it was left to the proprietor to make grants on such conditions as he chose — limited by the nature of his own patent, — to erect or permit the erection of manors, to devise the machinery necessary for surveying, issuing, and recording grants and collecting rents.

Preparatory to the exercise of the power thus bestowed in the charters, the proprietors issued so-called " concessions," or "conditions of plantation," stating the terms on which they would grant lands to colonists. As settlement progressed these were modified, either by new concessions or by instructions to the governors. These were not infrequently accompanied by statements of the physical advantages of the country and relations of recent voyages thither, all intended as a form of advertisement for settlers. Lord Baltimore issued conditions[1] of plantation in 1633, 1636, 1642, 1648. The earliest issue contained offers made to the first body of settlers before they left England, which when accepted became a contract between them individually and the proprietor. It provided that each free planter should pay the cost of his outfit and transportation, which amounted to about £20. To every married man who thus provided for the voyage, and for that of his family, the proprietor promised one hundred acres of land for himself, and one hundred for his wife, if she accompanied him ; one hundred acres also for each adult servant, and fifty for each child under sixteen years of age. Two thousand acres of land should also be given to each adventurer who, in the year 1633, should take into the province, for the purpose of settlement, five men between the ages of sixteen and fifty.[2] In 1636 these conditions were extended so as to apply to settlers who had arrived subsequent to 1633. One thousand acres were now promised for every five men whom a colonist or adventurer brought over. By each new issue, which came in the form of a proclamation or an instruction to the governor, former conditions were amended or revoked. In 1642 the amount of land promised to each individual settler of adult age was reduced

---

[1] Calvert Papers, I, 138. Md. Arch., Proceedings of Council, 1636–1667, 47, 99, 223.

[2] Proceedings of Council, 1636–1667, 47.

from one hundred acres to fifty acres. The conditions of
1648 were especially elaborate, and provided at length for
the erection of manors, the reserve of one-sixth of each
manor as demesne, and the grant of the remainder by the
lord to tenants under such terms as should not infringe on
the jurisdiction of the proprietor or prevent his collecting
the rents reserved in the original patents. These privileges
were to obtain in every grant of two thousand acres, though
under earlier conditions grants of one thousand acres might
carry with them manorial rights.

The conditions of plantation involved simply the renewed
application of the system of head rights, which obtained in
proprietary Virginia and continued in that province long
after it came under the government of the crown. As land
was the largest and most important factor in production
over which the proprietor had control, he could not do otherwise than dispose of it somewhat freely for the purpose of
encouraging emigration. The system served this purpose
well throughout the early history of all the provinces. Still
these rights were subject to transfer, and fraud was sometimes attempted or committed[1] in the proof of claims which
were alleged to have originated under them. For this reason,
among others, in 1683, by proclamation of the proprietor,
this method of obtaining land in Maryland was abolished.
Henceforth land could be procured only by the payment of
purchase or caution money, the sums being payable partly in
tobacco and partly in specie.[2]

The concessions which were issued by the proprietors of
Carolina, of the Jerseys, and Pennsylvania, differed in no
essential particular from those which had as their object the
encouragement of colonization in Maryland. In 1663 the
proprietors of Carolina offered one hundred acres of land to
every "present undertaker," fifty acres for every man servant, and thirty acres for every woman servant whom he
should bring or send into the province.[3] When, in 1665, the
Barbadians undertook to settle at Cape Fear, the proprietors

---

[1] Bruce, Economic History of Virginia, I. 518.
[2] Md. Arch., Proceedings of Council, 1667–1688, 391, 394.
[3] N. C. Recs. I. 45.

reached a special agreement with them.[1] It provided that five hundred acres of land should be granted in return for every thousand pounds of sugar which were subscribed toward the enterprise, and more or less in proportion to the amount of subscriptions. At the same time the conditions which were to apply to the entire province were prescribed in the Concessions and Agreement of 1665. In these provision was made for an elaborate system of head rights, varying with each successive year between 1665 and the close of 1667. Within the county of Clarendon the maximum for freemen should be one hundred acres and the minimum fifty acres. The larger amount should be bestowed on those who arrived in 1665, and the smaller on those who should delay till 1667. In Albemarle the corresponding offers were eighty and forty acres respectively. The Fundamental Constitutions, though they designated the areas of the baronial grants alone, were in the nature of a great territorial concession for the entire province. During the period when efforts were being made to put them into force, various instructions concerning grants of land were issued by the proprietors.

In 'New Jersey the Concessions and Agreement were put into force in 1665. Though the document was an almost verbatim reproduction of that issued the same year by the Carolina proprietors, in the provisions concerning land the grants offered in the form of head rights were larger by one-half than those which were intended for Clarendon county in Carolina. In both provinces they were modified or wholly abandoned by later instructions, while the later proprietors of both the Jerseys issued a variety of concessions of their own.

William Penn, as soon as he had secured the charter of his province, offered land for sale in "proprieties" of five thousand acres each, the price of each to be £100. Smaller estates of two hundred acres each would also be granted, subject to the immediate payment of a quitrent. Masters should receive fifty acres for each servant they brought over, and fifty acres should be given to each servant

[1] N. C. Recs. I. 77 *et seq.*

when his term of service expired.[1] The "first purchasers"
were those who took up land under these and other conditions which were issued before Penn left England on his
first visit to the province. In an elaborate series of "conditions," which were issued in July, 1681,[2] the proprietor
sought to regulate the granting of land both in town and
country. In one clause of these Penn insisted that every
grantee, within three years, should begin the settlement and
improvement of his land, or it might be granted to others.
A condition like this, whenever possible, was insisted on by
all proprietors. Penn was always careful to assert his right
to dispose of the land of his province on such terms as he
chose to make with would-be settlers, and this led to many
changes in the terms of grants. These were occasioned not
only by differences of location and soil, but by the wishes
of both parties to the contracts.[3] The same course was followed by all proprietors, and in each instance it furnishes an
additional illustration of the fact that the land of the province was always regarded as a private estate.

The course of development in New York differed somewhat from that of other provinces, owing to the fact of its
early occupation by the Dutch. The settlement of Dutch in
New Jersey, and of both Dutch and Swedes on the Delaware,
had a slight modifying effect there also. Penn confirmed
titles of this origin,[4] so far as they lay within his province.
New Netherland, as will be shown at greater length in a
subsequent chapter, was a Dutch proprietary province, of
which the West India company was the immediate proprietor. The company may be said to have inaugurated a land
system in New Netherland with the issue, in 1629, of the
Freedoms and Exemptions. They were the equivalent among
the Dutch of the conditions of plantation which were issued
by the English proprietors. Through them provision was
made for the extension of settlement outside of Manhattan
island and its immediate vicinity. The patroonships and

---

[1] Shepherd, Proprietary Government in Pennsylvania, 18.
[2] Hazard, Annals of Pennsylvania, 516.
[3] Huston, Land Titles in Pennsylvania, 5, 63.
[4] *Ibid.* 26.

colonies which originated under the authority of the Freedoms and Exemptions, together with villages and very many
small grants, the English found in existence when they took
possession of the province.   They were, therefore, not compelled to advertise for settlers, as was the case when the
colonization of a province had to be begun.   Both in 1664
and in 1674 Dutch titles were confirmed, and on both occasions there was a general renewal of patents.   By this means
tenure of the English proprietor, and afterward of the crown,
was substituted for the very similar Dutch tenure, and the
change was accompanied by the administration of the oath
of allegiance to the king.[1]

By confiscating the estate of the West India company —
one of Governor Nicolls's earliest acts — the proprietors secured all of the unoccupied land in the province.   Conditions
for new planters were issued by the governor, in which regulations were prescribed for the purchase of land from the
Indians, temporary exemption from taxes and settlement of
towns.   Special reference was made to land at Esopus, as
being ready for occupation.[2]   When, after the Dutch reoccupation, Andros became governor, he was ordered in the
assignment of lands to select his rules both from those which
were followed in New England and from those which obtained in Maryland.

Upon the conditions of plantation, and the extent to which
they were observed, depended the size and variety of estates
within the provinces.   In general, estates were much larger
in the provinces than they were in the corporate colonies.
The few score of acres which, as the result of a series of
town allotments, ordinarily came into the possession of a
New England farmer, were almost insignificant when compared with the princely estates of the Dutch patroons, with
the seigniories and baronies which the proprietors of Carolina
intended for themselves and their provincial nobility, with
the manors which the Calverts or Penn reserved for them-

---

[1] N. Y. Col. Docs. II. 250 ; N. Y. Col. Laws, I. 44, 57, 80, 93 ; State
Library Bulletin, No. 2, General Entries, I. 161.

[2] Smith, History of New York, ed. of 1829, I. 35. This does not appear
in any collection of sources.

selves or granted to their wealthiest colonists.   The territory   CHAP.
within the New England colonies was limited, when com-   II.
pared with the broad stretches which were included in many
of the proprietary grants.   Moreover, though exceptions appear in the cases of a few trusted magistrates and others, yet
generally the system of town grants in New England necessitated small estates.   We have already seen how it tended
toward agrarian equality.

The proprietary policy did not impose so strict a limitation.   The system of head rights was elastic, and it could
be made increasingly so by more or less illegitimate traffic
in them.[1]   In New England there was no opportunity for
proprietary reserves, but in the provinces they, with manors,
occupy a large place in the projects of all the proprietors.
In Maryland, prior to 1676, about sixty manors were erected,
containing on an average about three thousand acres each.[2]
As the special manorial privileges which accompanied those
grants were exercised in only a few cases, the great majority
of them were only large freehold estates.

In 1665 the proprietor issued instructions that in every
county at least two manors, each containing not less than
six thousand acres of land, be surveyed and set apart as
reserves for himself.[3]   These, in the beginning, were placed
under stewards, who leased them in parcels to tenants.   Reserves were also made by the proprietors for the purpose of
securing control of unusually rich land or land thought to
contain mineral deposits, or in order to confine settlement to
parts of the province where it was thought desirable that it
should be made.   Though parts of the proprietary reserves
were leased, they were not surveyed or named, as were the
manors.[4]   As all land was liable to escheat, measures were
adopted to secure the rights of the proprietor in this relation.

In the projects of the Carolina proprietors manors and
proprietary reserves occupied a leading place.   In the proposals of 1663, which were intended for Cape Fear, the board

---

[1] Bruce, Economic History of Virginia, I. 519.
[2] Mereness, Maryland as a Proprietary Province, 52, 105.
[3] Kilty, Landholder's Assistant, 95 *et seq.*
[4] Md. Arch., Correspondence of Governor Sharpe, I. 426.

announced that it would reserve twenty thousand acres of land near each settlement that might be formed, and this should be laid out for the proprietors by their agents in such a way as not to incommode the colonists. Later in the same year they announced that a tract of the same size should be located in Albemarle, near a town which it was proposed to found there. In the agreement of 1665 with the Barbadians, provision was made that the land of the counties of Clarendon and Albemarle, exclusive of cities, towns, and lots adjacent thereto, should be divided into tracts varying from twenty-two hundred to twenty-two thousand acres each, and one-eleventh of these by lot should be reserved for the proprietors. In the scheme of the Fundamental Constitutions the eight seigniories in each county — each consisting of twelve thousand acres — were intended to be proprietary reserves. The eight baronies in each county were to be bestowed on the provincial nobility. In order to keep these estates together, it was provided that, after 1701, neither proprietors nor provincial nobles should have the power of alienating or dividing their estates. Tracts of more than three thousand, and less than twelve thousand, acres might be erected into manors.

To the dozen or more individuals who in Carolina were created landgraves patents of a general character[1] were issued, calling in each case for a grant of forty-eight thousand acres. The same was done in the case of those who were created caciques, each patent in that case calling for twenty-four thousand acres. In many cases these grants were never located or surveyed, and later their legality was for this reason denied. The seigniories, likewise, dwindled to ordinary proprietary reserves, taking in a few instances the form of a project for a large plantation. In one instance an attempt was made to locate such a grant within one of the colonies.[2] Ashley, Carteret, and Colleton, who had formed a partnership for the purpose, ordered that forty-five hundred acres should be reserved at Port Royal, which they intended to people with servants. The reserve was actually

---

[1] Smith, South Carolina as a Royal Province, 35.
[2] Shaftesbury Papers, 125 *et seq.*

made at Albemarle Point, and it apparently contained only
four hundred and twenty acres.[1]   We lose sight of it when
the removal was made to Oyster Point, or Charlestown.
Later the Earl of Shaftesbury began a plantation at Locke
island, but in less than a year it was abandoned.[2]   We hear
of various grants ranging from one thousand to two thousand acres each; but of enormous estates, such as were contemplated in Locke's scheme, none took permanent form.

In New Jersey about fifteen thousand acres of upland and
meadow near the junction of the Hackensack and Passaic
rivers were granted to Captain William Sandford.   Adjoin-
ing it on the north another large grant was made to Captain
John Berry.   A large purchase which had been made in the
Dutch period, and which lay west of the Raritan,[3] was confirmed.   But neither these, nor other similar grants in New
Jersey, were organized as manors.   The proprietors, however,
announced that they would reserve to themselves one-eleventh
of all grants.

The sale of East Jersey in 1682 by the heirs of Sir George
Carteret to William Penn and his eleven associates[4] was followed by the settlement of the valley of the Raritan.   But
before their plans for this and for the building of the town of
Perth Amboy were completed, each of the twelve proprietors
sold one-half of his share in the province to a new associate,
thus making a board of twenty-four for East Jersey.   As
many of the new proprietors were Scotchmen, an appeal for
colonists was specially addressed to that nation.   Various
new concessions were published, the object of which was to
open the way for the grant of moderate-sized freeholds to
colonists, and to secure for the proprietors ample estates in
the province.   The grants ranged in most cases from three
hundred to two thousand acres each.   Many of them were
made to proprietors, and to individuals who were directly
associated with them in the enterprise.   Both the English

[1] Shaftesbury Papers, 269, 371.   Also the map.

[2] *Ibid.* 438–447, 468, 473, 474 ; Rivers, 387.

[3] Whitehead, East Jersey under the Proprietors, 54, 55 ; Winfield, Land
Titles in Hudson County ; East Jersey Deeds, Liber I, calendared in N. J.
Arch. XXI. 6, 7.   [4] Whitehead, 102, 314 *et seq.*

and Scotch proprietors made reserves for themselves,[1] individually and as distinct groups or partnerships. Successive divisions of unimproved land were made among the
proprietors in 1686, 1698, 1702, 1739, 1740, and 1744.[2] Each
proprietor sought to plant colonists, either as servants or
freeholders, on those parts of his share which he did not
choose to retain. By means of sale and inheritance very
many changes of ownership took place in the proprietary
shares. Many of them were divided and subdivided, till in
some cases they appear as a thirty-second or a fortieth of an
original twenty-fourth of the province.[3]

West Jersey consisted, at the beginning, of Fenwick's colony, and of the undivided nine-tenths of the province which
was held by three trustees. Fenwick's colony, which comprised one-tenth of the province, was founded among the
sparse settlements of the Dutch and Swedes near Salem. It
had a distinct land system, which was essentially that of a
manor. With the nine-tenths the trustees — Penn, Lawrie,
and Lucas — dealt more systematically than did the East
Jersey proprietors with their share of the original province.
In 1677 an elaborate set of Concessions and Agreements was
prepared, mostly by Penn himself, containing regulations for
the granting of land and organization of government in West
Jersey.[4] It was provided that this business should be actually done by commissioners acting under appointment from
the proprietors, assisted by such subordinate officials as might
be necessary. The land along the east bank of Delaware
river from Assunpink creek[5] to Cape May was divided into
ten equal parts, of which one went, as has been stated, to
John Fenwick. Each of these parts was known as a tenth.
They were gradually to be taken up as the number of settlers

[1] N. J. Arch. I. 464–469 ; Whitehead, 136 n.
[2] Whitehead, 145 n., 162 (map).
[3] The entire list of conveyances and inheritances, showing the descent of
title among the proprietors until 1745, is given in Schedule No. II, annexed
to the New Jersey Bill in Chancery. Instances of such descent are given in
the text of the bill. In N. J. Arch. I. 528, is a list of the proprietors with
their shares, as they were in April, 1687.
[4] N. J. Arch. I. 241 ; Grants and Concessions, 382.
[5] Smith, History of New Jersey, 131.

increased. To this end each tenth was to be divided into
ten proprieties, which might be disposed of piecemeal, or all
together, for the founding of what in Fenwick's case, and in
similar cases in other provinces, was called a colony. Provision was made for the customary system of head rights,
varying in extent with the date of the claims. The commissioners were ordered to reserve proper sites for towns, and
to see that the towns were regularly built. Settlement
within a specified time was required, later commissioners
insisting that it should begin within six months after the
survey.

The first considerable groups of colonists which came to
West Jersey were Quakers from Yorkshire and London.[1]
The Yorkshire people selected for their place of settlement a
tenth which lay immediately below the falls of the Delaware.
The colonists from London first established themselves in a
tenth near the later town of Gloucester. But, subsequently,
at the request of the Yorkshire proprietors, the Londoners
removed up the river, and the two companies united in the
settlement of the town of Burlington.

William Penn made provision from the outset for grants
of considerable size within his province. In the "conditions
and concessions" which he issued in England, and which
were intended for the "first purchasers," the purchase of
estates of a thousand acres or more was regarded as likely
in many cases to occur. Those who should take up five
thousand acres or more might be organized into townships.
For every hundred thousand acres which were granted the
proprietor announced his intention of reserving ten thousand
for himself.[2] The reserves in Pennsylvania were therefore
known as proprietary tenths. A considerable number of
estates from this land were organized as manors, though
none of them ever possessed manorial courts. A few grants,
as for example that to the Free Society of Traders, were also
known as manors, but they were never really anything more
than large estates of land on which lived certain rent-
paying tenants.

[1] Smith, 92.
[2] Shepherd, Proprietary Government in Pennsylvania, 18.

The only fully developed manors which ever existed within the English-American colonies were in New York. The institution was of Dutch origin, though it was perpetuated by the English until, in the eighteenth century, it became a leading feature of the land system of that province. In the Freedoms and Exemptions, which gave rise to the system, provision was made for two varieties of grants — patroonships and colonies. All land within New Netherland, outside of Manhattan island, might be granted under one or other of these forms. At first, steps were taken which seemed likely to make the patroonship — the large estate — the predominant form of grant. Presuming that, as elsewhere, the patroons would prefer sites along the river courses, it was specified that their grants might extend for sixteen English miles along one side of a navigable river, or eight miles on each of both sides, and as far back into the country as conditions might determine. It thus appears that no exact limit was set to the size of these estates. The grants of land should be absolute, with the right of perpetual inheritance in the grantee, and should carry with them high and low jurisdiction, fishing and milling rights, and liberty to dispose of the heritage by will. Adjacent lands might also be made use of by the patroons so long as they were not granted away by the company, and none could settle near their bounds without the consent of the patroons. The officials, free settlers, servants, cattle, and farming implements that were needed in the colonizing of these grants should be transported to New Netherland at specified rates in the ships of the company, or, if these were lacking, in vessels sent under license by the patroons. For ten years the colonists should be free from taxes and customs, and the patroons themselves should be exempt for eight years, except from customs on fish caught on the coast of New Netherland and exported. Though subject in many ways to the control of the company, especially in respect of trade and defence, the patroonships were intended to be centres of local government, and for that reason the lords were given the right to issue instructions to their colonists, though these must be in harmony with the law of the company and of the province.

In the patroonships many of the features of continental CHAP.
feudalism were reflected.   They carried with them more   II.
definite judicial powers than did any similar English grants,
while specific provision was made for the banalities and for
rights of trade.   The Exemptions also contemplated estates
which would be larger than any Virginia plantations, Maryland manors, or Carolina baronies.   They might easily reach
the area of two hundred thousand acres each, while about
fifty thousand acres was the maximum contemplated in Carolina grants, and eighty thousand or one hundred thousand
acres in the Virginia grants.   If many of them developed,
they would certainly imperil the supremacy of the company,
though they might well give rise to a certain type of colonization that was more vigorous and beneficial than any
which rested mainly on the fur trade.

Immediately certain wealthy directors of the company
secured grants, and the patroonships of Rensselaerswyck
and Pavonia on the North river, and that of Swaanendael
on the South river, were secured.   The area of the first soon
reached upwards of seven hundred thousand acres.   In order
to facilitate settlement two associations [1] were formed by
the patroons — Van Rensselaer, Godyn, Blommaert, and the
rest — among themselves and with other influential directors.
One of the associations was to assume charge of Rensselaerswyck and the other of Swaanendael.   Neither De Pauw, nor
his patroonship, was included.   But in 1634, a settlement
at Swaanendael having been destroyed by the Indians, the
rights of the patroons on the South river were bought up by
the West India company.   Three years later Pavonia and
Staten Island, with the small settlements which had been
founded there, came again into its possession in the same
way.   Rensselaerswyck alone remained — now in the exclusive possession of the Van Rensselaer family — to contend
with the company over its seigniorial rights.   A few smaller
patroonships were granted later; but these soon disappeared
and had no special influence on the development of the
province.   Owing to these events, toward the close of the
period of Dutch rule the manorial influence declined and

[1] O'Callaghan, History of New Netherland, I. 126.

ceased practically to exist in the southern part of the province. From time to time, however, both by Stuyvesant and by
the early English governors, grants of considerable size were
made. Some of these, notably Fordham, Pelham, and Phil-
lipsburgh in Westchester, assumed the name and to an extent
the organization of manors. Toward the close of the Dutch
period the Van Cortlandt family began to build up its large
estate. During the administration of Governor Dongan the
first grants were made which resulted in the development of
the Livingston manor. By these events the manorial system
began again to assume a prominence in New York like that
from which, since the dissolution of the early association of
patroons, it had declined. The social and political development of New York has been deeply affected by the family
alliances and the system of tenant right which, as the result
of these grants, extended so widely within its borders.

Provision was also made in the Exemptions for smaller
grants to private persons, who should settle in the province
on their own account or in the service of masters — not
patroons — who lived in the Low Countries. With the
consent of the director and council of the company in New
Netherland, they might take up as much land as they could
properly improve, and enjoy it, with the customary rights,
as their own property. In the end this form of grant played
a more important part in the development of the province
than did the larger fiefs for which such detailed provision
was made. In the Exemptions of 1640 greater stress was
laid on the necessity of encouraging small grants than was
done in the issue of 1629. Individual grants of moderate
size, followed later by organized settlement, were multiplied
at the western end of Long Island, on Staten island, and on
the west bank of the Hudson, in the northern part of Manhattan island, and in the region northeast of the Harlem
river.

If we compare the provinces as a whole, it will be clearly
seen that grants of moderate size vastly predominated within
them. They were larger than the average estate in New
England, but it will probably appear that the majority of
them did not exceed one thousand acres in extent. In

proprietary instructions we hear much of manors and large
reserves.   But in many cases the bounds of manors were not
surveyed, the rents of tenants who were settled upon them
were not collected, leases were lost, and the estates fell into
general neglect.   In not a few instances they had simply a
nominal existence, no effort being made to settle or organize
them under a system of lordship.   As the province developed and filled with population, the relative importance of
grants of this kind steadily diminished.   Varieties of soil
and contour, dearth of settlers, lack of means and enterprise on the part of both proprietors and grantees, all combined to defeat cut-and-dried schemes for the settlement of
provinces, whenever they were put forward.

During the first decade of Maryland's existence the presence there of Catholic priests involved possibilities in the
management of land, as well as of religion, which were of
considerable importance.   The work of the priests among
the Indians put them in the way of obtaining deeds from the
natives for large tracts.   The numerical and social strength
of the Catholic settlers was a guaranty to them of support in
a natural effort to procure large landed estates in the province for the Jesuit Order or for the church itself.   But these
hopes were crushed by the proprietor in the proclamation of
1648.   In this was a provision excluding from its benefits all
corporations, societies, fraternities, and guilds, whether temporal or spiritual, and forbidding any grantee, without license
from the proprietor, to alienate land to such a body for any
uses forbidden by the statutes of mortmain.   In no other
British-American colony was such a precaution necessary,
but it kept the land law of Maryland in harmony with that
of the mother country and of the other colonies.   Though
usually overlooked, it was really, for a Catholic proprietor,
a concession as important as the more famous toleration act
of the following year.   The two acts had their origin in
similar motives, and were complements the one of the other.

The private or strictly feudal income which was derived
by proprietors from the land thus granted assumed the forms'
of quitrents, purchase money, fines on alienation, income
from ferries, and port duties.   The last two call for no

special reference in this connection.   So far as the author
has been able to discover, fines on alienation were actually
enforced only in Maryland.   The proprietary instructions of
1658[1] in Maryland contained a requirement that, upon the
alienation of land thereafter to be granted, a fine equal to
one year's rent of such land should be paid.   If this was not
paid and duly recorded within one month after sale, the
alienation should be void.   The regulation continued in
force throughout the colonial period.   After 1671 the fines
became payable in tobacco at 2d. per pound.   They continued to be payable in this form until 1733, after which
date they were received in money.   In the other provinces
the only restraints on alienation were the few which were
intended to prevent the division of manors; and they seem
in most cases to have been inoperative.

In the early history of the provinces, where it was desirable to give the maximum of encouragement to colonists, land
was rarely sold.   In New Netherland and New York, in the
Carolinas and New Jersey, during the period of which we
are speaking, a price seems never to have been put upon the
land.   Land was sold in Pennsylvania from the very first.[2]
As soon as he had secured his title, Penn offered for sale
shares of five thousand acres at £100 each.   After 1684 this
land was also to be liable to a quitrent.   The practice of
selling land was steadily continued, the prices varying with
the period of time which had elapsed since the settlement of
the province, with the character and location of the land,
and with such other conditions as might affect a bargain.
After 1732 prices became more permanent.   For thirty years
from that date the price was £15, 10s. per hundred acres.
Prices were always fixed by the proprietor and his officials. ·

Until 1683 no price seems to have been fixed upon land in
Maryland.   But in that year, whether or not it was an imitation of Pennsylvania practice, the proprietor began to insist upon the purchase of land.   The price first set upon
land in the interior of the province was one hundred pounds

[1] Kilty, Landholder's Assistant, 56, 266 ; MacMahon, History of Maryland, 174.

[2] Huston, 4, 63, 195 ; Shepherd, 17, 34.

of tobacco for every fifty acres. At later dates the price
was somewhat increased, and in the eighteenth century the
form of payment was changed to money. Escheated land,
with such improvements as had been made upon it, was sold
at auction, and the larger part of the purchase money went
to the proprietor. It was a requirement in all the provinces
that land should be settled within a brief period — often
designated as three years — after the issue of the patent.
Squatters' rights, as evidenced by "improvement," were as
a rule generously recognized.

The most characteristic form of territorial revenue was
the quitrent, paid annually at a rate prescribed by the proprietor and received in lieu of all services. It appears in
all the provinces. Upon the Maryland grants which were
promised in 1633 the quitrent was twenty pounds of wheat
for every hundred acres. In 1642 the rate was changed to
2s. for every hundred acres, and in 1659 and 1660 to 4s.
sterling, on simple freehold as well as manorial grants. But
owing to the internal disturbances and a probable hesitancy
on the part of the government, not till a decade later
was it possible to begin the regular collection of rents
at the last-mentioned rate.[1] At the same time a pre-
mium was set on the status of a freeholder by the issue of
writs of election for the lower house in 1670 which restricted
the suffrage to freeholders. In 1671 the well-known act
was passed imposing an export duty of 2s. per hogshead
on tobacco, one-half of the revenue from which was to
go to the proprietor, provided he accepted, in payment of
his quitrents and alienation fines, good tobacco at 2d. per
pound.[2] By an act of 1669 it had been provided that tobacco
should be received in the payment of ordinary debts at the
rate of three halfpence sterling per pound, while its market
price was about one penny per pound. The law of 1671 was,
therefore, naturally regarded by the people of the province
with favor, and was continued in force till long after the beginning of the eighteenth century.

The quitrent which at the beginning was demanded by

[1] Mereness, *op. cit.* 78.
[2] Md. Arch. Proceedings of Assembly, 1666–1676, 284, 220.

the Carolina proprietors was one halfpenny per acre.[1] Governor Berkeley of Virginia, as the member of the Carolina board who was nearest to the province, was ordered to impose this rate upon the land which should be granted in the Albemarle settlement. But a large proportion of the colonists had come from Virginia, and there the quitrent was one farthing per acre. Having settled in Albemarle before Berkeley's instructions were published, or without special reference to their terms, they sought a reduction of the rate. The assembly of Albemarle county petitioned the proprietors that they might have their lands on the same terms as the inhabitants of Virginia. In 1668 the petition was granted, the "Concessions" being suspended to that extent. So valuable did this seem to the colonists, that they came to call the concession the great "deed of grant," and to regard it as irrevocable. The proprietors, however, did not so consider it, and in the Fundamental Constitutions provided that after 1689 the quitrent should be one English penny per acre. But as late as 1694 Governor Ludwell was granting land at the rent of one farthing per acre, and referred to the "deed" for his authority. Later still, in the eighteenth century, the question of the inviolability of this deed became an important issue between the colonists and some of the royal governors.[2]

In all transactions, and in all the colonies, the form of payment was a matter of importance to the people. So scanty was their supply of money, that payment in kind was always strongly their preference. The proprietors, and afterward the crown, always found their interest in securing money payments whenever it was possible. This in many cases gave rise to controversies over quitrents, which in turn occasioned the interference of the assembly in a matter which the proprietors claimed as exclusively their own. Such a dispute agitated South Carolina for several years previous to 1690. It arose from the omission of the words "or the value thereof" in the form of patent which in 1682 was sent over for use in land grants. The effect of the omis-

---

[1] N. C. Recs. I. 43, 51 et seq.
[2] Ibid. I. 238, 391 ; IV. 60, 91, 109, 183, 238, 336.

sion was to make rents payable in money.[1] At the same time strict regulations were issued for the payment of arrears. The agitation which followed contributed to the overthrow of Governor Colleton in 1690, and forced the proprietors to consent to acts which provided that rents should be paid in money or in certain designated staple products at fixed prices. The regulations concerning the payment of arrears were also made easier.

In all the provinces quitrents were an object of aversion. They were continually falling into arrears. Payment was avoided whenever it was possible; and it was not infrequently resisted. In the last resort payment could be enforced by distress, the assistance of the sheriff being called in for the purpose. In Pennsylvania, as in other provinces, these conditions were ever and anon recurring. But in the history of New Jersey the question of quitrents played a more important part than in any other province. This was due to the fact that the settlers of the Elizabethtown and Monmouth patents, who had previously received their grants from Governor Nicolls of New York, did not acknowledge the claim of Berkeley and Carteret to the province.

When, in 1670, quitrents first became due, the three towns within these grants refused to pay them, and declined in other ways to recognize the authority of the proprietors. The legal right of Berkeley and Carteret to administer government within the province was also in doubt. In Woodbridge the disinclination to take out patents from Governor Carteret was so great that he had to warn delinquents that they could not be regarded as freeholders or entitled to any of their privileges, and further that their lands might be disposed of to others. Some of the inhabitants of Elizabethtown,[2] alarmed by the demand for a quitrent, and by other acts of the governor which they considered to be encroachments on their privileges, tore down the fence about a lot which had been granted by the governor to one Richard Michell, who had been one of his servants. When summoned before the court on the charge of riot, the accused

[1] Smith, South Carolina as a Royal Province, 29.
[2] N. J. Arch. I. 80 *et seq.* ; Hatfield, History of Elizabeth, 137–139.

refused to plead, and in their absence were found guilty and
fined.   All the inhabitants of this town and of two towns
within the Monmouth Purchase claimed to hold their land
independently of the proprietors, while the Monmouth towns
claimed independence in all things.

So great was the confusion thus occasioned, that in 1672
Governor Carteret returned to England to make the situation
known and obtain fresh authority.   It was then proven to
the satisfaction of the Duke of York [1] that the Nicolls grants
were void in law, because they were issued later than his
grant of the province to Berkeley and Carteret.   Therefore the duke ordered the governor of New York to take
no further notice of those patents, and to inform the parties
concerned that he would in no way countenance their pretensions against the proprietors.   The king also wrote, commanding all persons within the province to obey "the laws
and government" of the proprietors, they "having the sole
Power under us to settle and dispose of the said Country, upon such Terms and Conditions as they shall think
fit."

Governor Carteret also obtained from the proprietors renewed declarations [2] that all land in the province must be
held of them, and that the rent due therefrom might be collected by distress.   As an interpretation of the sixth article
of their concessions, they declared that the governor and
council should have the exclusive power to admit persons to
be planters and freemen of the province, and that no one
should be counted a freeholder, or have the right to vote or
hold office, unless he held his land by patent from the lords
proprietors.   The proprietors, and their agent the governor,
in accordance with the practice in the provinces generally,
proceeded on the supposition that territorial affairs should
be regulated wholly by the executive.   According, also, to
the opinion just mentioned, the exercise of political rights
was to depend wholly on the form of land grants.   It is true
that in provinces where the territorial rights of the proprietors met with no opposition this practically followed as a
matter of course.   The proprietors were not forced to de-

[1] N. J. Arch. I. 98.   [2] *Ibid.* 99, 101, 107.

clare the principle according to which they acted. But in New Jersey a considerable element among the settlers insisted, not only that the exercise of political rights should be regulated by the legislature, but that certain of the towns had the exclusive right to determine who should be residents and freeholders within their limits. Owing thus to the peculiar way in which the northern part of New Jersey was settled, questions of land, of rent, of the relation between these and political rights, had, and were always destined to have, an unusual prominence.

The attitude of the board of twenty-four proprietors toward the claim of those who still clung to their grants from Nicolls was the same as that of Carteret had been. The settlers were told that purchase from the Indians gave them "no Right[1] but what is duly confirmed by us, or our legal Predecessors, unless you would renounce all Interest and Protection from the King of England, and so Subject your all to a just forfeiture." But such a result they deprecated, and instead referred the inhabitants of Elizabethtown and of the Monmouth Purchase to the scheme of government they had sent over for proof of the kindly spirit which the proprietors cherished toward them.

A general inspection of patents was discussed, but it was not undertaken, and quitrents in East Jersey continued largely in arrears.[2] The proprietors were never able satisfactorily to establish their rights to government, and that fact furnished a chronic incitement to agrarian troubles. The executive remained weak, even after the proprietors had resigned their political rights to the crown. Therefore, during long periods in the eighteenth century, New Jersey was plunged into anarchy by agrarian disputes which the government was too weak to control.

In the Dutch ground briefs no definite provision was made for the payment of a rent. In some of the patents the payment of a tenth of the products of the soil was required. In many only the general obligation of submission and allegiance was enforced, with some special duty, such as that

[1] N. J. Arch. I. 456.
[2] Grants and Concessions, 173, 214; N. J. Arch. I. 429.

of fencing the land.[1] The West India company owned six
boweries, which were situated on the east side of Manhattan
island outside the limits of the Dutch town. They were furnished with buildings and with cattle, and were leased for
short periods, with their stock and other outfit, on such terms
as were customary throughout the province.[2] The farms of
the colony of Rensselaerswyck were managed according to
the same system of stock leases. Some were let at a fixed
rent, payable in grain, beaver, or wampum, while others
were let at halves or thirds, including one-half of the increase of the stock and a few pounds of butter[3] as a recognition. The tenant was bound to keep the buildings and
tools in good repair.

The English conquest in 1664 resulted in no immediate
change in the land law of the province. The articles of
capitulation[4] provided that the Dutch should "enjoy their
own customs concerning their inheritances," and all public
writings which contained the record of them should be carefully preserved. In the Duke's Laws also the permanency
of property rights was carefully guarantied.[5] This, however, did not preclude the necessity of a general renewal of
patents and town charters, as a means of breaking the tenure
by which land had been held of the Dutch government, and
as an accompaniment of the oath of allegiance to the English
crown. Provision was made for this in the Duke's Laws[6]
and their subsequent amendments. "To the end all former
Purchases," it was declared, "may be ascertained to the
present possessor or right owner, They shall bring in their
former Grants, and take out new patents for the same from
the present Governoure in the behalf of his Royall Highness

---

[1] See patents in N.Y. Col. Docs. XIV. Translations of the original
Dutch patents which have been preserved are in the office of the Secretary
of State at Albany.

[2] N.Y. Col. Docs. XIV. 19 *et seq.*, 39 ; Valentine's Manual of the Corporation, 1866, p. 575.

[3] O'Callaghan, History of New Netherland, I. 323–326.

[4] N. Y. Col. Docs. II. 250.

[5] N. Y. Col. Laws, I. 57.

[6] *Ibid.* 44, 80, 93 ; State Library Bulletin, History No. 2, General
Entries, I. 161.

the Duke of York." It was also carefully provided that all
patents and bounds of towns, also surveys for new purchases, should be deposited in the office of records at the city of New York, as well as in the towns and in the custody of the courts of sessions. Wills, drawn now not according to Dutch precedents but according to forms which, for lands held by socage tenure, had been legal in England since Henry VIII, were likewise to be filed in the city of New York.

In the Duke's Laws also the fact was recognized that by 12 Charles II, c. 24, all military tenures in England had been abolished. Free and common socage was therefore the tenure which was substituted for Dutch law and custom.

Dutch ground briefs and transports were very generally submitted to the English officials for confirmation, and in most of the English patents or deeds which were granted in their stead no express mention was made of a quitrent.[1] This is emphatically true in the case of confirmation of city lots. Confirmations of Indian deeds and new grants were made subject to "the accustomed rent of new Plantations in this country," or to such payment and conditions as should be designated by the Duke of York and his officers. In some cases the annual payment of a lamb, or of a barrel of codfish or a bushel of winter wheat, was demanded. Confirmations of patents on the Delaware and the issue of new grants in that region were always accompanied by the condition that a quitrent should be paid in wheat.

At the close, in 1674, of the Dutch reoccupation there was another renewal of patents. But even then the system of quitrents was not fully introduced. In 1686 Governor Dongan reported[2] that the quitrents, at his arrival in the province, were very inconsiderable, the larger part coming from the Delaware region under the terms of the patents granted by Andros. But Andros even had renewed Indian purchases and township grants with the former reservation of a lamb only as a quitrent. Dongan, however,[3] insisted

[1] See Patents, Vols. I, II, and III, Office of Secretary of State, Albany, N.Y.; N.Y. Col. Docs. III. 303, 309.

[2] N.Y. Col. Docs. III. 401.

[3] Patents, Vol. V, Office of Secretary of State, Albany.

that all patents or deeds which were recorded during his administration should contain provision for a quitrent. No exception was made even in the case of city lots.

Rent in the city was made payable in money, but in the country it was payable in wheat, fish, or other commodities. Albany was made the place of payment for the northern part, and New York for the southern part, of the province. At first rents were payable to the duke, but later, after his accession, to the king. Dongan himself explains how he succeeded in increasing the quitrent in some of the towns. He found that certain tracts of land within their limits had not been purchased from the Indians and were at the disposal of the government. By threatening to grant them to outside parties, he induced the proprietors of the town to submit to an increase of rent. By these measures the system of quitrents was extended throughout New York, and its practice in this respect was brought into conformity with that of the other English provinces.

The fact that under this system the proprietor was the grantor of land and the recipient of revenue therefrom, necessitated the creation of an administrative body within the province for the performance of the duties which these rights implied. Under the conditions of plantation those who were entitled to head rights had to record their claims, and on the basis of them warrants were issued for the survey of the tracts to which the claimants were entitled. When the survey in each case was duly made and return thereof submitted, the patent or deed for the land was made out and title [1] was thereby conveyed. As the rents and other forms of income from land became due, provision had to be made for their collection.

During the early history of Maryland this work was done by the governor, council, and secretary — who was a member of the council, — and mainly through the secretary's office. Surveyors, and especially the surveyor-general, who was also a member of the council, were continuously called into requisition. Warrants and deeds were made out under the order of the governor, and the deeds passed the great

[1] Kilty, 66 *et seq.*; Mereness, 58 *et seq.*

seal of the province.   In the collection of rents the sheriffs
were brought into requisition, while in prosecutions the services of the attorney-general were sometimes needed.   In
1685 [1] an examiner was appointed, who signed the certificates
of survey.   Previous to that time this duty had been performed by the surveyor-general.

About 1670 there was a notable increase in the territorial
business of the province.[2]   In that year the secretary was
instructed to prove all claims to land ; to inquire after, and
enter on record, all escheats, also all proprietary manors and
reserves ; to prepare a rent roll, and in connection therewith to discover and report to the proprietor and governor
all attempts to conceal the obligation to pay rent ; to secure,
if possible, the payment of alienation fines and to enter upon
record a list of alienations.   In 1673 and earlier the sheriffs
were ordered to return lists of escheats for their respective
counties.   In 1671 the surveyor-general was instructed to
hold annually courts of inquiry in the several counties for
the purpose of examining titles, and ascertaining whether
more land was held than was due and what rents and services should be paid ; these facts should also be recorded
and one copy sent to the proprietor and another to the
receiver-general.[3]   At this date or a little later two receiver-
generals were appointed by the proprietor, with authority to
collect rents and dues and to appoint deputies to assist them
in the work.[4]   In 1678 the formation of a complete rent roll
was in progress, for then the clerks of the county courts
were ordered through the justices to transmit to the office of
the secretary a complete list of alienations of land within
their counties, which might be used for the purpose.

In 1680 this increased activity took shape in the organization of a land office which, though connected with the
office of secretary, should be distinct from it.[5]   The chief
clerk of the secretary's office was placed in charge of the
new bureau, under the title of clerk and register.   The land
records were transferred to his care, and he was authorized

[1] Kilty, 83.   [2] Md. Arch., Proceedings of Council, 1667-1688, 73.
[3] *Ibid.* 95, 122.   [4] *Ibid.* 1671-1681, 119.
[5] Kilty, 108 *et seq.;* Proceedings of Council, 1681-1686, 254 *et seq.*

to prove claims, issue warrants, and draw patents. In 1684, just before leaving the province, Charles Calvert, the lord proprietor, commissioned a land council of four members, all of whom were members of the council of state. This body received elaborate instructions concerning all matters relating to land, and were intrusted with full care of the proprietor's territorial interests. Two of its members, who were the secretaries of the province, were to sign warrants and examine all patents; two other members, who were keepers of the great seal, were, during the absence of the proprietor, to sign all patents. Thus the business of granting land, collecting the revenue therefrom, and keeping the land records was organized under one distinct office, which continued in existence until 1689, and after a suspension of five years was reopened and remained in activity, with certain administrative changes, as long as Maryland was a province.

In New Netherland territorial affairs were administered by the director and council, and no separate land office was organized. The same was true of the Carolinas, of New York, and of New Jersey prior to about 1680. In those provinces the governor, the secretary, the surveyor-general, and the receiver-general, with their subordinates, attended wholly to the making of surveys, the issue of patents, and the collection of rents. No evidence appears that in this capacity the governor and secretary acted under separate commissions. The procedure which was followed in the making of surveys and the issue of warrants and patents was much the same in all these provinces, and in all essential particulars it was the same as that of Maryland.[1] This included provision, especially in New York and in the Fundamental Constitutions of Carolina, for the registry of all leases, mortgages, and conveyances. New York also included wills under the requirement for registration. Florence O'Sullivan, the first surveyor-general of the Ashley River settlement, was ordered,[2] not only to survey

---

[1] N. C. Recs. I. 51 *et seq.*, 182; Shaftesbury Papers, 117–123; Smith, South Carolina as a Royal Province, 27.

[2] Shaftesbury Papers, 131. O'Sullivan was later removed on the charge of unfitness for the duties of his office.

all bounds and allotments under warrants from the governor and council, but to make a return of such surveys and keep a record of such returns in his office.

In New Jersey the office of surveyor-general was one of the first[1] to be created, while that of receiver-general was in existence at least as early as 1672. But owing to the large number of proprietors, after the division of the province into East and West New Jersey, it became necessary to delegate authority to a part of the board. In East Jersey authority was first given, in 1684 and 1685, to the governor and the proprietors who were resident in the province, with their deputies, to grant lands and settle disputes with the planters. This soon became known as the Board of Proprietors of East Jersey, and it continued to have the chief management of territorial affairs in that part of the original province.

In West Jersey the trustees, — Penn, Lawrie, and Lucas, — who for a time took charge of the province on behalf of the creditors of Edward Byllinge, appointed a board of commissioners to administer territorial affairs. Had that board been continued through appointment of their successors, West Jersey would have retained the form of other proprietary provinces. But such was not the case. In chapter third of the Concessions it was provided that, on March 25, 1681, the proprietors, freeholders, and inhabitants, resident within the province, should meet and elect from among themselves ten commissioners to take the place of those who had at first been appointed. This process should be annually repeated. Its effect was to give the control over territorial affairs into the hands of the inhabitants, to democratize the land system as well as the political system. In other words, it indefinitely multiplied the number of those who in the technical sense were proprietors; all grantees retained a joint interest in the enterprise. Therefore when, after settlement of the province had begun, commissioners are mentioned, a board chosen by the colonists is meant. West Jersey was like a New England town — greatly enlarged. It is possible that, during the interval between 1681 and

[1] N. J. Arch. I. 26, 106.

1687, the commissioners were not regularly elected. But in the last-mentioned year, forty or more of the proprietors met and resolved that eleven of their number should be annually chosen to act as commissioners and trustees for the entire body. In this act originated the Council or Board of West Jersey Proprietors, which has continued in existence from that time. This board, as well as that of East Jersey, may be regarded as constituting a land office, and neither the governor nor the other officers were *ex officio* members of it.

The course of policy which in these matters was followed in Pennsylvania was similar to that of Maryland and the Jerseys. Like them, Pennsylvania had a land office, though until after 1732 its affairs were very much in confusion. Even then records were kept and affairs were managed with less care than was shown by the Calverts and their officials. The long absences of Penn from his province made it impossible for him to attend in person to the details of selling and letting land and collecting rents. Not until 1741 was the care of these matters intrusted to the governors. Instead, a commission or board of property was from time to time designated, which acted as the special agent of the proprietor. The board consisted of a secretary, — who was at the same time secretary of the province, — the surveyor-general, and from three to five special commissioners. Closely associated with the board was the receiver-general, the keeper of the seal, and master of the rolls. The special duties of the commissioners related to the granting of lands, but, as their powers developed, they also became concerned with the collection of rents.[1] After 1741 the governors became members of this board, but their authority to act with it was conveyed through a special commission. In its divorce of territorial business from the office of governor, the practice of Pennsylvania and that of the Jerseys, as well as that of Maryland in its later history, were similar.

In all the provinces the land system was kept as free as possible from the control of the legislature. It was organized and regulated under instructions and proclamations of the proprietors and their appointees. Any attempt to regulate

[1] Huston, Land Titles, 68, 80, 85, 107 ; Shepherd, *op. cit.* 27 *et seq.*

it by legislation was resented and opposed.   It was regarded
as the private concern of the proprietor and its administration as distinctly an executive function.   Until 1690 it remained under executive control in Maryland, and few laws of
importance were passed for its regulation.   The most important act of the period affecting land was the one passed in 1671,
specifying the price at which tobacco should be received in
payment of quitrents.   In 1649 the principle always insisted
on by the proprietor, that titles should be derived from him and
not through Indian deeds, was confirmed by statute.   In 1642
an act was passed prescribing the time subsequent to a grant
when the payment of quitrent should begin.   The act was also
intended to prevent undue delays in surveying and recording
grants.   The same year the fees of the surveyor-general were
regulated [1] and acts for that purpose were repeatedly passed
thereafter.   Irregularities on the part of surveyors received
attention after 1660,[2] but no laws on the subject were passed.

In New Netherland, and in New York during its proprietary period, there was, of course, no question of executive
control *versus* legislative regulation.   In the absence of a
legislature such an issue could not arise.   But in the Carolinas, the Jerseys, and Pennsylvania it arose, and the occasion which usually brought it to the front was some dispute
over the payment of quitrents.   It was at this point that
the territorial regulations of the proprietor touched the
pocket of the colonist.   Like a tax, the rent was a constantly
recurring burden.   Over its amount and the form of its payment the individual desired in some way to secure such control as had been effected in the case of taxation.   Efforts to
secure this helped to initiate the process of legislation relating to territorial affairs.

Group settlements, which were so characteristic of New
England, appear in the proprietary provinces with very unequal prominence.   The towns of eastern Long Island [3] were

[1] Proceedings of Assembly, 1638–1664, 163, 194, 248.

[2] *Ibid.* 1666–1676, 85.

[3] See the Records of Easthampton, Southampton, Southold, Huntington,
Brookhaven, Smithtown, and Oyster Bay ; Thompson, History of Long
Island.   The records of all the towns above referred to, except those of
Oyster Bay, are in print.

exclusively of New England origin and type. The same may be said of the five English towns — Hempstead,[1] Gravesend, Jamaica, Newtown, and Flushing — which lay immediately to the westward and were settled under Dutch rule. The English towns of Westchester county[2] belonged, in the main, to the same class, as did Newark, Elizabethtown, Shrewsbury, and Woodbridge in northern New Jersey.[3] Viewed collectively, the towns to which reference has just been made were a projection of New England into the middle colonies. If the enterprise of New Haven on the Delaware had succeeded, one or more New England towns would have been planted still farther south. In so far as the inhabitants of these towns at a later time became subject to a quitrent, they departed from the New England model and approximated to the conditions of tenancy by which they were surrounded.

The fact that in the proprietary provinces land was granted by the proprietor and was held of him, could not fail, when it was really operative, to have an effect on the formation of group settlements. The system itself was preeminently favorable to individual grants. The economic impulse, under which the provinces were settled, operated upon individuals and families more than upon groups and entire communities. Migration and the progress of settlement within the provinces were, in most cases, distinctly individualistic in character. This is true among the Dutch, as well as among the English. In New Netherland individuals pushed out into unoccupied territory, extinguished Indian titles, and then obtained sanction from the company for what they had done. The form of early deeds implies this. To cite one among a large number of examples :[4] On

---

[1] The Records of Hempstead are in print. For the lay-out of Gravesend see Stiles, History of Kings County, I. 160 ; details from town records of Jamaica are in Munsell, History of Queens County, 194 ; Riker, Annals of Newtown.

[2] Baird, History of Rye ; Bolton, History of Westchester County ; Scharf, History of Westchester County.

[3] Town Records of Newark ; Hatfield, History of Elizabeth ; Middletown Town Book ; Dally, History of Woodbridge.

[4] N. Y. Col. Docs. XIV. 4. Many other similar deeds appear in this and in Vols. XII. and XIII. of the series ; also in various works on the local history of the region, and in the libers of the registries of deeds.

June 16, 1637, the director and council declared that certain
Indian chiefs, whose names are given, came before them and
stated that, with the consent of the tribe and in return for
certain merchandise which had been transferred to them,
they had conveyed to George Rapalje a piece of land upon
Long Island, with bounds loosely specified in the document.
This simple recognition by the director and council in writing of what private parties had done is the essence of the
Dutch ground brief, and in this case it sanctioned the first
step that was taken toward the settlement at Wallabout.

Similar steps were being taken elsewhere. On the open
flats, north of the present Coney island, Hudde, Van Corlaer, Gerritsen, and others took out patents, some of which
were afterward revoked, for tracts estimated at fifteen
thousand acres. A part of this was known as the plantation of Achtervelt, of the buildings, stock, and growing
crops on which, as they were in July, 1638, we have an
inventory.[1] After settlers in sufficient number had bought
or leased farms and built dwellings within these large grants,
rights of local government were bestowed by the director
and council, and the settlement became, not the manor, but
the village and town of Amersfoort, later called Flatlands.
Breuckelen originated in a similar way from grants to
individuals at Gowanus, Red Hook, The Wallabout, The
Ferry, and finally at a point some distance east of The Ferry,
where a church was built, and the village of Breuckelen
proper was founded. In 1667, after the English conquest,
these settlements were bound together into one bundle, and
made a town by a patent from Governor Nicolls.[2] The
other Dutch towns in Kings county consisted of grants to
individuals, made originally by the province, and at a later
time bound together by a town patent, itself also a grant
from the chief authority in the province. Haerlem and
Bergen[3] originated in a similar manner.

---

[1] N. Y. Col. Docs. XIV. 10 ; Stiles, History of Kings County, I. 65, 66.

[2] Stiles, History of Brooklyn, I. 154.

[3] The process can be traced in detail in the brilliant pages of Riker's
History of Harlem. For Bergen see Winfield, History of Hudson County,
New Jersey, and Winfield, Land Titles in Hudson County.

After a local magistracy had been established, and especially after the issue of the town patent, the locality itself granted land, though it had not the exclusive power to do this, and such grants might be subject to confirmation, to quitrents, or to other conditions under which land was generally held in the province. Within towns thus organized unoccupied land was treated as commons, and the system of common fields, pastures and woods, with town herds and common fences, appears, much as in New England. As time progressed the towns divided their commons by lot,[1] as they did in New England. A genuine village community system existed among the Dutch, as it did among the New Englanders. But in the two sections it came into existence in a somewhat different way. In New England, as a rule, the group of settlers was original, and secured the town grant and managed it from the first. Among the Dutch, as a rule, the villages originated from aggregations of farms, and attained their corporate life in consequence of such preëxistent aggregation. When the Dutch village community had once been formed, it exhibited most of the characteristics of the New England village, though it was always subject to certain limitations which did not attach to the latter. Moreover, in New Netherland the village was by no means the only form of settlement, and it did not determine the form of society to the extent which was true of the villages in New England.

As one passes to southern New Jersey, to Pennsylvania, and the provinces still farther south, he will find the village or town diminishing in importance, and the isolated farm or plantation appearing still more distinctly as the chief form of settlement. This tendency culminated in the tobacco-planting and rice-growing provinces south of Pennsylvania. Though such a form of settlement was in close harmony with the proprietary system in general, it was the result of natural and economic causes which are familiar, the working of which has often been explained.

[1] A typical instance is furnished by Brooklyn, in 1693; Liber I. of Conveyances, in Office of Register of Deeds; see also Stiles, Kings County, I. 92. Even the fragmentary records of Kings county which have been preserved furnish much evidence relating to the management of common lands.

When, in the provinces to which reference has just been made, the village or village community appears, it will in most cases be found to have originated after the manner of the Dutch rather than after that of the New Englanders. And yet one would not be warranted in inferring that the English of the provinces were in this feature of their colonization imitating their Dutch neighbors. It would be safer to infer that both Dutch and English were acting under similar conditions, both economic and administrative.

Perth Amboy, in East Jersey, was laid out by the proprietors, and lots were granted or taken up by them. Over the settlement of Salem John Fenwick exercised the control of a chief proprietor. After the location and general plan of the town had been decided upon by him in consultation with the intending purchasers, one-half of the site was set apart for their home lots and the other half was reserved by Fenwick, to be granted exclusively by him. Burlington and Gloucester were laid out by the proprietors — who were the principal freeholders of the tenths where they were located — in accordance with the democratic method [1] of procedure which was generally followed in West Jersey.

In Pennsylvania, as well as in Maryland, towns were laid out and lots in them were granted under the immediate authority of the proprietor and his appointees. In the case of Philadelphia this was literally true, and proportional allotments of land within the town were made in connection with the grant of country lots. Quitrents were reserved upon both alike. [2] When transfers were made from the original grantees to third parties, quitrents were also reserved, and they were payable directly to Penn. In reference to land the relations between the proprietor and individuals in Philadelphia proper was as direct as it was in any other part of the province. Land in the beginning was not transferred to the inhabitants of that city as a group, but as individuals. They came to form a city, because within that particular

[1] Johnson, First Settlement of Salem in West Jersey; Mickle, Reminiscences of Old Gloucester; Smith, History of West Jersey.

[2] Lewis, Original Land Titles in Philadelphia, 124 *et seq.*, 220; Exemplification Records, in Office of Recorder of Deeds, Philadelphia county.

tract settlement was compact and not dispersed.   When
Philadelphia was incorporated, the records of land titles
remained with the officials of the province, or in the custody
of the county of Philadelphia.

Germantown, on the other hand, originated as a group
settlement, and was not merely an aggregation of grants to
individuals.   The initial step was taken in Europe with the
founding of the Frankfort land company.[1]   Though none of
the members of that company, except Francis Daniel Pastorius, came to America, he, acting as their agent, bought
land of Penn, to which settlers came from Crefeld and other
points on the Rhine.   A patent was procured from Penn's
commissioners of property for 5700 acres.   This contained a
grant of 200 acres to Pastorius and 150 acres to Hartsfelder,
and provided for the transfer of the remaining 5350 acres to
Pastorius for the German settlers.   This tract was divided
into two equal parts, one half going to the Frankfort
company and the other half to the Crefeld purchasers.
From the entire grant a quitrent was reserved by Penn as
proprietor, though rents on estates within the tract were
frequently made payable to intermediate parties.   But the
surveying of the tract, the locating of streets and lots, and
the assignment of land to settlers was left to Pastorius
and his associates.   In October, 1683, they laid out fourteen lots for the first comers, and these were assigned.
Successive allotments were made as groups of colonists arrived, and three townships besides Germantown itself were
soon founded within the large tract.   Deeds were executed by Pastorius, or others, under the authority of the
Frankfort company or the Crefeld purchasers.   Records
of these grants[2] were kept, as was done, though less systematically, in New England towns.   In 1689, by charter
from Penn, Germantown was made an incorporated borough.
Authority was thereby given to the bailiff, burgesses, and
commonalty of the borough to manage and improve their

[1] Pennypacker, The Settlement of Germantown, 28, 91, 259 *et seq.* ; Lewis,
op. cit. 80.

[2] They appear in the *Grund und Lager Buch* of Germantown, which is
now in the office of the Recorder of Deeds of Philadelphia county.

lands and stock in trade.   A borough court was established,
with authority to issue local ordinances ; and in the exercise
of this power by-laws were passed which went as far in the
regulation of allotments and common lands as did the orders
of New England towns.[1] But local powers of this extent
were the exception in the provinces, and were the result
of special conditions.

In Maryland the straggling settlement at Saint Mary's
and the more compact and permanent town of Annapolis
were subject in all their territorial arrangements to regulations which were issued by the government of the province,
or by county officials who were acting under its authority.
Annapolis originated in a grant in 1649 of 250 acres to ten
families, led by Richard Bennett, who had recently arrived
from Virginia.   This tract was surveyed and divided into
lots, probably by surveyors who were acting directly under
authority from the proprietor.   Later, as the settlement
grew, other farms, on the lower course of the Severn, were
surveyed and occupied.   Thus the town grew by the
addition of homestead to homestead rather than by joint
and simultaneous acts of a considerable group of colonists.[2]
In 1683, when the rage for founding port towns was at its
height, an act was passed by the Maryland legislature which
provided a cut-and-dried scheme for the establishment of
towns in the various counties.   As, about ten years later,
the same plan was applied especially to Annapolis, and since
it well illustrates the methods by which in the southern
provinces attempts were made to found towns, a brief reference to it is necessary.[3]

In the act commissioners for each county were named, and
they were empowered to buy one hundred acres of land conveniently situated at each of a certain number of designated
points where it was believed that port towns could be devel-

[1] The charter is printed by Pennypacker, *op. cit.*, and also the beginning
of the court orders.   A manuscript copy of the Germantown Court Book is
in the possession of the Pennsylvania Historical Society.

[2] Riley, The Ancient City, History of Annapolis, 18.

[3] Md. Arch., Proceedings of Assembly, 1678–1683, 612 ; Bacon, Laws of
Maryland, Act of 1694, c. 8.

oped. After any one of the given tracts had been surveyed, the commissioners should cause it to be laid out in streets and alleys, reserving open places for a church, a market-house, and other public buildings. What remained of the tract should be laid out, as nearly as might be, into one hundred numbered lots, and these should be sold to intending settlers. For the period of four months the lots should be reserved for purchase exclusively by residents of the county in which the town was situated ; at the end of that time they should be thrown open to purchasers from outside. Prior owners of the land might be compelled to sell at an appraised value, while the grantees should be under obligation, not only to pay for their lots, but to build a house upon each of them within the period of two years. County surveyors should be required to lay off the lots, as well as the streets and commons, and a quitrent on the land should be reserved to the proprietor. By the act of 1694, relating to Annapolis and Oxford, provision was made in each case for purchasing and fencing a town pasture. A board of possibly resident commissioners was also designated for each town. But, as under the act of 1693, the laying out of streets and lots, and all else which was connected with the founding or extension of the town, was to be done under provincial rather than local authority. A town thus founded would be only a more densely settled area within a county. It would have little or no organic life apart from the county.

Although the plan of 1683 to promote town life within Maryland proved a failure, Annapolis survived, and in 1696[1] a board of resident trustees was created for it. They were incorporated and empowered to meet from time to time as a court to regulate town affairs and administer local justice. The resident freeholders were also recognized as freemen of the town, and were empowered to fill vacancies in the board of trustees. The trustees were authorized to buy land for common use, and from it or other ungranted land to sell lots to newcomers. By this measure Annapolis for the first time attained to the conditions of corporate life.

North Carolina, until near the close of the period which

[1] Bacon, Laws of Maryland, Acts of 1696, c. 24.

we are discussing, was almost destitute of group settlements.
On the Ashley river there was only one of importance —
Charlestown on Albemarle Point, which was afterward
removed to the site of the same name on Oyster Point.
This town was the residence of the provincial authorities,
and was the place where the legislature met, and where government centred.   Notwithstanding the fact that provision
was at once made for individual ownership in the management of its land, and in everything which pertained to its
life, Charlestown was quite as much under provincial control
as was Jamestown in Virginia.   Indeed, the remoteness of
Charlestown from the other English settlements, and its
exposure to attack, both from Indian and Spaniard, remind
one of Jamestown during the early decades of its existence.
The resemblance is strengthened when we find that the proprietors gave minute instructions concerning its settlement,[1]
and that these were followed as strictly as possible, though
the site which was chosen was quite different from the one
which the proprietors had in mind when the orders were
drawn.

The origin of the settlement at Albemarle Point cannot
be better described than in the words of the provincial council as written to the proprietors : [2] " When we arrived here,
we thought it most conducing to our safety to build a town,
where we are now settled, it being a point with a very convenient landing, and safely fortified, being almost surrounded
with a large Marsh and Creek, and after the first joint planting, upon our arrival, which necessity had soe put upon us :
that the people might have sufficient land to plant and keep
a small stock, and that we might keep as near together as we
could, for the better security of this place, we were forced to.
grant them town lotts cont: eleaven poles or thereabouts per
head, and Tenn acres per head to plant as aforesaid. which
tenn acre lotts were and are laid out to them and about the
Town from the South, westward to ye North, by which we
humbly conceive we shall prevent any sudden surpriseall."

We are told that no person was settled more than two
miles from the town, whether up or down the river.[3]   The

[1] Shaftesbury Papers, 125 *et seq*.   [2] *Ibid*. 284.   [3] *Ibid*. 274.

town enclosure itself, which was christened Charlestown, seems to have contained about nine acres, and was surrounded by a palisade.   It was located about midway of the settlement, where it was protected on three sides by marsh. A plan[1] which has been preserved in the *Shaftesbury Papers* shows that grants were made to the settlers, extending back in long, rectangular strips from the marsh adjacent to the river, and that these grants varied in extent from less than twenty acres to forty-two acres.   A list of sixty-two grants, apparently smaller than most of those which appear on the plan, has also been preserved.   This may be the list of town lots, while the plan shows outlying farms.   The largest grant which appears on the plan was one of 420 acres to the partners Ashley, Carteret, and Colleton, who had undertaken jointly to settle a plantation within the colony.   Of this, West, the storekeeper, took special charge, as the agent of the partners, and on the plantation their servants were settled.

Over the territorial arrangements at the second Charlestown — that on Oyster Point — the control of the proprietors was even more complete than it was over the settlement which has just been described.   In the fall of 1671 instructions[2] were issued to Sir John Yeamans, who was then governor, that he should have surveys made for a port town at the healthiest spot available upon the Ashley river, and the Point was selected as best meeting that condition.   This was in accordance with the provision of the Constitutions that there should be one port town on each navigable river in the province.[3]   The governor was instructed to lay out land for six colonies about it, — which would make a precinct, — but

[1] This is reproduced in Shaftesbury Papers; also in Ex-Mayor Courtney's volume, The Centennial of the Incorporation of Charleston, Charleston Year Book, 1883.   See also p. 140 *et seq.* of this volume.

[2] Shaftesbury Papers, 342, 361.   Page 379 contains a fine description of the advantages of Oyster Point as a site for a town, written by Joseph Dalton, secretary of the province.

[3] The proprietors declared that they intended that all vessels which entered Ashley river should unload at Charlestown, and also take on their cargoes there, except such bulky commodities as timber, which could not be brought to the port.   In this way trade should be conducted on all the large rivers.   *Ibid.* 361.

not to grant any seigniories or baronies among them.   The CHAP. town, according to the plan of the proprietors, which was II. known as a "grand model," should be regularly laid out in plots three hundred feet square, on each of which one house might be built.

The squares should be separated from one another by streets and alleys.   With each square as a town lot should also be granted eighty acres in the colony of which the town formed a part, and four hundred acres in some of the other five colonies of the precinct.   The town should be palisaded, and outside the palisade should be a ditch.   Immediately without the palisade the land, for the breadth of one-third of a mile, should be left common, and in order to insure its being cleared, the inhabitants might be temporarily allowed to plant or make gardens there.   But its final and permanent use should be as a common for the cattle of the town, and the grantee or grantees of every square in the town should have their proportional share in the use of it.

Preparatory to the settlement on Oyster Point, the surrender of a few tracts of land which had already been occupied there was procured.   References appear in the council records to gradual progress in the occupation of the new site.   The inland boundary of the "new town" was at a line corresponding to Hasell and Beaufain streets in the modern city.   The first buildings were erected along the eastern side of the peninsula.   Many creeks and marshes obstructed settlement even here.   But the seat of government was removed to the new town, and the settlement at Albemarle Point was officially abandoned.[1]   In 1679 and 1680 the proprietors issued the decisive orders which changed its name to Charlestown, removed the government offices, and made it thenceforward the chief town in the province.   A general removal of the inhabitants from Albemarle Point — the older Charlestown — followed.   No town in this province during the period which we are discussing was made a borough, or in any way enjoyed distinct corporate rights.

[1] Shaftesbury Papers, 385, 388, 391; Colls. S. C. Hist. Soc. I. 102, 103; Rivers, 128, 129.

CHAPTER III

THE OFFICIAL SYSTEM IN MARYLAND

PART
III. HAD governmental powers not accompanied the territorial grants which have been described, those grants would have lain wholly within the domain of private law. They would have been estates of land, unusually large, no doubt, but nothing more. In cases where the governmental rights of proprietors were suspended or resigned into the hands of the crown, they remained thereafter only private landlords. But the fact that rights of government were bestowed with the land gives to the regulations concerning the latter a significance in constitutional history. The proprietor was made thereby the political head of his province. In fact, the territory became a province by virtue of the rights and institutions of government existing in and connected therewith. The bestowment of grants of land by the proprietor not only carried with it the obligation to pay quitrent, but to take to him the oath of fidelity. Had it been possible for a territorial nobility to develop in the American provinces, its creation would have shown here, as in Europe, how the granting of land could have been utilized as a means of strengthening the government and checking the growth of democracy.

In the discussion of the corporation as a form of colonial government it was necessary to dwell first and chiefly on the legislature. The general court was the central feature of that organism, for in that the freemen, who were the grantees of power, found their embodiment. But with the proprietary province the case is different. The king established this form of colony by delegating to the proprietor the right to exercise certain functions of the prerogative within the province. It is true that the proprietary charters contained more hints con-

cerning the form of government which should obtain in the
province than did the charters of the corporations; but the
existence of an assembly, and hence the enjoyment of political
rights by the colonists, was not in any of the charters guarantied in mandatory terms.   In the charter of New York
it was not mentioned.   The powers which were definitely
bestowed were executive in character, — the ordinance
power, the power to appoint all officers, to establish courts, to
punish and pardon, to organize a military force and defend the
province, to bestow titles of honor, to found churches and
present to livings.   These made the proprietor the executive
of the province, and for the most part left it to him to
determine how and under what forms the governmental
powers which he had received should be exercised.   That he
did this alone, without advice, or apart from the social and
political conditions of the province, is not claimed.   That in
none of the provinces, save New York, was there or could
there have been much delay in calling an assembly, is true.
But in all cases the assembly was called by the proprietor,
and without such action of his it could not legally meet.
What control he had over its organization and work, when
once in existence, will appear in the sequel.   The fact here
insisted upon is, that the bestowment of power upon an
individual instead of a corporation assembled in general
court, and its transmission through him to the colonists, made
the executive, instead of the legislature, the centre from and
around which development in the province chiefly occurred.
It gave to the proprietor an importance, especially at the
outset, which was analogous to that enjoyed by the general
court in the corporate colony.   It made him in a derived
and inferior sense the source, within the province, of office
and honor, the fountain of justice, the commander of the
military, the recipient of the provincial revenue, the constituent part of the legislature.   These were the *jura regalia*
of the proprietor, which made his position that of a count
palatine.   They were in kind the power of the English mon-
arch; and, when used according to the precedents of the
county palatine, they made the province monarchical in
form.

Of the proprietary provinces which attained permanent form and development, Maryland was founded prior to the Restoration, while all the rest were established subsequent to that event. The Calverts and the Duke of York were the only proprietors who did not issue elaborate concessions as to government. As we have seen, they all published the terms on which they would grant land ; the Carolina and New Jersey proprietors and Penn made similar announcement of the conditions under which government should be administered. With one exception, — the Fundamental Constitutions of Shaftesbury and Locke, — these documents have a decidedly modern form and purport. They were apparently issued for the purpose of attracting settlers, and may have contained features which were suggested by those who expected to live as colonists under them. They approach as near formal compacts as is possible in the case of documents within the domain of public law. One cannot imagine a mediæval count palatine issuing to his vassals such grants as these. In them the organs of the government which it was proposed to establish, and their powers, were described, in some cases very minutely, while provisions for amendment were included. They were, in fact, *octroi* constitutions, and were issued as an expression of the will of the proprietors, but also with a view to the interests and demands of those who, under new and strange conditions, were to inhabit the provinces. In these rudimentary constitutions, then, we note the first significant innovation in matters of government, which occurred when the palatinates were reproduced in the American colonies. The Calverts and the Duke of York, by refraining from their issue, kept more strictly in the line of precedent, and, on that account, for a time at least, they were able better to control the exercise of political power. They conceded less at the outset than did the proprietors of Carolina, New Jersey, and Pennsylvania.

In Maryland, as in the other provinces, the effective exercise of government began with the appointment of the governor. Between two and three hundred colonists came thither on the first vessels in 1634.[1] Before they left England, a

[1] Calvert Papers, I. 131 *et seq.*

governor, a secretary, and a surveyor were appeared. Closely
associated also with the governor were two commissioners,
Jerome Hawley and Thomas Cornwallis, who were likewise
appointed in England.   They were called " commissioners
for the government of the province," and were the germ of
the executive council.   The first instructions extant were
issued by the proprietor to the governor and commissioners
jointly.   According to the instructions the appointees were
enjoined to keep the peace on board ship during the voyage,
to choose a place for a settlement on their arrival, to land the
colonists, cause them to assemble to hear the patent read,
take charge of Indian relations, and of relations between the
colony and its English neighbors.

In April, 1637,[1] a general ordinance of government, containing a commission for a governor, a council, and a secretary, as well as direction for calling an assembly, was issued.
This clearly shows what the powers of the governor were.
The military function was placed in the foreground.   The
governor was designated as lieutenant-general and admiral,
and as such was within the province the chief commander
of its militia, its forts and vessels of war.   Indian relations
fell partly under this head, and partly under the powers
relating to trade.   The second power mentioned was that of
chancellor.   By virtue of this the governor was keeper of
the seal of the province, and from him all patents, territorial
and governmental grants, writs for elections and original
processes, licenses, and many other public documents took
their origin.   As chancellor also the governor was judge in
equity for the province, with power, if he saw fit, to call the
council to his aid in its exercise, a discretion which the governors of Maryland never chose to exercise.   From 1661 to
1689 the office of chancellor was distinct from that of governor and was held by another individual.   This was also
the case during two brief intervals at a later time.   But
with these exceptions the two offices were united in the
same hands throughout the entire history of Maryland as
a province.

Under his authority as chief justice the governor was

[1] Council Proceedings, 1636–1667, p. 49 *et seq.*

chief common law judge, with power to hear and determine all cases, civil and criminal, as if the proprietor himself were present. When life, member, or freehold were involved, the councillors should sit as judges with him. The fact that the governor was intrusted with the pardoning power, save in cases of high treason, at the same time that he was judge, shows how limited was the official personnel of the province in the early period of its existence.

The title of chief magistrate apparently refers to the power of the governor as leading conservator of the peace in the province, and to the fact that from him proceeded the authority which was exercised by the sheriffs, constables, and justices of the peace in arresting, detaining, and binding over offenders. Closely connected with the governor's magisterial authority was his general executive power; that is, his power to issue and execute ordinances, to establish ports, harbors, markets, and fairs, to care for the interests of the province and control its administration in general, supplementing in all needful ways the work done under the functions already specified, so as to make a rounded whole. Under this head fell the power of the governor, as the constituent part of the legislature, to call, prorogue, and dissolve it, and to accept or veto its acts. The last-named power was also exercised by the Maryland proprietor on such acts as passed the governor. This right was of special value to the proprietor,[1] in that it enabled him to review acts which established, confirmed, or changed officials in the province, or infringed any of his rights. Later commissions made no material change in the governor's powers, though the gradual expansion of the official system made it necessary that in time some of his authority should be shared by others.

Within the province, especially in the early time, the governor was the centre from whom radiated military, judicial, administrative, and, to a considerable extent, legislative activity. He was the proprietor's commissioner or agent for all purposes of government. Power was transmitted to him by a commission, and he was guided in the use of it by instructions. Instructions might be given him at the time

[1] Council Proceedings, 1636–1667, 154, The Commission of 1644.

of his appointment or at any later period. The letters written by the proprietor to his governor were informal instructions. As cases in point, may be cited the detailed instructions given to Leonard Calvert and his associates before they left England in 1634, the various conditions of plantation, a long list of instructions concerning grants of land, the reorganization and management of the land office, and a less number relating chiefly or wholly to matters of government.[1] Appointments to office, relations with Claiborne and with the Jesuit priests who accompanied the early settlers to America, Indian affairs, relations with Virginia and with the Dutch, internal disturbances and attacks on the proprietor's authority, the calling of assemblies, measures the passage of which would encroach on his prerogative — all these and many more affairs of a public nature are referred to in a manner more or less imperative in the proprietor's letters and formal instructions. Since the early governors of Maryland were in several instances members of the Calvert family, instructions were most frequently conveyed through the informal channel of letters, and these often refer in detail to the management of the private estates of the proprietor,[2] the purchase and sale of stock and products, building of houses, servants, control of trade, and the like. The correspondence with the secretary and with some of the councillors also partakes largely of this character.[3] These give an informal aspect to the communications between the proprietor and his subordinates which reminds one that, even under the system of individual property, the province had not lost all the characteristics of a plantation.

The governor, in return, was expected to report his doings to the proprietor, and to keep him informed concerning all

---

[1] Those relating to territorial affairs will be most easily found in Kilty, Landholder's Assistant. All are printed in the Council Proceedings under their respective dates. The letters, so far as preserved, will be found mainly among the Calvert Papers, and some specimens of them have been printed. A few instructions appear among the Proceedings of the Assembly. Examples of Maryland instructions may be cited as found in Proceedings of Council, 1636–1667, 51, 99, 135, 139, 324, 329, 335, 385 ; Assembly Proceedings, 1637–1664, 321–323 ; Council Proceedings, 1667–1678, 54, 63, 94.

[2] Calvert Papers, I. 211, 229.   [3] Ibid. I. 194.

affairs, public and private, in the province. This, with the aid of the secretary and other officials, he did, and in the same informal manner which characterized the instructions. The governor, like all other officials, held office at the proprietor's pleasure, and was in no respect legally independent of him. Of this the first Cecilius was not slow to inform his brother, Leonard Calvert, when in 1641 he had granted some land to the Jesuits contrary to the proprietor's express order. "Certainly," he wrote,[1] "I have the power to revoke anie authoritie I have given you, either in whole or in part, . . . for you are but meerly instrumentall in those things to doe what I direct, and not to compel mee to doe what you thinke fitting." "I shall earnestlie therefore desire you to bee more observant hereafter of my directions, and not to expect that I should satisfie your judgment by acquainting you still with my reasons why I direct anie thing; for then my power there were no more than any mans else, who may with reasons persuade you to doe or forbeare anything as well as I."

In order to the existence of proprietary government, it was not necessary that the proprietor should reside in the province. Wherever the governor was, there was the proprietor. The governor brought the proprieter into the province, for every public act of the governor, if legally performed, was done in the name and by the authority of his superior. Anything which the proprietor could lawfully do, he could require his governor to do ; and at the outset the proprietor was limited only by the very general, though in the sphere of private rights the comprehensive, terms of his charter. In the provincial system, then, provision was made for instructions before it was decisively made for legislation, and it was only through instructions that legislation could legally begin and be continued. Instructions were as normal and regular a part of the system as was lawmaking. Not only were they sent to the governor, but, when necessary, to all other officials appointed by the proprietor. Any official in the province might also send them to his subordinates.[2]

[1] Calvert Papers, I. 219.
[2] Council Proceedings, 1636–1667, 141, 147, 161, etc.

So far as Maryland is concerned, reference to the official oath will furnish additional evidence that the relation between the proprietor and the governor was such as has been indicated. The oath which was prescribed in 1648[1] bound the appointee to defend and maintain the jurisdiction and seigniory of the proprietor to the utmost of his power, and never to " accept of nor execute any Place, Office, or Employment, within the said Province anyway Concerning or relating to the Government of the said Province from any Person or Authority but by from or under a lawful Authority derived or to be derived from time to time under the hand of his said Lordship or his heirs and Assigns." The oath of 1669[2] was drawn in the same terms. This furnishes additional evidence that, unlike the governor of the corporate colony, the head of the proprietary province derived his official status, not from the colony, but from the proprietor. He was head of the province by virtue of his being intermediary between it and the proprietor.

It has already been stated that at the time when the office of governor was brought into existence provision was made for a council. Of this body the governor was *ex officio* a member. By the commission of 1637 he was commanded to advise with its members " as he shall see cause upon all occasions concerning the good of our Said Province and of the people there." That it was associated with the governor in the discharge of the highest judicial functions we have seen. The councillor's oath, as formulated and administered in 1639, bound him to bear true faith to the proprietor and defend his rights, maintain the peace and welfare of the people, assist in the administration of justice, give good advice to the proprietor and his governor, and keep secret the affairs of state.[3] This oath proves that the council was an important part of the provincial executive, and that as such it was under obligation to uphold the rights of the proprietor. It

[1] Council Proceedings, 1636–1667, 209.

[2] *Ibid.* 1667–1688, 39.

[3] The oath was prescribed in one of the bills which in 1639 just failed of final passage through the assembly ; but it was later used. Proceedings of Assembly, 1637–1664, 44 ; Proceedings of Council, 1636–1667, 85 ; Bozman, II. 140.

stood toward the governor in a relation analogous to that occupied by the privy council toward the king in England. In 1642 the council received for the first time a commission[1] distinct from that of the governor. In this it was called "our privie Councell within our said Province of Maryland," and its members were empowered to meet with the governor when and where he should direct, "to treate, consult, deliberate and advise of all matters, causes and things which shall be discovered unto you, . . . as well concerning the quiet government and regulating the people there, as for the good & safety of our said Province of Maryland." The peculiar function of the council, therefore, was to advise the governor and through him the proprietor, and without that advice the governor should not act. The councillors in early times also occupied the status of justices of the peace in their respective counties, their judicial powers in this connection being set forth in the commissions of the governors.[2] The powers of the council as the upper house of the legislature will require notice in another connection.

The council was never a large body. Its existence began with three members, and by 1690 it had reached the number of nine or ten. Its actual membership never exceeded this. Its extant records, prior to 1660, are so fragmentary that little idea of its composition can be obtained. Its journal subsequent to that date reveals the fact that business was usually transacted in the presence of from three to six, among whom the governor, chancellor, and secretary would in most cases be found. The councillors were appointed by the proprietor, usually on the recommendation of the governor. They were appointed for indefinite terms, and death or resignation were as a rule the only causes which brought their official careers to an end. The board met at irregular, but frequent, intervals, and during the seventeenth century it did a great variety of business. By it or in its presence

[1] Council Proceedings, 1636–1667, 114. Substantially the same language was used in the commission of 1644. *Ibid.* 157, 159.

[2] *Ibid.* 1636–1667, 159. They are called in this commissioners for conservation of the peace, with authority individually or collectively to arrest, detain, and bind over; but when the time for trial came the governor must be associated with them.

counties and hundreds were erected, offices and courts were established, commissions and instructions were issued to officials, oaths were administered, trade and fees were regulated, petitions and complaints heard, pardons and licenses granted, ordinances issued, advice given with respect to calling, proroguing, and dissolving the assembly, orders were issued for expeditions against the Indians and protection against the other enemies or rivals of the province.[1]   In the eighteenth century the governor and council were deprived by legislation of many of their earlier powers, but in the seventeenth century they formed altogether the leading organ of the provincial government.

During the seventeenth century, when internal peace permitted, the expansion of the official system, under the action of the proprietor, governor, and council, kept even pace with the growth of the province.   By the ordinance of April, 1637, provision was made for a secretary, whose duties were closely connected with the original functions of the governor as chancellor.   The first incumbent of this position was also made judge of probate, register of the land office, and receiver of the proprietary rents, profits, and customs, while he acted also as surveyor-general and attorney-general.   A treasurer was also appointed, apparently by a separate commission.[2]   In 1642 the original office of surveyor was elevated to that of surveyor-general,[3] and separated from the office of secretary.   The same year the governor, council, and secretary received separate commissions.[4]   About the middle of the century the office of attorney-general was separated from that of the secretary, while in 1673 that of judge of probate was temporarily attached to the chancellor's office, though ultimately made a distinct function.   In 1676 two receiver-generals were appointed, and the secretary ceased to perform that function.   Four years later the secretary ceased to act as register of the land office, and that

CHAP.
III.

---

[1] See entries in the first two volumes of Maryland Archives, Proceedings of the Council. The summary is given by Mereness, Maryland as a Proprietary Province, 175.

[2] Calvert Papers, I. 153.

[3] Council Proceedings, 1636–1667, 101.   [4] *Ibid.* 108.

became a separate position.   In 1685 the office of examiner-general was separated from that of surveyor-general.[1] Toward the close of the century, naval officers began to be appointed, a part of whose duties was to collect customs which were levied under acts of assembly.   Two treasurers were appointed, one for each shore, and their functions became distinct both from those of the naval officers and of the receiver-general.

The multiplication of lower offices was one of the results of the organization of counties and hundreds, of the establishment of courts and the development of a fiscal and a militia system.   These, in nearly all cases, like the central executive offices of the province, antedated the legislature, and derived their origin from the proprietor.   They were created by act of the proprietor, or of the governor and council proceeding with his approval, and in imitation of corresponding English institutions and offices.   At first the entire west shore of Maryland was treated as one county under the name of Saint Mary's,[2] while it may be said that the east shore was treated in the same way under the name of Kent, or Kent island.   These names appear also as the designations respectively of a hundred, a fort, and a town.   The settlements, as they grew up on either shore, were organized as hundreds,[3] and were used in early times as territorial units for elections, public levies, and the preservation of the peace. The chief officer of the hundred was an appointee of the governor, and, whether he went by the title of constable or conservator of the peace, had the powers of one or more justices of the peace in England.   The chief officer of Saint George's hundred was called a justice of the peace, and received authority to appoint a constable as his subordinate.   The justice of the hundred could arrest, try, and punish for petty crimes, and bind over grievous offenders to the county court for trial.

The bounds of Saint Mary's county were gradually defined by the formation of outlying counties.   Of the order of 1650,

---

[1] Kilty, *op. cit.* 83 ; Proceedings of Council, 1667–1688, 542.

[2] Council Proceedings, 1636–1667, 61.

[3] *Ibid.* 59, 70, 89, 91 ; Assembly Proceedings, 1637–1664, 2, 87 *et seq.*

and that of 1654, repealing the above ordinance and estab-   CHAP.
lishing the bounds of Calvert county, the record has been   III.
preserved.[1] The orders for the erection of Somerset county
and for the attempted erection of Worcester county on
Delaware bay are exceptionally detailed.[2] But the more
important act in the establishment of a county was the
erection of the county court. Though the detailed consideration of this subject more properly belongs in a later
chapter, it may here be said that, prior to 1690, the county
courts of Maryland, with one exception, were created by the
executive. By the governor their officers were appointed,
and by him their jurisdiction to an extent established.

The same was true of the military officials. The governor's commission implied that he should possess full power
of appointment, and that all should obey him as lieutenant-
general and admiral. Thomas Cornwallis, the councillor,
commanded the first expedition against Claiborne. In May,
1638, John Boteler was appointed captain of the Kent island
militia. In May, 1639, on the eve of a conflict with the
Indians, Giles Brent was appointed captain of the military
band of Saint Mary's. This expressly gave him immediate
command for purposes of training over "all Inhabitants of
Our Said Colony able to bear arms, those only of our
Council excepted." After several more subordinate appointments, in August, 1642, Thomas Cornwallis was commissioned, with the power of a captain-general, to levy men and
lead them on an expedition against the Indians. His
authority for this purpose seems to have extended throughout the province. The following spring he was commissioned again for the same purpose, while Thomas Baldridge
was at the same time ordered to take the assize of arms and
ascertain the number of persons within his hundred who
were able to serve. During the perturbed state of the
province, between 1646 and 1657, we know that the gov-

[1] Council Proceedings, 1636–1667, 259, 308.
[2] *Ibid.* 553–555 ; *ibid.* 1667–1688, 108. By the assembly of 1654, which
was held under the parliamentary commissioners, Patuxent county was
created by legislation. This was done when the authority of the proprietor
was suspended, and Patuxent does not appear in the later list of counties.
Proceedings of Assembly, 1637–1664, 369, 381, 396.

ernors repeatedly appeared at the head of the provincial
forces, as did Calvert in 1646 and Stone in 1655. Whenever outrages were committed by the Indians, or serious
outbreaks on their part occurred, especially also when,
because of conflicts between the Five Nations and the
Susquehannas, the peace of the northern part of the province was threatened, armed expeditions were fitted out
under the authority of the governor and council. Instances
of such action during the period under review were the
expedition of 1652 against the Indians of the eastern shore,
of the spring of 1661 to aid the Susquehannas at Susquehanna Fort, of the summer of 1664 and 1665 against raiders
presumably from among the Five Nations. The despatch of
Henry Coursey to Albany in 1677 to negotiate with the Five
Nations was caused by the almost yearly repetition of their
attacks, which necessitated defensive operations. These all
were carried on directly under the authority of the executive and of the commissions and instructions which he
issued.[1]

By the process and to the extent thus indicated was the
official system developed in Maryland prior to 1690. It constituted at once the provincial executive and judiciary, and
was dependent almost wholly on the proprietor. The support of its members was largely derived from fees, and in
addition from the appropriation by the legislature of a poll
tax or the proceeds of a customs duty. Repeatedly during
the decade between 1640 and 1650, and during the years
between 1662 and 1670, such taxes were levied for the support of the government.[2] Occasionally special grants of
land were made to the governor, and he, with the other
leading officials, was so situated that large favors of this
kind could be procured. It was the intention of the assembly that one-half of the revenue from the export duty of
2s. per hogshead on tobacco, for which provision was made
by the act of 1671, should go to the support of the governor
and council and for a supply of arms and ammunition. For

[1] Proceedings of Council, 1636–1667, 75, 86, 87, 88, 102, 104, 106, 132,
148, 282, 411, 502, 522 et seq.; ibid. 1667–1688, 21 et seq.; Bozman, II. 287.
[2] Mereness, op. cit. 171 et seq.

this purpose it was presumably used.   During the period
under review no question of the proper support of officials
arose ; it did not become an issue, and the action of the executive was not modified or hampered by it.

Prior to 1690 no effort was made to limit the proprietor's
right of appointment, except in the case of sheriffs. The duties
of the sheriffs were then large, for, besides being the executive
officers of the courts, they held elections for members of the
lower house and collected all direct taxes, officers' fees, and
dues of the clergy.   For a time, also, about 1671, they were
concerned with the collection of quitrents.   In 1642 an act
was passed requiring that the governor should appoint sheriffs from lists presented by the provincial court and by each
county court.   An act of 1662 added to this provision one
forbidding any person to serve as sheriff longer than one
year.   Both of these were temporary acts and soon expired.
But during the period of the Restoration complaints of the
oppressive administration of sheriffs continued and multiplied, so that in 1678 an act was passed forbidding any one
to serve in that office longer than one year, unless at its end
he procured from the court of his county a certificate that
he had performed the duties of his office with justice.   This,
though it was kept on the statute book, was evidently not
an effective limitation; but it was the only one which, before
1690, was applied to the appointing power of the proprietor.

By the creation of offices and the appointment of their
incumbents the influence of the proprietor was extended
through the province and was consolidated.   Those who held
the higher offices were for the most part large landholders,
while conversely the holding of office was very likely to
facilitate the increase of the incumbent's estates.   In other
words, under the Maryland system, there was a tendency
toward the identification of the large landholders with the
official class.   But at the same time the higher offices were
concentrated in the hands of a few persons, and these, in
addition to being large landholders, were in many instances
relatives of the proprietor.   The last-mentioned feature of
the system appears very clearly after 1660, when Charles
Calvert was governor and afterward proprietor.   Before

that time the only conspicuous instance of that kind was
the appointment of Leonard Calvert, brother of the first
proprietor, as governor.   About 1660 Philip Calvert was
appointed first as secretary, then governor, and, when his
service in that capacity ended, he retained the chancellorship
as a distinct office.   Between 1669 and the overthrow of
the proprietary government in 1689 the system of family
government, with accompanying privileges and cliques, was
at its height.   During a part of this time Charles Calvert
and his brother Philip were on bad terms and acted to an
extent as rivals.   In 1669, among the members of the
council — which was also the upper house — were Charles
Calvert, Philip Calvert, and William Calvert, Baker Brooke,
who was brother-in-law of William Calvert, and the firm
friends of the family, Jerome White and William Coursey.[1]
Soon after the arrival of Charles Calvert in the province,
his intimate friend, Henry Sewall, was made[2] secretary and
a member of the council.   Sewall married a daughter of
Vincent Lowe, who was later a councillor and surveyor-
general.[3]   By her he had four daughters and one son.   On
Sewall's death Charles Calvert married the widow.   In due
course the children all married, and the husbands of the
daughters — Dr. Jesse Wharton, Colonel Benjamin Rozier,
Colonel William Chandler, and Philip Calvert — found their
way either into the council, the provincial court, or the
offices of sheriff and colonel of militia.   William Burgess,
whose daughter Nicholas Sewall, the son, married, became
a councillor.   Thomas Notley, a strong friend of the proprietor, was for some time speaker of the lower house and
later became a member of the council.

The accumulation of offices in the same hands also contributed toward the concentration of political power.   Secretary
Lewger, who by his capacity and intelligence contributed not
a little to the early success of the provincial government, received, in addition to his chief office, those[4] of receiver-gen-

[1] Proceedings of Assembly, 1666–1676, 157 ; Sparks, Maryland Revolution
of 1689, J. H. U. Studies, XIV.

[2] Proceedings of Council, 1636–1667, 439.

[3] *Ibid.* 1667–1688, 309 *et seq.* ; Sparks, *op. cit.*   [4] *Ibid.* 1636–1667, 55, 60, 71.

eral, judge of probate, justice of the peace, deputy governor,
while he was at the same time a member of the council.
The members of the council constituted also the provincial
court.   They might or might not act with the governor
as a court of admiralty.   Reference has already been made
to the union of large judicial powers with his many executive
duties in the hands of the governor.   It has also been stated
that the members of the council were *ex officio* justices of
the peace.   It is true that they, with their immediate connections, held in many instances the positions of colonels of
the county militia.[1]   The control of the proprietor over the
personnel of the sheriffs was almost complete.   It therefore
appears that, from the attainment of internal peace about
1660, until 1689, official power in Maryland was centred
in a few hands and these belonging to the proprietor's own
family or his immediate political connections.   The official
system was at that time an instrument which he and his
governor could use almost as they chose.   That it was used
to hold in check all manner of popular movement which was
favorable to change or reform in the province, is indicated
by the numerous arrests and prosecutions for seditious conduct which occurred after 1670.   The spirit of the administration under Charles Calvert was narrow, and toward those
who refused quietly to submit to the pretensions of the government it was oppressive.   The feeling of agitation and
suspense which presently began to pervade the province was
faintly suggestive of conditions which at the same time
existed in England.

[1] Proceedings of Council, 1667–1688, 309.

CHAPTER IV

THE LEGISLATURE IN MARYLAND AND ITS RELATIONS WITH THE EXECUTIVE

THE charters which the proprietors received from the crown went farther toward guarantying the existence of legislatures within the colonies than did those which created the corporations. The latter made no reference to any assembly except the general court of the company, leaving it wholly to the latter to grant or withhold the benefits of a colonial legislature. In the proprietary charters, beginning with that of Maryland, the grantees were empowered to make laws and to do so with the assent of the freemen of their provinces, and it was declared to be the will of the king that they should be called together for the purpose. But it was left to the option of the proprietor to determine when, where, and how he should exercise this power. A proprietary instruction or concession was therefore necessary to bring the legislature into existence and to continue its activity. The existence of a parliament in England did not legally necessitate the existence of assemblies in her colonies, though it greatly increased the difficulties of governing them without assemblies. Moreover, their origin is not to be found in the natural or preëxistent rights of Englishmen. Like all their other organs of government, the legislatures of the provinces developed as the result of social and political causes operating upon the proprietors and in the provinces themselves. Though not original in the sense in which the executive was, events soon showed them to be instruments of government which were indispensable to proprietors as well as provincials, and about their development centre events of the greatest interest in the history of the provinces. Their study reveals the operation of forces which were to

74

transform the fief and thus to open the way for the growth CHAP.
of modern democratic institutions. The rise of assemblies IV.
in the English-American colonies is an event of great significance in the history of the world. Its importance will be
evident to any one who takes the trouble to compare events
as they occurred in these colonies during the seventeenth
century with the trend of institutional development at the
same period, especially on the European continent.

The form of the legislature in the corporate colony was
determined by the organization of the general court of the
trading company from which it developed. The form of
the general assembly in the province was determined by
the concessions of the executive, and by the form which the
executive had assumed when the legislature had reached its
full development. The first step toward calling a general
assembly was taken by the proprietor, who, if he was not in
the province, instructed his governor to issue writs of election, with such other summonses as might be necessary.
The electors to whom these writs were issued were not
freemen in the technical sense of being members of a corporation, but were such in the broad and general sense which
attaches to that term. In the beginning they were literally
free men, but the law soon came to define them as freeholders.

When met in regular form the legislature consisted of
the governor, the council or upper house, and the assembly
or deputies. The latter, who were sent by the localities,
constituted the only representative part of the legislature.
Its other elements were, as a rule, appointed, were a part
of the executive, and were in existence before the legislature
met. In both tenure and functions the governor and council were legally independent both of the deputies and of the
electors. They held their offices at the pleasure of the
proprietor, and were or might be guided by his instructions. Engaged as they were in the permanent work of
government, they would naturally be swayed by a regard
for the interests of the proprietor and by some sense of
administrative traditions and needs. Though a component
of the legislature, the council was also the legal adviser of

the governor and through him of the proprietor. As the governor, unless specially limited by law, had the sole power of calling, proroguing, and dissolving the general assembly, the council might advise him in such a way as to destroy the body itself or thwart its plans. The joint work of the council and assembly was subject to the veto power of the proprietor, or of both the proprietor and his governor. The legislature of the province, therefore, differed materially from the general court, though in practice this was somewhat offset by the fact that in the New England colonies the magistrates were in the majority of cases reëlected for a long series of terms. In the province, as in the kingdom, the legislature was in a sense an expansion of the executive, developed out of it, and was to an extent controlled by it. Out of this relation arose the possibility of conflict between the two parts of the legislature—that which represented the people and that which represented the proprietor.

The policy of the first proprietor of Maryland apparently was to call assemblies frequently, but to control their proceedings by retaining in his own hands the exclusive right to initiate legislation. Not until the close of the disturbed period of the Commonwealth and the restoration to Lord Baltimore of the powers, the exercise of which had been suspended at the advent of the commissioners of parliament, did the legislature of Maryland assume its final and permanent form. In its early sessions it consisted of only one house and that was variously organized. In 1658, so far as the legislature was representative, the hundred was the unit of representation ; but the representative element in the body throughout those years was decidedly fluctuating. For the general assembly of January, 1638, — the earliest whose records have been preserved, — both personal writs and writs of election were issued, but the only one which has been preserved was that directed to Captain Evelyn,[1] commander of Kent island. It commanded him to assemble the freemen of that locality and to persuade such as he should think fit to attend in person ; the others he should authorize either to go themselves or to elect and send deputies. It was left

[1] Md. Arch., Assembly, 1638–1664, 1.

wholly to the freemen of the localities to decide how many deputies they would send, but a record of the election and of all else which was done should be returned by them to the secretary of the province. The assembly was attended by the governor and the members of the council, by the commander of Kent island and one of his council, by two other officials, together with twenty gentlemen and planters and one artisan, all of whom came in response to writs addressed to them personally. The rest of the freemen, so far as they took any action at all, sent proxies, and many of the proxies were held by officials. Those who did not appear, either in person or by proxy, were fined. On every day until the close of the session cases occur of the admission of freemen to seats ; the membership roll of the assembly was never closed. The body seems not to have contained a single representative ; it was substantially a primary assembly, with the governor as its president. Though summoned in a different way, it, to an extent, resembled the New England court of election.

But in the legislature of February, 1639, the above model was almost wholly abandoned. Elections were held in nearly all the hundreds, and the assembly which resulted was largely representative. Individual writs were apparently sent to only three besides the members of the council. Two were admitted without election or special writ. An enactment was passed at this session and became law, to the effect that the general assembly should consist of the lieutenant-general and secretary, of gentlemen summoned by special writ, and of one or two burgesses chosen out of every hundred. Included in a list of bills, already referred to, which failed of final passage, was one providing for triennial assemblies, and one providing that the general assembly should have within the province the same powers as the House of Commons in England.

From this time until 1650 the legislature fluctuated in its organization between the primary and the representative form, while a small proportion of the members attended in response to personal writs. The general assembly of October, 1640,[1] was almost wholly representative. It was continued in existence by successive prorogations until March,

[1] Archives, Assembly, 1638–1664, 89.

1642. In July, 1641, however, elections were held in Kent island and in two of the hundreds, and from one of these, Saint Clement's, Thomas Gerard, lord of the manor, was returned in the place of Robert Vaughan. Vaughan thereupon asked " to have a voice in his own person," but was refused. Gerard, as lord of the manor, was also summoned in person, by virtue of the proprietor's authority to specially summon "gentlemen of able judgment and quality." Writs of election for a new assembly were issued in January, 1642,[1] but, for some reason which is not stated, early in March they were superseded by a proclamation of the governor requiring all freemen either to attend the assembly personally or to send proxies. This was obeyed and the legislature which resulted was organized substantially as that of 1638 had been. A resolve was passed that it should not be adjourned or prorogued without its own consent, and it adjourned itself from day to day. At the close of a short session, during which it manifested some independence toward the proprietor, it was dissolved.

In July, 1642,[2] writs of election were issued and personal writs were sent to nine individuals. Elections were held and burgesses were returned from all the localities of the province. No proxies seem to have been sent to this assembly, except one or two by those who were personally summoned. A natural result of the adoption of this form of organization was the proposal made by Robert Vaughan in the name of the burgesses that the general assembly should be divided and the representatives sit by themselves and have a negative voice; but the governor would not agree to it. The unsettled condition of affairs was again shown when a new general assembly was called in September, 1642. Under the authority of the governor's proclamation the proxy system was entirely restored.[3] In this body there seem to have been no representatives. One hundred and eighty-two persons were entitled to seats, of whom eighteen were individually summoned, eighty-eight attended without personal summons or sent proxies, and seventy-six were fined twenty

[1] Archives, Assembly, 114, 115.   [2] Ibid., 1638–1664, 127, 129.
[3] Ibid. 167 ; Bozman, II. 237.

pounds of tobacco each because they failed to be present.
The proxy system seems to have been retained until 1644,[1]
or possibly a year later. Records of the sessions between
April, 1644, and December, 1646, are lacking. The general
assembly of the latter date, which was called by Governor
Hill at Saint Inigoe's Fort, and continued by Calvert, contained burgesses, and one would infer from the fragmentary
record which remains that it consisted of two houses. It is
stated that Governor Calvert, " in the upper house," with
two councillors, called the burgesses before him and assured
them that they might consult as freely as in any earlier
assembly. But in January, 1648, the representative system [2]
was again abandoned, and in that body there is no trace even
of personally summoned members. The general assembly
held by Governor Stone in April, 1649, the one which passed
the famous act concerning religion, seems, on the other hand,[3]
to have consisted of council and burgesses. In the proclamation by which the assembly of April, 1650, was summoned,
it was left to the option of the freemen to choose delegates [4]
or to attend personally or by proxy. All the hundreds now
showed their preference for the representative system by
electing burgesses. This legislature did not stop there, but
as soon as it met organized in two houses and passed an act
confirming what had been done. This, as it proved, committed Maryland permanently to the representative system
and to the normal provincial legislature of two houses; the
upper house consisting of the council, presided over by the
governor, and the lower house consisting of the burgesses.
Only during the brief period when affairs were administered
by the commissioners of parliament did the legislature meet
again in a single house.

The upper house, in its legislative as in its executive
capacity, supported the interests of the proprietor. In its
sympathies it represented him rather than the people of the
province, and was really a projection of the executive into
the legislature. It was a small body, consisting wholly of
the governor's nominees and of the proprietor's appointees,

[1] Archives, Assembly, 1638–1664, 201, 205, 209.
[2] *Ibid.* 214.   [3] *Ibid.* 238 *et seq.*   [4] *Ibid.* 259 *et seq.*, 272.

all holding during pleasure. Though subsequent to 1675 the governor[1] ceased to be a member of the upper house, it was still easy for him to control it. Neither house made much use of committees till near the close of the seventeenth century, and the upper house needed them scarcely at all except for the purpose of negotiating with the lower house. The lower house contained the representatives of the free-holders of the province, and through it taxes were voted and their desires and interests found expression.

At the outset it was the intention of Lord Baltimore to control the proceedings of his legislatures, not only by his right of appointing and instructing the governor and mem-bers of the upper house, by his veto[2] power and the influence which he could exert in many other ways, but by retaining in his own hands the exclusive right to initiate legislation. He attempted at the beginning to exercise this power on a large scale. Whether his rejection of all the acts of the general assembly of 1635 was due to the fact that they originated with that body, we cannot tell. But he caused to be submitted to the general assembly of January, 1638, — the second legislature which met in the province, — a series of twelve bills which he desired to have enacted.[3] They were read and debated, and finally, by a majority of the mem-bers, led by Captain Cornwallis, they were rejected. Only the votes of the governor and Secretary Lewger, and the proxies which they held, were cast in favor of their passage. Then the question arose, by what laws the province should be governed. Some said that they would do well to agree upon certain acts, which should be in force till they heard again from England. The governor at once denied that the assembly had such power. Captain Cornwallis then sug-gested that in the interim they be governed by the laws of England. To this the governor replied that by his commis-sion he was empowered to proceed in civil causes according to the laws of England, and in criminal causes also if they did not involve life or member. In cases of this nature he

---

[1] Proceedings of Council, 1671–1681, 10.

[2] Ibid. 1636–1667, 51, 111, 154, 203, 543 ; ibid. 1666–1676, 161, 173, et seq.

[3] Ibid. 1638–1664, 6 et seq.

could proceed only by the laws of the province, and if these
were lacking, great crimes could not be punished. On
examining the commission, this was found to be true. In
spite of the assurance from some that such crimes could hardly
be committed without mutiny, and in that case they might
be punished by martial law, the prospect was apparently not
reassuring. When, the following afternoon, a motion was
made that some bills be considered with a view to their transmission to the proprietor, the governor went so far as to advise
that a committee be chosen to draft them. This was done.

When the discussion of the subject was resumed, on motion
of this committee the bills sent over by the proprietor were
again considered, because it was found that their rejection
had been due to the existence of misunderstanding concerning them. Between thirty and forty new bills, prepared by
this and a later committee, were considered along with them.
The result was the passage of a considerable number of acts at
the close of this session, all of which, however, were rejected [1]
by the proprietor, probably as a further assertion of his claim
to the right of initiative.

But before the general assembly of the next year met Lord
Baltimore apparently became convinced that it was unwise,
if not useless, to longer contend for the claim in the extreme
form in which he had asserted it. Therefore, after organization,[2] the first business of that session was to listen to a
letter in which the proprietor authorized the governor to assent
to acts originated and passed by the general assembly, and that
they should be in force in the province until Lord Baltimore
or his heirs should express their dissent. An act declaring
the substance of this concession as it applied to the existing
assembly was at once passed. When the commission of the
governor was reissued by the proprietor,[3] it was made to con-
form to the regulation thus established.

And yet these acts, in the proprietor's opinion, did not deprive him of a right to a share in initiating legislation, for, in
1649, moved apparently by the disturbances recently created
by Claiborne, Ingle, and their Puritan supporters, he sent

---

[1] Bozman, II. 67.　　[2] Proceedings of Assembly, 1638–1664, 31, 32, 75.
[3] Proceedings of Council, 1636–1667, 111.

over under his great seal sixteen bills which he instructed
the governor to lay before the assembly for its acceptance
as perpetual laws.   Among these were a number, the intent
of which was to secure the right of the colonists to freedom
of conscience, freedom from martial law except in camp and
garrison, exemption from taxes, and especially from contributions to wars outside the province without the consent
of the assembly, and freedom of trade with the natives on
reasonable conditions.   There was also among them an act
in recognition of the royal charter, and another providing for
an oath of fidelity; and the expressions "absolute lord and
proprietary" and "royal jurisdiction" which were contained
in these at once provoked criticism.[1]   In a long letter the
assembly insisted on its right and on the necessity of making
a selection from among the measures which the proprietor
had sent over, and adding others of its own which might be
less elaborate, but, in their opinion, better suited to the condition of the province.   In view of the stringent oaths which
the proprietor had directed to be taken, the assembly asked
to be let off with "as little Swearing as Conveniently may
be."   The proprietor was also requested not to send over
bodies of laws "which serve little other end than to fill our
heads with suspitious Jealousies and dislikes of that which
we understand not."   Instead, they urged that "some short
heads of what is desired" might be sent, and they pledged
themselves in dealing with these to give the governor all reasonable satisfaction.   A part of the proprietor's bills were
selected — among them perhaps the one concerning religion
— and others were added; the whole number was then
passed and sent to England.

The reply of the proprietor to this was a long declaration,[2]
which was laid before the assembly of 1650.   In this he
defended his royal jurisdiction and attributed the failure of
the preceding assembly to pass all the sixteen bills to the
machinations of his enemies.   He offered, if the sixteen
bills were passed, to release the province from one-half the
tobacco duty appropriated in a recent act.   But this did not
have the desired effect.   The assembly of 1650 substantially

[1] Proceedings of Assembly, 1638-1664, 238 et seq.   [2] Ibid. 262.

repeated the policy followed by its predecessor ; a selection
was made from among the bills sent over by the proprietor,
and others which were initiated by the legislature were
added.   With this Lord Baltimore abandoned his effort,
and the independence of the legislature, so far as it was
possible under the Maryland system of government, was
attained.   Its competency for all questions of local legislation was asserted.

But before this point was reached events had occurred
which reveal the extent to which the whole course of legal
and constitutional development within a province depended
on the relations between the legislature and the executive ;
in other words, on the comparative extent, at the outset or at
any point along the road, of the realm covered by statute and
of that covered by ordinance.   The legislature of February,
1639, as we have already intimated, advanced to a stage preliminary to the third reading a large number of bills,[1] the
object of which was to provide thus early a statutory basis
for all the institutions of the province; to take them, so far
as possible, out of the sphere of the prerogative, of custom,
and the common law, and to define and guaranty them
through positive legislation.   Thus it was sought to guaranty the liberties of the church, the liberties of settlers as
English subjects, the title of the proprietor to the lands of
the province, to assure titles in general to lands and goods,
to establish offices and courts and prescribe their duties, to
provide official oaths, regulate fees, establish ports, and provide a system of military discipline.   These elaborate measures did not then become law.   Instead, a few summary
enactments and such as were ineffective for the purpose
were passed.   The ideal, a glimpse of which had been thus
revealed, was left to be striven for, chiefly by the representatives in the lower house, during the entire period of provincial government.   A programme had been formulated,
and the most important part of the history of the province,
that part which gives the story unity and meaning, consists
in the record of the efforts that were made to carry it into
execution.

[1] Proceedings of Assembly, 1638-1664, 39-84.

Suggestions of the possible attitude of the lower house toward the executive appear in 1642. In the first session of that year, when a bill providing for an expedition against the Indians was read, the majority voted that the management of the enterprise should not be left to the discretion of the governor and council.[1] When, in the second session of that year, great opposition appeared among the burgesses to a proposed military expedition,[2] the governor told them that "he did not intend to advise with them whether there should be a march or not, for that Judgment belonged solely to himself as appeared by the Clause of the Patent touching the power of war and peace, but to see what Assistance they would contribute to it in case he should think fit to go."

A temporary act had been passed which regulated the granting of permits to leave the province. That law having expired, in the third session of 1642 Giles Brent, in obedience to the sentiment of Kent island, moved that it be re-enacted. The governor not only objected[3] to any attempt being made to decide such a question in the assembly, but refused to put Brent's motion. He declared that the freemen were not judges of the question, and, following English precedent, asserted that it was the right of all inhabitants to depart from the province, unless they were in debt or liable to punishment, or unless, for some reason connected with public safety, the proprietor or governor might temporarily, and in particular cases, overrule the right. This implied that the principle of the writ *ne exeat regno* should be applied to the province, and, notwithstanding a formal protest from members of the house, the contention of the governor prevailed.

Viewed from the constitutional standpoint, the most significant proposition yet made emanated from the lower house in the spring of 1660. Encouraged by a favorable turn of affairs in England, the lord proprietor had reached an agreement with Cromwell's commissioners in Maryland, by virtue of which proprietary government was restored. Josias Fendall had been appointed governor, and Philip Calvert, a

[1] Proceedings of Assembly, 1638–1664, 118.   [2] *Ibid.* 130.
[3] *Ibid.* 171, 173, 180.

brother of the proprietor, secretary. It was supposed that
the proprietory régime which had been interrupted nearly ten
years before would now be permanently reëstablished, and the
proprietor had ordered the bestowment of suitable rewards
in the form of land on those who had specially suffered in his
cause. In imitation of the practice in Virginia, it was proposed by some that the members of the council, with a part or
all of their families, should be exempted from taxation.[1] The
proprietor also resolved that an export duty should be levied
on tobacco. The two preceding acts of this nature had been
passed in 1647 and 1649. The former provided for a duty
of 10s. on every hogshead exported, and the latter, which
was to continue in force for seven years, limited the duty of
10s. to that tobacco which should be exported on Dutch
vessels bound for foreign ports.[2] But the act of 1649 did
not expressly repeal its predecessor. In 1659 the proprietor
instructed Fendall to procure an act levying 2s. on every
hogshead of tobacco exported to Great Britain or Ireland,
and 10s. per hogshead on that sent to any other ports. As
the law of 1647 had not been expressly repealed, the cry was
at once raised that the intention was to revive that act, and
Fendall played into the hands of the opposition. More than
a year previously, Thomas Gerard, of Saint Clement's Manor,
a prominent Catholic, had declared that Fendall would yield
to the Puritans of Ann Arundel anything they might desire,
however injurious it might be to the rights of the proprietor.[3] For this he was prosecuted by the attorney-general;
but, being a friend of the governor, he was not punished. The
organization of the assembly which was called to consider
Baltimore's instruction concerning the export duty, and
Fendall's attitude toward the plan which it then proposed,
revealed only too clearly the truth of Gerard's statement.

The writs called for four delegates from each county, but
Arundel county was represented in the assembly of Feb-
ruary, 1660, by seven members, at the head of whom was
William Fuller, the late Puritan governor. All except three

[1] Proceedings of Council, 1636–1667, 323, 333, 341.
[2] Proceedings of Assembly, 1638–1664, 420, 252.
[3] Proceedings of Council, 1636–1667, 355.

delegates from Saint Mary's county were opponents of the proprietor, and their election was contested, though without important result. In the upper house, the interests of the proprietor were supported by a small majority. A bill presumably embodying the instructions respecting the repeal of the act of 1647 was introduced, and that act was repealed the following year.[1]

The lower house then sent to the upper house a declaration to the effect that it considered itself a lawful assembly, without dependence on any other power in the province, and the highest court of judicature therein, and if any objection could be made to this they desired to hear it. The upper house inquired in return whether the paper was addressed to the council as the executive or as a part of the legislature, whether they considered themselves a lawful and complete assembly without the governor and upper house, whether they believed themselves independent of the proprietor. The lower house in reply to this desired a conference. In the conference Fendall, Gerard, and Utye supported the claim of the burgesses, while Philip Calvert, Baker Brooke, and Price stood by the proprietor. Fendall declared that in his opinion neither the proprietor nor his deputy should be present in the legislature or have a casting vote, and that the governor should not exercise the veto power; that laws should be passed by the freemen or their deputies, and when published should go into force till such time as the proprietor might express his dissent. Later declarations of the lower house showed that its object was to have the upper house join with it as a single chamber under the presidency of the speaker; that the speaker should have the power to dissolve the assembly, while the governor should lose his veto power and as a member of the single house should receive in its place only a double or casting vote. To this Fendall was ready to agree. But Philip Calvert absolutely refused to enter into such an arrangement for destroying the proprietor's share in the legislature, and with Baker Brooke he left the conference.[2]

[1] Proceedings of Assembly, 1638-1664, 381 *et seq.*
[2] *Ibid.* 388 *et seq.*

For the time the lower house was left supreme. It commissioned Fendall as governor, and appointed Gerard, Utye, and Slye, the speaker of the house, as his executive council.[1] Thus a movement toward independence, similar to that which had occurred a few years before in Virginia, seemed to have succeeded. But the triumph of Fendall and his associates was short. About two months later Charles II returned to the English throne. This insured the restoration of the proprietor's authority and the suppression of all tendencies toward a commonwealth. Philip Calvert was appointed governor and assumed office in the autumn of 1660. A council was appointed, and vigorous steps, military and administrative, were taken to prevent insurrection and to insure the reëstablishment of the proprietary régime. As it was, a "mutiny" occurred among Fendall's neighbors in Charles county, and John Jenkins, a captain of militia there, was outlawed. In response to severe instructions from the proprietor, several arrests were made among the opposition leaders, and Fendall and Gerard were sentenced by the provincial court to lose all their real and personal estate and to be banished from the province. Later, however, on advice of the council, they, as well as their less guilty associates, were pardoned, though Fendall and Gerard were forever disfranchised and forbidden to hold office in Maryland.[2] Fuller escaped arrest by flight, but his family continued for some years to live in Maryland. Fendall remained in the province, and, when occasion offered, continued to be a centre of opposition to the proprietor and his policy.

Reference to the account already given of the executive will suggest the points against which, during the next thirty years, the opposition directed its attacks. The influence of favoritism and privilege, as revealed in the concentration of offices in so few hands, and those so largely belonging to members of the Calvert family, was a constant source of irritation to many. The fact that the proportion of Catholics among the officeholders was much larger than their proportion among the population at large, gave an added point to the criticisms

[1] Kilty, Landholder's Assistant, 20.
[2] Proceedings of Council, 1636–1667, 396–409.

of the Protestant, and especially of the Puritan, element among the people. Maryland, between 1660 and 1690, was ruled by a family clique, a body which closed in and formed its ranks with great celerity after the protectorate in England and the period of civil strife within the province came to an end. The executive and the higher courts were wholly under its control. It managed the land system and military system and collected the public levies. Reference has already been made to the manifold duties of sheriffs and to their influence over elections and returns. Local government, save in a few localities, was under its control. Over the selection or removal of these officials and the determining of their policy, the colonists as such had no control, and little, if any, influence. The narrow and exclusive spirit in which, under Charles Calvert, the province was governed, strengthened in the mind of the ordinary colonist the impression that the official system was imposed from without. Its essentially monarchical or "absolute" nature was revealed in the fact that the appointing power of the proprietor and his governor, with their power to create offices, was so broad and inclusive. Until 1690 it was practically unlimited. Such legal talent as existed in the province was enlisted on the side of the government, and that strengthened the natural aversion of the farmer class to lawyers. The burden of the fee system, by which officials were mainly supported, was felt by all who had to employ their services. In many ways, besides the direct interference of sheriffs, officials could influence elections and the proceedings of the lower house. In 1671 Charles Calvert, as governor, congratulated himself much on the return to the assembly of Thomas Notley and John Morecroft from Saint Mary's county, and the election of the former as speaker. " Now I have gott Mr. Nottly into the Chaire," he wrote to his father, the proprietor, " I have Assured him, That with your Lordships Leave, I am Resolved to Keepe him there as longe as hee and I live together." [1] The bitter opponent of the proprietary régime who wrote the "Complaint from Heaven with a Huy and crye," not unnaturally declared that Notley was one of the " instruments " with which Lord Bal-

[1] Calvert Papers, I. 265.

timore worked, under the cloak of assemblies and the consent of freemen, to convert the common good to his private ends.[1] The Puritans as a body, together with some others, constituted a permanently dissatisfied element, which became active when Indian attacks and other causes made the imposition of taxes necessary.

When the assembly met in April, 1669, a communication from the lord proprietor was submitted,[2] stating that he disallowed a number of acts which had been passed in 1663,[3] more than five years before, and which were intended to secure interests of considerable value to the people at large. At the time of their passage the governor had given his assent, and upon that they had gone regularly into force. But that assent, under the proprietary system, was only provisional, and was liable at any time to be set aside by the veto of the proprietor himself. This involved a condition of perpetual uncertainty as to the status of the laws. Only those to which the proprietor had assented could be regarded as fixed, requiring as they did an act of assembly for their repeal. But the proprietor could choose his own time for declaring his assent, and until then there was no assurance of permanency. To this evil was added another, arising from the fact that in 1668 a public levy had been raised for defence under the authority of a perpetual law and without a special vote by the freemen. Complaints were also abroad

[1] Proceedings of Council, 1667–1688, 141. The complaints raised concerning informers throw a somewhat sinister light, at this period, upon the proprietary government. Its policy was narrow and selfish ; and, had the issues with which it dealt been larger, it might have been corrupt and oppressive.

[2] Proceedings of Assembly, 1666–1676, 157 *et seq.*

[3] The general intent of these laws had been to protect purchasers or heirs in the possession of their estates in spite of informalities of conveyance, to guaranty for orphans proper guardianship and care of their estates, to throw the lands of Baltimore county open more freely for settlement, to require the filing of actions and petitions at the beginning of proceedings before the courts so that defendants might have copies, to require adequate proof of the authenticity of bills — especially those coming from England — for the payment of which suit was brought in the province, to designate the secretary of the province as a public notary in order to facilitate the attestation of private papers and copies of public documents under the lesser seal. Proceedings of Assembly, 1638–1664, 487–506.

relating to the charges connected with the probate of wills, the fees of officials, the activity of privileged attorneys and vexatious informers, and the seizure of tobacco by sheriffs on the pretence that it was due in payment of public debts.

For these reasons the lower house came together in 1669 in a mood for aggressive action. Charles Nicholett, a clergyman, in a sermon preached before the house, held up before them the example of the Commons of England, with the liberties it had won, warned them of the sin of permission, and declared that the overburdened people expected great things from this house. For this utterance the clergyman had to crave the pardon of the house, and submit to the payment of a fine. But at the same time the assembly permitted an outsider to impeach before the upper house John Morecroft, an assemblyman, but at the same time an attorney who was in favor with the officials. The ground of the impeachment was that he was taking too many and exorbitant fees. The upper house, after hearing Morecroft's defence, declared him innocent of the charges, and levied costs on Morris, who had impeached him, to the amount of 1422 pounds of tobacco. While the proceedings against Morecroft were in progress, the grievances to which reference has already been made were formulated by the assembly, and laid before the upper house. The latter in reply justified the conduct of the provincial authorities on all the points, as being consistent with the charter. It then resolved that it would transact business with the lower house no longer until the latter should erase from its journal the mutinous and seditious votes contained in its list of grievances. During a conference on the subject the upper house roundly declared that the assembly was not to conceive that its privileges ran parallel to those of the Commons in England, for they owed their existence to the charter of the province, and would rather take rank with the common council of the City of London; both bodies were equally bound by the terms of their charter. Presently, after examining the province charter, the assembly showed itself to be in a more submissive mood, and declared its readiness to have its journal expunged or obliterated, or their form of stating the grievances

changed in any way, if thereby the weight of them could be CHAP.
removed from the province. The upper house then modified IV.
its demand, so as to require only that the complaints about
the exercise of the right of veto and assent by the governor
and proprietor, and about the raising of the levy the year
before, should be expunged. To this the assembly agreed,
the upper house on its part promising to use its influence
with the proprietor to secure a limitation of certain fees and
court charges. But this promise resulted at that time in
nothing of importance.

In 1671, however, acts were passed which embodied some
of the important features of those disallowed in 1669. These
included acts for the quieting of possessions, for the enrolment
of conveyances and securing the estates of purchasers, for
the preservation of orphans' estates, and for a public notary.
Sheriffs and clerks were prohibited practising as attorneys
before the courts. At this time also, and during the next few
years, the legislature made some progress in regulating fees.
In 1671 a beginning was made with the fees of coroners and
clerks of the county courts. In 1676 a somewhat extended
act was passed prescribing the fees chiefly of the chancellor
and secretary; in part also those of the judge of probate, the
surveyor-general, and deputy surveyors, sheriffs, and coroners. Two years later those of county clerks were again
limited. In 1674 it was provided by law that the governor
should appoint a certain number of attorneys to practise in
the higher courts of the province, and others should be appointed by the commissioners of the county courts to practise
in the courts of the counties. A special oath was prescribed
for them, and also the maximum fees which they should take.
But in the matter of fees none of these acts was exhaustive,
and that question was left unsettled till a later time.[1]

Throughout the period between the Restoration and the
English Revolution the large powers of the sheriffs and the
oppressive manner in which they sometimes exercised them
were a frequent subject of complaint. Sheriffs were charged
with seizing more tobacco than was due for the public levies,

[1] Proceedings of Assembly, 1666–1676, 276 *et seq.*, 322, 409, 477, 532;
ibid. 1678–1683, 19, 73.

with the detention sometimes of a man's whole crop when it
was ready for export, thus unnecessarily involving great delay
and loss.   In 1671 a sheriff of Talbot county, and in 1676
one of Cecil county, were removed from office and punished
on complaints of this character — some involving downright
extortion and oppression — which were presented by the lower
house.   In 1676 an act prohibiting undue seizures of tobacco
was passed; and two years later a proclamation was issued
against the oppressive conduct of sheriffs in general, and
recourse to the provincial court for their punishment was
encouraged.   The same year also an act was passed limiting
their term to a single year, unless at its close they could
produce a certificate from the justices of their respective
counties that they had conducted themselves fairly and
honestly in office.[1]   This, however, did not wholly remove
the evil.

Reference has already been made to the act of 1671, by
which the proprietor secured a permanent revenue in the
form of a grant during his life of an export duty of two
shillings per hogshead on tobacco, one-half of which should
go toward the defence of the province.   It was at the same
time provided that, so long as this act remained in force, no
public levy should be laid except with the prior consent of
the freemen in open assembly, and the act requiring that
expenditures for defence should be met by levies upon the
province should remain suspended.   This meant that the
cost of defence should be defrayed out of the revenue from
the two-shilling duty, the remainder going to the support of
the governor and council.   In 1676 the same duty was continued to the new proprietor for life, but the disposition of
it was changed when royal government was established.
But, owing to the influence of the proprietor and council
over the lower house, the provision that the cost of defence
should be met exclusively out of the revenue of the two-
shilling duty was occasionally violated.   In 1675 a direct
tax was voted to meet the charges of an expected war with

[1] Proceedings of Assembly, 1666–1676, 246 *et seq.*, 490, 499, 520;
Proceedings of Council, 1671–1681, 201; Proceedings of Assembly, 1678–
1683, 69.

the Susquehanna Indians, and the following year a similar
levy was ordered for the general purposes of defence against
the savages. In the last-mentioned law, however, the novel
device was included, that the governor and council should
summon one of the members of the lower house from each
county, and one from the city of Saint Mary's, to see that the
tobacco levied was used exclusively for the purpose intended
by the act. In all the appropriation acts [1] of this period,
as will be shown hereafter, the objects of expenditure were
specified in great detail, the budget of expenses being stated
in full in each act. In the military appropriation act of
1676 the wages of officers and soldiers were designated at
amounts previously agreed upon between the two houses.
We also find a joint committee on accounts becoming prominent about this time.

One of the fundamental causes of difference between the
lower house and the executive in Maryland arose from the
attitude which they respectively assumed toward written
laws as definite rules of action. The retention of power by
the executive, in other words the possession by it of the
opportunity to exercise discretion, depended largely on its
ability to hold in check the development of statutes, of
definite enactments. We sometimes see the executive in
this province seeking to direct legislation in its own chan-
nels, or vigorously opposing some unwelcome bill, but more
often we see it maintaining an attitude of passive resistance toward legislation in general. As we have seen, the
long delays of the proprietor in expressing his final decision
concerning the acts submitted to him kept the province in
uncertainty as to what was law or was not law. In 1674 the
suggestion of the upper house that a list of English statutes
should be prepared and put into force to guide the provincial
court in criminal cases, led to an inquiry as to the number of
laws to which the proprietor had actually given his assent,
and the lower house could find but thirty. Therefore,
in 1676, an act was passed repealing 127 laws and confirming 70, with the provision that they should remain in

[1] Proceedings of Assembly, 1666–1676, 284, 462, 497, 558 ; *ibid.* 1678–
1683, 148, etc.

force till repealed by the joint action of the proprietor and the two houses.[1] But on the plea that he was about to return to England and could not assent to any perpetual statutes without consulting his counsel-at-law, the proprietor confirmed all the acts of this session simply as temporary laws.

In consequence of this, the question was again brought up by the lower house in 1681.[2] Of this body Kenelm Cheseldyne and John Coode were members. It urged the passage of an act providing that a law passed by the two houses and assented to by the proprietor should be repealed only with the consent of the two houses, and also that the act of the governor in assenting to a law should be binding on the proprietor. To both of these propositions the upper house objected, to the former as useless and to the latter as dangerous, and cited Virginia, Pennsylvania, and Ireland as dependencies the governors of which did not possess the final veto power. In its reply to this the lower house, after insisting upon certain temporary and technical points, concluded with the broad statement of principle, "This house doth answer that nothing can or ought to be Satisfactory to us, or the Freemen of this Province (whom we Represent) unless we are Ascertained of the Validity force and Continuance of the Laws of this Province under which we live, and from whence we Expect protection and Safety and to the Enacting of which we have been and Still are Lyable to So much Trouble & Expence." From the stand which it had taken in favor of maintaining the existing system, the family group which practically constituted the upper house could not be moved, though it did signify its willingness to urge the proprietor to publish his dissents in the province as soon as possible. A promise from the proprietor that, when in the future he should be absent from the province, he would have his assent or dissent to any acts published there within eighteen months after their passage, was all the lower house gained by its effort.

[1] Proceedings of Assembly, 1666–1676, 374, 512, 542.
[2] Ibid. 1678–1683, 152–182.

CHAPTER V

THE OFFICIAL SYSTEM IN PROPRIETARY NEW NETHERLAND

THE distinguishing characteristic of New York as a pro- CHAP. V.
prietary province was the prominence and strength of its
executive. During nearly the whole period of its existence
under a proprietor, the executive officers and the council, together with the courts, were the only organs of government
which New York possessed. A legislature existed for a brief
time, but the share which it bore in the history of the province,
when compared with the other colonies, appears to have been
unimportant. This fact throws much light on the entire
course of New York history during the colonial period and
on the attitude of many of its people at the time of the
Revolution. Its government, in reality as well as in theory,
was more autocratic than that of any other colony. In New
York, especially during the early decades of its history, the
principles of the Tudors and Stuarts came nearer to reali-
zation than elsewhere in English America. The official
element was always strong in her governmental system, and
until comparatively late it was not adequately counter-
balanced by popular tendencies and forces. This characteristic was imparted to the province not solely by the Duke
of York and his officials, but it was also an inheritance from
the period of Dutch rule. When New Netherland passed
into English hands, in the part which became New York
the titles of officials were gradually changed, and readjust-
ments were made in order to secure conformity with English
practice, but the spirit of the administration remained practically unchanged. Reference to the main features of the
Dutch system and a comparison of them with those which
existed under English rule will make this evident.

New Netherland, like Virginia, was a proprietary province, of which a trading company was the proprietor. Though, corresponding to the federal system in the Netherlands, the stockholders of the Dutch West India company were organized into five chambers or groups, the Amsterdam chamber was the most important, and it had immediate control of New Netherland. Through this body its affairs were mainly transacted, and character was given to the political and commercial policy of this province. The general executive board of the company as a whole was the College of Nineteen. A very close connection was maintained between the company and the States General, and therefore the province was in a very real sense under their joint regulation and control. The establishment of the company was one of the results of a long political struggle. When founded, it was used mainly as an instrument for the prosecution of the war with the Spanish power in Brazil and the West Indies. In the charter provision was made for subsidizing the company by the state, and for the service, in emergencies, of government troops and ships on its expeditions. One of the members of the College of Nineteen was a deputy of the States General, and sometimes several of its deputies were in attendance at meetings of the college. The director-general of the colony, while selected and instructed by the company, must be approved by the States General, and from that body he received his commission.[1] In a variety of other ways provision was made in the charter for the exercise of control by the States General[2] over the accounts of the company and the transaction of its business; while it is also true that the company was created only for a term of years.

---

[1] N. Y. Col. Docs. I. 104, 175, 178.

[2] One of the clauses of the charter provided that if, at any meeting of the Nineteen, a weighty matter should come before them, upon which they could not agree, or in case the votes were equally divided, it should be left to the decision of the States General. A translation of the charter is in O'Callaghan's History of New Netherland, I. 399. The documents illustrating the control exercised by the States General will be found in N. Y. Col. Docs. I and II. Those which illustrate the relations between the company and its colony will be found both in those volumes and in Vols. XII, XIII, and XIV of the same series.

It is evident that the States General was informed respecting the business which was to come before the company
at its meetings, even if it did not assist in preparing the
programmes. The proof of this will be found in the *Pointen
van Beschryving*, several of which prior to 1645 are accessible
in the *Holland Documents*. These were calendars of business which demanded consideration and which related to all
the settlements within the sweep of the company's jurisdiction.[1] The States General used its influence with the provinces to secure the payment of the subsidy which was due
to the company.[2] Diplomatic relations in which the interests
of New Netherland were involved and defence lay especially
within its province. On one occasion the States General even
went so far as, by formal resolution, to permit the sending
of one hundred muskets to New Netherland.[3] In August,
1643, the company was ordered by it to permit no hostilities
between the Dutch and the inhabitants of New England.
Appeals were frequently made to the States General, and
on many subjects, by parties resident or concerned in New
Netherland; and the petitions thus presented furnished the
most common occasion for administrative action. In June,
1634, the complaints of the patroons[4] that the freedoms and
exemptions of five years before had not been observed by
the company were brought in this way before the States
General and led to an extended inquiry. Four years later,[5]
as a result of special information on the subject, it resolved
to adopt measures which should promote the increase of
population in New Netherland. This resulted in the issue
of articles abolishing the monopoly which the company had
hitherto possessed over the trade of New Netherland and

---

[1] N. Y. Col. Docs. I. 45, 68, 100, 117, 132, 135, 138, 163. None later than
the date mentioned occur in this series.

[2] *Ibid.* 93.

[3] *Ibid.* 397. Familiar illustrations of the activity of the States General
in foreign relations are its correspondence with England over the affair of the
Eendragt in 1632; in its controversies with England over boundaries and
the counter claims to New Netherland, and in the long series of acts which
followed the occupation of New Netherland by the English. Defence also
received its special attention at this time and during the war of 1652 to 1654.

[4] *Ibid.* 83–96.   [5] *Ibid.* 106, 110, 115; O'Callaghan, I. 176 *et seq.*

throwing it open to all Dutch subjects, with their allies and friends. The petitions of the Eight Men, followed by those of Melyn, Kuyter, and Van der Donck, occasioned by the Indian war of 1643 and the misgovernment of Kieft, led to inquiries and action by the States General which extended over many months and involved important results for the province.[1] The petition of Van Dincklage in 1636 for the payment of three years' salary as fiscal in New Netherland,[2] the petition of Henry Van Dyck in 1652[3] for redress because of his removal from the office of schout fiscal by Director Stuyvesant, furnish good illustrations of appeals to the States General of an administrative nature.   A judicial appeal,[4] however, made by Van der Capelle in 1653 to recover property of his which he alleged that Director Stuyvesant had caused to be unjustly seized in New Netherland, though at first allowed by the States General was afterward held not to lie.   In pursuance of a declaration of the states of Holland and West Friesland it was ordered, the same year, by the director and council that a writ of appeal from judgments pronounced in New Netherland ought in no case to be granted by the States General.   It thus appears that governmental control, which when exercised by the English monarchs over trading corporations has sometimes occasioned surprise, was an everyday matter at Amsterdam and The Hague.

Although the great body of the records of the West India company have been lost, enough remains to show that, especially after the appointment of Stuyvesant, a voluminous correspondence passed between the Amsterdam chamber and the director.[5] It was more extensive and minute than that

---

[1] N. Y. Col. Docs. I. 139, 141, 188 *et seq.*   The documents and other writings called forth by this affair furnish us with our chief information concerning the internal condition of New Netherland.

[2] *Ibid.* 103, 138.   [3] *Ibid.* 491 *et seq. ;* XIV. 107.

[4] *Ibid.* I. 528, 534–537 ; O'Callaghan, Laws and Ordinances of New Netherland, 147.

[5] The letters which have been preserved and are now in print will be found chiefly in N. Y. Col. Docs. XIV. A few appear in Vols. XII and XIII. They consist mostly of letters from the company, the replies from the director having probably perished.   About seventy of these letters have been preserved.

which English proprietors ordinarily kept up with their
agents in the provinces, and reminds one more of the memo-
rials which, in the time of Colbert, passed between the ministers in Paris and the officials of New France. The director
was required to present full reports of all the occurrences in
the province which affected the interests or rights of the
company. Upon the basis of these and of information
which it received from other sources, and from petitions and
complaints in the Netherlands, its advice and directions were
formulated. Few formal instructions appear, but orders
were transmitted in the letters concerning grants of land,
recall of grants, the despatch of vessels, admission of emigrants, duties and all the minutiæ of trade relations, claims
and suits against the company, dealings with the Indians,
relations with the English on the north and the south and
with the Swedes, the appointment and removal of officials,
the claims of the patroons. The attack of Kuyter and
Melyn on the company and its director also received much
attention. The internal affairs of the province in all
departments, as well as its external relations, were reviewed
in these letters. Though the director is sometimes reproved,
in general relations of high respect and confidence existed
between him and the company. The government at New
Amsterdam appears to have been most negligent in submit-
ting accounts, and finally Secretary Van Tienhoven was
removed amid strongly expressed suspicions respecting his
official honesty. About 1645 the company, because of its
vast expenditures in Brazil,[1] had become bankrupt, and for
that reason could give little positive assistance to New
Netherland. That province, in comparison with interests
in the Spanish seas, was always an object of minor importance. Still, the company continued to send its long letters
of advice and command, and to receive letters of warning
from Stuyvesant, occasioned by the weakness of the province,
until the encroachments of the English ended in their taking
possession of the whole territory. It is worthy of note that,
in the exercise of their joint control, the States General stood
for a broader and more statesmanlike policy than did the

[1] Netscher, Les Hollandais en Brésil.

company, and in part by its insistence the company was forced to abandon some of the narrowest features of its own commercial policy.

Within New Netherland governmental authority was exercised through the director-general and council and a small body of officials who were immediately dependent upon them. The director, as has already been stated, received his authority primarily from the company, though his appointment must be approved by the States General and from it he received his commission. The career of Stuyvesant shows that, when the States General and the company differed upon matters of policy, the director was the servant of the latter. The company then protected him as its agent and in general assumed responsibility for the line of conduct which, under its instructions, he had pursued.[1] On the appointment of Stuyvesant, in 1647, the office of vice-director was created, but its power did not essentially differ from that of a councillor.

The council, which was closely associated with the director in all his acts, was a small body. Usually it consisted of five persons, though during the administration of William Kieft it as a rule contained only one or two members. The schout fiscal, when not acting as prosecuting officer, had a seat in the body, but no vote. For the trial of certain cases it was customary to admit some of the inhabitants or officials to the board. In the early part of Stuyvesant's administration he was in the habit of calling captains of the company's ships, when on shore, to a seat and vote in the council.[2] The secretary of the province usually acted as secretary of the council, but he was not *ex officio* a member of it. In later years the receiver-general held also an appointment as councillor. The members, whoever they might be, were virtually the director's appointees, though legally their own power proceeded from the same source as his. The director and coun-

---

[1] The letters of the company contain reproofs of Stuyvesant for having taken up the quarrels of Kieft, and the company did not justify the way in which the Indian war had been brought about. But it shielded Stuyvesant when he was summoned to answer in Holland, and sought in no respect to make him its scapegoat.

[2] N. Y. Col. Docs. I. 308; O'Callaghan, Register of New Netherland, 11.

cil together were invested with local legislative, judicial, and CHAP.
administrative powers, subject in all administrative affairs, V.
and under the conditions already explained, to the control of
the Amsterdam chamber and the College of Nineteen.   The
relations between the councillors and the director were
legally the same as those existing between governors and
appointed councillors in the English provinces.   In executive
matters the director took their advice, but he was not bound
by it.   In Kieft's council there were for a time but three
votes, of which the director had two and the other member
one.

Kieft, says Van der Donck,[1] "imagined himself, or would
fain persuade others, that he was Sovereign, and that it was
absolutely in his power to do or to permit, everything."
The conduct of Van Twiller in securing for himself and
friends very large grants of land [2] without the knowledge
of the company, and the accounts which have been preserved
of Kieft's share in the origin of the Indian war, show that
in their time no recognized authority existed within the
province which could override the director.[3]   By fear or
favor, when he chose, he was able to play the autocrat.
Kieft relied on his commission from the States General to
justify an idle boast that he was independent of the company.   If Councillor La Montagne stated, as he is reported
to have done, that the power of the director in the province
was greater than that of the Prince of Orange in the Netherlands, he was well within the truth.

But the administration of Stuyvesant furnishes the largest
number of illustrations of the autocratic power and manners of the director,[4] as well as his paternal care of the
province and its inhabitants.   These proceeded from the
personal qualities of the worthy director himself, as well as
from the character of his office.   His critics called him the
"great Muscovy duke," and told many tales of his threats

[1] N. Y. Col. Docs. I. 304.

[2] *Ibid.* XIV. 119, 121, 132.

[3] *Ibid.* I. 194 *et seq.;* De Vries in 2 Colls. of N. Y. Hist. Soc. III. 114
et seq.

[4] N. Y. Col. Docs. I. 211, 302, 307, 348, 352, 453, 495 ; II. 152 ; Broad Advice, in 2 N. Y. Hist. Colls. III. 264 *et seq.*

to hang, or make shorter by a head, those who happened to incur his displeasure. He had the habit, on occasion, of browbeating opponents into submission. His state papers were not always precisely truthful; and his relations with Van Tienhoven show that he could long retain a faithful and able official in service, even though the private life of the man had been proven to be corrupt. But this was only a faint reflection of the conditions existing in the official systems of the European states at that time.

The delegates from the English and Dutch towns who prepared the remonstrance of 1653 to the States General[1] described the executive system under Stuyvesant as follows. Though somewhat hostile in tone, it is the best contemporary description which has come down to us. " The entire government of this country is directed and controlled exclusively according to the pleasure and caprice of Dr. Stuyvesant or one or two of his favorite Sycophants ; in divers cases decisions were given without the knowledge, yea frequently without summoning his adjoined Councillors, who have no further power to decide except as the Director permits them, his will being a Law absolute, whereby everything is controled ; even if the Burgomasters and Schepens were sometimes summoned to the Council when occasions presented, to dispatch business with the Director General and Council, it is, in fact, rather to approve of his plans than to assist in consultation upon them; for notwithstanding the Burgomasters and Schepens may dissent and differ from his opinion, the Director decides without them, declaring it must be so ; moreover, if any resolution be adopted with the consent of the Burgomasters and Schepens, 'tis changed and altered without their knowledge, at the pleasure of the Director ; and lastly, to show how great an appearance there is of the establishment of an arbitrary government among us, 'tis considered sufficient that a Director, a fellow-subject of a Free State, tho filling a high and honorable office, with arrogant words disclaims his fellow subjects who are assembled with his previous knowledge for the good of the country, and are thereunto convoked beforehand by the lawful Rulers

[1] N. Y. Col. Docs. I. 554.

of the first and most important City in this country, and CHAP.
present an humble Remonstrance, declares their Assembly   V.
illegal, protests against it, forbids the Members and Deputies
thereof to meet again, orders and commands them to disperse forthwith on pain of his highest displeasure and arbitrary punishment, as if they were, by their acts guilty of
resisting authority and had conspired to revolutionize the
State and reduce it under another Ruler and government."

It required the spontaneous efforts of the colonists, operating through the slow and roundabout process of petitions to
the company and the States General, to check the director in
any disastrous course or to secure redress.   Experience also
showed that in such cases it was doubtful if the interest of
the company could be enlisted in behalf of reform until it
was spurred to action by pressure from the States General.
By that time much of the evil had been done, and the belated
and partial reform would effect little change.   It was for
this reason that the more intelligent colonists, who realized
that the province had become something more than a group
of trading factories, desired that the council might be
enlarged[1] till it was permanently fixed at least at such a
number as the councils in the cities of the Fatherland. This
object, after the close of Kieft's administration, was reached;
but the further effort to add to the council a representative
body, thus establishing a legislature, failed.   The history of
this experiment, with that of the opposition from which it
originated, will, in a later chapter, throw additional light on
the character of New Netherland government.

The functions of the director and council were coextensive
with the government of the province.   Working on the basis
of the Roman-Dutch law, and under the limitations set by
acts of the States General and the orders of the company
affecting the province, they issued ordinances[2] concerning
all matters which fell within the scope of government.   A
real legislative power was thus exercised by them.   They
legislated concerning trade more than any other subject,

[1] N. Y. Col. Docs. I. 202.
[2] These will be found in O'Callaghan's Laws and Ordinances of New
Netherland.

prescribing the regulations under which it should be carried on, import and export duties, excises, the sale of liquors, fraud and smuggling, trade in all varieties of commodities with the Indians, and the despatch of runners into the Indian country ; the importation of negroes, trade with the English on the north and south and with Brazil, Curaçoa, and other Dutch possessions, the maintenance of a staple port at New Amsterdam for the purpose of securing the interests of the company as a commercial monopoly. By ordinances concerning land, provision was made for the extinguishment of Indian claims, for the issue of patents, for the annulment of extravagant and unimproved grants, for the fencing of land, for the levying of tenths and other taxes upon it, for the collection of rents, and the prevention of trespass. Courts were established under the authority of these ordinances ; their jurisdiction was prescribed, and provision was made for their officials. Provisions for land grants and for courts, when combined, led to the origin of local government within New Netherland. The villages of the province owed their origin as administrative units to grants of privileges from the director and council, while the affairs of New Amsterdam, after as well as before the grant of municipal privileges, were minutely regulated by them. Duties and fees of officials throughout the province were subject to their regulation. They made general provision for defence, as well as for meeting particular attacks of the Indians and peril from Europe or from neighboring colonies. The conditions under which religious worship should be celebrated were also subject to their control, as well as schools, Sunday observances, and general public morals.

The ordinances, the scope of which has just been indicated, it was the duty of the director and council, with the aid of the local and provincial officials who were subordinate to them, to execute. Though only fragments of the executive records of the council have been preserved, we know from correspondence and other sources — from the general character of the provincial system as well — that the administrative activity of the director and council was continuous, and that it reached all phases of the colony's life.[1]   The restraint

[1] O'Callaghan, History of New Netherland, I. 244.

of swine in the streets of New Amsterdam, as well as the
enforcement of the rights of the company in Rensselaerswyck
and the overthrow of the power of the Swedes on the South
river — things small and great alike — engaged its attention.
To describe its administrative activity would be to write the
political history of the province. When we add to this the
statement that the director and council constituted the highest judicial tribunal in the province, with civil and criminal
jurisdiction and the powers of a surrogate court and a court of
admiralty, and that either originally or on appeal all important cases came before it, the importance of this body and the
simplicity of the governmental system in New Netherland
will both be apparent.

The other officials of the provincial civil list in New Netherland were the secretary, the schout fiscal, the receiver-
general, the surveyor-general, the commissaries of stores, and
in the later years of the province the farmers of revenue.
They were such as the union of commercial and political
functions in the hands of the company made necessary.
With the exception of the schout fiscal, their titles indicate
their duties, and those were substantially the same as the
duties performed by officers bearing similar titles in an
English province. The schout fiscal — an appointee of the
company — was both prosecuting officer, or attorney-general, and sheriff, and was thus an important functionary.[1]
In the former capacity it was his duty to defend the rights
of the company before the director and council, in whatever
judicial capacity they might sit, and in all questions of
police, justice, and finance. In his double capacity he was
to see that all placards, ordinances, resolutions, military
regulations, and commands of the States General and the
West India company were executed and obeyed. To that
end he should inform himself concerning the delinquencies
of officials of the company, both on water and land, and pay
particular attention to the conduct of commissaries in the
loading and unloading of cargoes. In respect to prize cases
he should exercise special care. Information of all his

[1] See the commission of Hendrick Van Dyck and the instructions to him
as schout fiscal in 1645 ; N. Y. Col. Docs. I. 494, 504.

doings should be sent to the company, to be used in cases brought by appeal or petition before it. Though the schout fiscal was an appointee of the company, and was intended to act as a check upon all other officials, the statements of Van Dyck, who was removed by Stuyvesant in 1652, show, if true, that the director had been able from the first to prevent him from performing his duties; that he had been almost wholly ignored, and that the director had assumed almost exclusive control of business.[1] The fact, however, that Van Dyck was dismissed for drunkenness and inattention to duty decidedly weakens his case, though it does not make it improbable that Stuyvesant assumed all the authority which his office would bear. Upon the dismissal of Van Dyck, the director appointed his confidant, Van Tienhoven, to the office.

Within New Netherland, as we have seen, several well-defined sections existed. It is easily conceivable that each of these might have become a subordinate administrative district, a county, or group of counties. But such was not the case during the period of Dutch rule. The manor of Rensselaerswyck and the colony of New Amstel, the latter of which was separately organized in 1656, made provision in part for local government in the remotest districts of the province. Elsewhere a village system of government, in imitation of that of the Netherlands, was established, though with modifications in a few instances which were borrowed from New England custom. This was a direct result of the grant in the revised Freedoms and Exemptions of 1640, which provided for the establishment of colonies under masters who should bring over five adult colonists and establish them in the province. If such settlements should so increase as to become towns or villages, the company was bound to grant them "subaltern or municipal government," with magistrates and ministers of justice.[2] The process of

---

[1] N. Y. Col. Docs. I. 495 *et seq.*, 512. When on shipboard, as Stuyvesant was coming to New Netherland to assume office, Van Dyck offered his services, and he states that he was met with the response, "Get out! whenever I need you I'll call you."

[2] *Ibid.* I. 119.

bestowing village rights upon such communities began
among the English towns within Dutch territory on Long
Island in 1644.   In that year such rights were bestowed on
Hempstead, in 1645 on Flushing and Gravesend.   Breuckelen, in 1646, was the first Dutch settlement to receive a court
of justice.   In 1652 a court was erected at Fort Orange,
with jurisdiction over Beverwyck.   In the same year a
court was granted to Middleburgh, later Newtown, on Long
Island.   In 1654 Amersfoort (Flatlands) and Midwout (Flatbush) were granted a joint court, which became two separate courts in 1661.   In 1656 Westchester (Vreedland) and
Jamaica (Rustdorp) were granted similar privileges.   In
1660 a town court was granted to Haerlem.   In 1661 courts
were established at Bushwick, Wiltwyck (Kingston), Bergen,
and New Utrecht ; and one was granted to the settlers on
Staten Island in 1664.[1]

The village institutions thus created conformed in all
cases to the same general model.   The ordinances provided
in more or less elaborate terms for the establishment of town
courts consisting of a board of magistrates, called schepens,
and a prosecuting officer and sheriff, called a schout.   In a
few of the villages the officials were called commissaries.
The ordinance relating to Flushing declared that the schout
should have the powers of a Dutch schout or English constable.   These officials were in all cases appointed by the
director and council from lists of nominees — presented by
the freemen of the village.   In many cases, according to a
well-known Dutch custom, the list contained double the
number of names which were requisite to fill the offices.
The officials held office for one year.   The magistrates as a
town board had authority to pass ordinances concerning
lands, fences, highways, schools, churches, and other local

[1] O'Callaghan, Laws and Ordinances of New Netherland, 42, 48, 53, 58, 97,
389–391, 395, 403, 422 ; O'Callaghan, History of New Netherland, II. 183 ;
N. Y. Col. Docs. XIII. 65.   Of the village charters, the two which were
granted to Hempstead and Gravesend were identical.   The same is true of
those which were issued to Wiltwyck and Bergen.   Those which were
granted to Haerlem, Bushwick, and New Utrecht were also drawn from a
common model, but one which differed somewhat from the others that have
been mentioned.

affairs, subject to the approval of the director and council.
They acted also as a local court. The magistrates were
appointed from among the worthy men, freeholders of the
locality, and took a special oath of submission to the States
General and company. Legally all their acts were subject
to review by the provincial government,[1] and they had little
independence. Really, however, the localities seem to have
enjoyed a considerable degree of freedom. This was secured
by the tolerant disposition, or sometimes even indifference,
of the director and council, by the difficulties of communication, and by the very weakness of the province itself and the
need which its authorities felt that population should be increased and outlying settlements multiplied. It should also
be remembered that a large proportion of these villages were
inhabited by Englishmen, whose plans of domination the
Dutch always feared. And yet their need of colonists
forced them to be tolerant, even when their power was being
undermined.

New Amsterdam, though in size and population a village,
was the seat of the provincial government, and its affairs
were administered directly by the officials of the province.
The fact that it was the residence of the director and council
always affected its status to a certain extent. This delayed
for a time the full enjoyment of its liberties. In 1653 the
Amsterdam chamber[2] granted it municipal rights. This
grant took the form suggested by the clause of the Provisional Order on this subject and provided that the officers of
the new city should be one schout, two burgomasters, and
five schepens ; that they should be elected by the burghers,
as in old Amsterdam, and act as a court of justice with right
of appeal in certain cases to the supreme court of judicature.
In the absence of a single executive head, like the mayor of
an English city, the burgomasters acted as the general representatives of the municipality. But contrary to the intent
of the grant, Stuyvesant retained the appointment of burgomasters and schepens in his own hands. Van Tienhoven,

---

[1] Abundant examples of this appear in Vols. XII, XIII, and XIV of
N. Y. Col. Docs.
[2] O'Callaghan, II. 192 ; N. Y. Col. Docs. I. 391.

the schout of the province and Stuyvesant's chief supporter,
was appointed schout of the city.   On the plea that he had
not been definitely instructed to that effect or that he did
not wish to disturb the peace, and later that some of those
who were nominated were obnoxious to him, Stuyvesant
continued, until 1658, to delay the time when he must consent to the appointment of burgomasters and schepens from
a list, presented by the city magistrates, of double the number required to fill the offices.[1]   The concession was finally
made only after persistent solicitation on the part of the
citizens.   The city did not secure even this restricted control over the choice of its schout until 1660.

At first the city had no control over the revenue which
was raised within its limits.   But after some controversy,
and before the end of 1653, the director and council were
brought to agree that the excise on wine and beer consumed
within the municipality should be paid into the city treasury.[2]   But this concession was limited by the condition that
from this revenue the expenses of the churches and salaries
of the officials of the city should be paid, and the public
works kept in repair.   It should also be farmed out to the
highest bidder.   The right to determine the rate of the excise, or otherwise to tax the inhabitants of the city, remained,
of course, with the director and council.[3]   In 1654 the city
secured from the director and council the right to grant conveyances and mortgages of lots within its limits, but returns
of these had to be made to the provincial authorities.   The
regulative and ordinance power of the director and council
for the exigencies of defence, care of the streets, preservation
of the peace, trade, and other matters seems to have remained
without definite limits.   The records would indicate that the
chief function of the city magistrates was judicial.   The
business of a municipal court seems to have occupied the
most of their attention.

The settlements on the South river, with which communi-

[1] O'Callaghan, II. 257, 311, 322, 370 ; Records of New Amsterdam, I. 144,
156, 218, 233, 281 ; II. 16, 26, 109, 121, 282 ; III. 199 *et seq.*

[2] Records of New Amsterdam, I. 129, 130, 218 ; O'Callaghan, II. 255, 298.

[3] Records of New Amsterdam, I. 166, 192, 224, 232.

cation, whether overland or by sea, was quite as difficult as that with the outpost at Fort Orange, were first governed through a commissary. His duties were not light, for, in addition to keeping the peace among the colonists and with the Indians, he was forced to protect the commercial and territorial interests of the Dutch in that region against the encroachments of the Swedes and the English. He was subject to instructions from the director, and corresponded with him concerning all affairs of importance. Trade with the Indians he was bound to encourage, as he was also required to enforce the prohibition of the sale of arms and ammunition to them. No one was permitted to sail from Manhattan to the South river without a permit from the director-general, or to make the return voyage without a passport from the commissary.[1] Over defence, the granting of land, the administration of justice in the outposts along the river, the commissary, though as a subordinate officer,[2] had immediate control. The English from New Haven were also trying to establish settlements on the east side of the bay near Salem creek, and on the Schuylkill. The Swedes also occupied Fort Christina, Tinicum, and other points along the bay and river. As no party concerned had a definite grant from a power which could assert authority, traffic with the Indians was virtually open to all, and the representatives of each nationality were entitled to as much land as they could permanently occupy.

These were the problems which Jan Jansen of Ilpendam, the first commissary, had to face during the seven years between 1638 and 1645 when he held the office. He, with the support of the director, prevented the English from obtaining a permanent foothold, but was forced to accept the Swedes as neighbors. Finally he was removed on a charge of fraud and neglect of duty, preferred by the fiscal. Andries Hudde was appointed to the place, and Jan Jansen was sent to Holland for examination before the directors.

[1] Hazard, Annals of Pennsylvania, 50 ; N. Y. Col. Docs. XII. 120.
[2] Land patents for that region, as for other parts of the province, for example, were issued by the director and council. N. Y. Col. Docs. XII. 177.

Hudde[1] held the position, keeping up active rivalry with
the Swedes all the time, until 1655, when Stuyvesant destroyed the Swedish power on the Delaware. Then a vice-
directorship of the South river was created, and Jean Paul
Jacquet, who for years had been an agent of the company in
Brazil, was appointed to the place. Hudde was now made
secretary and surveyor. A commissary was also appointed,
and these officials, together with two of the most intelligent
freemen, formed a local court for the trial of civil and criminal cases,[2] and a council for general administration. When
a military offence was to be tried two sergeants were substituted for the freemen. All questions were decided by
majority vote, the vice-director having a double vote in case
of a tie. All important cases might be appealed to the
director and council. The minutes of this court from
December, 1655, to March, 1657, have been preserved.[3]
They show how petty civil controversies among the mixed
Swedish and Dutch inhabitants of this part of the province
were adjusted, and with what mildness their crimes were
punished. Drunken soldiers were at one time charged with
disturbance and mutinous talk. Illegal sale of liquor to
the Indians occasioned more than one trial. Suits for debt
appear more frequently than any other complaint, and of
these Isaac Allerton, the former merchant of Plymouth,
appears most frequently as plaintiff. He had long been
trading on the river, and many were indebted to him for
goods. Many against whom he now brought suit acknowledged the obligation, but said they could not pay till the
tobacco crop was sold or they became in some way possessed
of means of payment which they at the time wholly lacked.
In a petition[4] to the vice-director, Allerton states that some
twelve thousand guilders were due him, and some of this
had been owing for eight years. He was now more than
seventy years old, would soon have to give up travelling, and
must bring his affairs into order or he would leave his wife

[1] N. Y. Col. Docs. XII. 23, 25, 26 ; Hazard, Annals of Pennsylvania, 41,
61, 83 ; Acrelius, History of New Sweden, 58, 59.

[2] N. Y. Col. Docs. XII. 114 *et seq.* ; Hazard, 205.

[3] N. Y. Col. Docs. XII. 133–162.   [4] *Ibid.* 60.

and children in distress.   These entries afford the last glimpse that we get of an adventurous trader whose career is not the least interesting among those which present themselves in the seventeenth century.

The arrival of a Swedish ship, the *Mercurius*, in the spring of 1656, and its passage up the South river to a point above Fort Casimir, and that contrary to the command of the Dutch, aroused the attention of the director and council. De Sille and Van Tienhoven [1] were sent as special agents to investigate the case, and also to do whatever else seemed necessary for the security of the settlements on the South river.   For the time being by these agents the vice-director's authority was virtually suspended.   About a year later various complaints [2] were presented against Jacquet, alleging that he had been guilty, in certain cases, of arbitrary and oppressive conduct.   These were brought before the director and council by the fiscal, and Jacquet was arrested.   On his preliminary examination he declared that the charges originated largely in party spirit, and Director Alrichs of New Amstel afterwards expressed a similar opinion. [3]   He was discharged from arrest and allowed to return to the South river, but was required to submit his accounts for examination and must stand ready to make a full defence.   When soon after a large part of the territory along the South river was transferred to the immediate care of the city of Amsterdam, Jacquet was removed, and William Beekman of New Amsterdam took his place, though with the double title of vice-director and commissary. [4]   These events illustrate the extent and method of control which the provincial authorities exercised in this remote section.

The establishment, in 1657, by the city of Amsterdam of the colony of New Amstel introduced a new jurisdiction upon the South river, and greatly reduced the territory which was directly administered by the company.   The territory on the west side of the bay from Christina Kill southward now passed under the direct control of the city and its officials.   The vice-director of the company took up

[1] N. Y. Col. Docs. XII. 120–129.
[2] *Ibid.* 167–173.
[3] *Ibid.* 173.
[4] *Ibid.* 219 ; Hazard, 233.

his residence at Fort Christina, now called Altona,[1] and CHAP. administered the affairs of the few struggling Swedish and Dutch[2] outposts above the bay and along the eastern shores. At Fort Casimir, now called New Amstel, Jacob Alrichs, as the appointee of the city of Amsterdam and with the title of vice-director, administered the affairs of the city's colony. As was so common in such cases, the magistrates of Amsterdam intended that its colony should enjoy full municipal rights.   Provision was made for resident boards[3] of burgomasters and schepens, and, when the city should reach a population of two hundred families or more, for a common council.   The schout should be appointed by the director-general, under power of attorney, from the deputies of the city of Amsterdam who were members of the governing board of the West India company.   By means of this appointment, and the right of appeal in criminal cases and in civil suits involving more than $40 to the director and council, the subordination of the city to the province in judicial matters was to be maintained.   The company also claimed jurisdiction over the rivers and waters of the bay, and retained its right to inspect all goods bound for New Amstel.   The repression of smuggling was therefore an important object of its policy.   Stuyvesant visited the South river in the spring of 1658, and adjusted to an extent the relations between the company and the city's colony.[4]   This, with the active correspondence which Alrichs maintained, shows that the director, notwithstanding the divided jurisdiction, continued to exercise a general superintendence over all affairs on the South river.

The simple form of government through vice-director and council which Alrichs found in existence, was continued

---

[1] The negotiations between the company and the city of Amsterdam in reference to this colony may be traced in N. Y. Col. Docs. I. 612 *et seq.*   The correspondence of Jacob Alrichs, director at New Amstel, with Stuyvesant is in N. Y. Col. Docs. XII. 173–285.   The correspondence of William Beekman with the director follows in the same volume.   Hazard, 220 *et seq.*, gives a full documentary history of the enterprise.

[2] N. Y. Col. Docs. XII. 211.

[3] Laws and Ordinances of New Netherland, 241.

[4] O'Callaghan, History of New Netherland, II. 372.

until August, 1657.[1] Then seven city councillors were elected, and from them three new schepens were chosen. Another secretary and schout were also appointed, with two elders and two deacons for the management of church affairs. Thus municipal government was instituted at New Amstel, though at the close of the first year of the city's administration it was only a village of one hundred houses. In 1658 the population of the colony was somewhat more than five hundred. But its prosperity was checked by a series of disasters which remind one more of the sufferings at Jamestown and Plymouth than of the experiences of later colonies. Two wet seasons in succession almost destroyed the crops, and caused sickness so to prevail as to cripple the colony. Scarcity and discontent followed. Discontent was increased by the issue of certain modifications in the conditions of settlement. The English from Maryland threatened to take possession of the country. The vice-director, though struggling against adverse conditions, was accused by many and on many charges. A general exodus of the settlers to Virginia, Maryland, or to other parts of New Netherland was threatened. These events, together with complaints of the defenceless condition of the South river, led Stuyvesant to send commissioners to further regulate affairs in that quarter[2] and to negotiate concerning the claims of Maryland.

At the close of 1659, worn out by cares and losses, Alrichs died, and left as his successor Alexander d'Hinoyossa, a man who of late had occupied a prominent place among his accusers. D'Hinoyossa was only prevented by the opposition of the other magistrates from seizing all the estate of Alrichs. The city of Amsterdam had already become tired of its experiment and had sought to retransfer the colony to the company. But the latter shrank from again assuming responsibility for it. Because, however, of the friction which existed between the magistrates of the colony and those at Altona, it was felt that one or the other must be removed from the region. Finally, after full discussion, the

---

[1] O'Callaghan, History of New Netherland, II. 337.

[2] N. Y. Col. Docs. XII. 205, 226, 228, 231, 236, 245 et seq., 259, 266, 272 ; Md. Arch., Proceedings of Council, 1636–1667, 366.

directors of the company, in February, 1663, conceded to the burgomasters of Amsterdam all the Dutch territory on the west side of the river, and a tract three miles broad extending along the entire east bank.   This they were to hold, on condition that they should not alienate it, should send over annually four hundred settlers, and should assume the responsibility for its defence.   As the result of the agreement[1] the officials and soldiers of the company were removed from Altona, and a few months before the English conquest D'Hinoyossa, as representative of the city, became director for the entire South river.

The remoteness of the settlements on the North river from the seat of the provincial government, together with the exigencies of defence and of the fur trade, should have established between them and the director relations similar to those which he maintained with the South river.   But this was not altogether the case, and the reason for its not being so will be found in the feudal pretensions of the colony of Rensselaerswyck.   Fort Orange antedated by several years the establishment of the patroonship, and, like Fort Nassau or Fort Casimir on the South river, was a military and trading outpost, governed by a commissary, and occupied by a few soldiers and fur traders.   The purchases of land which Kiliaen Van Rensselaer made under the authority of the Freedoms and Exemptions, enclosed this little fort on all sides.   The colony had its distinct administrative system and claimed many privileges.   Its general court, which consisted of two commissaries and two councillors or schepens, performed executive, legislative, and judicial functions.   Connected with the court was a secretary, a schout fiscal, and a court messenger or constable, while the chief resident official held the title of director.   These all received their appointments from the patroon or from the court itself, and were in no respect officially dependent on the director and council. In this they differed from all village officials, and from those of New Amsterdam during nearly all of the Dutch period. At the outset even those of New Amstel were more dependent on the director.

[1] N. Y. Col. Docs. II. 165–215.

But in addition to these facts, it was the desire of the authorities of the manor wholly to exclude provincial officers and control from its limits.   Their ambition was not merely territorial, but chiefly to monopolize the fur trade along the upper Hudson.   The regulations of the colony against unlicensed trading with the natives were as rigid as those of the company.   But licenses could easily be procured by residents of the colony on condition that they should bring all furs to the patroon's magazine, whence they were shipped to him in Holland.   He and his partners were also the sole importers of European goods for the colony, and, owing to the neglect of the company, for Fort Orange as well.   Thus within ten years after the founding of the colony it had developed an independent organization and policy.   Attempts were made to prevent appeals to the court of the director and council.   In 1644 a fortification, called Rensselaers-Stein, was built on Beeren island, at the southern limit of the manor, for the purpose of enforcing the claim of staple-right.   Vessels passing up and down the river were obliged to lower their colors at this point, and a toll of five guilders was imposed on every trading craft.   This at once aroused protest at New Amsterdam, and through the schout fiscal maintenance of the fort and the enforcement of the exaction were both forbidden.   But the orders of the director and his officials were defied, and the pretensions at Beeren island were continued for several years.

Stuyvesant's prolonged controversies with Van Slichtenhorst, the director of Rensselaerswyck, began over a protest of the latter that the inhabitants of the colony were not bound to obey a proclamation which the director had issued for a general fast.   Though Stuyvesant visited the colony in person, he was unable to bring the sturdy director to terms.   The visit, moreover, called Stuyvesant's attention to the fact that the houses of Beverwyck, the patroon's village, were clustered so closely about Fort Orange as to encroach on the sovereign rights of the company there and to interfere with the range of the guns. The director protested vigorously against this and ordered that all houses within the distance of a cannon-shot — later he contracted the limit to that of a musket-shot — should be demolished.   Over this question a long struggle ensued, in which force was used on both sides.   It finally resulted in Stuyvesant bestowing village rights on Beverwyck, and thus withdrawing it, as well as Fort Orange, from the jurisdiction of the patroon.   Attempts, also, of the officials of the colony to secure additional tracts of land near Claverack and Katskill and to issue leases there to tenants were resisted by the provincial authorities.   The director ordered the collection of the excise within the colony, but that was refused.   In 1651 he ordered the payment of a subsidy by Rensselaerswyck, and this also was refused on the ground that it was a violation of custom and grossly unfair, since the colony, by a fiscal system of its own, provided for all its needs.   When on this occasion Van Slichtenhorst went to New Amsterdam to remonstrate, he was detained as a prisoner for four months by Stuyvesant.   The question was not settled during the period of Dutch rule, save in the practical way that no provincial taxes were collected within the colony.   In connection with these disputes it repeatedly happened that the service of writs and orders and the posting of placards by the officers of the company were resisted. Van Slichtenhorst's crowning act of offence was that of tearing down the placard which announced that a court of justice was established for the village of Beverwyck independent of the colony.   Soon after this he was dragged from his house by a body of the company's soldiers and carried a prisoner to New Amsterdam.   He was not again restored to office, and no such doughty champion of feudal rights as he had been appeared among the later directors of Rensselaerswyck.   Stuyvesant's attention was soon diverted by events and questions of larger import, and thus the controversies of an earlier time were allowed to drop without a settlement in express terms of the points at issue between the two parties.[1]

Thus, as the close of the period of Dutch rule approached, the authority of the director and council was withdrawn from the South river, and it failed to receive full acknowl-

[1] O'Callaghan, I. 319; II. 68, 159, 173.

edgment at the northern extremity of the province. The English were at the same time rapidly securing control of the towns at the western end of Long Island. These changes, however, resulted more from lack of resources sufficient to maintain its sway, than from change in the theory which was held as to its extent. Had the Dutch been left to themselves, the government of the province would probably have continued for an indefinite period unchanged.

CHAPTER VI

THE TRANSITION FROM DUTCH TO ENGLISH GOVERNMENT.
THE EXECUTIVE IN PROPRIETARY NEW YORK

THE transition from Dutch to English rule in New York
can best be understood if we follow events in the order of time.[1] The royal charter of March, 1664, provided for the substitution, when the province should have been conquered, of an English duke as proprietor in the place of a group of Dutch merchants. To the proprietor were given rights of subordinate government, without mention of a representative legislature, and with the express reserve on behalf of the colonists of the right of appeal to the king. Under this character, Colonel Richard Nicolls was appointed governor.[2] As soon as the authorities at New Amsterdam had surrendered, a council of four members, two from England and two from Long Island, was appointed; Matthias Nicolls was appointed secretary, and Thomas Delavall collector and receiver-general. Cornelius van Ruyven, who had been the last to hold the office of secretary in the Dutch province, together with Johannes van Brugh, one of the schepens of New Amsterdam, were sometimes called in for advice.[3] Since Nicolls's instructions as governor of New York, if they ever existed, have been lost, it is impossible to say what directions or restrictions were imposed upon him.

The articles of surrender fully guarantied[4] the rights of private property to all free inhabitants, and to the Dutch

---

[1] This subject is suggestively treated by Robert Ludlow Fowler in his introduction to the Grolier Club edition of Bradford's Laws of New York, 1694. The facts are given by Brodhead.

[2] His commission is printed in Brodhead, II. App. 653.

[3] Brodhead, II. 43.

[4] Bulletin of New York State Library, General Entries, 95 ; N. Y. Col. Docs. II. 250 ; O'Callaghan, II. 532.

"their owne Customes concerning their Inheritances."
Full recognition should be given to their public records and
to the judgments which had been rendered in their courts.
Contracts and bargains made previous to the day of surrender should be interpreted and executed according to Dutch
law. All inferior civil officers and magistrates should continue in their places till the time of the next election should
come, and then new ones should be chosen by themselves, provided the new incumbents should take the oath of allegiance
to the English king. Free exit was allowed to those,
soldiers or others, who desired to leave the province, while
for six months intercourse might be freely kept up with the
Netherlands. The benefits of these articles were extended
to the inhabitants of Albany and Rensselaerswyck, and,
though under a separate commission, to those on the South
river.[1] As, however, it was expected that the great body
of the Dutch inhabitants would remain in New York, Governor Nicolls, beginning with the magistrates of New Amsterdam, insisted that an oath of allegiance should be taken to
the king of England. To this some objected, unless a clause
was added implying that the oath did not involve the withdrawal of any of the privileges conceded in the articles of
surrender. After a discussion on this point between the
burgomasters and the governor, the latter, to make assurance doubly sure, issued a declaration, signed by himself
and the magistrates of the city, stating that the articles were
not in the least degree broken by the terms of the oath. The
administration of the oath then went on unobstructed.[2]

These acts insured for a time to the Dutch inhabitants in
many parts of the province the continuance of their system
of law and local government. In Albany the officials were
soon appointed regularly from lists of nominees submitted
by the locality.[3] But within the English section of the
province, the governor and council could immediately set
at work. The English component of the population was

---

[1] General Entries, 112, 119; N. Y. Col. Docs. XII. 457; *ibid.* XIV. 559;
Hazard, Annals of Pennsylvania, 364.

[2] Records of New Amsterdam, V. 143; General Entries, 118.

[3] N. Y. Col. Docs. III. 143.

increased by the inclusion of the towns at the eastern end of
Long Island.   The addition of such remote dependencies as
Martha's Vineyard, Nantucket, and Cornwall signified little
to the province of New York itself.   The loose authority
which Connecticut had exercised over some of the eastern
towns was withdrawn, and the process of incorporating them
with New York began.   The authority of Connecticut was
again revived during the fifteen months of Dutch reoccupation (1673–1674), but on the restoration of English government it was finally abandoned and their fortunes were
permanently joined with those of New York.   Within Long
Island, though it was inhabited partly by Dutch ; in Staten
island, which contained a small Dutch population ; and in
Westchester, which was wholly English, Governor Nicolls
began the introduction of English institutions.   The process
commenced with the organization of this region as a great
English county under the name of Yorkshire.   It was
divided into three ridings, — the east riding comprising the
present Suffolk county ; the west riding comprising Staten
island, the present Kings county and the town of Newtown
in Queens ; the north riding including the rest of Queens
county and Westchester.

On March 1, 1665, before a meeting of deputies from
Westchester and all the towns of Long Island, the " Duke's
Laws " were proclaimed.[1]   Within that region, as well as in
Staten island, — though it had no deputies present, — the
laws were at once put into force.   This code was probably
prepared by the governor, with the assistance of the secretary and members of the court of assizes.   It was compiled
from the codes of the New England colonies, with probably
some additions from English sources, and the whole was
thrown into such form as best to meet the needs of officials
in a proprietary province.   Under sections alphabetically
arranged it set forth carefully the forms of judicial business
and procedure ; also the various civil actions classified as

[1] N. Y. Col. Docs. XIV. 564 *et seq.*   The text of the Duke's Laws is in
1 Colls. of N. Y. Hist. Soc. I. 305–428.   Another copy is also printed in the
volume entitled Charters and Laws of Pennsylvania.   The last-named copy
is followed by some of the orders later issued by the court of assizes.

was then the custom in English law, and a criminal code which was less severe than that of contemporary England. It also contained the law which was to prevail in the English part of the province concerning ecclesiastical relations, the Indians, military affairs, the courts, taxation, and the oaths and fees of officials. For the enforcement of the law within Yorkshire the governor and council appointed a high sheriff for the whole of the county, an under-sheriff and a board of justices for each of the ridings. The justices held a court of sessions in each of the ridings three times a year. The highest judicial body of the province, as well as the closest approximation which it had to a legislature, was the court of assizes. This met once a year at New York, and consisted of the governor, the council, and the justices of the courts of sessions. It was this body, or more truly the governor and council within it, which formulated the "Duke's Laws" and subsequently revised them. At its meetings new laws were published, and important public business was done or the fact that it had been done was announced. The officials of the new county government were at once appointed, and it, with the court of assizes, was set in operation.

The substitution in the Dutch towns of officials with English titles and powers, in the place of the schouts and schepens, accompanied the process which has just been described. The Duke's Laws provided for the election by the freeholders of each town of a board of eight overseers and a constable to hold for one year. One-half of the board of overseers should retire from office annually, and from the retiring list the constable should be chosen. The overseers and constable possessed judicial powers, as did the local officers of the Dutch village. We find that by December,[1] 1665, the change had been effected in Brooklyn, Flatbush, and Flatlands, and it is probable that the other Dutch towns on the island did not fall much behind in this matter. The English parish system in a somewhat modified form was legalized throughout this section.

Even earlier than this a similar change was effected in

[1] N. Y. Col. Docs. XIV. 573.

the city of New York, this encroachment of English usage
upon a town that was still essentially Dutch being due, we
may suppose, to the residence there of the officials of the
provincial government, as well as to instructions from England. In June, 1665, for government by schout, burgomasters, and schepens, was substituted[1] government by
mayor, aldermen, and sheriff, all appointed for one year by
the governor. The statement in their commission that
they were to govern the city " according to the Generall
Lawes of this Government," and such special ordinances as
might be thought convenient or necessary, was sufficiently
ambiguous to open the way for the gradual substitution
of English for Dutch law and usage in the city. Even
the restricted right of choice which the city had previously
enjoyed in the election of its magistrates was taken away.
For this reason, and because the new measure seemed to
violate the clause in the articles of surrender which provided that existing magistrates should continue as they
were till the time of election, and that then new ones
should be chosen in their places, objection was made by
some to the installation of the governor's appointees. But
he met the objection by stating that the election referred
to had been held the previous February, and by it the
requirement in the articles of surrender had been fully
met. He also declared that the duke had instructed him
to establish the government of the city in conformity with
the law of England. This silenced objection, and the English mayor, Thomas Willett, with the Dutch sheriff and the
two English and three Dutch aldermen, took their oaths of
office.

The work of introducing English law and officials did not
proceed farther than this during Nicolls's administration.
Not until July, 1667, the date of the treaty of Breda, did
England hold the territory of New Netherland by any title
save that of conquest. The course which she pursued during that interval conformed with the dictum of the lawyers
respecting the mode of introducing English law into con-

[1] General Entries, 172, 173 ; Doc. Hist. of New York, I. 602 ; Records of
New Amsterdam, V. 248 *et seq.*

quered territory. The change was effected by the act of the conqueror. But it is certain that the course pursued by the officials in New York differed in no vital respect from the measures by which we have seen that English government was established in other colonies. In the light of comparative study, the assertion of the lawyers, which was intended to apply exclusively to conquered territory, becomes broadened into a statement which applies in general to the entire process by which English law was introduced into the colonies. Not all of English law was introduced into any of the colonies. It was introduced into them all in various proportions, and by methods which differed in detail. The process in its main features was the result of conscious, purposed action. This statement, however, does not involve a denial of the probability that in the case of a conquered territory, of New Netherland itself in fact, the change was effected with greater care and more conscious intent than would appear in the history of most of the other colonies.

By the treaty of Breda New Netherland was left in the possession of the English in exchange for Surinam, which was restored to the Dutch. England thenceforward held New Netherland by a title which was valid by the law of nations. In the year following the conclusion of the treaty, Nicolls resigned the governorship, and was succeeded by Colonel Francis Lovelace. He brought with him a confirmation of the Duke's Laws, and an instruction to make no changes in the system of government which Nicolls had established. This order was obeyed. But the reoccupation of the territory by Evertsen and Binckes, which brought the administration of Lovelace to a close, restored Dutch law and institutions, and they continued in existence for more than a year. By the treaty of Westminster, February, 1674, New Netherland was ceded to England, and thus the Dutch title was finally extinguished. By being a party to this act, England may be considered to have abandoned her former position, that the Dutch had never had any rights on the Hudson, and to have acknowledged that the original title of the Duke of York was defective. In order now to remedy this defect, a new charter was issued to him in 1674, which

was an almost verbal copy of its predecessor. Under its CHAP.
authority Edmund Andros was appointed governor, and by VI.
him English law and institutions were not only restored, but,
under instructions from the proprietor, were gradually extended throughout the province. In 1674[1] the Duke's
Laws were introduced in the city of New York. By 1678
they had been put into force on the Delaware, in the towns
at Esopus, and at Albany and Schenectady. On the Delaware English official titles had superseded the Dutch, though
at Albany and Schenectady the latter survived for some
time longer.[2] Many of the forms of Dutch procedure and
provisions of their law continued long after this time, especially in the northern parts of the province, but the decisive
steps toward the supremacy of English practice had now
been taken. Strengthened thus by the perfected title of the
duke, Andros also summarily quelled the opposition of a
few who objected to taking the oath of allegiance, and it was
administered to all Dutch subjects.

Executive action is much the same the world over. Especially is this true in the governments of two nations which
in origin and type of culture were so much alike as the
Dutch and the English. The course pursued by Stuyvesant
and that followed by Andros — both men of the military
type — were in their general character the same. Both, up
to the measure of their powers, served their chiefs with the
utmost fidelity. The autocratic and exclusive power of the

---

[1] N. Y. Col. Docs. III. 218, 260 ; *ibid.* XII. 575, 581 ; *ibid.* XIII. 471.
In June, 1677, the magistrates of Newcastle on the Delaware express the
desire that "the sending of the Law book may not be forgot, there being
great occasions for the same." Andros replies that in September they may
expect to receive a copy.

[2] *Ibid.* XIII. 485, 500, 514, 532, 533. Considerable evidence on this point
exists in the records of Albany county, a manuscript calendar of which for
the period now under review exists in the State Library at Albany. The
officials of the local court at Albany, from about 1680, bore the English title
of justices, but their powers were substantially the same as those of the earlier
Dutch commissaries. The transition from Dutch to English local government in northern New York was made very gradually, almost imperceptibly,
and the changes which it involved were not great. The system, under whatever names it existed, was of course worked by Hollanders, and the Dutch
language was used by all.

executive within the province was jealously maintained by both. Under the English system the crown held aloof from interference in the affairs of the province much more than the States General had done. Though the duke sought revenue and trade, his administration was scarcely characterized by the narrow and monopolistic spirit which a trading company is likely to exhibit. In New York as a proprietary province land-grabbing, so far as we know, never assumed the dimensions to which it attained in the time of Van Twiller and his associates. Indian relations developed on a much larger scale than during the Dutch period, and they were managed with much greater wisdom than was shown by Kieft. It is certain that under the English the people were more systematically trained in the use of arms than they had been under Dutch rule. The English executive was stronger, and its work more effective than that of the director and council, but that was largely due to the fact of conquest, and to the support which the officials received from the proprietor. The Duke of York compares very favorably not only with the Dutch West India company, but with other English proprietors as well.

The affairs of the Duke of York, especially after 1673, were regularly transacted[1] in England through a secretary, a treasurer and receiver-general, an attorney-general and solicitor-general, and commissioners of the duke's revenue. By these officials, in the issue of commissions and instructions and in correspondence, the forms of the English chancery, and of the government offices in general, were followed. Thus the transaction of business in proprietary New York was characterized by greater regularity and observance of form than appears in any other proprietary province except Maryland, and the forms observed were distinctly like those of the later royal provinces. The conquest of New York resulted from the direct initiative of the crown, and Nicolls as the commander of that enterprise acted under a commission from Charles II. He acted at first in a double capacity, as royal commissioner and as proprietary appointee. Justice was administered in New York in the name of

[1] N. Y. Col. Docs. III. 214, 224, 228 et seq.

the king, and all warrants, writs, and executions ran in his
name.[1] The right of appeal to the crown was guarantied
in the charter.   Care was also observed, not only that the
Dutch should take the oath of allegiance to the king, but
that all officers of the province should do so as well.[2] These
facts, when taken in connection with the relationship which
existed between the duke of York and the king, show that
New York always stood on the borderland between a proprietary and a royal province. Political motives also contributed to the same end. It was considered desirable by
those who were best informed that New York should act as
a curb on New England. Near the close of 1668 Governor
Nicolls, finding it impossible to induce Massachusetts to
embody its militia as a precaution against the possibility of
French attack, wrote to Secretary Arlington, "My Lord, the
foresaid discouragements fall heavy upon us poore mortalls
that know no interest but his Majesty's, and are ready every
houre to sacrifize our lives for his honour and service.
When His Majesty is truly informed how advantageously
wee are posted by scituation to bridle his enemies and secure
all his good subjects, I humbly presume to thinke that his
Majesty would afford much countenance and regard unto
us notwithstanding that his Majesty hath graunted the
whole tract to his Royal Highness." [3]

Richard Nicolls was eminently qualified for the discharge
of the delicate task which was imposed upon him. The
record of his acts, as well as the testimony of his contempo-
raries, shows that he possessed that combination of firmness
with a conciliatory spirit which make the successful adminis-
trator. Law and power were wholly on his side, and he was
not slow to make it evident when necessity required. When
a spirit of opposition in the towns of Southampton, Easthampton, and Southold manifested itself in what he regarded as an
unjustifiable delay in the choice of constables and overseers,
Nicolls wrote,[4] "I am much more troubled to heare that such
wicked designs should have Generall Influence upon those
three Townes, contrary to the Duty they owe to his Majesty,

---

[1] N. Y. Col. Docs. III. 219.   [2] *Ibid.* 218.   [3] *Ibid.* 167.
[4] *Ibid.* XIV. 577.

whose crown and dignity, wisdom & power I must and
will assert, not only against his publique but his private
Enemys. . . . " If the neglect were continued, " I shall
bee necessitated," he wrote, "to declare against the dissenters
therein, as mutinous contemners of the Lawes Established,
and disturbers of the peace of this Government, and shall
(with God's Assistance) proceed against any or every person
according to Law, in those cases provided."   In a different
spirit he wrote to the inhabitants of Jamaica respecting
a controversy which that town was having with Flushing
over a parcel of land recently bought from the Indians: [1] " I
am very tender in giving credit to the reports on one part
till the other is heard, and I am also very unwilling to putt
the Magistrates or Inhabitants to the trouble of coming
hither this Winter Season to Answer what those of Flushing
have objected, but rather to recommend to you the Silencing
of former Divisions betweene Neighbors, and no(t) beginning any new occasion of difference. . . . "

To the constable and overseers of Oyster Bay,[2] who had
objected to an order of the governor increasing the public
rate for the year 1666 to a penny in the pound, and who had
probably objected also because they were being taxed without their consent, Nicolls wrote that he would never be
unwilling to manifest the openness both of his ears and
heart to the humblest man in the world who complained of
oppressive treatment.   After insisting that the trust committed to him by the king was sufficient warrant for what
he had done, and that he had done it in order that the public
debts might not run into arrears or men complain that they
must wait two years for payment, he continued, " You see
how ready I am to satisfy your scruples, and therefore I
cannot but expect your complyance to my directions, whose
dayly meditacon it is, which way I can best serve the country, and without any other expectation of benefit from them
than a good name and no such peevish dispositions which
may render them refractory to his Majesty's Government."
He closed with a declaration that before God and the world
he would justify what he had done, and would uphold the

[1] N. Y. Col. Docs. XIV. 562.   [2] *Ibid.* 574.

officials of the town in executing it.   When, at the close of
his short term, Colonel Nicolls was returning to England,
Samuel Maverick, his associate upon the royal commission,
wrote [1] concerning him to Secretary Arlington, "After his
abode here four yeares (where he hath lived with great
reputation and honour) hee is now returning home, I must
needs accompany him with this character, that hee hath done
his Majesty and his Royall Highness very considerable service in these parts, having by his prudent management of
affaires kept persons of different judgments and of diverse
nations in peace and quietnes, dureing a time when a great
part of the world was in warrs.   As to the severall Nations
of the Indyans, they were never brought into such a peaceable posture & faire correspondence, as by his means they
now are."

Edmund Andros, who was appointed to the governorship
after the close of the Dutch reoccupation, possessed the
strong and imperious will of Nicolls, but without his conciliatory manners.   The two were alike in their fidelity to
the rights and interests of their superior.   Both were also
men of the military profession, and fond of autocratic rule.
Andros possessed less of the gentlemanly instincts and sense
of justice than did Nicolls.   Nicolls was better able to conceal the harsh features of absolutism than was Andros.   But
both men were willing servants under the same régime.

During his administration of seven years as proprietary
governor Andros visited England twice, and reported upon
the condition of New York.   His report [2] on the first occasion — in 1678 — was made to the committee of Trade and
Plantations, and was occasioned by the charges made by
Massachusetts that, during the recent Indian war, the
people in the neighborhood of Albany had furnished·ammu-
nition and other material for war to Philip and his men.
Upon petition of Andros, Stoughton and Bulkley, the agents
of Massachusetts, were called upon to justify the charge, but
were unable to do so.   Thereupon an order in council was
issued declaring that none of the inhabitants about Albany
should lie under such an imputation unless Massachusetts

[1] N. Y. Col. Docs. III. 174.   [2] *Ibid.* 258 *et seq.*

should prosecute them thereon to a legal conviction within one year, and that the government of Massachusetts should be immediately informed to that effect.   The Puritan colonies never responded to the challenge.   The relations between them and Andros had never been cordial, and, in fact, could not be so with any governor of New York, so long as by charter its northeast boundary line was the Connecticut river.   In the testimony, moreover, which Andros gave before the English authorities concerning the colonies in general, he urged the importance from the military standpoint of the crown regulating the militia of the colonies in such a way as to secure united action.   This foreshadowed the course which was later to be taken, and this, with other free criticisms, still further prejudiced New Englanders against Andros.   The confidence of the crown in his ability and fidelity was, however, shown by the bestowment on him at this time of the honor of knighthood.

The second visit of Andros to England, and the one which closed his administration, was caused, in 1680, by a direct summons from the duke.[1]   The occasion of this was the circulating of charges by private persons, including certain Quakers, Captain Christopher Billop — who for misconduct had been discharged from his office as commander on the Delaware — and others, to the discredit of Andros.   It was said that in trade regulations he favored Phillips and Van Cortlandt, who were councillors and wealthy Dutch merchants; that he caused ordinances to be issued which were harmful to the English; that he traded directly himself or admitted Dutch ships promptly, while unduly detaining those of Englishmen.   Offers had also been made to farm the duke's revenue in New York, and the estimates of its amount contained in these offers differed greatly from the reports of Andros.   As the information which had reached James concerning the province was loose and scattered, Andros was ordered to return and fully explain all matters. At the same time John Lewin, supposed to have been a London attorney, was commissioned as the special agent of the duke, to go to New York and thoroughly inform himself

[1] N. Y. Col. Docs. III. 279 *et seq.*

concerning the administration of the revenue of the province and its amount.   He was carefully instructed to examine records, and officials and private individuals as well, and if possible ascertain whether or not the duke had been defrauded or private traders wronged in the administration of the customs.   Andros was ordered to give him all possible countenance and assistance, and did so just before he himself sailed for England.   Lewin submitted a long report,[1] in which he treated several of the charges as substantiated, and presented a complaint of his own that various records and other sources of information had been withheld from him.   To Lewin's report Andros presented a reply, denying the charges seriatim, and shifting the responsibility on other officials and their conduct after he had left the province. William Dyer, the collector of the customs at New York, having meanwhile been sent to London under a charge arising from illegal collection of the revenue, he, with Andros, Lewin, and others, was examined by John Churchill on behalf of the commissioners of the duke's revenue.   Churchill could not find that Lewin and his friends were able to sustain any of their charges against either Andros or Dyer, and both were discharged.   But, though the fidelity of Andros to the proprietor was proven, Colonel Thomas Dongan was selected to carry on the government of the province, and to finally quench the hostility of the English merchants to the customs regulations of the duke, from which Andros had suffered, by calling a representative assembly.   Dongan's career in the province proved that James had again chosen wisely.   He proved to be one of the very best of all the colonial governors.   So far, then, as its chief magistrates were concerned, New York was fortunate so long as James Stuart held the power of appointment.

The council of New York, like that of New Netherland and those of the other English proprietary provinces, consisted of few members.   The secretary, Matthias Nicolls, was sworn in regularly as councillor, and with him on the board, as first organized, were Captains Robert Needham and Thomas Delavall, who had accompanied the commissioners from England,

---

[1] N. Y. Col. Docs. III. 302.

Thomas Topping of Southampton, and William Wells of Southold.[1] The board usually numbered from six to eight. At executive sessions sometimes only two were present, as the governor and Mr. Whitfield ; again, the governor, Mr. Whitfield, and the secretary ; still again, the governor, Mr. Delavall, Mr. Willett, and the secretary; or the governor, Mr. Mayor, Mr. Steenwyck, and the secretary.[2] Passing to the administration of Governor Andros, we find that on October 23, 1675, the governor, the secretary, Captain Dyer, and Mr. Phillips were present. On May 5, 1676, the governor, Captain Brockholls, the secretary, Captain Dyer, and Mr. Phillips were in attendance.[3] These entries fairly indicate the members who regularly attended. Attention to the personnel of the council will reveal the additional fact, already familiar from the study of other colonies, that this body consisted almost wholly of officials. Among the members just referred to as in attendance were the secretary, the mayor, and one of the aldermen of the city of New York — both appointees of the governor ; also a lieutenant-governor, who was at the same time the major of a militia company and the collector of the customs. The mayors of the metropolis were regularly appointed councillors. Of the council, as first organized, the high sheriff of Yorkshire was a member. The heads of the rising families of the province, — merchants and large landowners, — especially if they lived in the vicinity of the city of New York, were almost sure to be members of the council. Frederick Phillips and Stephen Van Cortlandt in early times are good examples of members of this class. At the beginning the council was largely composed of military officers and lawyers direct from England. As time passed, its membership came necessarily to consist chiefly of permanent residents of the province. Men of Dutch as well as English descent were appointed, provided they showed themselves loyal to the established government. Of the loyalty of Nicholas Bayard, Andros at first had doubts, but in 1685 Bayard was appointed

[1] Brodhead, II. 43.
[2] Council Minutes, Sept. 2, 1668 ; Sept. 9, 1669 ; N. Y. Col. Docs. XIV. 623, 635, 644.　　　　　　[3] *Ibid.* 703, 719.

mayor of New York, and at the same time began his career
as a councillor.[1] It would appear that the council in New
York was aristocratic and exclusive in character, and the
official spirit strongly prevailed within it.   Sessions of the
council were held in any part of the province where the governor happened to be and where it was most convenient that
business should be done.

CHAP.
VI.

The directing influence of the governor and council was
continuously felt in all sections of the province.   In Long
Island its attention was chiefly devoted to the settlement of
boundary disputes and other conflicting claims between
towns.   There also it had to contend with the sensitiveness
of the people on the subject of prerogative taxation, and over
the requirement that land patents should be taken out anew
from the English authorities.   In the valley of the Hudson
the council was largely concerned with the Indians, and
with the founding of new settlements and the regulation of
affairs at the Esopus.   Relations with New Jersey naturally
came in for a large share of attention.   On the Delaware
relations with the Swedes and with the inhabitants of Maryland, who claimed the territory as far north as the fortieth
degree of latitude, land grants, the maintenance of peace and
trade with the Indians, the appointment of English officials
and establishment of courts, and finally the controversy with
John Fenwick over his settlement on the east side of the
bay, occupied very much of the attention of the council.   A
somewhat more extended reference to certain typical examples of the business thus transacted will throw light on the
history of the times.

One of the most difficult tasks which the New York executive had to undertake was that of establishing a uniform
system of control over the towns of Long Island.   It was
necessary to impose it, not only on the towns which were
inhabited by Hollanders and had been under Dutch rule, but
on the English towns at the east end of the island, which
had hitherto been practically independent.   The system of
control in itself was no more searching than that which the
executives of the New England colonies exercised over their

[1] Brodhead, II. 428.

towns, but it did not proceed from men of their own choice, acting under laws of their own making ; neither from men of their own religious confession, or those whose political views were in harmony with the desires of the people who were to be governed. In a word, it was imposed by an outside power instead of being part of a system of self-government.

It was fortunate that when the first encounter between the towns and the provincial executive occurred, a man with the temper of Nicolls was in the office of governor. Under the lead of Howell of Southampton and Young of Southold, these towns, together with Easthampton, refused to choose town officers or to pay rates. John Underhill, who at the time was high constable of the east riding, sympathized more or less with them, and there was widespread aversion to the Duke's Laws and to the way in which they had been imposed by executive action at the meeting which was held at Hempstead in March, 1665. The oaths of the town over- seer and constable bound them to obey and enforce these laws, together with the orders of the executive and courts, and the obligation to take the oaths was especially offen- sive. Personal jealousy of William Wells of Hempstead, who had been appointed high sheriff of Yorkshire, and per- haps of other fellow-townsmen who had gained the confidence of the government, probably had an influence with some. At any rate, the discontent was widespread, leading to utterances and acts which savored of sedition. At Seatalcot (Brook- haven) the constable, while executing the duties of his office, was assaulted by citizens in a riotous manner. Nicolls met this crisis with a combination of firmness and conciliation. He declared to people and officials alike his resolution to en- force the law and maintain authority. Disturbers of the peace were threatened with immediate punishment. But at the same time he ordered that the requirement that town officers should take the oath should be suspended until further action by the court of assizes. The result was that quiet was soon restored, and open opposition to the establishment of government in the duke's name among the towns ceased.[1]

But when English authority was restored after the Dutch

[1] N. Y. Col. Docs. XIV. 574–582.

reoccupation, the trouble revived.[1]   Governor Andros received a letter from the same towns, in which they declared
that when New York had been surrendered in a cowardly
manner to the Dutch, and its authorities had thereby failed
to afford protection, the assistance of Connecticut had again
been sought.   By means of this the towns in question had
been able to save themselves from the necessity of submit-
ting to the Dutch, and now they declined to renew their connection with New York without the consent of Connecticut.
This was the reply which they made to the command of
Andros that they should reinstate the constables and overseers who were in office when Fort James was surrendered
to the Dutch.   It was true that Captain Manning, the officer
in command at New York when Evertsen and Binckes appeared, was guilty of cowardice in its surrender, and was soon
after convicted of the charge and dismissed from the king's
service.   But that, of course, afforded no justification for the
present conduct of the eastern towns.   The Connecticut
government, moreover, claimed no permanent interest in the
towns or control over their administration.   On the other
hand, they were a part of the province of New York, and
Andros in asserting authority over them was ˙obeying the
instructions of his superior.   Acting therefore upon the
advice of the council, he ordered Mulford, Howell, and
Young, who had signed the letter of the towns, to answer
at once before him at New York on penalty of being treated
as rebels.   The towns in question were again ordered to
reinstate the constables and overseers in office.   A special
commissioner was sent thither to administer to them the
oaths of office, to assure the inhabitants of the just intentions of the governor, and to report upon the state of feeling
which he found in the towns.   This prompt action, together
with the knowledge that Connecticut would not interpose on
their behalf, proved decisive.   There could be no further
thought of resistance, though the spirit of opposition continued to show itself in the refusal to renew land patents.

It was a fundamental law of New York as a proprietary
province that all land should be held of the proprietor, as

[1] N. Y. Col. Docs. XIV. 681 *et seq.*

the grantee of the king.   Only in this way could a title
which was good in English law be secured.   The land would
then be subject to a quitrent or other payments, such as the
proprietor, with due regard to the possibilities of the case,
might impose.   This phase of the system, however, was
peculiarly obnoxious to all New Englanders.   The fact that
purchases had been made from agents of Lord Stirling also
played a part in the controversy.   As has already been stated,
it was found impossible, at this time, to collect quitrents
of any amount from Long Island grants,[1] or even to specify
the obligation.   But it was the duty of the governors to
insist upon a general renewal of patents, while, on the
other hand, this met with much opposition.   The towns
of Southold and Southampton in particular maintained
passive opposition to the demand from the time of Lovelace
until 1676.   In that year Southampton[2] formally presented
to the governor its objections to taking out patents.   The
inhabitants claimed that their title was already valid, that
the step they were required to take was new and strange,
that it involved uncertainties and seemed to subject them to
the arbitrary will of another.   " Wee cannot bee free," they
said, "to pass over our owne proper rights to our lands into
other mens hands and put ourselves and successors into a
state of Servitude, which, if soe, whoe will pitty or helpe
us."   The paper was laid before the court of assizes.   That
tribunal in response declared that the said towns had forfeited all right to the lands in question, unless within a
fortnight they acknowledged their error and promised obedience.   This brought the required submission ; patents were
accepted from the proprietor, and the question of land titles
was finally settled.   But, as will later appear, the spirit which
lay behind this opposition readily lent itself, not many years
after, to the successful demand for a representative assembly.

The administrative work of the governor and council of
New York was of the ordinary prosaic sort.[3]   One of the

---

[1] N. Y. Col. Docs. III. 303, Lewin's report.   [2] *Ibid.* XIV. 723.

[3] See Journal of the Executive Council, Ms. I. 1668–1678 ; II. 1683–
1688 ; also some material in the Records of the Court of Assizes, 1665–1672.
The larger part of the journal and correspondence of the governor and council prior to 1685 has been printed in N. Y. Col. Docs. XII, XIII, and XIV.

earliest entries in their records which has been preserved — September, 1668 — reveals them engaged in the task of prescribing conditions on which trade with the other colonies, especially those of the West Indies, could be carried on. It then considered a dispute [1] between John Archer, who afterward was the grantee of the manor of Fordham, and the town of New Haerlem, over the possession of land, some of which lay near Spuyten Duyvil, and it was decided, after examination of the ground briefs and patents, that the land in question belonged to the town. The ferry at Haerlem not having answered the ends proposed, commissioners were sent to view the passage over the Haerlem creek at Spuyten Duyvil, to see how it could be made more commodious for travellers and cattle. A few months later we find commissioners appointed, by joint action of governor, council, and bench, to lay out a wagon road from New York to Haerlem. At the same meeting — which was held at Haerlem — a dispute between the town of Westchester and William Willett concerning Cornell's neck, and between the same town and Thomas Hunt about his commonage and a washing place on Throgmorton's neck, was to have been heard, but Westchester did not appear. Therefore a committee was appointed with power to adjust the disputes, and the governor would confirm their decision.

At about the same time steps were taken to settle by arbitration a dispute over the boundary between the towns of Gravesend and New Utrecht. The claim of Oyster Bay to a certain neck of land, which was also in controversy between grantees of the Dutch government on the one hand and of the Earl of Stirling on the other, came before the council and later before the courts for settlement.[2] Shortly before the general meeting of March, 1665, at Hempstead, one important object of which was the adjustment of boundaries, the magistrates of Jamaica and Flushing were summoned[3] to meet the governor for the purpose of discussing a boundary dispute between those towns. The boundary between New York and Connecticut was also under consideration. One of the most important suits over land titles which came in the

[1] N. Y. Col. Docs. XIII. 421.   [2] *Ibid.* XIV. 557–560.   [3] *Ibid.* 563.

early years before the council and the courts was that
between the town of Huntington and Richard Smith, the
founder of the distinguished Long Island family of that
name, over a claim to land on the west bank of Nesaquake
river.[1] In 1669 controversies over the possession of land
between Newtown and Hempstead, Newtown and Bushwick,
as well as the one between Gravesend and New Utrecht,
came before the governor and council. On petition, controversies between individuals and between towns and
individuals, respecting a variety of matters, were also
brought before the same body. Some of these naturally
passed to the courts for adjustment.

The formation of villages and towns, either by new settlements in the wilderness, or by separation from towns previously existing, was regulated by the governor and council.
By that body Shelter island[2] was set off by itself, while
during the year 1669 and later they were much occupied
with the organization of Marbletown and Hurley, two villages in the Esopus region near Kingston. The immediate
care of this latter business was intrusted[3] to commissioners.
This involved the laying out of lots, the adjustment of land
titles, the allotment of land to disbanded soldiers and others,
provision for the defence of the settlements and their relations with the Indians, and the direction of the local magistrates in many things relating to the duties of their offices.
All matters connected with the beginnings of town government on the frontier came in this way within the sphere of
the governor and council. Under Governor Andros, instructions were freely issued to the commissaries at Schenectady ;
and a general court, or judicial tribunal, was organized, to
consist of the commander and justices or commissaries of
Albany and Rensselaerswyck, with those of Schenectady.[4]

The beginnings of New Dorp on Staten island[5] and of the
precinct at the Whorekills[6] on the Delaware came in a
similar way, though not in such detail, within the purview of
the same authority. Throughout the Dutch sections of the

---

[1] N. Y. Col. Docs. XIV. 613, 615, 640, 644.

[2] *Ibid.* 566.

[3] *Ibid.* XIII. 428 *et seq.*

[4] *Ibid.* 485, 500 *et seq.*

[5] *Ibid.* 415 *et seq.*

[6] *Ibid.* XII. 507, 562, 604 *et seq.*

province, local magistrates were appointed by the governor,
either directly or from lists nominated by freeholders of the
localities. This involved the creation of local courts by the
same authority. On the Delaware, when the Dutch magistrates had been superseded by sheriffs, constables, surveyors,
and other officials for keeping the peace and administering
justice, three courts were thereby organized. Each was provided with justices, a sheriff, and a coroner, and had jurisdiction over an administrative district. One of the courts was
established at Upland, another at Newcastle, and a third at
the Whorekills. Sessions were held with considerable regularity. The records of the court at Upland have been preserved,
and show that it continued without interruption till it became
the court of Chester county, Pennsylvania. Newcastle also
was known as a county as early as 1678. By 1682 the region
from Newcastle southward had become organized as the
Three Lower Counties of Newcastle, James (later Kent),
and Deal (later Sussex), and in that form it was annexed to
Pennsylvania.[1] The organization of counties within the
province of New York itself was not carried beyond the
rudimentary stage until the process of legislation by a representative assembly began.

Fiscal affairs in the various sections were regulated by
the governor and council. Full provision was made in the
Duke's Laws for the annual levy of rates under the authority of the governor, transmitted through the high sheriff to
the constables, and for their collection under warrants to the
constables. The enforcement of payment rested both with
the governor and the courts. The governor appointed commissioners to collect taxes on Long Island which were due
to Connecticut. From time to time instructions were issued
to sheriffs and constables concerning the levy and collection
of rates, whether for general or special purposes. The towns
of the west riding of Yorkshire were ordered to contribute
what was necessary for the building of a session house. The
justices of the north riding were empowered to make a rate

[1] N. Y. Col. Docs. XII. 561, 572 *et seq.*; V. 544, 551, 572 *et seq.*; *ibid.*
2 Pa. Arch. IX. 644 *et seq.*; Record of the Upland Court, Memoirs of
the Hist. Soc. of Pa. VII.

for a similar purpose. The constable and overseers of Huntington were empowered to levy by distress both their town rate and a rate for the support of the minister.[1] As early as April, 1665, John Underhill was appointed surveyor of customs on Long Island,[2] and sub-collectors were later appointed for Easthampton and Southampton. At Esopus and the settlements about Albany the Dutch excise was continued until the English laws were fully introduced, and its collection was annually farmed out under orders of the governor and council.[3] Customs duties and quitrents were collected on the Delaware under authority from the same source.[4]

The control of the governor and council over military affairs was equally complete.

[1] N. Y. Col. Docs. XIV. 573, 583, 590, 591, 597, 602–605, 626, 734.
[2] *Ibid.* 566, 608, 637.
[3] *Ibid.* XIII. 430 ; Council Recs. Ms., March, 1671.
[4] N. Y. Col. Docs. XII. 475, 483, 490, 495, 501, 506, 609, 619.

CHAPTER VII

THE BEGINNINGS OF A LEGISLATURE IN PROPRIETARY
NEW YORK

THIS subject, as well as the early history of the executive
in New York, cannot be properly understood without somewhat extended reference to the experience of the Dutch in
New Netherland. The government of that province throughout its entire existence centred in the director and council.
It was, at least in theory, a centralized and autocratic system. The council itself was a small body, filled mainly by
the director's appointees and subject to his control. The
director himself received his authority from a mercantile
company in the Netherlands; he naturally shared in its
exclusive and monopolistic instincts, was its more or less
faithful agent, and received its support in return. By
directors and company alike, attempts of the colonists at
large to influence or regulate the conduct of the government were resented; no place was made for this in the
system of provincial government as originally planned. In
the charter, as in those which were issued to early English
trading companies, no provision was made for an assembly.
As the West India company cared far less for the larger
and more permanent interests of New Netherland than did
the London company, when under the administration of
Sandys and Southampton, for those of Virginia, the Dutch
province was allowed to remain with a governmental system
that was fit only for a trading post. Action on the part of
the people beyond that of isolated petitions for favors was
discouraged, and the organization of a legislature persistently
opposed. Secretary Van Tienhoven expressed the truth
when, in defending Stuyvesant and his policy against attack,
he declared, "No one comes or is admitted into New Neth-

erland except on this condition, not that he shall have anything to say, but that he shall acknowledge the sovereignty
of their High Mightinesses, . . . and obey the Director
and Council for the time being, as a good subject is bound
to do." [1]   And yet an opposition was formed, in which both
Dutch and English shared, and by means of it efforts were
made to limit the power of the director and council; but
this did not result in the union of the localities into a permanent representative system.   The origin and nature of
this movement it is now necessary to explain.

It began amid the perplexities of an Indian war.[2]   By
1640 the extension of settlement had brought the colonists
into closer contact with the natives.   Isolated boweries and
small groups of plantations had been settled at various points
in the midst of the Indian country.   At Pavonia and Achter
Col, on Staten island, and on the upper part of Manhattan
island, such outposts existed.   As in Virginia before the massacre of 1622, the colonists lived on familiar terms with the
Indians, taking them into their employ, even admitting them
into their houses and to their tables.   The lands of the settlers being, in many cases, unfenced, their cattle frequently
broke into the cornfields of the Indians and did much damage.   Guns and ammunition were sold, first, it is said, to
the Mohawks about Fort Orange, and then to the river
Indians to enable them to defend themselves against the
Iroquois, who now, with the help of firearms, were better
able than ever to assert their superiority over the river
Indians.   The sale of liquor followed.

The irritation of the natives was increased by a contribution of maize, furs, and wampum which Kieft, without the
knowledge, as it was alleged, of the company, levied upon
the river Indians.   Petty outrages began to be committed
by them.   The whites retaliated, a considerable proportion
of them, it seems, being in favor of exceedingly harsh measures toward the Indians.   Director Kieft either approved of
this policy from the outset, or yielded to it under pressure.

[1] N. Y. Col. Docs. I. 425.

[2] The Journal of New Netherland, in N. Y. Col. Docs. I. 179 *et seq.*; De
Vries, Voyages, in 2 Colls. N. Y. Hist. Soc. III. 113.

After the worst seemed to have been averted by a truce with
the natives who lived immediately north of Manhattan island, the director assented to a proposal to massacre a large body of river Indians who had taken refuge, as they supposed, under Dutch protection from the assaults of the Iroquois. This outrage, in which about 110 of the savages were slain, was committed on the night of the 25th of February, 1643, at Pavonia and Corlaer's Hook.

Though the earlier acts of the Dutch might bear favorable comparison with the raid of Endicott against Block island and into the Pequot country, the massacre of February, 1643, was madness itself.   De Vries, whose settlement on Staten island had already been the scene of outrages by both parties, exclaimed to Kieft, "Stop this work ; you wish to break the mouths of the Indians, but you will also murder our own nation, for there are none of the farmers who are aware of it. My own dwelling, my people, cattle, corn, and tobacco, will be lost." But his protest was of no avail.[1] The massacre set the province in a flame, and two years elapsed before peace was restored.   Boweries and settlements throughout Manhattan island and the adjacent regions of the main-land and Long Island were destroyed, and the Indians advanced to the gates of New Amsterdam.   The fort there was described at the time as being entirely "out of order" and "rather a mole-hill than a fort against an enemy."[2] The weak and poorly organized force of fifty or sixty Dutch militiamen was unable to hold them in check in the open country.   But offensive operations were finally undertaken by the Dutch in coöperation with the English of western Long Island, and these culminated, in February, 1644, in the destruction of an Indian stronghold near Stamford, Con-necticut, and the slaughter of possibly five hundred of the sav-ages.   This, as an achievement, ranks with the destruction of the Pequot fort in 1637 and the Swamp Fight of 1675. It was followed by the gradual cessation of hostilities and finally by peace.   It was amid the agonies of this struggle that a political opposition in New Netherland was born.

In August, 1641, early in the conflict, Kieft called together

[1] N. Y. Col. Docs. XIII. 10.   [2] *Ibid.* I. 190.

the masters and heads of families who resided in New Amsterdam and its vicinity, and submitted to them the question, whether or not steps should be taken to avenge the recent murder of Claes Smits by the Indians, and what they should be. After presenting their reply, the commonalty chose twelve men [1] to coöperate with the director in carrying out their suggestions. De Vries was named their president. The director considered that this board was called to advise him about the best way in which to attack the Indians, and for no other purpose. He did not regard them as a permanent body,[2] or as a part of the council, or consider that they should thwart his plans. In order the better to assure himself of their assent to an immediate offensive war, he called the members of the board before him individually. But failing even then to secure the consent of the majority, he had to postpone action till winter. Then they as a body consented to an expedition, provided the company would furnish the ammunition and provisions, and the director would accompany it.[3]

But the Twelve were not content with this temporary function. Acting on the supposition that they were representatives of the commonalty for the purpose of securing reforms, they at once petitioned [4] the director that annual musters should be held, that the membership of the council should be increased, that from the Twelve four should be appointed in rotation to represent before the council the interests of the commonalty, especially in the matter of taxation, freedom of trade with neighboring colonies, and a few other minor reforms. While assenting in general to these propositions, Kieft stated in his reply that he was not aware that the Twelve Men received fuller powers from the commonalty than simply to give their advice concerning the murder of Claes Smits. This clearly revealed his view of the power of the board and foreshadowed the end. About

---

[1] 2 Colls. N. Y. Hist. Soc. III. 103 ; N. Y. Col. Docs. I. 183, 414 ; O'Callaghan, History of New Netherland, I. 241.

[2] N. Y. Col. Docs. I. 304, Van der Donck's Remonstrance of New Netherland.

[3] *Ibid.* 415.   [4] *Ibid.* 201.

two weeks later — February 8, 1643 — the director issued CHAP.
an order dissolving the Twelve, because their meetings VII.
tended to dangerous consequences and the weakening of
authority. Further meetings were forbidden on pain of
corporal punishment. It was shortly after this act that
three members of the late board petitioned the director to
order the massacre of the Indian refugees, a proposition to
which he was only too willing to yield.[1]

The following September, owing to the pressure of the
war, it became necessary to summon the commonalty again.
They now chose a board of Eight Men to consider the propositions submitted by the director and council.[2] The previous board had consisted entirely of Hollanders; upon this
board two Englishmen had seats, Thomas Hall and Isaac
Allerton of Plymouth fame; Joachim Pietersen Kuyter, of
the settlement that was to be New Haerlem, and Cornelis
Melyn of Staten island were also members. Jan Jansen
Dam, one of the Twelve who had counselled the massacre,
they voted to exclude from membership. The Eight voted
to meet weekly, and at once resolved that a larger body of
men should be raised for the war. They also adopted regulations against taverns and drunkenness and in favor, for
a time, of more religious services. These, however, were
not put in execution. They also desired that all possible
help should be procured from Europe, and that the crews
on two of the company's ships which had just arrived should
be put into the service. To the latter proposal Kieft would
not consent. As the Indians continued to spread destruction, slaying Mrs. Hutchinson and her family, and attacking
Gravesend, petitions for aid were sent by the Eight to the
States General and to the company. In these the sufferings
of the colonists and the impotence of the government were
clearly depicted as related phenomena. The appeal to the
authorities at home, as well as the inclination of the board
to interfere in affairs within the province, offended the
director, and the Eight were not called together again on
public business until June, 1644. In a subsequent letter to
the Amsterdam chamber, they state that during the interval

[1] N. Y. Col. Docs. I. 193.   [2] *Ibid.* 192, 139, 209, 212, 185.

the director treated them with manifest disrespect.[1] " No sooner did they open their mouths to propose anything tending in their judgment to the public good, than the director met them with sundry biting and scoffing taunts ; and sometimes had them summoned without asking them a question, thus obliging them to return amidst jeers and sneers, as wise as they went."

Finally, on June 18, 1644, the director summoned the Eight Men and told them that additional taxes must be laid or the English soldiers would have to be discharged. They declared in reply that the people were too much exhausted by the war to pay more, and besides they did not consider that their powers extended to the imposition of new taxes, a question which must first be decided by the company. At this the director became enraged, and asserted that his authority in the province exceeded that of the company, and he could do what he pleased. The Eight then agreed to his proposition, but suggested that it would be better to levy upon the profits of private traders to the province than upon the exhausted commonalty. But this he rejected, and the ordinance levying the first excise in New Netherland — on beer, wine, and beaver [2] — was issued. The excise was to continue until peace, or until aid should come from Holland. This latter condition was soon fulfilled by the arrival of 130 soldiers from Curaçoa, who had recently been sent thither from Brazil. But in order to provide clothing for them, Kieft and the council ordered an increase of the excise on beer,[3] and also that the brewers should make return to the receiver of all the beer they had manufactured before any of it could be sold. This created strong opposition. Payment was refused, but the schout fiscal, after long trials, obtained judgments from the director and council against the offenders, and they were forced to submit. Feeling, however, was very bitter, and a faction of determined opponents to Kieft, at the head of which were Kuyter and Melyn, was formed. Remonstrances were addressed to the company and to the States General, setting

[1] N. Y. Col. Docs. I. 212, 206.   [2] *Ibid.* 189 ; Laws and Ordinances, 39.
[3] Laws and Ordinances, 40.

forth the waste condition of the province and the evil policy of the director.[1] The reports of the massacre and its disastrous results had already drawn from the States General an order to inquire into the condition of New Netherland. The Assembly of Nineteen ordered the temporary recall of Kieft to answer charges. The chamber of accounts of the company, to which the matter was referred, reported in favor not only of improved defence, the encouragement of emigration and of settlement in villages, freedom of trade with Brazil, and harmonious relations both with the Indians and the English, but that a permanent scheme should be devised for keeping the director and council in touch with the various colonies and sections of the province.[2] Article 28 of the Freedoms and Exemptions of 1629 provided that the colonies of each section should delegate one or two persons annually to report their condition to the director and council. The chamber of accounts now recommended that such delegates should be summoned every six months for consultation with the director and council, concerning all matters which related to the welfare of the province. But this wise suggestion met with no response. Soon after the conclusion of permanent peace with the Indians, Kieft's administration terminated, and Stuyvesant came to take up his quarrel and to assert to the utmost the autocratic power of the director.

Though the Eight Men had been able to put no direct check upon the doings of Kieft, their appeals to the authorities at home had arrested attention. Kuyter and Melyn, the leaders of the opposition, now petitioned Stuyvesant to investigate Kieft's conduct and policy. Naturally Stuyvesant was opposed to this, and had no difficulty in persuading the council to share his opinion. By their decision not to attempt the investigation, Kieft, who was still in the province, was encouraged to demand [3] that Kuyter and Melyn be prosecuted for libelling himself and the government in their petition of October 28, 1644, sent in the name of the Eight Men to the company in Holland. Stuyvesant took up the case, and

[1] N. Y. Col. Docs. I. 144, 148, 209.
[2] *Ibid.* 154 ; Laws and Ordinances, 9.   [3] N. Y. Col. Docs. I. 203, 205.

the accused, under an indictment prepared by the director and council themselves, were tried by the same body on the charge of *læsa majestatis*, or seditious attack on the government. They were found guilty, and Stuyvesant gave as his opinion that Melyn should be punished with death. But both of the accused were finally sentenced to fine and banishment.[1] They immediately sailed for Europe on the same vessel with Kieft. The ship was wrecked off the Welsh coast and Kieft perished, but Kuyter and Melyn were saved. At once they repaired to the Netherlands and lodged an appeal with the States General against the judgment of the director and council in their case. The sentence against them was suspended,[2] and Stuyvesant was ordered to appear in person or through an attorney at The Hague to defend the action of the court, and in the meantime to permit the accused the enjoyment of all their rights in New Netherland.

While these steps were being taken in Europe, Stuyvesant, as one of his many reform measures, undertook the repair of the fort at New Amsterdam. But the commonalty showed itself unwilling to bear the expense. In order the better to secure the money, the commonalty was ordered,[3] in September, 1647, to choose eighteen men, from whom the director and council selected the Nine Men. This was the third body of its kind which the exigencies of defence and fiscal needs had brought into existence in New Netherland. The Nine Men, for the first year, were all Dutch in origin and were selected from the merchants, citizens, and farmers of Manhattan, Breuckelen, Amersfoort, and Pavonia. Augustine Heermans, Govert Loockermans, Jan Jansen Dam, Jacob Wolfertsen van Couwenhoven, and Jan Evertsen Bout were prominent among their number. Though the existence of this board was as dependent on the will of the director and council as that of its predecessors, a somewhat fuller description of its functions was expressed in the order which created it. Its members,

---

[1] N. Y. Col. Docs. I. 213, 349; the Breeden Raedt, or Broad Advice, 2 Colls. N. Y. Hist. Soc. III. 265 *et seq.*

[2] N. Y. Col. Docs. I. 248 *et seq.*

[3] O'Callaghan, History of New Netherland, II. 37; N. Y. Col. Docs. I. 309 *et seq.*; Laws and Ordinances, 75.

as tribunes of the people, were to confer with the director and
council about means for promoting the welfare of the community. Such advice they were to give only when regularly convened by the director and only upon matters brought before them by him and the council. At their meetings the director or his representative should be present, should support the proposals of the government, take the vote, and report to the council. When civil suits were on trial before the council, three of the Nine Men, selected monthly in rotation, might attend for the purpose of becoming acquainted with cases wherein they might be called upon to act as arbitrators. The director and council might abolish the board whenever they saw fit, and in the meantime vacancies should be filled by the joint action of the board and the director, without again calling the commonalty together.

It is impossible to state how long the board of Nine Men continued in existence. Traces of it appear in the records as late as April, 1652.[1] It concerned itself somewhat with Stuyvesant's plans of local improvement. At its first meeting it assumed the expense of building a church and starting a school, but it refused to repair the company's fort. At a later time the board[2] called the attention of the director to alleged evils of allowing such as were not permanent residents to trade freely in furs within the province. This led to the issue of regulations confining internal trade to permanent residents, save at the market in New Amsterdam on the weekly market days; and permitting the sale of imported goods from the decks of the vessels which had just brought them to port, provided all duties upon the goods had been paid. Hints appear of a few other acts of this board, of minor importance.

But the Nine Men are chiefly to be remembered for the share they took in the efforts to procure redress and assistance from the home government.[3] In the winter of 1649

---

[1] N. Y. Col. Docs. XIV. 112, 145, 155, 163, 177; *ibid.* I. 444–461.

[2] O'Callaghan, History of New Netherland, II. 42, 59; Laws and Ordinances of New Netherland, 86.

[3] N. Y. Col. Docs. I. 258, 315 *et seq.*; Broad Advice, 2 N. Y. Hist. Colls. III. 268, 270.

Melyn returned to New Amsterdam, bringing with him the mandamus which was to be served upon Stuyvesant. Much to the chagrin of the director, this was read in the church in the presence of the commonalty, and gave rise to a dramatic scene. The feud between Stuyvesant and Melyn now became more bitter than ever, and every effort was made to prevent Melyn from securing the rights guarantied to him by the States General, while his friends felt the vengeance of the government. Melyn returned to the Netherlands, while the director appointed Van Tienhoven to answer there for him.

Under these conditions there seemed to be no prospect of reform, or that the necessities of the province would be relieved. For this reason the Nine Men, among whom Adriaen van der Donck, formerly commissary of Rensselaerswyck and now patroon of Yonkers, was a member, resolved to send a delegation of their own to the Netherlands. Preparatory to this, they asked that they might consult the commonalty, but the director objected to this and insisted that they must act in conjunction with him. Members of the board now went from house to house to gather the sentiment of the community. Van der Donck, who, with Van Couwenhoven and Bout, was selected as delegate, drew off some rough notes which he intended to use in the preparation of a formal statement of the condition of the province. Stuyvesant was so enraged when he learned of the independent course which the delegates were taking that he seized Van der Donck's papers, and had part of them read at the next meeting of the Nine Men. A violent debate followed, in which Van Dincklage, the vice-director, took part in opposition to Stuyvesant. Van der Donck, however, because of the alleged libellous statements which were found in his notes, was expelled from the board and imprisoned.

At this juncture Stuyvesant was charged with being engaged in the sale of arms to the Indians, a form of traffic which he had rigorously prohibited by recent orders. This confirmed the desire of all to strengthen the appeal to the home government. The pressure became so strong that for once the director could not resist it. Van der Donck was

set free, and in the summer of 1649 departed with his associates for the Netherlands.   There the "Remonstrance of
New Netherland," containing an able arraignment of the
province as a commercial enterprise, was laid before the
States General.   The argument of the opposition was here
stated in full, and it amounted to this : New Netherland had
only a small population, which in numbers and resources
were unequal to its defence.   Its government was autocratic.
Its trade was burdened with excessive regulations.   It
needed many more Dutch colonists, freer trade, provincial
and municipal institutions like those which existed at home.
It would also be relieved from its greatest peril if the boundaries of the province could be definitely fixed and maintained.   The administrations of both Kieft and Stuyvesant
were reviewed at length, and the specific charges against
them were brought out in full array.[1]

Both the directors of the West India company and Van
Tienhoven, Stuyvesant's agent, replied[2] to these charges.
They were able to show that many of them were exaggerated
or based on misapprehension.   We can now perceive that
some of the most serious causes of weakness and disturbance lay in the very nature of things, and could not be
removed without changes far more radical than any which
even the opposition contemplated.   It is not probable that
any policy which the company could have pursued would
have greatly stimulated the flow of Dutch population to New
Netherland.   The trade regulations do not seem to have
been excessively severe for the times, especially when we
consider the necessity of maintaining a staple port at New
Amsterdam.   The high prices which prevailed for European
goods were due to the heavy cost and risk of their transport
across the ocean and the correspondingly high rate of profit
of the merchants.   There is nothing to show that prices or
the rate of profits were higher in New Netherland than in
the neighboring English colonies.   Van Tienhoven was able
to show that New Englanders were taxed more heavily than
were the Dutch.

Finally, it is now apparent that the boundary question —

[1] N. Y. Col. Docs. I. 295 *et seq.*, 332 *et seq.*   [2] *Ibid.* 338, 422.

the most important problem of all — could not be answered in a way which would satisfy the Dutch colonists in New Netherland. Had the Dutch government and the West India company, prior to 1650, been fighting England instead of Spain, had they centred their efforts on New Netherland instead of Brazil, a Dutch province might have been permanently established on the North American continent. But by 1650 the die had been cast, and the question was already receiving a different answer. The West India company had expended its resources on a grand but futile enterprise in South America. It was now bankrupt, and during what remained of its existence could only make a pretence of colonization. In the light of such considerations it is possible to see why the complaints of the Nine Men could not receive a favorable answer. The States General showed itself, as always, to be well disposed, but the Company conceded little, and that only after delay. It supported Stuyvesant, as in duty it was bound to do, for he was a faithful servant and exponent of the system which the company had established and was resolved to see maintained. Though, as the result of the efforts of Melyn, Van der Donck, and their associates, another order for Stuyvesant's recall was sent out, it was soon revoked.[1] A new set of Freedoms and Exemptions[2] was issued by the company, which provided for a few changes in detail, but left the territorial system and trade regulations of the province substantially as they had been since 1640.

The views of the States General were set forth in a report of its committee on New Netherland affairs, issued in 1650, and known as the Provisional Order.[3] Besides certain requirements for the better arming of the inhabitants and for the encouragement of agriculture, this document set forth the necessity of enlarging the provincial council by the addition of two councillors appointed for four years from a list presented by the patroons, or their agents, and the deputies of the commonalty. It was also proposed that the board of Nine Men should be continued in existence three years longer, and should be given jurisdiction as a

---

[1] N. Y. Col. Docs. I. 390, 471, 475.   [2] *Ibid.* 401.   [3] *Ibid.* 388.

court over suits not involving more than fifty guilders, and for higher amounts under privilege of appeal.   When the increase of population should justify it, a provincial court of justice, distinct from the director and council, should be established.   The town of New Amsterdam should receive municipal rights.

These were wise measures, and they were referred to the various chambers of the company for their action.   The Amsterdam directors received them with disfavor because of the source whence they came.   The administration of the province had been committed to them by the Council of Nineteen, and they were jealous of interference by the States General.   They regarded Melyn and the delegates from the board of Nine Men as restless agitators who were seeking personal advantage.   This was the view which Stuyvesant held concerning them, and while Van der Donck was laboring in the fatherland for Stuyvesant's recall, the director himself was jeering and scoffing at the members of the board, trying to punish them for their share in the " Remonstrance," and substituting appointed selectmen for the original board.[1]   The company informed the director that the Provisional Order was not to be enforced.   But, as the result of the persistence of Van der Donck, continued for a period of two years, views were elicited from the other chambers of the company which suggested the possibility of the withdrawal from the Amsterdam chamber of its exclusive control over the province.[2]   This convinced the Amsterdam directors, and Stuyvesant as well, that some concession must be made, and this took the form of a grant of municipal rights to New Amsterdam.   But the prolonged efforts which were necessary before its advantages were fully secured have already been described.

With the outbreak of war between England and the Low Countries in 1652, and the resulting activity of the Indians and of freebooters on Long Island sound, the English of Long Island began to take a more active share in the politics

[1] See extracts from letters of the Nine Men to Van der Donck during the years 1650 and 1651, *ibid.* 444 *et seq.*

[2] N. Y. Col. Docs. I. 462–468.

of New Netherland. Their object was to secure from the
Dutch government protection for themselves, or, if that was
impossible, to seek it elsewhere. The military weakness of
the Dutch, as well as the lack of representative government
in the province, and the extent to which the director and
council ignored the expressions of local need, seemed to make
such action necessary. But it was suggestive of sedition,
and was sure to be unfavorably regarded by the director.
At Flushing delegates assembled from that town, Hempstead, Middleburgh (Newtown), and Gravesend, and opened
communication with the magistrates of New Amsterdam.
This action led to a meeting at the city hall on November 26,
1653, which was attended by two delegates from each of the
towns mentioned, as well as two from the burgomasters and
schepens[1] of New Amsterdam. George Baxter of Gravesend was credited with being the prime mover in the enterprise. Stuyvesant sent La Montagne and Werckhoven to
attend on behalf of the council. When they attempted
to guide proceedings, the English delegates refused even
to recognize them as members of the convention. The same
delegates then sent in writing to the director a statement
that, as he would not protect them, they must provide for
themselves. For this reason, while still professing allegiance
to the States General and the company, they thought they
were no longer under obligation to pay taxes to the provincial government. Not content with this declaration, and
apparently with the intent of putting it at once into practice, they proposed a firm alliance with the magistrates of
New Amsterdam. To this the delegates from New Amsterdam gave no answer, but reported what was said to the
director. That drew from him the declaration that, though
the burghers might still confer with the English, he would
at the next election grant courts of justice to Breuckelen,
Amersfoort, and Midwout, so that delegates from Dutch
towns to future assemblies of this kind might outvote the
English. This promise was reasonably well kept.[2] In
reply to the director's further statement of his willingness

---

[1] N. Y. Col. Docs. XIV. 223–240; O'Callaghan, II. 238.
[2] Ordinances of New Netherland, 159.

to protect his people, the delegates cited recent outrages by small bands of savages which had gone unpunished, as poor evidences of his ability in that direction.   At the concluding session on the following day, when La Montagne and Werckhoven were not present, the delegates from New Amsterdam objected to forming an alliance with the English until the other Dutch towns, as well as the director and council and Amsterdam chamber, had been consulted.   The Englishmen replied that if the city did not join them and the director protect them, they would form a union among themselves on Long Island.   But in order the better to ascertain the sentiments of the Dutch on the subject, an adjournment was taken until the tenth of December.

The burgomasters and schepens of New Amsterdam now requested the director to summon delegates from all the Dutch towns and settlements to the forthcoming convention, that they might prepare such remonstrance to the Amsterdam chamber as seemed wise.   This elicited from Stuyvesant and the council a long protest against false statements alleged to have been made by the English at the recent meeting, and on the peril of allowing subjects to form an offensive and defensive alliance without the knowledge and consent of the government.   But they consented to the holding of the meeting.   Four Dutch and four English towns met on December 10 and prepared their remonstrance.[1]   The contents of this remarkable document clearly reveal the influence of the English delegates who shared in its preparation.   The argument begins with the claim that they had settled in New Netherland on a mutual covenant with the lords patroons, to which the natives from whom they had purchased the soil had assented.   Being thus not a conquered or subjugated people, but such as had voluntarily put themselves under the protection of the laws of the province, they considered that they were entitled to privileges equal with those of the inhabitants of the Netherlands.   After this introduction, which suggests the reasoning of a century later, the remonstrants state their charges against the government of New Netherland.   The only

[1] N. Y. Col. Docs. I. 550.

important complaint was that its government was arbitrary, that is, absolute, in form and spirit; officers were appointed without nomination by the people; orders and proclamations were issued without the approval, and in many cases without the knowledge, of the people. "'Tis contrary to the first intentions and genuine principles of every well regulated government, that one or more men should arrogate to themselves the exclusive power to dispose, at will, of the life and property of any individual, and this by virtue or under pretence of a law or order he or they might enact, without the consent, knowledge or election of the whole Body, or its agents as representatives. Hence the enactment, except as aforesaid, of new laws or orders affecting the commonalty or the inhabitants, their lives or property, is contrary and opposed to the granted Freedoms of the Dutch Government and odious to every freeborn man, and principally so to those whom God has placed in a free state on newly settled lands, which might require new laws and orders, not transcending, but resembling as near as possible those of Netherland. We humbly submit that 'tis one of our privileges that our consent or that of our representatives is necessarily required in the enactment of such laws and orders."

It was impossible that the sentiments expressed in this remonstrance could be other than irritating to Stuyvesant, for they proceeded from the supposition that by natural right the constitution of New Netherland should be other than it was; that it should possess a representative, tax-granting assembly. The director and council, on receiving the document, peremptorily ordered the convention to disperse. It was told not to meet again, or use the titles "general assembly" or "delegates of the land." It was declared to be illegal, because it had not been called by the director and council. It was only a conventicle. To the statement that by nature all men had the right to assemble for the purpose of promoting the public welfare, Stuyvesant opposed the doctrine that only officials, not men in general, could do this. All political action which did not proceed with the knowledge and consent of the recognized authorities he repudiated. The director and council stood squarely

on the authority of their commission and instructions, and
refused to share in the doings of any " self-created unlawful
gathering." The town of Gravesend now laid its complaints
before the Amsterdam chamber, while the magistrates of
New Amsterdam sent a mild representation[1] to the burgomasters of Amsterdam, in which they dwelt wholly on the
right which the city claimed to share in the choice of its
magistrates and to control the revenue from the excise on
wine and beer consumed in the city.   Thus ended the first
effort, in which Englishmen prominently shared, to limit in
some way the discretion of the executive in New Netherland.
Like the earlier efforts, it resulted only in an empty protest.

Ten years now passed, during which the English from the
north made great encroachments on the territory of New
Netherland, and at the same time developed great political
independence and activity on Long Island.   In the Connecticut charter, which had recently been issued, the existence
of New Netherland was entirely ignored.   A troublesome
Indian war also prevailed at intervals on the middle Hudson,
while in 1655 the savages had done much damage on Manhattan itself and in its immediate vicinity.   Stuyvesant had been
able to destroy the power of the Swedes on the South river,
but his energies and resources were wholly inadequate to
the task of holding the English in check on Long Island and
in Westchester.   The Dutch had long since ceased to protest against his autocratic rule, because they now saw the
necessity of union in the presence of a threatening rival.
The authorities at home could be induced to do nothing for
the province except to utter pious wishes for its welfare.
Stuyvesant, with wholly inadequate military and financial
resources, was left to fight the battle alone.   He was inces-
santly active, showing much address in dealing with the
English and not a little conciliation.   But it was clearly
a losing battle, and he was forced to yield point after point.
During this crisis it was well that his discretion was unlimited.   As the protagonist of the Dutch cause in North
America during the years previous to its extinction, the
figure of Peter Stuyvesant assumes something of the heroic.

[1] O'Callaghan, II. 253; Records of New Amsterdam, I. 144.

It was in the last stage of this struggle that, with the full consent of the director, another effort was made to secure joint action by the localities.

On November 1, 1663, the magistrates of New Amsterdam, Haerlem, Breuckelen, Midwout, Amersfoort, New Utrecht, Bushwick, and Bergen met and sent a remonstrance to the Amsterdam chamber.[1] It was intended that magistrates from the settlements on the upper Hudson should be present, but the lateness of the season prevented this. The remonstrance set forth in strong language the dangers which threatened the province, and arraigned the Amsterdam directors for their failure to keep the promise made in the Freedoms and Exemptions to protect the colonists and their property against usurpation and force. But practical result it had none.

As the prospect continually grew darker, on April 10, 1664, the first and only assembly of delegates from all the localities in the province was called at New Amsterdam.[2] The summons was issued by the director at the request of the burgomasters and schepens, and two delegates were chosen from each of the towns. This was properly a representative body, a *Landtdag*. Jeremias Van Rensselaer was its president. The convention asked the government to protect the inhabitants against the Indians and the English. The director and council replied that, in their efforts to do this, they had already exceeded their powers. They called in turn on the assembly to furnish supplies for a regular force, or, if not, that every third man in the province should be called out. The assembly asked whether it should address the company or the States General. Stuyvesant insisted that the inhabitants had not contributed toward the defence of the province, while the company had expended upon it far more than the revenue amounted to. But the assembly declined to vote supplies, and adjourned without contributing anything of value toward the solution of the difficulties. With this event disappeared the last chance of the growth of representative institutions in New Netherland.

[1] O'Callaghan, II. 490 ; N. Y. Col. Docs. II. 477.
[2] O'Callaghan, II. 505.

The position of the Dutch as a conquered people within the province of New York made it impossible for them, during more than a decade after the English occupation, to join in any movement favorable to the limitation of the power of the executive.   Therefore such demands for reforms of this character as were made on the proprietary governors of New York came from the English settlers in the province.   Long Island, with its New England inhabitants, traditions, and institutions, was the section where they originated.   Protests against the autocracy of the Dutch government had been heard from that region.   The advent of the English brought the towns of the east, as well as those of the west, end of the island under the control of government at New York and within reach of this question.

Governor Nicolls at once showed his appreciation of this fact by the efforts he made to conciliate the people of this section.   In his earliest proclamation and letter,[1] not only were the privileges of English subjects promised to all who made due submission, but it was stated that deputies from the Long Island towns should in convenient time be summoned "to propose and give their advice in all matters tending to the peace and benefitt" of that section.   " They may assure themselves," wrote the governor on another occasion, " of equall if not greater, freedomes & Imunityes then any of his Majesty's Colonyes in New England. . . ." These utterances naturally led those to whom they were addressed to believe that a representative, tax-granting assembly would be conceded.

This feeling was strengthened by the call for the meeting of March 1, 1665, at Hempstead.[2]   In this call the governor ordered that deputies should be chosen by the freeholders, Dutch and English, of the several towns on the island, to meet him at the designated time and place, and that the result should be a settlement of all controversies and the propagation of the true religion.   The summons called for the presentation of such documents as would make

---

[1] Bulletin N. Y. State Library, General Entries, 79, 100, 132 ; Journal of Legislative Council of New York, Introduction.

[2] Bulletin, General Entries, 154 ; N. Y. Col. Docs. XIV. 564, 565.

possible the settlement of boundary disputes between towns
and the establishment of all important territorial rights.
Beyond that it did not go. It made no general grant of
legislative power. The "general meeting" which resulted
was in no sense a legislative body. It listened to the
promulgation of a code of laws, and, so far as the fragment
of its records which has been preserved would indicate,
took some steps toward the settlement of boundary controversies between the towns.[1] It also sent to the duke a
declaration of submission to his rule.[2] The close of this
meeting without further action was doubtless a disappoint-
ment to its members. As time passed and the duke himself, with the governor and council, continued to legislate
for the province, and rates which the proprietor or his
council really had determined were regularly assessed by the
town overseers and collected by the constable under orders
from the sheriff, it became evident that New York was existing under a system different from that of the New England
colonies, Maryland, and Virginia. But Nicolls had no authority to change it, for the royal charter made no mention
of an assembly, and his instructions, though now lost, must
have been silent on this subject. The most he could do
was to commend the autocratic system which he was sent to
enforce by a just and mild administration, and this he accomplished to a very marked degree.

In 1669, however, soon after the accession to office of
Governor Lovelace, petitions[3] were presented by Hempstead,
Oyster Bay, Flushing, Jamaica, Newtown, Gravesend, with
Westchester and Eastchester, the two English towns on the
mainland, craving a redress of several grievances. First
among these was a demand that the promise which Nicolls
and the other royal commissioners had made when English

---

[1] Nicolls, in a letter to John Underhill dated May, 1666, implies that the
meeting not only accepted the method of levying rates which was prescribed
in the Duke's Laws, but agreed that, if the sum mentioned would not satisfy
the public charge, an additional rate should be levied and in the same way.
In a report on the state of the province prepared in 1670, the statement is
made that the rate of public charges was agreed to in a general assembly.
N. Y. Col. Docs. XIV. 580 ; III. 188.

[2] N. Y. Col. Docs. III. 91.   [3] *Ibid.* XIV. 631 *et seq.*

sovereignty was established, namely, that the inhabitants of
Long Island should enjoy such privileges as other English
subjects in America enjoyed, should be fulfilled.   These
privileges the petitioners claimed to consist in the annual
election, by the freeholders of the towns or parishes, of
deputies who should coöperate with the governor and council in the passage of laws, and in the publication of those
parts of the governor's commission (and presumably also of
his instructions) which directly concerned the colonists.
The reply which these petitions elicited revealed the use-
lessness of pinning faith to vague and general statements.
Colonel Nicolls, it was said, had not made the alleged
promise, for he had been directed by his instructions to
make no change in the system of government which had
been agreed upon before his arrival.   The supremacy of the
executive and the binding force of the governor's commission — which had often been read to them — was then
asserted to the fullest extent.   Nothing, it was said, was
required but obedience and submission to the laws as they
appeared in the duke's commission.

Before a year had passed the towns had an opportunity to
express their opinions still more pointedly.   Through the
justices in the courts of sessions the court of assizes ordered
a levy for the repair of the palisade of Fort James, which had
fallen into decay.   Immediately the inhabitants of Southold,
Easthampton, Southampton, Jamaica, Flushing, and Hempstead either protested against the demand as illegal, because
it called for a grant without their consent, or expressed
themselves as willing to pay the tax provided they might
have such privileges as colonists in New England enjoyed.
Though no seditious sentiments were directly expressed in
these papers, both the court of sessions of the west riding
and the governor and council pronounced them scandalous,
illegal, and seditious, and the last-named ordered them to be
publicly burned before the city hall in New York.   Southampton and Southold, which had not yet taken out new
patents for their land from the English authorities, now refused to do so.   The court of assizes declared titles in Southampton to be invalid unless a patent was taken out within a

specified time. Against this decree fifty of the inhabitants issued a remonstrance, complaining not only of the order of the court, but of the fact that they had no deputies. The governor appointed three of the councillors a committee to confer with the remonstrants,[1] but no further steps were taken to enforce obedience. Here the discussion of the points at issue ceased until after the close of the Dutch reoccupation and the appearance of Edmund Andros as governor.

Andros was at once met with the demand for an assembly, and it came, as before, from the Long Island towns. The governor discouraged the movement, and for this action received the approval of the duke.[2] The latter wrote on at least two occasions that he considered such bodies likely to prove dangerous, that they would assume many privileges and thus disturb the peace of the province. Neither did he believe an assembly to be necessary, because all grievances could be redressed by the courts or the governor in the province, or by appeal to himself. There the matter rested until 1680, when Andros was recalled to answer certain charges growing out of his administration of the revenue. Hitherto orders had regularly been issued once every three years for the collection of the duke's customs. The last order for this had been issued in 1677.[3] Before Andros sailed, while commanding that everything should remain "as then settled," he neglected to expressly mention the customs. They therefore expired by limitation in November, 1680.

In the spring of 1681 certain merchants of the city of New York began to refuse the payment of customs on an incoming cargo. Brockholls, the commander-in-chief, at the time was in Albany; Dyer, the collector, was sick; Lewin was still in the province, pretending that he had found proof of the dishonesty of Andros. When, on Brockholls's return, the question of the legality of the customs was submitted to the council, instead of ordering their collection until word

---

[1] Ms. Records of Court of Assizes, II. 646, 653.

[2] N. Y. Col. Docs. III. 230, 235.

[3] *Ibid.* 246, 287–289, 292 ; *ibid.* XIII. 549 ; Commissions, Orders, Letters, etc., Ms. 43, 45, 53, 54.

could be obtained from the duke, they decided that there was no authority to continue them without orders from his Royal Highness. If this is not to be considered as an actual breach of the law, it at least involved gross neglect of the interests which the councillors had sworn to uphold. Its effect was to encourage refusal to pay customs, and other taxes as well, throughout the province. Dyer, the collector, was sued for detaining goods for customs, and was finally brought before the court of assizes on the extravagant charge of treason against the fundamental laws of the realm as set forth in Magna Carta, the Petition of Right, and other statutes. This was naturally too weighty a charge for the court to pass upon definitively ; and since Dyer questioned its authority in the case, after the examination of witnesses it remanded him to England for trial before the privy council. The court also petitioned the duke that the province might in the future be ruled by a governor, council, and assembly to be elected by the freeholders, as was the custom in the other colonies. The court stated that the inhabitants of the province had " groaned " under the " inexpressible burdens " of " arbitrary and absolute power "; that, by means of revenue exacted against their wills, their trade had been burdened and their liberty destroyed, until they had become a " reproach " to their neighbors in the other colonies.

Brockholls meantime was seized with a panic. In July he wrote that not a penny of customs was paid in the province and that it was scarcely possible to keep the peace. There was a general demand for an assembly, and Brockholls was sure that quiet would not be restored until the government was greatly strengthened or changed to suit the popular will. Early in August a commission was received from Andros, specially empowering Brockholls to receive the duke's revenue, and commanding all to obey him. Encouraged by this, Brockholls sent orders for the collection of the excise at Esopus and Albany. In his letter to the commissaries at Albany, however, he was not imperative, but threw doubt on the legality of the excise by referring to the fact that no provision for it could be found in any law book in New York ; it rested on custom and the orders of a

succession of governors. The consequence was that Brockholls's orders met with little or no response. His subsequent
letters to Andros show with the utmost clearness that
authority had collapsed, that the judges and all other
officials were scared. Disorderly meetings were held in
various towns on Long Island. Disturbances were also
reported at Esopus. Several magistrates from Long Island
were summoned to appear on the charges of refusing to
perform their duties, promoting sedition, and attacking the
government. Josiah Hubbard of Easthampton, the high
sheriff, to an extent justified such conduct on his own part,
and was bound over for trial. For nearly a year the government showed itself to be weak, if not almost in collusion
with its opponents. Dyer, of course, was exonerated[1] as
soon as he reached England, but the large reduction of the
revenue brought the duke to terms. The English towns of
Long Island had initiated the effort, and it was carried
through to success by the action of the merchants of New
York City.[2]

In the spring of 1682, on the duke's return from Scotland,
he wrote[3] to Brockholls that it was his intention, through
the calling of an assembly and other measures agreeable to
the laws of England, to give to residents in New York and
traders thither all the privileges which were enjoyed by the
inhabitants of other American plantations. But he also
warned Brockholls that he expected the colonists to support
the government and to clear off the arrears which had ac-
cumulated since the obstruction to the collection of duties
began. Preparatory to the execution of this measure,
Colonel Thomas Dongan was appointed governor in the
place of Andros, the latter receiving an appointment at court.
Dongan's instructions[4] contained the duke's plan of reform.
In addition to the appointment of a council which should

---

[1] N. Y. Col. Docs. III. 318-321.

[2] General Entries, Ms. 1680-1682, contain Brockholls's letters during this
crisis, and much additional material. Some of the letters have been printed
in N. Y. Col. Docs. XIII and XIV ; Brodhead, II. 351 et seq.

[3] N. Y. Col. Docs. III. 317.

[4] Ibid. 331.

contain the most eminent men of the province, the governor
was instructed to issue writs in the name of the proprietor for the election by the freeholders throughout the province of an assembly of not more than eighteen representatives. This body should enjoy freedom of debate and of voting on all matters respecting which legislation would be proper for New York and its dependencies. Its acts should be subject to the assent and dissent of both the governor and the proprietor. The right of summons, prorogation, and dissolution should rest wholly in the hands of the governor, though it might be exercised under instructions from the proprietor. No law for raising a revenue should be passed without an express mention of the fact that the grant was made to the proprietor ; and no act reducing the revenue should be passed without the express prior consent of the duke. No public money should be paid out without warrant under the governor's hand. The passage of temporary laws should, as far as possible, be avoided. In this body of instructions originated many of the most important features of the constitutional law of New York. They had the precision which characterized the later orders of the crown concerning the legislatures of the royal provinces, and in the case of New York were revived when, as a royal province, it came to have a permanent legislature.

As soon as possible after Governor Dongan's arrival in the province, writs of election were issued,[1] for each of the three ridings of Yorkshire, for the city of New York and Haerlem, for Esopus, for Albany and Rensselaerswyck, for Schenectady and dependencies, for Pemaquid and dependencies, for Martha's Vineyard, Nantucket, and the other neighboring islands. Thus not only was the province of New York itself, but all its dependencies, except that on the Delaware, to be represented. Three members were returned from each of the ridings of Yorkshire, four from the city of New York and Haerlem, two from Esopus, two from Albany and Rensselaerswyck, and one from each of the remaining groups of settlements. The general assembly met at Fort James in the city of New York on October 17, 1683, and remained in

[1] Journal of Legislative Council, Introduction, ix.

session for about three weeks. Of its members a majority were of Dutch descent.[1]

The journal of this assembly has been lost, but the fifteen acts which it passed have been preserved, and constitute the beginning of the statute law of New York.[2] Those which are of greatest importance in this connection relate to the organization and powers of the general assembly and the guaranties of civil rights which it immediately sought to establish. The entire province and its dependencies were divided into counties, their names and boundaries remaining in most cases permanent. In the so-called "charter of liberties" — the first statute that was passed — provision was made for the representation of the freeholders of the province in the assembly by counties. The whole legislature was given a statutory basis, and provision was made that the assembly should meet at least once in three years. To the governor, council, and assembly should belong the supreme legislative power within the province. At the beginning of a series of clauses which were intended to secure to all inhabitants the jury trial and the civil rights which it had been the object of Magna Carta and the Petition of Right to guaranty, stood the declaration that no tax, custom, or assessment should be levied on any subject within the province without the consent of the governor, council, and representatives in general assembly met. In pursuance of this enactment a free and voluntary grant was made to the governor for one year of one penny in the pound on all real and personal estate in the province. Commissioners to make this levy in each county were designated in the act, and their duties were specified. By another act provision was made for a new tariff of customs duties and excise, at rates generally higher than those prescribed by the duke, and specific rather than ad valorem.[3] Thus with a bold hand and according to the best English traditions this assembly assumed the full exercise of the taxing power, and that under the form

[1] Brodhead, II. 382.

[2] The Colonial Laws of New York, I. 111.

[3] Compare N. Y. Col. Docs. III. 217, with Colonial Laws of New York, I. 117.

of an annual grant of the internal or direct tax. It also
provided for the establishment of county and local courts
and began the work of defining their jurisdiction. By this
act the legislature assumed to remodel the judicial system
of the province and to give it also a statutory basis.

The important measures of this session received the approval of the governor and were sent to the proprietor. They
were examined by him and his council in October, 1684. The
so-called "charter of liberties," and probably the other acts,
was approved by the duke; his approval was countersigned
by his secretary, Sir John Werden, and was sent to the duke's
auditor to be registered preparatory to its being despatched
to New York.[1] Meantime the approval of the governor
brought the acts provisionally into operation. But before
the duke's approval reached New York, Charles II died and
the duke became king. This closed the period of proprietary government in New York.

One of the first acts of the Committee of Trade and Plantations, after the accession of James II to the throne, was
to examine[2] the provisions of the so-called "charter of liberties" to ascertain whether they so far conformed with the
privileges enjoyed by the plantations generally, and·agreed
with the purposes then entertained by the home government concerning the colonies, as to admit of its final confirmation. It was found to contain clauses which asserted too
absolutely the legislative supremacy of the governor, council, and assembly, which insisted too strongly on triennial
sessions, which referred to "the people" as the source
whence the assembly sprang, and which seemed to imply
that the governor could not act without the consent of the
council. The powers thus asserted were believed to be
greater than those generally enjoyed by colonial legislatures,
and might be understood to imply a denial of the legislative
supremacy of parliament. But, while these considerations
of themselves might have seemed weighty enough to the

---

[1] Brodhead, II. 416 n.

[2] N. Y. Col. Docs. III. 354, 357. The paper entitled "Observations on
the Charter of the Province of New York" errs in several particulars in its
statements concerning the contents of the act.

crown to induce it to disallow the act, the really decisive
consideration must have been the resolve, which was then
taking shape, that assemblies in all the colonies should be
dispensed with.   For this reason the acts of 1683 were not
finally confirmed ; neither were the thirty-one acts of a later
session, and the six acts of a second assembly,[1] which Dongan
held before the transition to the consolidated royal province
was completed.   Finally, when, in 1686, Dongan was commissioned [2] as royal governor, he was expressly empowered
to exercise the full legislative, as well as executive, power,
in conjunction with the council.   Thus with the beginning
of royal government New York, by action of the home government, was forced back into its original condition and remained without a representative assembly as long as James II
occupied the throne.

New York consisted as yet of a number of loosely connected sections.   The two components of its population —
Dutch and English — had not yet grown together into a
political whole.   They spoke different languages.   Many
differing forms of religious faith existed within the province.
The larger part of its people had long been accustomed
to autocratic rule.   The charter guarantied nothing different.   Commercial interests predominated in the city, where,
if anywhere, continued and successful opposition to autocratic government could be maintained.   New York, moreover, formed the centre and starting-point of a great
imperialist scheme of colonial union, and it was without
power to resist.   For these reasons the permanent establishment of representative institutions in that province was
postponed until it could be achieved by a government in
England which favored their maintenance in all the colonies.
At that late period within this province began in permanent
form the development of institutions through statutory enactment.

[1] Laws of the Colony of New York, I. 142–178.
[2] N. Y. Col. Docs. III. 378.

CHAPTER VIII

THE GOVERNMENTAL SYSTEM OF NEW JERSEY

ON the threshold of this subject the inquirer is met by a question of fundamental importance, one which does not assume prominence in the history of any other proprietary province. The question is this, did the proprietors of New Jersey legally possess rights of government? The question arose from the fact that New Jersey, unlike the other colonies, New Hampshire excepted, did not originate from an immediate grant of the crown. The charters which were issued to the Duke of York contained no authority for a delegation by the grantee of governmental powers. Indeed, they could hardly have contained such a provision, for it was and is an accepted principle of English law that the right to exercise powers of government in the full and proper sense of the term can pass only by express grant from the king himself. In strict point of law a royal charter affords the only sufficient basis for the exercise of such powers, and a royal charter the proprietors of New Jersey never received. The nature of the grant which was made to them will be revealed by an examination of the documents that were issued.

The deed of release which was granted by the Duke of York to Berkeley and Carteret in 1664 was in point of law a permanent grant of the soil and nothing more. The phrase in that document,[1] " with their and every of their appurtenances in as full and ample Manner as the same is graunted to the sayd Duke of Yorke," referred only to the land and its appurtenances. By this and the accompanying lease the Duke of York effected a sale of all his rights in the soil of New Jersey, but nothing more. No expression which can

---

[1] N. J. Arch. I. 12.

be understood to convey rights of government appears in the lease or release, and if such words had appeared, they would have been inoperative.   In this fact lay the strength of the claim of the inhabitants of the Elizabethtown and Monmouth patents, in so far as their agitation was directed against the exercise over them by the proprietors of strictly governmental powers.

In consequence of the opposition with which the efforts of the proprietors to exercise powers of government were met, they procured in 1672 a letter[1] from Charles II to Deputy Governor John Berry and the council of New Jersey.   By this all inhabitants of the province were commanded to obey the laws and government which had been established there by the proprietors, who had the sole power under the king to settle and dispose of the said country as they should think fit.   This of course did not amount to a legal conveyance of rights of government, though it was intended to strengthen the hands of the proprietors by a public assurance that the king was ready to support their claims.   But the reoccupation of New Netherland by the Dutch immediately destroyed the effect of this letter.   It also was held to have annulled the royal charter to the Duke of York, and that the rights which had existed under that grant did not revive with the conclusion of the treaty of Westminster and the retirement of the Dutch.

It would therefore seem that, during the interval between February, 1674, when the treaty of Westminster was concluded, and June 29 of the same year, when the second charter to the Duke of York was issued, the entire territory which had been New Netherland was an English royal province.   But during that interval — that is in March, 1674 — Lord John Berkeley sold[2] for £1000 his undivided half of New Jersey to John Fenwick in trust for Edward Byllinge. As, however, the royal charter to the duke was not issued until the following June, it is difficult to see what was transferred by this act save an equitable claim to the land of one undivided half of New Jersey.   The royal charter,

[1] N. J. Arch. I. 107.
[2] Leaming and Spicer, Grants and Concessions, 64 ; N. J. Arch. I. 209.

when issued, conveyed again to the duke, and in terms identical with the charter of 1664, the territory between the Connecticut and Delaware rivers, with additions which [1] have already been mentioned. Immediately after, on July 1, 1674, Edmund Andros was appointed governor and his commission [2] empowered him to administer the affairs of this entire region.

Inasmuch as in 1662 a royal charter had been issued to Connecticut by which a valid grant was made at least of the territory then occupied and usually claimed by the inhabitants of that colony, the charter of the Duke of York could not be legally operative there. But no similar charter protected the grantees of New Jersey. On June 13, 1674, Sir George Carteret obtained a letter [3] from the king commanding all persons within the province to yield obedience to the laws and government which he had established or should establish there. But apart from the fact that this could not effect for him what the charter of Connecticut had secured for its grantees, it implied that Carteret had authority over the whole of New Jersey, a claim which could not be valid now that Berkeley had sold his share of the province.

On July 29, 1674, the Duke of York granted a release [4] to Sir George Carteret of the eastern half of New Jersey, and in terms identical with those which had been used in the release of ten years before. It must be held, both from the origin and the wording of this document, that, in point of law, it conveyed to Carteret only the soil of East Jersey and the rights of a private owner over the same. Fenwick, Byllinge, and their associates, the purchasers of West Jersey from Berkeley, did not seek even to procure deeds of lease and release from the Duke of York, and therefore for a time, if our previous interpretations are true, must be regarded as squatters on the territory of the Duke of York. These con-

[1] When Fenwick was tried in New York in 1677, he could not produce Berkeley's deed, but the fact that the grant was made is proved by a statement in the grant issued by the Duke of York to Penn, Lawrie, and Lucas in 1680. N. J. Arch. I. 237, 326. A copy of the deed itself is in Salem No. 1, p. 9. See N. J. Arch. XXI. 559.

[2] N. J. Arch. I. 156.   [3] *Ibid.* 153.   [4] *Ibid.* 163.

siderations explain the efforts of Governor Andros to administer government and exercise political control over both East and West Jersey. They also justify those efforts, so far as considerations of mere legality may justify any course of conduct. He attempted faithfully to obey his commission and instructions; and if any one should be censured for an ambiguous course of conduct, it should be the Duke of York himself.

Affairs continued in this uncertain state until the summer of 1680. Then, it will be remembered, Andros was recalled to England. Among the charges concerning the collection of revenue in the duke's possessions, which were then urged, were the complaints of the proprietors of West Jersey that the payment of duties had been illegally enforced by New York officials on the Delaware. The question was referred to the attorney-general, Sir William Jones, and his opinion, based on the supposition that full governmental powers had gone with the grant, was that the duke was not entitled to the customs, because he had not expressly reserved the right to them, in the original deeds of lease and release issued in 1664.[1] It is needless to say that this opinion was hastily formed, and ignored some important elements in the case. But it led to the issue, in the following August and September, of almost identical deeds of release both to the proprietors of West Jersey and to the younger Sir George Carteret, who was then the proprietor of East Jersey.[2] By these documents the duke assigned to the grantees the free use of all bays, rivers, and waters within their respective limits for navigation, free trade, and fishing, and transferred to them all the "powers, authorities, jurisdictions, governments, and other matters and things whatsoever" which he had been granted by the king. Sir John Werden wrote to Andros that by these grants the duke intended to convey all his governmental and other rights in the premises, that they were valid and not surreptitiously obtained. These were the last concessions ever issued by the Duke of York to the New Jersey proprietors, and though they were regarded by the grantees as decisive in their favor,

[1] N. Y. Col. Docs. III. 285, 286.   [2] N. J. Arch. I. 324, 337.

it is certain that in point of law they did not convey powers of government, and therefore that they left the question as unsettled as it was at the beginning.   Having thus outlined the strictly legal aspects of this controversy, it is now time to describe the steps which the New Jersey proprietors took in the assertion of their claim to rights of government. This will reveal the practical political aspects of the question, which for the time at least were decisive.

The grant of a province like that of New Jersey would have been useless without rights of government.   No effort was made by the Duke of York until after 1674 to administer its affairs through his own appointees, and even then it was done only at intervals and imperfectly.   The proprietors, on the other hand, assumed rights of government, and from the outset acted as if they had been fully entitled to them. This assumption was acquiesced in by the king and the Duke of York, and was expressly approved by the former.   The Duke of York himself, between 1680 and the time when the Jerseys were incorporated within the great consolidated province which, as king, he was building up, insisted upon no rights over that region except those which concerned his revenue and the interests of New York as a port.   Through the assumption and continued exercise of political authority Berkeley and Carteret came for all practical purposes into its possession, though their right to it was for a long time challenged from various quarters.   The struggle which resulted from these conditions chiefly determines the character of early New Jersey history and helps to make it unique among American proprietary provinces.

The first step which the New Jersey proprietors took in the establishment of government was the same as that taken by the proprietors of Carolina.   The Concessions and Agreements which Berkeley and Carteret issued in 1665 were the same as those issued that very year by the Carolina proprietors and put into force at the Cape Fear settlement and partially also in Albemarle.   The influence of those Concessions, as a precedent favorable to liberty, was felt through the entire proprietary period of Carolina history.   In New Jersey, however, though they contained the provisions already outlined

for a representative legislature, with authority by statute to
establish and regulate all the institutions of the province,
they were viewed in many quarters as expressions of arbitrary power.   This arose from the way in which the Elizabethtown grant and Monmouth Patent originated, and from
the uncertainty which prevailed concerning the right of the
proprietors to governmental powers.   In other words, the
social conditions under which the Concessions and Agreements were enforced in Carolina differed from those which
existed in New Jersey, and a correspondingly different result
followed.

The first act of the proprietors under the Concessions was
the appointment of Philip Carteret, a relative of Sir George
Carteret, as governor.[1]   He was authorized by them to select
a council, raise and command troops, appoint officers, and do
all other things belonging to the office of governor, as fully
and freely as any governor had done.   Though only fragmentary records of this time are now accessible, enough has
been preserved to indicate how the official system of the province was developed.   Six councillors were appointed, and
from time to time vacancies in their number[2] were filled.
John Bollen was appointed secretary and Robert Vauquellen
surveyor-general.   This was done in February, 1665.   Later
a provost marshal or high sheriff of the province[3] appears.

Local governments were organized in the towns which
had been settled by the Dutch, or under grants from Nicolls,
and the proprietors sought to establish a control over these
localities which should be more than nominal.   Charters
were granted to Woodbridge and to the jurisdiction of Bergen.[4]   These provided that the freeholders should choose
deputies to a general assembly, elect magistrates who should
assist the local justice of the peace in the administration of
justice, and choose their own ministers.   The Woodbridge

[1] N. J. Arch. I. 20.

[2] Mulford, History of New Jersey, 141.   Record of later appointments of
individual councillors has been preserved in East Jersey Records, Ms. Liber
III. 4, 7, 13, 28, 52.   The contents of this volume are in part calendared in
Calendar of New Jersey Records, 1664–1703, N. J. Arch. XXI.

[3] N. J. Arch. XXI. 35, June 14, 1673.

[4] Whitehead, East Jersey under the Proprietors, 286, 293.

charter also provided for town meetings. The resident justice of the peace, who was also president of the local court,
was to be an appointee of the governor, though in most, if
not all, cases the locality exercised the right of nomination. Thus a great degree of liberty was enjoyed by the
towns.

Rights fully equal to those of Woodbridge were exercised
by Elizabethtown and Newark,[1] though without the guaranties of a charter. The towns of the Monmouth Patent,
under authority [2] claimed by virtue of Governor Nicolls's
patent, not only had their town meetings and equipment of
officials after the New England model, but they now claimed
to be virtually an independent jurisdiction. Everywhere,
indeed, the conditions of settlement were such that a large
degree of local liberty must necessarily be conceded by the
proprietors.

But such authority as it was possible for Governor Carteret and his council to exercise through grants of land, the
appointment of officers, and the administration of the oath of
allegiance was maintained. In 1665 Nicholas Verlett, who
was also councillor, was appointed president of the court of
Bergen and its jurisdiction. In 1668 justices of the peace,
on nomination by the inhabitants, were appointed for Woodbridge, Newark, Elizabethtown, and the settlements on the
Delaware. In 1669 local magistrates of Woodbridge were
commissioned in the same way. In 1672, at the request of
the inhabitants, justices of the peace were appointed for
Middletown and Shrewsbury.[3] In January, 1665, James
Bollen, the secretary, was appointed justice of the peace for
the province in general, an indication, if the record be correct, of the looseness of existing relations. Occasionally a
constable received appointment from the governor. From
time to time militia officers were appointed for some of the
localities. Deputy surveyors for the localities were also
appointed by the governor, and one who was designated for

---

[1] Hatfield, History of Elizabeth, 54 ; Records of Newark, published by
N. J. Hist. Soc.

[2] Leaming and Spicer, Grants and Concessions, 662 ; N. J. Arch. I. 88.

[3] The citations are all from East Jersey Records, Ms. Liber III.

Elizabethtown, where the governor resided, was ordered to act wholly under his direction.

These appointments, occurring as they do in considerable number, and representing the chief civil functions as they were under the simple relations of those times, show that the proprietors were gradually developing a framework of government throughout their province. In some localities, especially those of the Monmouth Purchase, we know that the proprietary officials were scarcely recognized. But elsewhere they met with a fair degree of recognition. The oaths of allegiance and fidelity were administered to all who would take them,[1] and strenuous efforts were made to induce all settlers to recognize the proprietors by receiving land patents from them, paying rent, and at the same time pledging their submission by the oath of fidelity. Evidence appears of the recall by the governor of various commissions, apparently because the appointees were not considered faithful to the proprietary cause. The proprietors lost no opportunity to declare [2] that only those who held land of them, and had taken the oaths, could hold office or enjoy the privileges of freeholders.

No general provincial court existed in New Jersey prior to the Dutch reoccupation. In April, 1670,[3] Governor Carteret tried temporarily to supply the place of one by enlarging the jurisdiction of the court of Woodbridge. In February, 1672, for the trial of disturbers of the peace, a special court, consisting mainly or wholly of members of the council, was held at Elizabethtown. In June, 1673, under authority, it is said, of an act of assembly, a similar court was held at Bergen.[4] Concerning other judicial tribunals of this character, no evidence appears.

The first body calling itself an assembly which met within the territory of New Jersey consisted of deputies from Middletown, Shrewsbury, and Portland Point,[5] the towns of the

---

[1] N. J. Arch. I. 48.   [2] Ibid. 59, 64, 103.   [3] Ibid. 62.   [4] Ibid. XXI. 35.
[5] Portland Point is now the Highlands of Navesink. See a paper on Monmouth County during the Provincial Era by Hon. Joel Parker, 2 Proc. N. J. Hist. Soc. III. The Middletown Town Book, from which Parker quotes at length, is also in print. The records of the so-called assembly of the Monmouth Patent are in the office of the clerk of Monmouth county.

Monmouth Patent. It met in June, 1667, and was called
the "General Assembly of the Patentees and Deputies."
Sessions continued at intervals for a number of years.
Local orders were passed, judicial functions performed, and
grants of land were made. The existence of this body
affords curious proof of the obstacles against which the New
Jersey proprietors had to contend.

The first assembly which met under the authority of the
proprietors was convened at Elizabethtown in May and
November, 1668. It was called by the governor, and he,
with the council, sat apart from the deputies. At the May
session deputies were present from Bergen, Newark, Elizabethtown, Woodbridge, and the towns of the Monmouth
Patent. At the November session two representatives also
appeared from Delaware river, but Middletown and Shrewsbury were unrepresented. In addition to the passage of a
number of "capital laws," which, in their severity, remind
one of Puritan legislation, a brief act was passed for the
maintenance of the authority of the proprietors. Rates
were voted, the same to be levied by quotas upon the towns,
and the prices of commodities in which they should be paid
were specified. A province treasurer was designated to
receive and disburse the rates, John Ogden of Elizabethtown
being the second appointee to this office. The general obligation of keeping firearms was enforced, and provision was
made for trainings. A beginning was made in legislation
concerning the Indians. By an order of the first session, the
time when the second session should begin was designated.

A message from the deputies to the council, which was
sent toward the close of the second session, shows that the
usual amount of friction had existed between the two houses.
"We," say the deputies, "finding so many and great Incon-
veniences by our not setting together, and your apprehensions
so different to ours, and your Expectations that things must
go according to your opinions, though we see no Reason for,
much less Warrant from the Concessions, wherefore we think
it vain to spend much Time of returning Answers by writings that are so exceeding dilatory, if not fruitless and end-
less, and therefore we think our way rather to break up our

meeting, seeing the Order of the Concessions cannot be attended unto." The governor and council desired that a joint committee might be appointed to consider in what respect they had violated the Concessions. But to this the deputies apparently paid no attention, and instead carried out the resolution they had already formed to finally adjourn. This they did without the coöperation of the governor.[1]

The relations between this assembly and the towns of the Monmouth Purchase throw much light on the political conditions of the times. James Grover and John Bowne attended the assembly in its May session, claiming to be deputies from Middletown and Shrewsbury. The inhabitants of Middletown, however, at their next town meeting, declared[2] that Grover and Bowne had been chosen by only a few of their friends hastily summoned for the purpose, and that neither their election nor their departure for the assembly was known to the town at large. For this reason their acts as deputies were repudiated. Shrewsbury sent no delegates of its own, leaving Middletown to act on its behalf.

Two deputies from each of these towns were chosen to attend the November session of the proprietary assembly. But before the local election was held the inhabitants of Middletown in town meeting instructed their deputies not to take the oath or subscribe a declaration of fidelity unless it contained a reservation of the privileges claimed under the Nicolls patent. When the deputies, however, insisted at Elizabethtown upon the addition of the proviso to their oath, they were not allowed to take their seats. Another event which contributed to the same course of action was this, that the two towns had refused to pay a tax of £5 each which had been levied by the proprietary assembly in its spring session to meet the needs of the province. Therefore two commissioners, Luke Watson and Samuel Moore of Woodbridge, were sent thither to collect the arrears, by distress if necessary, and to demand if the towns in question intended to submit to the authority of the proprietors. Middletown replied to this by the adoption of a resolution

[1] Leaming and Spicer, 77–91.　　　[2] Middletown Town Book.

in its next town meeting[1] requiring all the inhabitants to assist in securing the property of one and all against any attempt to levy upon it by distress, for the collection of the province rate. If any individual should be summoned before governor or court because of his giving such assistance, the town would pay his expenses and his business should be cared for during his absence. Moore and Watson were also informed in further resolves that they would receive no assistance, and that no inhabitant should be carried away by force until the town had taken further action. A formal reply to the demand of the proprietors that full submission should be made was also prepared by a committee and adopted by the town. In this document, which was drawn with ability, full reliance was placed on the validity of the patent from Nicolls, with its guaranty of property and of the right to pass by-laws. To the obligation to pay rent to the new proprietors and to submit to the " absolute " authority of their government, the remonstrants declared that they could not submit. If they did this, they would be proving false to their patent. But if security could be granted, — by which was meant exemption from the payment of proprietary quitrents, and a guaranty of rights of local government, — the towns would submit to the proprietors.

In November, 1671, an assembly was held, of which no record has been preserved. It, however, passed an act in which the towns in question were charged with contempt of authority. When this became known to them, together with the fact that a summons to elect delegates to attend a later session had been issued, the towns declined to hold the election,[2] but sought to excuse previous failures of their deputies to attend. In an assembly which was held the following year, the Monmouth towns were also unrepresented. This, however, told in their favor, for since 1670 the quitrents had fallen due, and great disorder occurred in connection with attempts to collect them. Though nearly all the records of the time have been destroyed, enough remains

[1] Middletown Town Book ; 2 Proc. N. J. Hist. Soc. III.
[2] Middletown Town Book.

to show that riots occurred, and that the prospect of the overthrow of the government which the proprietors had partially established was imminent. The fact that James Carteret, the reckless son of the proprietor, allowed himself to be made president of the province, and to appear as leader of the malcontents, shows the extent to which the opposition was able to go. Under his authority they even held an assembly. Governor Philip Carteret was forced to return to England for advice and support, leaving John Berry as deputy governor. From the proprietors Carteret procured a declaration confirming the Concessions, and so interpreting them as to sustain the claims which the governor had been making. This, with the letter from the king, brought about the temporary submission of the Monmouth towns to the authority of the proprietors. They abandoned for the time the claims they had urged under the Nicolls patent, and received grants of land from the proprietors.[1] In return for this, existing property rights and rights of local government among them were confirmed, and it was ordered that patentees who had expended money in the purchase of land from the Indians should have grants of five hundred acres each. James Carteret now withdrew, and quiet was restored throughout the province. Soon after the attainment of this result, the Dutch reappeared and again temporarily set up their power.

When, in 1674, Philip Carteret returned as governor of East Jersey under a single proprietor, he brought instructions[2] confirmatory of the rights which Berkeley and Carteret had previously asserted, and explanatory of their Concessions. In reference to government it was declared in this document that the governor and council, to the exclusion of the assembly, should have the power to admit all persons to become freemen of the province, and to grant and confirm all rights of incorporation. The latter clause meant that town charters should be granted by the execu-

---

[1] Leaming and Spicer, 53; N. J. Arch. I. 88; Whitehead, 71.

[2] N. J. Arch. I. 167, 173. For a sharp and prolonged debate between the Council and deputies in the general assembly of 1681, over the right of the proprietors to make these changes, see *ibid.* 354; N. Y. Col. Docs. III. 293.

tive, while the former provision made it all the more necessary that land in the various towns should be rapidly
surveyed, and patents for it secured from the proprietors.
The council soon ordered the surveyors to attend specially
to this business.[1]

It was also declared that to the governor and council
belonged the power of summoning and adjourning the general assembly at such times and to such places as they
chose. The general assembly, moreover, should continue
to sit in two separate houses. They also were authorized
to establish town courts, but courts of sessions and assize
should be established only by the governor, council, and
assembly acting in conjunction. Over the establishment
of fees, the appointment of officials, the surveying and
granting of lands, the calling out of the militia to repel
invasion or suppress rebellion, the governor and council
should have exclusive control. They should also approve
the ministers who were chosen and settled over the churches
within the province.[2] All these provisions indicated a
strengthening of the executive, or distinctly proprietary,
element in the province, as a means whereby the tendencies
toward disorder and revolt which had manifested themselves
might be restrained. Those who had shared in occasioning
the disorders of 1672, unless they at once made amends,
should be proceeded against in the courts. The letter which
Charles II sent at this time from England tended in the
same direction, for it commanded[3] all persons whatsoever
within the province to yield obedience "to the laws and
government which are or shall be established" by Sir George
Carteret.

On November 6, 1674, the royal letter and instructions
from the proprietor were published at Bergen in the presence
of commissioners from all the towns except Shrewsbury.[4]
On the 9th of the following March a proclamation was issued
by the governor and council, convening at Elizabethtown a
general court of oyer and terminer for the province.[5] The
immediate purpose of this act was to create a tribunal by

[1] N. J. Arch. I. 178.   [2] *Ibid.* 174.   [3] *Ibid.* 154.
[4] New Jersey Bill in Chancery, 40; Whitehead, 83.   [5] N. J. Arch. I. 176.

which those who defied the authority of the proprietors could be tried and punished.　To aid in the work, constables were sworn for the different towns.　Samuel Moore, as provost marshal, was ordered to collect the fines for riotous conduct which had been imposed by courts in 1671 and 1673, and was given power to imprison those who refused to pay.　In this task also the constables were to assist.　Justices of the peace and presidents of local courts were also commissioned. In June, 1675, another[1] commission for a court of oyer and terminer was issued.　In July various military commissions were issued to officers in the localities, and orders for forming and training the militia, these being occasioned by the outbreak of Philip's war in New England and by rumors of the restlessness of the Indians along the Delaware.　In October still another commission for a court of oyer and terminer was published.

These measures restored and helped to develop the administrative system of the English province after its final relinquishment by the Dutch.　They were accompanied by a return of quiet.　The proprietary claims were also strengthened by the arrival from England of an opinion, signed by eight prominent lawyers, which was unfavorable to the claims of the Nicolls patentees.　Under these conditions it appeared safe to again summon an assembly.　It met at Elizabethtown in November, 1675, and between that time and the close of 1679 no less than eight assemblies were held.[2]　They met, not only at Elizabethtown, but at Woodbridge and Middletown.　At first members elected from Shrewsbury refused to qualify by taking the necessary oaths. They were dismissed; and by the assembly of October, 1676, a law was passed making a town which should send such deputies liable to a fine of £10.　The following year the deputy who was elected from Shrewsbury did not attend.[3] He was fined 10s. for every day's absence during the session.　Shortly after this, provision was made for the payment of wages to governor, councillors, and deputies during the sessions of the assemblies, but it is not probable that

[1] East Jersey Records, Liber III.　　[2] Leaming and Spicer, 93–137.
[3] Ibid. 121, 123.

this or improvements in facilities for travelling materially changed the attitude of Shrewsbury toward the claims of the proprietors. Slowly and with the lapse of time the old animosities weakened and the eastern province grew together into a unit. In 1675 an act of oblivion was passed covering all acts between 1670 and June, 1673, the purpose of which was the overthrow of the government of the proprietors.

By the assembly of 1675 also the northern part of the province was divided into four counties, and provision was made for a court[1] in each of them, which should hold two sessions a year. Their jurisdiction was loosely defined, and fees were prescribed for their officers. The judges of these courts were elected from their respective counties and were commissioned by the governor. By the same assembly monthly courts of small causes, with exclusive jurisdiction over cases involving less than forty shillings, were created, as well as a court of assize, which should be the supreme civil tribunal of the province, and meet once a year. This body was distinct from the council, though councillors were doubtless frequently appointed as its judges. The council as such acted as the highest court of appeals. The governor here, as elsewhere, possessed the powers of a chancellor.[2]

Provincial rates were regularly voted by these assemblies, annual public charges increasing from £30 in 1668 to £196 in 1680. Among the items of expenditure was the governor's salary, which was annually fixed by the assembly. Provision was made in 1676 for its payment by the towns in kind, the constables collecting the same. A province treasurer was annually designated by the assembly.

It is to be remembered that in 1676 West Jersey was by the Quintipartite Deed fully separated from East Jersey and began its distinct career. But before it had more than entered on its separate existence, the resolution of Governor Andros to assert his control over New Jersey renewed dis-

---

[1] The jurisdiction of Bergen received one of these courts, Elizabethtown and Newark a second, Woodbridge and Piscataway a third, Middletown and Shrewsbury the fourth. In 1683 the names Bergen, Essex, Middlesex, and Monmouth were given to these jurisdictions.

[2] Field, The Provincial Courts of New Jersey.

turbance in the eastern province, while it aroused quite as strong protest in West Jersey. This interference with conditions in the Jerseys themselves must next be considered.

The first encounter was between the government of New York and John Fenwick, the grantee of Lord Berkeley and trustee for Edward Byllinge. Fenwick had been one of Cromwell's officers, but was now a convert to Quakerism. In the summer of 1675 he had arrived in the Delaware river with his family and a small additional group of settlers. They had taken possession, on the east bank of the Delaware, of the post known to the Dutch as Varcken's Kill, and later to the Swedes as Elsingborg, and named it Salem. This was the beginning of Fenwick's colony. Early in the following December the governor and council at New York, having been informed that this colony had been founded without its consent, resolved that Fenwick should not be acknowledged as proprietor, with authority of his own to grant land and exercise rights of local government. But, if he paid the duties, as other subjects did, he should be treated civilly, and if any of his colonists desired land it should be surveyed and granted to them under the authority of New York. The customs duties of New York should be levied on the east as well as the west shore of the Delaware, and exemption from them should not " be allowed in any case to the smallest vessell, boate or person." [1] It is certain that in no event of his career does the resolute and autocratic character of Edmund Andros appear more clearly than in his dealings with the New Jersey governments during the next five years. William Dyer had been commissioned to collect customs [2] throughout the duke's territories as specified in his charter, and this, with the authority granted in the governor's own commission, Andros was resolved to maintain to the fullest extent.

In the summer of 1676 the duke's secretary, Sir John Werden, wrote [3] that his master was not inclined to let go any part of the "prerogative," that is, of the governmental rights which Andros and his predecessors had asserted on

[1] N. Y. Col. Docs. XII. 542 ; N. J. Arch. I. 185 *et seq.*
[2] N. Y. Col. Docs. III. 221.　　　[3] *Ibid.* 240.

the duke's behalf.   When the settlers challenged the right of the New York authorities to levy duties on their goods, they were met with the argument that it was a conquered country, and that the king had vested his absolute power to make laws for such a country and to raise money within it in the duke.   But in reply to this, the question was further asked, Did these laws extend to the English as well as to the conquered inhabitants?   If so, they must be limited by the condition that a subject's goods could not be taken without his consent.   If this limitation were ignored and an absolute power asserted, then, demanded the Quakers of West Jersey, what security have we for anything we possess?   We can call nothing our own, but are tenants at will.   Their removal into the colonies had then been a transition from good to bad conditions; and if the duke's officials persisted in the course they were following, their province would never reach true greatness.   In opposition to these claims, the settlers affirmed that with the conveyance to them had gone true rights of government, for without these they could not have been induced to buy, and colonists could not have been induced to remove into the country.   With such arguments as these, anticipating in all essential points those which were used a century later against England, the inhabitants of New Jersey opposed taxation without representation.[1]

John Fenwick seems to have ignored the command of the governor and council of New York for nearly a year. He continued to act as proprietor, that is, to survey and grant out lands and collect rents therefrom, and there is no evidence that he or the inhabitants of his colony paid customs to the duke.   Jean Paul Jacquet complained that he had been dispossessed of land by the newcomers.   Therefore, in the autumn of 1676, a warrant[2] was issued to the commander on the Delaware to arrest Fenwick and bring him to New York.   To Captain John Collier, when he went

[1] The argument will be found in a memorial from the proprietors of West Jersey to the commissioners of the duke's revenue, presented in 1680. Smith, History of New Jersey, 117.

[2] N. Y. Col. Docs. XII. 559, 565 ; N. J. Arch. I. 189-204.

to serve the warrant, Fenwick declared that he had nothing to do with the governor of New York, and that he would obey no order except one that came from the king or the Duke of York. The latter statement weakened his case, but the old Cromwellian stood so on the defensive, finally bolting his door and speaking through "a small scuttle hole at the end of the house," that the sheriff had to take a lieutenant and twelve soldiers to Salem to arrest him.

When he was brought to New York, in January, 1677, a special session of the court of assizes[1] was called. Fenwick was found guilty of riotous conduct, fined £40, and ordered to be kept in custody till he could give a bond of £500 to keep the peace. His claim both to soil and government broke down because of his failure to produce the original of his deed of grant from Berkeley. Fenwick refused to give the security demanded, and was kept for some months in prison.[2] There is no proof that he ever prosecuted an appeal before the privy council, though he threatened so to do.

Fenwick was finally released on parole, his bond was remitted, and he was allowed to return to the Delaware country on condition that he would not assume power of government there until he could produce from England more authentic proof of his right to do so than he had hitherto offered. But he at once resumed the administration of his colony as before. Complaints were again preferred against him,[3] and after some threats of resistance he came to New York. His case was again heard, this time before the council, but nothing decisive seems to have been done. In October, 1678, Andros, according to his custom, appointed certain inhabitants of Salem to act as town overseers there. They were placed under the immediate jurisdiction of the magistrates at Newcastle, on the west bank of the river, who were virtually county officers within an important "appendage" of New York.[4] Beyond this, no steps

[1] N. Y. Col. Docs. XII. 568.　　[2] N. J. Arch. I. 199.
[3] N. Y. Col. Docs. XII. 592–602, 610; N. J. Arch. I. 193 et seq., 275.
[4] N. Y. Col. Docs. XII. 610; N. J. Arch. I. 284; 2 Pa. Arch. V. 708. The commission to the overseers, which was for one year, was renewed in 1679.

seem to have been taken, and Fenwick continued to grant[1] land as usual.

Similar measures were adopted by Andros toward Thomas Olive and the Quakers associated with him, who came over in the summer of 1677 for the purpose of settling that part of West Jersey which lay north of Fenwick's colony. When they appeared before him at New York, he asked them if they had anything from the duke. On their replying that they had no special grant, but only his conveyance to Berkeley and that of Berkeley to Byllinge and his associates, the governor replied that he could not resign jurisdiction over West Jersey without express orders from the duke. To this he adhered, though he permitted them to go thither and proceed with their settlement until full authority could be obtained from England. He also commissioned Thomas Olive and seven other leaders of the enterprise to act as overseers of the settlement for one year, holding courts, appointing constables, surveying and granting land, and performing all other necessary duties. On any extraordinary occasion they might apply to the commander and magistrates at Newcastle, and give notice to the governor and council at New York. Appeals were to be allowed in the more important criminal and civil cases from their court to the court of assizes at New York.[2] This commission was renewed and the vacancies in the board were filled on May 22, 1681. By those who held the commission Burlington was founded. Thus Andros, as long as he remained governor, sought to retain at least a formal hold on West Jersey.

Over East Jersey the control of New York was for a time extended much farther. After the restoration of English government, in 1674, the payment of duties and the entering and clearing at New York of vessels which were trading with

[1] N. J. Arch. XXI. 339, 541, 567, being the Calendar of Town Grants, New Salem, Fenwick's Surveys, and Salem Deeds, Liber "B."

[2] The council minute in which an account is given of the interview between Andros and the would-be settlers is printed in N. Y. Col. Docs. XII. 579, and in N. J. Arch. I. 239, but the commission to Olive and his associates appears nowhere in print. It is recorded in Orders, Letters, and Warrants (Ms.), August 7, 1677.

East Jersey were regularly insisted on.   This was borne
without manifest show of resistance until April, 1679.   At
that time the legislature of East Jersey passed an act to the
effect that, if any vessel, for the offence of entering and
clearing at Elizabethtown, should be seized by the New York
authorities, its owners should be indemnified at the expense
of the colony.[1]   Governor Carteret declared that all vessels
might trade freely with East Jersey.   On the strength of
that proclamation a ketch from Barbadoes was sent thither
loaded with rum ; but it was compelled to enter and pay
duties at New York before its cargo could be landed.
Andros soon after proposed to take possession of Sandy
Hook, erect a fort there, and set up beacons.   This implied a
decisive assertion by New York of a right to Staten island
and the Kill van Kull, as well as to the Narrows.   To this
Carteret replied that Andros in the prosecution of his plan
would be resisted, and the East Jersey governor proposed to
appeal to the king.[2]   Andros proceeded at once to the extreme of forbidding Carteret to exercise jurisdiction anywhere within the limits of the duke's province as specified
in the charter and his own commission, and forbade any one
to assist or obey him.

On April 5 Andros went to Staten island with a number
of councillors, officers, and merchants, and two days later
crossed over to Elizabethtown.   There he met Carteret and
his council, who were accompanied by a number of armed
men.   A conference was held, at which both sides produced
legal documents on which they based their respective claims.[3]
Andros insisted that the King's letters patent were of greater
force than the lease and release and the letter from the king.
The point upon which the East Jersey men insisted was that
Sir George Carteret was the duke's assignee, and as such had
as ample rights of government as the duke himself.   They
insisted on being left in possession until an appeal could be
taken to England and the question finally settled.

---

[1] Leaming and Spicer, 131 ; N. Y. Col. Docs. IV. 382.

[2] Leaming and Spicer, 673, 674.

[3] N. J. Arch. I. 299 *et seq.*; Leaming and Spicer, 677 *et seq.*; Whitehead,
92.

But Andros resolved not to wait for the regular course of proceedings. Ignoring the entire series of precedents since 1665, which told so strongly in favor of the essential right of the New Jersey proprietors to powers of government, he ordered the arrest of Carteret. Carteret himself relates how a party of soldiers from New York came to Elizabethtown, broke open his doors at dead of night, and with much show of brutality haled him out of bed and took him away to New York to prison.[1] A special court of assizes was called, and he was brought to trial on the charge of unlawfully exercising powers of government within the Duke of York's patent. Andros presided, and the trial was held before a jury. Carteret at first protested against the jurisdiction of the court, but being overruled, he finally pleaded not guilty. His commission and instructions, with other documents,[2] were submitted to the jury, and they brought in a verdict of not guilty. Andros then sought to change the verdict by sending the jury out three times with repeated charges. But he was finally compelled to record the original verdict. Carteret was then released, but only on condition that he would not assume any authority or jurisdiction in East Jersey.

Meantime writs had been issued for an assembly to meet at Elizabethtown on June 2. Andros accompanied Carteret back thither, and, with members of his own council, held this session of the assembly. His own commission was read, and the Duke's Laws were presented to the deputies for their acceptance, Andros at the same time urging that an act be passed to confirm past judicial proceedings and for the continuance of the courts. He also promised indemnity for all who had shared in previous acts of government. The deputies were told that, if they would submit to New York, they should retain the right to make local prudential laws, the court of assizes passing orders concerning important

CHAP.
VIII.

---

[1] Leaming and Spicer, 678 ; N. J. Arch. I. 316 ; Journal of Dankers and Sluyter, Pubs. of L. I. Hist. Soc. I. 346–352.

[2] During a colloquy between the two governors, Carteret is said to have produced letters in which, during the previous years of their friendship, Andros had addressed him as governor. This rather nonplussed the New York executive.

matters.   The deputies, who did not refuse to act in conjunction with Andros, insisted upon a guaranty of all the privileges which the people had enjoyed under Carteret, and in particular that assemblies should continue to meet in October of every year, as had been the custom.   All acts passed by former assemblies should also be confirmed, and the book of laws of New Jersey, including the Grants and Concessions, was presented as a counterpoise to the Duke's Laws.   Long and repeated conferences were held by Andros and his council with the deputies, but he did not find them disposed to intrust themselves to his tender mercies, except with all the guaranties which they had possessed.   An argument extending through about two hours was held between the governor and John Bowne of Middletown, speaker of the assembly, in which the latter pleaded the rights and privileges of the deputies and the claims which were connected therewith.   A bill was prepared for the confirmation of all existing laws and privileges, but to this Andros and his council were not willing to agree.   Finally the council resolved, "that nothing offered by the Assembly is for the King's or Country's service, but the contrary, particularly reflecting upon his Majesty's letters patents and the authority thereof."   Upon this the assembly was dissolved.

Andros, however, continued for some time thereafter to perform acts of government for East Jersey.   On presentation by the inhabitants he commissioned overseers, constables, militia officers, and justices of the peace, some or all of these, for Elizabethtown, Newark, Bergen, Woodbridge, and Piscataway.   In one instance petition was made for an appeal from the court of sessions at Elizabethtown to the authorities of New York.[1]

The aggressive measures of Andros, both in West and East Jersey, forced the proprietors to make urgent representations on their case at home.   It was at this time that the argument of the West Jersey proprietors, already referred to, was presented.   The influence of Penn was exerted with effect.   Though Sir George Carteret was now dead, his widow and her friends exerted themselves to

[1] N. J. Arch. I. 318–322, 334–336.

redress the wrongs of Philip Carteret. The anti-Catholic excitement which followed the revelation of the so-called Popish Plot, together with the struggle over the Exclusion Bill, embarrassed the Duke of York, and led him to withdraw for the time the support which he had undoubtedly been extending to Andros and his policy. In consequence of the opinion rendered by Sir William Jones, the additional deeds of release, to which reference has already been made, were issued in August, 1680. Andros was soon after recalled to meet other charges. In March, 1681, Governor Carteret proclaimed the cessation of all authority by New York,[1] and New Jersey was again left to the natural course of its development. With this, the efforts of New York officials to exercise full powers of government in New Jersey came to an end. But their attempts, backed by the merchants of New York, to secure the annexation of New Jersey to that province continued for years to come.

We have now reached the time when, as the result of an auction sale in London and for the sum of £3400, East Jersey was sold by the trustees of Sir George Carteret to William Penn and eleven associates, mostly Quakers. The province then contained about thirty-five hundred inhabitants, grouped together in eight communities which extended from the shores of the Hudson and New York bay to the Raritan. For about fifteen years they had lived under such government as Carteret had been able to provide, enjoying throughout the time a large degree of local independence. Now, by a transaction in which they had no share, similar in all respects to the purchase of an estate of land, these people were subjected to the rule of a new and quite different proprietary body. By other transfers, which took place a few months later, this body was increased from twelve to twenty-four proprietors. In nationality, professions, and religion they not only differed widely among themselves, but were quite unlike Berkeley or Carteret. No province except East Jersey, after the process of settlement had progressed so far, was subjected in this sudden fashion to such a change of rulers.

[1] N. J. Arch. I. 346.

The new proprietors, moreover, not content with accepting the system of government which had already been worked out, constructed a frame of government of their own, and under the name of the Fundamental Constitutions attempted to impose it on the province. This document, as well as the Concessions and Agreements which were issued by the proprietors of West Jersey in 1677 and the Frames of Government of Pennsylvania, embody many of the ideas of the seventeenth-century Quaker concerning government. We may suppose that William Penn himself had a hand in the framing of them all. If one were taking a broader survey of schemes of government in that prolific century, these documents would have to be brought into comparison with the Agreement of the People and other manifestoes which proceeded from the Levellers in England between 1647 and the Restoration. They express in a crude way the yearning of the middle and lower classes of that day after proper guaranties of civil liberty.

The Concessions of East and West Jersey were largely occupied, it is true, with provisions concerning the granting of land and the collection of rents. The East Jersey document gave the proprietors a considerable share in the government. But both of these constitutions, as well as those which were issued in Pennsylvania, provided with scrupulous care for the protection of property and for personal liberty. The Concessions of West Jersey provided that the clauses which contained its guaranties of liberty should be read at the opening and close of every session of the general assembly and four times a year in the presence of the people of every locality ; that no laws should be passed which were in the least degree inconsistent with the guaranties, and that, if any member of the assembly should attempt to secure the passage of such a law, he should be proceeded against as a traitor.

The familiar phrases of Magna Carta recur, elaborate provision was made for jury trial, simplicity and publicity in all judicial proceedings were insured, and care was taken to give the accused every advantage which justice could demand. The West Jersey Concessions gave the com-

plainant, whether in a civil or criminal case, the right to CHAP.
forgive the accused and remit his penalty, even after judg- VIII.
ment.   The East Jersey Constitutions provided that litigants
might plead their causes in person, or employ a friend for
that purpose.   No one should take money for pleading or
advice in such cases.   In order to avoid an accumulation of
statutes, which of itself might make lawyers a necessity, it
was provided that no law should remain in force more than
fifty years without renewal.   The taking of oaths was of
course dispensed with.   Freedom of conscience was guarantied.   The Indians were to be treated mildly and justly.
The obligations of military service were ignored, or were
so stated as to excuse those whose consciences forbade them
to bear arms.

Another characteristic feature of all these plans of government was the prominence which they gave to election as a
method of filling offices.   The provisions of the West Jersey
Concessions and of the Pennsylvania Frames of Government
on this subject must be reviewed when those provinces come
up for consideration.   Those of the East Jersey instrument
were substantially the same as the plan which Penn was
then devising for his province across the Delaware.   Their
nature can be made clear by reference to the part which election was to play in the organization of the executive and of
the legislature.   The offices of governor and deputy governor were made appointive.   The secretaryship and several
of the other subordinate offices also remained appointive.
Robert Barclay was appointed governor for life, and his
deputy was to hold office for seven years.   But thereafter
the term of the governor was to be limited to three years.
The governor was then to be appointed by sixteen of the
proprietors from a list of nominees presented by the whole
board.   The governor's council, or common council as it was
called, was to consist practically of all the proprietors who
were resident in the province, or their proxies, and the proxies
of all the other members of the board, together with twelve
freemen chosen by ballot from the great council.[1]   The
thirty-six members of this body were to be organized into

[1] N. J. Arch. I. 399.

three committees, one on manners, education, and the arts, one on trade and the treasury, and a third on plantations. There is no evidence that the common council was to have legislative power.

The legislature of the province was to be known as the great council, and was to consist of the proprietors or their proxies, and at first of 72 members — later to be increased to 144 — who should be chosen by the freeholders of the province. The elected members should hold office for three years, one-third retiring every year. The election in each locality should be by lot. The council should meet annually in April and adjourn itself. Its session might be prolonged for two months. The governor and common council might extend it beyond that time, or call extra sessions. Bills could be passed only by a two-thirds vote, which should include the votes of twelve of the proprietors. All laws affecting the liberties or property of the inhabitants must pass this council.

This combination of a council, a part of which was elective, with so large a legislative body was cumbersome and to the highest degree impracticable. Both bodies were far too large for the capacities or needs of the province. Penn's effort to administer government under a similar system in Pennsylvania failed. There is no accessible proof that in East Jersey the proprietors ever seriously tried to put their scheme into operation. The colonists had not the slightest interest in it. The institutions which already existed were sufficiently well adapted to their needs. An official system was in existence of which the proprietors availed themselves. Commissions of local officers which were issued by Gawen Lawrie and his successors in the governorship have been preserved. Writs of election dating from the same period are also in existence. The journal of the legislative council from and after 1682 as well as the laws which were passed during that period have been preserved.[1] The evidence which they furnish is conclusive to the effect that in the actual organization and workings of the government under the twenty-four proprietors the Fundamental Constitutions were ignored. The

[1] Leaming and Spicer, 227 *et seq.*; N. J. Arch. XIII.

small council, holding by appointment and exercising both legislative and executive powers, was retained.[1] The lower house was organized on the same plan as that which existed in Carteret's time, and the functions of the two were the same as they were during that period.

In 1682 and again in 1688 acts were passed which further extended the process of dividing the province into counties. Renewed legislative sanction was given to county courts and courts of small causes. By another act provision was made for a new supreme court of the province, with the title of the court of common right, and its jurisdiction was specified. A long list of general laws was passed, the contents of which do not agree with the Fundamental Constitutions. None of them materially changed the institutions of the province.

The provisions relating to government which were promulgated in the Concessions of West Jersey were at once simple and democratic. The executive authority was lodged in a board of commissioners, who were at first appointed by Penn, Lawrie, and Lucas in England, and were sent over to purchase lands from the Indians and prepare the way for settlement. After the settlement had been made the commissioners were to be chosen annually by the resident proprietors and freeholders in general assembly.[2] By the assembly, also, all the other officers of the province were to be elected, the commissioners of the public seals, treasurers, chief justices, sheriffs, and collectors. Justices of the peace and constables were chosen by the people of the locality, though one engagement of justices of the peace has been preserved, who were chosen by the assembly to act as justices of what later became Salem county.[3]

The strictly representative part of the general assembly, when developed, consisted of ten members chosen by the freeholders of each tenth. During the period of which we

[1] See the commission of Governor Thomas Rudyard to the council in December, 1682. N. J. Arch. XIII. 3.

[2] *Ibid.* I. 220, 241, 265, 266; Clarkson, Life of Penn, Chap. 13.

[3] See Ms. volume entitled West Jersey Concessions, etc., 1681–1699, in the office of the Secretary of State at Trenton.

are speaking, only five [1] out of a possible ten tenths had been settled.   One of these was Fenwick's colony, and the others were the jurisdictions settled by the groups of Quaker colonists from London and Yorkshire.   In the assembly of 1683, the governor, council, or commissioners, and representatives sat together in a single house, [2] the governor presiding and having a double vote.   But this practice does not seem to have been adhered to.   The formal right of assenting to acts seems also to have belonged to the governor.   During the intermissions of the assembly the governor and council administered the affairs of the province.   They also prepared bills to be submitted to the general assembly, publishing the same through the province twenty days before the beginning of the session when they were to be discussed.   It is clear that the general court in the New England colonies was no more truly the source of power than was the West Jersey assembly.   That body expressly asserted its right even to amend the Concessions.

For a time, however, the operation of this system was hindered by a claim of Edward Byllinge to the rights of governor. These seem to have originated in the grant from Berkeley and to have been strengthened by the language used near the close of the Duke of York's grant of West Jersey to Penn and his associates in 1680. [3]   It was stated that in order the better to enable Edward Byllinge, his heirs and assigns, to settle the province and govern it, the duke granted and transferred " to the said Edward Byllinge all and every the same Powers, Authorities, Jurisdictions, Governments " which had been granted to him by the king.   Penn and his associates as trustees, in order to quiet the claims which Byllinge had, chose him governor of West Jersey. [4]   Byllinge appointed Samuel Jennings as his deputy.   By him an assembly was called which met in November, 1681.   This body affirmed, under the title of " fundamentals," the principles of government which had been stated in the Concessions. [5]

---

[1] Five tenths were represented in the Assembly of 1686.   See West Jersey Concessions, 1681–1699.   [2] Leaming and Spicer, 474.

[3] N. J. Arch. I. 331 ; Mulford, History of New Jersey, 234.

[4] Smith, History of New Jersey, 125, 126.   [5] Leaming and Spicer, 423.

These were to the effect that a general assembly should meet
annually and that to it should belong the exclusive power to
legislate on all matters of provincial concern.   The governor
should not attempt to legislate, or make war, raise money or
have dealings with other colonies, tribes, or states without its
consent.   No grant of revenue should be made for a longer
period than one year.   The assembly, moreover, should elect
all officers of the province ; full liberty of conscience should
be enjoyed and none should be excluded from office for ecclesiastical reasons.   The assembly was not to be prorogued
without its own consent, and the governor must confirm its
acts.   It was only on the acceptance of these conditions that
Jennings was permitted to act as deputy governor.

But still Jennings was Byllinge's appointee, and it seemed
possible, notwithstanding the Concessions, that a non-resident
as proprietor might secure control of the executive of the
province.   This uncertainty, accompanied by anxious dis-
cussions of the subject, continued until 1683.   The assembly
of that year determined to settle the question, to decide
once for all that government went with the land, and that
authority for it was derived from the body of freeholders.
Therefore, upon the advice of William Penn, it was resolved [1]
that the assembly should choose Samuel Jennings governor,
and that he should solemnly promise to execute the office
diligently and according to the concessions.   This was
done, the required engagement was taken, and six hundred
acres of land were granted to Jennings in recognition of his
services as governor.   This act was also accompanied by the
adoption of a long series of resolves to the effect that the
Concessions should be obeyed, and that Byllinge should be
induced to sign a paper conceding this point.   This meant
that government had been transferred with the land, and
that authority for its exercise should proceed from the general assembly.   At the same session it was resolved that the
general assembly should consist of governor, council, and
assembly.   Since the previous year the members of the council
had been chosen by the assembly.   Now the office of governor was filled in the same way.   At this very session also

[1] Leaming and Spicer, 466–472.

the justices of the respective tenths, the commissioners for dividing and regulating lands in each tenth, the commissioners for buying lands of the Indians, the two treasurers of the province, the recorder for the Salem jurisdiction and another for the rest of the province, a high sheriff for the Burlington jurisdiction and another for the Salem jurisdiction, a surveyor, and constables for the first, second, and third tenths were elected. The entire civil list of the province, except some local officers at Burlington and more in Fenwick's colony, was thus filled by the assembly. This process was annually repeated by the assembly — when its sessions were not interrupted by outside interference — so long as West Jersey continued to be a distinct province.

But it was found impossible to induce Edward Byllinge to abandon his claims as proprietor. The assembly in 1684 [1] chose the governor, Samuel Jennings, and Thomas Budd to go to England as agents and present a formal demand for the abandonment of Byllinge's claims. An appropriation was made to meet the expense of the agency. Thomas Olive was chosen deputy governor, to hold during the interval, until the meeting of the next general assembly, and it was voted to continue the existing system of government. During Jennings's absence it was indeed further perfected by laws for the levy and collection of taxes by officials elected by the people of the tenths, and an act authorizing the levy of local taxes and the building of highways within the Salem tenth.

Byllinge sent over a new charter and some additional bills, but he would not agree to abandon his claims. [2] He appointed John Skene governor, while he, with three others who were apparently non-resident proprietors, insisted that proxies should be admitted to the assembly on their behalf. The assembly referred them to the committee which was inspecting the new charter. The only fragment of the proceedings of a West Jersey assembly which has been preserved relates to the session of 1686. [3] From this it appears that the committee reported that each proprietor might have one proxy

[1] Leaming and Spicer, 485.   [2] Ibid. 497, 502, 503–505.
[3] West Jersey Concessions, 1681–1699.

in the assembly and no more, provided such proxy were resident on the proprietor's land. The bills and charter which had been sent over by Byllinge were also read, and a report of the committee against accepting them was unanimously adopted. The view was expressed that, irrespective of their contents, it would be improper to accept these proposals, since they came from a proprietor who lived so far away. Furthermore, if Byllinge might make void the Concessions which he and the other proprietors had already issued, he might with more ease recall those which he now sent. A committee was then appointed to write to Byllinge, asking him to instruct his deputy governor to approve such laws as the assembly and deputy together should consider necessary for the good of the province. The letter which they prepared was read and approved. On this particular subject no further entry appears.

The death of Byllinge the following year closed the controversy with him. His governor, Skene, by appointing certain rangers to take up stray horses and cattle, brought down on himself the rebuke of the assembly of 1686. They told him that such an act was an intrusion on the rights of the public, and required him to desist. They then resolved that rangers were necessary, and chose six for the four upper tenths. Immediately after this they declared to the governor that the right to choose officers belonged to themselves, and proceeded to elect Thomas Revell clerk and recorder. The governor and council were also ordered to prepare a table of fees for officers, and to submit this to the assembly for amendment and confirmation.

Upon the death of Byllinge, Dr. Daniel Coxe, who was already a proprietor of West Jersey, bought the entire interest of Byllinge and his heirs in the province.[1] With this went his claims to government. Coxe took the advice of counsel and urged upon the colonists a full recognition of these claims. But before the controversy with him had proceeded far, such governmental rights as the proprietors had were surrendered to the king, and all New Jersey was joined to the great dominion which he was constructing.

[1] Smith, History of New Jersey, 190 ; Mulford, 248.

CHAPTER IX

CAROLINA AS A PROPRIETARY PROVINCE. THE CAPE FEAR
AND ASHLEY RIVER SETTLEMENTS, SOUTH CAROLINA

WHEN Virginia became a royal province the unoccupied
territory south, as well as north, of the latitude of Point
Comfort again became subject to grant by the king. In
1629, not far from the time when Lord Baltimore was
prospecting in Virginia, the first Carolina grant was made [1]
to Sir Robert Heath, attorney-general and afterwards chief
justice of common pleas. Though he had been concerned
in the dissolution of the London company and was one of
the royal commissioners appointed after the revocation of
the charter for the government of Virginia, Heath never
took sufficient interest in colonization to undertake the settlement of his province. A plan in which the Vassalls, a
prominent Puritan family to which reference has already been
made, were interested for the settlement [2] of a body of Huguenot refugees within its limits failed. After that Sir Robert
Heath assigned his interest in the province, according to one
account,[3] to Samuel Vassall and to the heirs of Sir Richard
Grenville, and according to another to Lord Maltravers, the
heir of the Earl of Arundel, from whom it passed to the Duke
of Norfolk and his family. Both claims were quite shadowy.
Though the province was thus neglected by the immediate
grantees, the faint beginnings of settlement were made within
the northern part of the region by emigrants from Virginia,
while certain New Englanders became interested in trade and
colonization [4] near Cape Fear. Thus early, and in both these

[1] N. C. Recs. I. 5.

[2] Cal. of State Papers, Am. and W. Indies, Entries, 1627 to 1635.

[3] N. C. Recs. I. 35, 519.

[4] Hening, Statutes of Virginia, I. 262, 380, 422 ; N. C. Recs. I. 18–20. In
Hawks, History of North Carolina, II. 132, will be found interesting papers

localities, a certain nonconformist trend was given to the development of the province.

When, in 1663 and 1665, the Earl of Clarendon, the Duke of Albemarle, Lords Craven, Ashley, and John Berkeley, Sir George Carteret, Sir William Berkeley, and Sir John Colleton procured their patents for Carolina, an order in council was issued for the institution of legal proceedings against the claims of the early assignees.[1] Under the new grantees the work of colonization actually began.

The fact that, unlike Maryland and New York, Carolina was granted to a board of proprietors, had no small effect on the course of its development. With that system, which Carolina shared in common with the Jerseys, the consistency and strength that was possible under a single proprietor was scarcely attainable. The attention of all the members of the Carolina board was far more absorbed by English affairs than they were by those of the province. With one or two exceptions they could no more be regarded as experts in colonization than could the great majority of the members of the New England council. In fact, between these two bodies, as well as between the policies which they pursued, more than one suggestive resemblance may be traced. Ashley alone devoted himself seriously to Carolina affairs, and that for only a limited period. Sir William Berkeley for a brief time had a somewhat intimate connection with the Albemarle settlement. Of the original board Colleton died in 1666, Albemarle in 1669, Clarendon, after having lived in exile seven years, died in 1674. Lord John Berkeley took no interest in the affairs of the province after the lapse of the first five years. Of the original grantees

from the records of the court of chancery of North Carolina, respecting early grants of land to George Durant and George Catchmaid in what was later Perquimans precinct.

[1] Shaftesbury Papers, Colls. of S. C. Hist. Soc. V. 9. The Heath patent was never revoked by legal process. In 1696 Daniel Coxe of New Jersey came into possession of such rights as existed under it. The validity of his claims was twice acknowledged by the board of trade. In 1768, in settlement of them, the heirs of Coxe received a hundred thousand acres in Tioga and Oneida counties, New York. N. C. Recs. I. 519; N. Y. Col. Docs. VII. 926.

the Earl of Craven survived the longest.[1] Within a period
of less than twenty years the process of natural inheritance
almost entirely changed the *personnel* of the board. Their
shares passed to heirs, the transfer sometimes occasioning
litigation or necessitating appointments of trustees for heirs
who were under age. Under these conditions it was impossible to maintain the interest in the province which was felt
by the board as first organized. The transfers also brought
in men of little weight or influence, and of widely differing
opinions. Meetings were held at irregular intervals ; little
attempt, except the impractical one set forth in the Fundamental Constitutions, was made by the proprietors to
organize themselves for business. Few records were kept,
and business, so far as any was done, fell naturally into the
hands of small groups[2] within the board. These facts
explain in a large degree the vacillation which is discernible
in the policy of the Carolina proprietors, and the looseness
which characterized their administration.

Soon after the issue of the first charter to Clarendon and
his associates, negotiations were opened with them by two
groups or associations of would-be colonists. One of these
consisted of New Englanders who, in connection with certain
adventurers resident in England, had already been concerned
in a temporary settlement near Cape Fear, and wished, under
conditions agreed upon with the proprietors, to establish a
permanent colony on or near that part of the coast. The
others were colonists from Barbadoes who had sent an
explorer to the Carolina coast, and desired to remove thither
if satisfactory conditions could be obtained from the proprietors. Peter Colleton — a brother of the proprietor — and
Thomas Modyford were interested in this plan, while both
the Barbadians and the New Englanders seem to have employed Henry Vassall as an agent in England.

The ideas which the two bodies held concerning government
and the relation in which they would like to stand toward
the proprietors were not unlike. Both desired a grant of
land within the province and a distinct status therein, thus

---

[1] McCrady, South Carolina under the Proprietary Government, 268.
[2] During a part of its history, provision was made for a quorum of three.

reminding us of arrangements long before made by Gilbert
and Raleigh, and later in some cases by the London company
and the New England council. The Barbadians asked to be
called the corporation of Barbadian adventurers, and wanted
a county or "corporation" in which to settle. They also
desired that the governor and the members of the council
should be removable only by their official associates.[1] On
behalf of the New Englanders it was stated that they had
ever enjoyed the benefits granted to corporations; and
among those benefits were mentioned full liberty to choose
their own governors, and make and confirm their laws, together with immunity from all except self-imposed taxes.
In addition to unfavorable reports which were in circulation
about Cape Fear, it was said that the New Englanders would
probably abandon the enterprise if they had none of the
privileges just mentioned. The Barbadians stated that,
as many of their number were " of good quallity " and were
thus fit to manage the government, they expected " to have
sole power of electing all delligates, Governors and officers,
and making Lawes, and governing amongst themselves according to the tenor and Priviledges of the said Graunte or
charter from his Majestie. . . ." If such policy were pursued, the petitioners thought it would promote the settlement " of many other considerable corporations " within
Carolina. Colleton and Modyford suggested that the proprietors appoint persons to treat with the petitioners, and
bring them to accept the right to make by-laws only, and to
elect such officials as, for example, the county of Exeter had,
while general laws should be made by the inhabitants of the
whole province of Carolina. These suggestions,[2] together
with the design of the proprietors to secure colonists from
all possible quarters, gave a decidedly liberal tone to the
"declaration and proposals " which were issued in August,
1663. These had special reference to Cape Fear, and, so
far as provisions relating to government were concerned,
were not intended for the northern part of the province.
Besides the provisions concerning grants of land, with
proprietary reserves and a quitrent, the proprietors in this

[1] N. C. Recs. I. 40 et seq., 58.   [2] Ibid. 41, 43, 53.

document agreed that the colonists should present to them
the names of thirteen persons from whom they would appoint
one to be governor and six to be councillors.   Both governor
and councillors should hold for six years, and at the end of
that time a new list of names should be submitted.   Provision
was also made for freedom of conscience and for the election
of an assembly which should have the usual powers.   But the
New Englanders, as an association, did not take advantage of
these proposals, though there is evidence that individuals
from that section took up their residence in the settlement.[1]

Before the proprietors had come to a definite agreement
with the body of colonists from Barbadoes which first negotiated with them, a second group, led by Sir John Yeamans
and Major William Yeamans, submitted conditions.   These
were accepted in 1665, and by Yeamans and his associates a
settlement was founded near Cape Fear.

This was the beginning of Clarendon county.   But in addition to this jurisdiction the proprietors had planned, as we
have seen, for a county of Albemarle on the north, and a county
possibly to be called Craven on the south.   The provisions
of the elaborate Concessions and Agreement of 1665, which
were issued for all these counties, must now be reviewed.[2]
In this document provision was made, not only for an executive organized in a way similar to that already in existence
in Albemarle, but for the immediate calling of an assembly
and for its annual sessions thereafter.   This body, though
consisting of freeholders, was to be elected by the freemen
of the province, without designated property qualification.
The powers bestowed upon the assembly were such as to
make it from the outset the centre of the colonial government.   It could appoint its times and places of meeting,
adjourn itself, pass all laws ; establish courts and determine
their jurisdiction, together with the number of their officers,
their fees and salaries; levy all taxes and provide for the
payment of all expenses of the government ; erect baronies
and manors, with their courts ; divide the province into
counties, hundreds, and parishes, designate the amount of
land to be granted to individuals, and make rules for the

[1] N. C. Recs. I. 36–59, 144–149.   [2] *Ibid.* 77 *et seq.*

issue of such grants ; erect forts, build towns and cities, CHAP.
provide in all ways for defence, and enact all other neces- IX.
sary laws. In the exercise of their administrative powers
the governors and councils were to be guided by the laws,
were to execute them in detail, and were to see that all
subordinate officials obeyed and enforced them.

The difference between this document and any which proceeded from the Calverts or the Duke of York is very noticeable. According to these Concessions the judicial, military,
and financial systems, and the organs of local government,
were to be created by and through legislation. To the governor and other officials — the representatives of the proprietors — was left only the task of carrying into execution
the commands of the legislature. The proprietors seem not to
have thought of reserving the right of initiative. Had this
scheme been carried into permanent and complete operation,
the governments within Carolina would at once have assumed
the form which the provinces generally did not reach till
some time in the eighteenth century. From the outset the
assembly would have occupied a position which elsewhere it
won only as a result of prolonged effort and the accumulation of many precedents. Neither Lord Baltimore nor the
Duke of York committed themselves at the outset on the
subject of government. The Concessions of which we are
now speaking are the earliest example of their class, and we
know that they also served for New Jersey.

Were it not for the subsequent issue by the Carolina proprietors of the Fundamental Constitutions and their continued
attempt to enforce them, it would be natural to attribute the
issue of the Concessions and Agreement of 1665 to their
liberal views concerning colonial government. One might
argue that the development of legislatures in the other colonies, and the express recognition of parliament by the Restoration government as a permanent feature of the English
system, had convinced the proprietors that it would be best
to make all necessary concessions at the outset. In English
politics Clarendon, and especially Ashley, were standing for
such recognition of facts, while many of the letters and instructions of the board of proprietors during the early years

of its existence have a certain broad and liberal tone. But the history of the Fundamental Constitutions, as well as the hints we have concerning the origin of the "proposals" of 1663, would seem to necessitate the inference that the liberal features of the Concessions and Agreement were due as much to the Barbadians as to the proprietors. Indeed, the document itself expressly purports to be an agreement, a covenant, between proprietors and settlers as two parties, the conditions of which the proprietors promise to fulfil. In the terms of public law it was a grant, but one which was made very liberal. The reputation of the Barbadians as supporters of royal government against the Commonwealth naturally convinced the proprietors that such men would be safe custodians of power. In a suggestive letter written by the proprietors to the adventurers in January, 1665,[1] they state that William Yeamans had been very careful of the latter's advantages, and by his ingenuity, "hath prevalyed with us to consent to more than severall people would have accepted from us." But of this the proprietors declare that they did not repent, because of the forwardness of the adventurers to settle near Cape Fear and later to form another settlement south of Cape Romania. In the case of the Carolinas more spontaneousness appears on the part of the settlers, together with less rigid and continuous control by the proprietors, than is observable in the early history either of Maryland or New York.

As soon as the Concessions and Agreement were issued, Sir John Yeamans was appointed governor at Cape Fear, with jurisdiction also over all the southern part of the province. In the fall of 1665 he landed at Cape Fear a body of colonists from Barbadoes, and possibly some from others of the West India islands. Yeamans himself soon returned to Barbadoes and did not visit the colony again, except possibly in the summer of 1666, when there is some evidence that he held an assembly at Cape Fear. But the shipping, both on the first voyage and in the later voyages, suffered greatly from the storms and shoals along the coast.[2] A voyage of

[1] N. C. Recs. I. 98.
[2] *Ibid.* 95, 118 *et seq.*, 145 *et seq.*; Hawks, II. 42, map.

discovery commanded by Robert Sanford, the secretary and
register of the colony, revealed anew the attractiveness of
the coasts as far south as Port Royal. This probably
strengthened a desire, already existing in the minds of the
settlers who had come under the lead of Yeamans, to remove
to some place farther south. Though the colony of 1666 is
said to have numbered eight hundred settlers, and was
apparently on the road to permanence, dissensions existed
from the start. They arose from the presence among the
colonists of representatives of the New England interest, of
those Barbadians who had negotiated with the proprietors in
1663, as well as the larger body of Barbadians who had
secured the Concessions. The older elements complained of
the provisions in the Concessions which related to the allotment of land. They declared that these regulations not only
interfered with their antecedent rights in the soil, but that
the existence of so much waste and swampy land made an
unidecimal division of the whole by lot to appear unjust.
An appeal on the subject was sent to the proprietors, which
Yeamans neither disapproved nor openly and expressly
supported. The opposition charged him and his party with
lack of interest in Cape Fear and with the desire to remove
to the south. Under these conditions, and with practically
unanimous consent, the colony was abandoned in 1667, the
colonists withdrawing to Albemarle, Virginia, and New England. By this event Clarendon county, the middle region,
was left vacant, and the first and decisive step was taken
toward the separation of Carolina into two distinct provinces.[1]

At this juncture the Earl of Clarendon was driven from
office and from public life in England, and the Earl of
Shaftesbury, with the assistance of John Locke, became for
a few years the most active member of the board of proprietors.[2] Shaftesbury's interest was chiefly directed toward
the southern part of the province, and his efforts, together
with those of Sir John Colleton and the Barbadian adven-

[1] N. C. Recs. I. 146 *et seq.*, 159, 161.
[2] Clarendon, however, did not sell his rights as proprietor to Seth Sothell
until more than ten years later. Hawks, II. 483.

turers, resulted in the founding of the Ashley river settlements. Previous to this time the efforts of the proprietors
to settle their province had not been especially successful.
Notwithstanding liberal concessions,[1] the Cape Fear settlement had proved a failure, and Albemarle county contained
only a few hundred people. The vast coast region of the
province, with its sand-bars and narrow inlets, its deep
rivers and inaccessible stretches of swamp and forest, still
remained almost untouched. The proprietors now directed
their attention chiefly to two objects, the settlement of the
region south of Cape Carteret and the development of the
province as a whole according to the most elaborate feudal
model. In July, 1669, the Fundamental Constitutions[1] were
issued, and that with the intention that they should take the
place of all earlier concessions. Four later editions of the
Constitutions were prepared, and for the next thirty years
the proprietors made it one of the continuous objects of their
policy to induce the colonists, especially of the southern part
of the province, to accept them. They embodied a distinct
and express reaction against the liberal policy which had
hitherto characterized the attitude of the proprietors toward
the province. In the preamble it was declared that the
purpose of the proprietors in issuing them was to make the
government of the province " more agreeable to the Monarchy under which we live " and to " avoid erecting a numerous democracy."

The Fundamental Constitutions have a significance which
is derived both from what they reveal concerning the nature
of provincial institutions in general and from their influence on the history of Carolina in particular. They set
forth, more clearly than any other document we possess, the
feudal and monarchical idea of the province. Shaftesbury
repeatedly stated that he considered them the best concessions which had been issued in any colony.[2] According
to the plan which they contained, political power was, so far

[1] This set, with corrections, is printed in Shaftesbury Papers, 93. The
issue of March, 1669-1670, is in N. C. Recs. I. 187. Rivers, Historical Sketches
of South Carolina, 83.

[2] Shaftesbury Papers, 207, 399.

as possible, to be concentrated in the possession of the nobility and the proprietors.   The board of proprietors itself was organized under the headship of a count palatine, while among the remaining seven the powers of government, which in the case of Maryland were concentrated in a single hand, were distributed.   A copy in miniature of the English court, with its treasurer, chancellor, justice, high steward, constable, admiral, was thus formed.   The proprietors acting jointly as the palatine's court had, among other powers, those of appointment, pardon, and the calling of parliaments.   Each proprietor, in conjunction with certain commissions, was to be the head of a distinct court in which the business that was especially intrusted to him was transacted.   The proprietors as a whole, together with the councillors of all the proprietors' courts, formed a grand council.

The creation of this imposing executive was immediately connected with a change in the policy of the proprietors respecting the legislature.   An effort was now begun to bring it into greater harmony with the earlier traditions of the county palatine, with the feudal type of government the acceptance of which the proprietors through the Constitutions sought to enforce.   For the name "general assembly" was substituted that of "parliament."   Provision was made that it should meet biennially, and that it should consist of the proprietors or their deputies, the provincial nobility, and one representative from among the freeholders of every precinct.   The electors should possess fifty acres of land each, and the property qualification of a representative should be the ownership of five hundred acres of land lying within the precinct for which he was chosen.   The members should sit and deliberate together, but should vote in four distinct groups.   If the majority of any one of the four estates — the proprietors' deputies, the landgraves, the caciques, the representatives — should vote that a measure was not consistent with the Fundamental Constitutions, it should not pass.   Provision was also made that all matters which were to be brought before parliament should be prepared in and approved by the grand council.   This body, as we have seen, consisted of the proprietors resident in the province

— or their deputies — and the councillors of the proprietors' courts. As in Maryland, so in this plan, the right of initiative was thus reserved by the executive. The palatine court was given the right to negative acts of parliament, except in two cases, and none of its acts should go into force till ratified by the palatine or his deputy, and by three of the other proprietors or their deputies. Moreover, the legislative sphere of the parliament was much less broad than that of the general assembly as specified in the Concessions of 1665. There is no recital of its powers in the Constitutions, but from the provisions of the document in general [1] it appears that it was to have only the formal power to regulate the granting of land, the erection of manors and baronies, the establishment of offices and courts, the making of war, and the doing of other things which were specified in the Concessions as fully within the sphere of the legislature. It voted taxes, and that of course was a powerful lever; but the evident intention of the framers of the Constitutions was, by the creation of machinery above it, to reduce the power of the Carolina legislature to a shadow.[2]

Of the Constitutions, two editions were prepared: one dated March 1, and the other July 21.[3] The latter was an amended copy of the former, and was the edition which the proprietors first sent into the province as "the unalterable forme and rule of Government forever." But notwithstanding this emphatic statement, in 1687 four of the proprietors, led by the Earl of Craven, issued a statement to the effect that the text of the Constitutions which was issued in 1669 was imperfect and not considered to be final. This, however, was denied by the colonists, and it was said that in no transaction with them had the proprietors exercised greater care than in the issue of the Constitutions of 1669.[4]

With the issue of the Concessions and Agreement and of the Fundamental Constitutions the custom was initiated among the proprietors of outlining at the beginning, and in more or

---

[1] See the powers of the various proprietary courts, Art. 33, and those which follow.   [2] N. C. Recs. I. 193, 196, 199 et seq.; Arts. 33, 51, 73–79.

[3] N. C. Col. Recs. I. 187; Shaftesbury Papers, 93; Rivers, 418.

[4] Col. Recs. of S. C. Ms. II. 190; Rivers, 419.

less idealistic fashion, the general features of the system of government which they proposed to erect. The custom was imitated by the proprietors of East and West Jersey and by William Penn. It gave character to much of later proprietary history, and helps to distinguish it from that of Maryland and New York. In the last-mentioned provinces no elaborate programmes, favorable or unfavorable to popular rights, were published, but government was suffered to adjust itself to conditions as they developed. In South Carolina, the Jerseys, and Pennsylvania an effort was made by the proprietors to anticipate the course of development, and to guide it in certain definite lines. The documents in which these plans were set forth, whether known as constitutions, concessions, or frames of government, stood on the border line between instructions and statutes. They were charters of government, or *octroi* constitutions, issued under the general authority which the proprietors had received to govern their provinces. Their provisions in many cases were elaborate, and in some cases were grotesquely ill adapted to the conditions of new settlements. In the end they all had to be modified or abandoned, while the fact that they were ever issued furnishes sufficient evidence of the impractical notions of many of the proprietors. In South Carolina the efforts of the proprietors to put the Fundamental Constitutions into force were continuous and very prolonged. Partly because of the reactionary character of the document, these efforts were persistently, and in the end successfully, opposed by the colonists. Since it is true that, until after 1690, the institutional development of the province was to a large extent conditioned by this struggle, it is necessary to outline its chief features.

Actually and by means of instructions the proprietors put some of the provisions of the Constitutions wholly or partly into force in South Carolina. When the decision was reached to found a colony south of Cape Romania, the proprietors sent a blank commission to Sir John Yeamans, with the request that he would insert the name of him whom he thought most suitable for governor.[1] Yeamans, though he still

[1] Shaftesbury Papers, 117 *et seq.*; Rivers, 340–347.

retained the title of governor of Carolina, was at this time in the Barbadoes; moreover, because of his abandonment of the settlement at Cape Fear, he was distrusted by the proprietors. After having given assistance to the colonists who were about setting out from Barbadoes for Carolina, Yeamans accompanied them as far as the Bermudas, where he designated William Sayle as governor. In the documents accompanying this commission the proprietors admitted that the number of people who were expected at Port Royal would be so small that the Constitutions could not at once be put into force. There were as yet no landgraves or caciques among the colonists. For this reason, as a compromise, the proprietors, acting individually, appointed five deputies, and an instruction was issued that, as soon as they reached Carolina, the freemen should be called together and should elect five other deputies to be joined with those appointed by the proprietors to form the council. All officials were required to swear or subscribe fidelity to the proprietors and to the form of government by them established.

The instructions also provided that those who received grants of land within the province should, with their oath or declaration of fidelity, acknowledge their submission[1] to the Constitutions. This implied that the acceptance of the Constitutions was to be a condition without which colonists would not be permitted to settle in Carolina. It further implied that the proprietors intended to treat the Constitutions as executive orders, and that, if this theory prevailed, they would never be submitted to an assembly of the province for its acceptance or rejection. Many of the provisions of the document related to the organization of the council and courts, to the powers and titles of officials, to the granting of land, to the creation of a provincial nobility. These all were matters over which, after the abrogation of the Concessions and Agreement, the proprietors claimed full control.

By the instructions of 1669 provision was also made for a parliament of twenty members, elected by the freeholders of the province. Its acts, when ratified by the governor and three of the five deputies of the proprietors, should be in

[1] Rivers, 349, 420.

force as provided in the Fundamental Constitutions. According to the plan contemplated in the Constitutions, the executive should possess the sole right of initiative. This right the proprietors soon began to claim, and continued to insist upon it as long as there was any prospect that it might be secured. Considerations such as these show how the proprietors might plan to secure their object solely by executive action.

But the royal charter provided that the proprietors should legislate with the assent of an assembly. The colonists, falling back on this, insisted that the Fundamental Constitutions must be regarded as a bill, and if they were ever to go into force it must be as a statute. They did this the more promptly, because it was the only way in which they could protect themselves against the reactionary provisions of the document, and ultimately secure what had once been granted in the Concessions and Agreement. They met the proprietors substantially with the demand that the Constitutions be abandoned, or be submitted to the parliament for its action.

This demand was formulated very early. While the colonists were at Port Royal, and before they decided to abandon that place for Albemarle Point, the elective members of the council were chosen. William Owen, one of the defeated candidates, challenged the legality of the election, and it was held a second time without change of result. With Owen soon became associated William Scrivener, one of the council and a deputy of Lord Berkeley.[1] These men were dissatisfied because Yeamans had appointed Sayle, a Puritan, as governor, instead of retaining the office himself. They also came to insist, as has already been stated, that all attempts to govern according to the Constitutions, until they were accepted by the colonists, violated the provisions of the charter concerning legislation. It followed from this, as they thought, that the people of the province were still legally entitled to the benefit of the Concessions of 1665. In the light of the early acts of the proprietors there was indeed much to be said for this view, and, as has been indicated,

[1] Shaftesbury Papers, 290, 300.

it practically determined the attitude of the colonists through-out the province toward the Fundamental Constitutions.

In the summer of 1670 Governor Sayle and the council, wishing to restrain the profanation of the Sabbath and other abuses, considered whether or not, as provided in their special instructions, an assembly should be called. But they found that there were not sufficient freeholders in the settlement to admit of the election of twenty members. Therefore it was resolved that the necessary orders should be issued by the council. But while the orders were being discussed and published before an assembly of the people, Owen held an election and returned the names of those who were chosen as representatives.[1] No notice, however, was taken of this, and the orders were duly published. The dissentients then protested against the legality of this procedure, but without immediate result.

In the spring of 1671, after Sayle's death and the accession of West to the governorship as a temporary appointee, Owen and Scrivener again sought to alarm[2] the colonists, especially certain newcomers, by the plea that, as the seal of the province had not yet been received, they had no assurance of their lands unless a parliament was chosen which should pass an act in confirmation of the grants. To this the governor replied that he considered that the instructions of July, 1669, gave him sufficient authority, with the advice of the council, to guaranty estates until the seal should arrive; then all grants should be sealed. This, with the declaration that it was his intention to call a parliament when a proper time came and when it became evident that the settlement needed laws, quieted opposition. But so angered was the governor and some of the councillors by this attack that both the assailants were declared incapable of holding public office till further orders, and Scrivener was suspended from the council. That Owen and Scrivener, however, were among the most intelligent men in the colony and not mere agitators, is evidenced not only by the arguments they used, but by the fact that both of them soon appear again as members of the council. In July, 1670, a parliament was held, but of its proceedings we know nothing.

[1] Shaftesbury Papers, 176.   [2] Ibid. 293, 302, 303.

In August, 1671, after the agitation caused by Owen and Scrivener had subsided, Captain Halsted brought to the colony from the proprietors a set of temporary laws.[1] These reveal anew the fact that the board intended to force upon the province the most important provisions of the Constitutions. These temporary laws provided for an elaborate official system like that of England, for the development as rapidly as possible of the provincial nobility and its incorporation with the council, and for the exercise by the council of the right of initiation and the other powers prescribed for the grand council in the Constitutions. Parliaments were to be called biennially. The creation of landgraves also began at this time, and the governor and council were ordered to have their baronies surveyed when any of the provincial nobility should desire it.

Among the first group of landgraves was Sir John Yeamans. About the time of his elevation to that rank Yeamans appeared in the province, and by virtue of his title took a seat in the council and claimed the governorship.[2] But West's administration was popular, and Yeamans's claim was viewed with disfavor by some of the colonists. Therefore the landgrave retired to his country house in disgust, but was presently called forth by his election as speaker in the parliament which West called in the early summer of 1671. There a contest seems to have occurred between the friends of the governor and those of the landgrave. Some, notwithstanding an express instruction to the contrary,[3] thought that West's appointment had not been made in the way prescribed by the proprietors' instructions, and the parliament was for a time irregularly adjourned in order to permit a general discussion of the question. At the close of this discussion Yeamans announced that, according to the instructions, the consent[4] of three of the appointed deputies was required to confirm the acts of the parliament; but only two,

[1] Rivers, 351–369 ; Shaftesbury Papers, 322 *et seq.*

[2] Shaftesbury Papers, 337 *et seq.*

[3] *Ibid.* 119.

[4] See commission and instructions to Sayle, *ibid.* 118, 121.   Also West's account of these events, *ibid.* 337.

besides West himself, who was deputy for the Duke of Albe-marle, were living. The way out, as suggested by Yeamans, was that West should resign the office of governor and act as the third deputy. But this West declined to do. Then the parliament broke up, and the recently elected members of the council also withdrew from service. West at once ordered the parliament to meet again to elect members of the council, and in this body Yeamans urged the choice of such men as would " stand at the greatest distance from the Governor."

In December, 1671, Yeamans in the council declared [1] that, as sole landgrave who was resident in the province, he was vice-palatine and hence entitled to the governorship. But it was resolved to make no change till positive directions came from the proprietors. They, as the event proved, had already taken action; for, as soon as they heard of the death of Governor Sayle, they issued a commission to Yeamans as his successor. This reached [2] Carolina in April, 1672, and at once terminated West's first administration. In the instructions which were sent over at the time, the enforcement of the Constitutions and temporary laws was again commanded, and in particular the maintenance of the initiative of the council was required. " For there is nothing to be debated or voted by the Parliament but what is pro-posed to them by the Council." John Culpepper came into office as surveyor-general when Yeamans received his com-mission as governor.

In the governmental system of South Carolina as actually organized the unique feature was the council, which took the place of the grand council of the Constitutions. Its organization, consisting one-half of appointed and one-half [3] of elected members, has already been described. The intro-duction of the elected members involved an important departure from the form of the executive which existed in Maryland and New York. Though the introduction of this

---

[1] Shaftesbury Papers, 359, 360.

[2] Calendar of State Papers, 1669–1674, Aug. 21, 1671 ; Shaftesbury Papers, 330, 367.

[3] Shaftesbury Papers, 323, 367.

group of members was a temporary device, they continued to form a part of the council for twenty years. They were elected by the parliament for an indefinite term, and in their case, as well as in that of the deputies, the right of removal was vested in the proprietors. Through them it was possible for the parliament and the colonists to make their wishes felt in the deliberations of the colonial executive. They tended to ally the council with the colonists. The council, as thus organized, could prepare bills for the assembly, expend money which had been voted by the parliament, levy military forces, and declare war or conclude treaties with the Indians. Its functions were almost legislative in character.

In addition to their place in the grand council the deputies of the proprietors were also organized as a substitute for the palatine's court. As such they could call, and later prorogue or dissolve parliaments, pardon offences, elect to offices which were at the palatine's disposal, erect forts, expend funds which were not specifically appropriated, negative acts of the grand council and assembly, and consent to legislation. In short, they could exercise all powers which were not otherwise granted. With the governor they constituted a majority in the grand council.[1] Though in the history of the province we hear but little of the palatine's court, it is evident that in the plan of the Fundamental Constitutions it was intended to be a stronger body than the council.

Another feature of the council, of which we hear more in the records of the time, was this: As provided in the "temporary laws" of 1671 and 1672 the governor was named by the palatine, while each of the deputies was the nominee of an individual proprietor. This fact was held by Shaftesbury[2] at least to give the deputies a certain equality with the governor. The governor might be regarded as himself only a deputy. The expression of this view by Shaftesbury was occasioned by efforts of Yeamans to play an unusually prominent part as governor. He prepared or set on foot several improvements, such as the building of works of de-

[1] Bassett, in Johns Hopkins University Studies, XII. 148 ; N. C. Col. Recs. I. 193, 239.

[2] Shaftesbury Papers, 401.

fence, organizing a militia, building a house for the governor and one for the entertainment of strangers.[1] These would involve larger expenditure and would call for additional contributions from the proprietors. Yeamans was also charged with subordinating the interests of Carolina to those of the Barbadoes and his own trade with that island. The letters of West and others informed the proprietors of the controversies which had preceded Yeamans's appointment and of his ambitious policy as governor. This drew from Shaftesbury the statement that the distinction between the governor and the rest of the deputies was " a thing rather of order than of overruling power," and the governor had no more right than any of the council to depart from the rules laid down by the proprietors. In the face even of a pro-prietor as governor the deputies should maintain the rights of the proprietary board, and not become partisans of the chief magistrate. This certainly emphasizes the conciliar element in Carolina to an extent which would scarcely have been possible in Maryland or New York. When this is taken in connection with the fact that the governor and council, so far as possible, exercised the right of initiating legisla-tion, and that the council sometimes practically named the governor, one sees that the proprietors were justified in terming the council the " Senate of Carolina," as they some-times did.[2] But the event showed that the affiliations be-tween the council — half elective as it was — and the commons in parliament were so strong that they stood together as a unit against the acceptance of the Fundamental Constitutions. The proprietors' deputies were *ex officio* members of parlia-ment, but the elected councillors necessarily had no seats there.[3]

Of West, Shaftesbury spoke in high terms, and presently added to his offices of storekeeper and deputy that of reg-ister or secretary. As the reports came in of the alleged extravagant schemes of Yeamans, the proprietors began to look about for his successor. In 1674 they made West a landgrave and appointed him governor.[4] At the same time

---

[1] Shaftesbury Papers, 397, 416.   [3] Shaftesbury Papers, 405.
[2] Rivers, 396.   [4] Colonial Papers, 1669–1674, April 25, 1674.

seven of the proprietors adopted articles binding themselves
to contribute annually £100 each for the period of seven
years, to be expended partly in reducing the debts due from
the board on previous expenditures and the rest in supplies
which should be sent to the province for sale through an
agent.   This step was accompanied by repeated statements
to the effect that they expected the province to soon become
self-supporting and would incur no more debts among its
inhabitants.[1]   A return of eight per cent on their invest-
ment was expected.   A set of agrarian laws, sent over at
this time, provided for the laying out of seigniories, baronies,
and colonies along the course of rivers in such proportions
as to give the proprietors and nobility two-fifths of the land.

In 1682, under the influence of Benjamin Blake, Daniel
Axtell, and Joseph Morton, a body of several hundred
Presbyterians and other dissenters came to South Carolina
from Somersetshire and other districts in England.   Their
purpose was to escape from the dangers which they feared
would result from the prospective Catholic revival in England.   In reward for their services the leaders of this
enterprise were made landgraves, while Morton was in
addition made governor.

A few months later certain Scotch Presbyterians, in
order to escape from persecution by the Duke of York
and Claverhouse at home, proposed to remove to the province under the lead of Lord Cardross.   Though the number
who actually came was not large, an emigration of several
thousand was expected.   In order to encourage them in this
plan, the proprietors made a few changes in the Fundamental Constitutions.   Of these the most important was one
providing that, in case the council should neglect to propose fitting laws to be passed by parliament, the grand juries
of the counties should submit the desired propositions; if
the council should then neglect to initiate them, the parliament itself might take them up and pass them.[2]   A
prospect of exemption from the payment of rent after 1689
was also extended to settlers.   This slightly liberalized edition of the Constitutions was now twice submitted in various

[1] Shaftesbury Papers, 431–438 ; Rivers, 356.   [2] Rivers, 396, 409.

ways to the colonists. Among the elaborate orders which
were issued for the granting of land was one repeating the
condition that no one should receive an allotment until he
had sworn submission to the Constitutions. This also was
made a condition of admission to the council. The Scotch
settled their colony at the fated Port Royal, where they
were permitted to establish themselves to a large extent
independent of the Ashley river settlement. Lord Cardross even claimed authority coördinate with that of the
officials at Charlestown. This, when taken in connection
with the natural aversion of Englishmen at that time
toward the Scotch, and the fact that the advent of the
new colonists had been accompanied by a renewed attempt
to put the Fundamental Constitutions into force, occasioned
much jealousy toward the new settlers. How serious or
prolonged this might have become the brief existence of
the new settlement makes it impossible to affirm. The
really important consequence of the advent of the Scotch
appears in the fact that it contributed toward the development of a system of local government in the province.

In 1682 the proprietors ordered that the province should
be divided into three counties, Berkeley, Colleton, and
Craven. Berkeley county should embrace Charlestown and
extend from Sewee bay on the north to Stono creek on the
south. Colleton was located to the south of this and Craven
to the north. Though Colleton county was intended to
include the Scotch settlement at Port Royal, not until near
the close of the colonial period were steps taken to organize
local government for any of the counties except Berkeley.
Those, we shall see, were extremely imperfect. Until 1683
elections for parliament were held exclusively at Charlestown, freeholders coming thither from all the settlements
to vote, or sending their proxies. This was now becoming
a great hardship or an impossibility. An order was therefore issued that votes in the election of 1683 should be
polled, not only at Charlestown, but at London in Colleton
county.[1] In order to avoid attempts to vote in both counties,
they also ordered that voting at the two localities should

[1] S. C. Public Recs. Ms. I. 242 ; Rivers, 135.

occur on the same day.   Ten members should be chosen
from each of the counties.

The first part of the instruction was satisfactory to the
colonists at Ashley river, but the second requirement, which
gave to the sparsely settled Colleton equal representation
with Berkeley county, aroused their opposition.   Governor
Morton and the council showed their sympathy with the
settlement on Ashley river by disregarding the instruction
and holding the election as usual.   The parliament thus
chosen passed several acts, among them being one for the
protection of the colonists against prosecution for debts
contracted out of the colony.   This, as well as the conduct
of the governor and council concerning the election, greatly
offended the proprietors, and they ordered that the parliament should be dissolved and no other chosen except in
compliance with their instructions.   Governor Morton was
removed from office, and a successor for him was diligently
sought.   Sir Richard Kyrle, a knight of Ireland, was appointed, but died six months after his arrival in America.
Robert Quarry, afterward prominent in the admiralty and
customs service, was elected to the office by the council, and
discharged its duties for a brief time, though without appointment from the proprietors.   Quarry, however, was soon
charged with harboring pirates, and in September, 1685,
West entered upon a brief third term as governor.   He
became involved in the controversy over the payment of
quitrents, to which reference has been made in another
connection.   To him also the proprietors repeated their
orders, that the revised Constitutions of 1682 should be
subscribed and put into force.   Realizing that the task imposed upon him was hopeless, West very soon resigned the
office and left the colony.[1]

Landgrave Morton was now restored to office, and called
the parliament together in November, 1685.   In obedience
to instructions he required its members to subscribe the Constitutions of 1682.   Twelve of the nineteen representatives
refused to do so, on the plea that they had already subscribed
those of 1669.   Thereupon Governor Morton expelled them

[1] 5 Colls. Mass. Hist. Soc. V. 116, Sewall's Diary.

from the house. The remaining seven, with the deputies, transacted the business of the session. But these measures were to no purpose. It was again found impossible to procure the acceptance of the Constitutions by the colonists, and Morton in his turn had to give way to James Colleton, a brother of the proprietor.

In the summer of 1686 a Spanish force from Saint Augustine made a descent upon the coast, plundering the country about the Edisto river and destroying Stuart Town, the settlement of the Scotch at Port Royal. The colonists at Charlestown and vicinity, forgetting for the time their domestic quarrels and their disputes with the proprietors, under the lead of Morton began fitting out an expedition of reprisal against Saint Augustine. They were absorbed in the task when Colleton arrived and assumed the governorship.

The governors who preceded Colleton had been provincials themselves, or men who identified themselves quite fully with the colonists. Colleton, though he had been a resident in Barbadoes,[1] was the first who failed conspicuously in this respect. His failure, however, is partly to be accounted for by the attitude which he found it necessary to assume toward the expedition against Saint Augustine. As England and Spain were then at peace, Colleton felt compelled to forbid the expedition, though the colonists considered that their honor demanded its prosecution. The governor thereupon threatened to hang any who persisted in it, and by this means forced its abandonment. In their chagrin some of the colonists later attributed his course of action to the desire for "a little filthy lucre" which might accrue from Spanish trade.

Colleton was a man of resolution, capable of arbitrary measures and made bold by his consciousness of the support of the proprietors. Through him they made one more effort to procure an acceptance of the Fundamental Constitutions. In the parliaments of 1686 and 1687 a committee undertook the task of proposing such changes as would make them acceptable, but their report soon became so voluminous that

[1] Colonial Papers, 1675–1676, 169, 210, 254.

it was laid aside. Then Colleton, "in some passion," produced a letter from the proprietors in which, apparently
because of their desire to secure the acceptance of the
revision of 1682, they repudiated the edition of 1669 as an
imperfect copy. The elected members of parliament then
unanimously declared that the government should be directed
solely according to the royal charter. They even went so
far as to deny to the council the right of initiative. But
during two sessions the proprietary deputies insisted on
maintaining the initiative. Finally the proprietors ordered
Colleton to call no more parliaments without instruction
from them, unless some very extraordinary occasion required
it. Therefore no laws were passed, the temporary laws were
allowed to expire, and by 1690 no statute was in force in the
province.

Colleton now undertook to govern the province alone, or
with the aid of the appointed deputies, who he knew would
support him. His rigorous exaction of quitrents, prohibition of the Indian trade, and punishment of discussion
provoked an uprising. Paul Grimball, the secretary, was
imprisoned and all the records were seized. On the inspired
petition of a number of colonists and the advice of the proprietors' deputies, and without calling the parliament, Colleton now proclaimed martial law. But so strong was the
feeling in opposition to him, that he did not dare to attempt
its enforcement or to keep the civil courts closed. In fact,
it was only through the people acting as a militia that martial law could be enforced, and they were well-nigh unanimous in opposition to it.[1] Government had practically
broken down, when Seth Sothell, the proprietor who had
bought the share of the Earl of Shaftesbury, arrived as a
fugitive from the Albemarle settlement.

The proprietors had already abandoned Colleton and had
appointed Thomas Smith governor. He was one of the
richest men in the province, and was soon after made landgrave. But Sothell brought with him a certificate of the
proprietors that, by virtue of the clause in the Fundamental
Constitutions which provided that the oldest proprietor who

[1] Rivers, 416, 423 ; Statutes of South Carolina, II. 49.

happened to be resident in Carolina should be governor, he must be obeyed as such. If the Constitutions, so dear to the proprietors, were to be obeyed, Sothell's claim must be recognized. But Sothell came as a refugee from the Albemarle settlement, whence he had been banished for alleged rapacity and gross misgovernment. Colleton and his adherents at once arrayed themselves against him. The opponents of Colleton, led by Andrew Percival, by Muschamp, the king's collector of customs, and by others, supported Sothell in the hope thereby of escaping from the tyranny of Colleton. Sothell assumed the governorship, removed the deputies who opposed him, and called a parliament.

A violent conflict now ensued between the Sothell and Colleton factions. Sothell was publicly charged with treason, and the colonists were called upon to refuse obedience to his authority. But the parliament supported Sothell. He removed some of the deputies and procured from the parliament acts banishing Colleton and disqualifying Bull, Grimball, and Charles Colleton — who had recommended the proclamation of martial law — from holding office. By an unprecedented assumption of authority the ex-governor was required by an act of assembly to present himself for trial before the king's bench at Westminster. But, notwithstanding the arbitrary character of some of those measures, a considerable number of laws [1] were passed by Sothell's parliament which were of decided utility for the province. They related to the militia and defence of the province in general, to the building of roads, to taxation and the regulation of trade, to the fees of the governor, while among them was one for the naturalization of French and Swiss Protestants among the colonists. However questionable had been his career in Albemarle, Sothell's conduct at Charlestown, so far as we know it, redounds to his credit.

But the proprietors, notwithstanding the provision of the Constitutions, refused to recognize Sothell, though at first they did not go farther than to order him to come home and answer charges. This command he did not obey. All the acts passed by his parliament relating to officials, courts, and

[1] Statutes of South Carolina, II. 39–73.

elections were disallowed.   This not only left the French
and Swiss aliens as before, but defeated the efforts of Colleton's opponents to punish him and his associates.   After
Sothell had been in office about thirteen months, 1690–1691,
he was ordered to give place to Philip Ludwell, who was
formerly secretary of Virginia and an adherent of Governor
Berkeley.   From him an adjustment and quieting of strife
within the province was expected.

The accession of Ludwell to office marks the beginning of
a change in the course of Carolina history.   Both public and
private instructions[1] in elaborate form were given to him,
and for more than a decade thereafter these orders were
referred to as standing rules of government.   In the instructions themselves the proprietors state that they intend them
to make void in the southern part of the province all former
orders and temporary laws, and to be the only rule of government, save in the granting of land, till they should otherwise direct.   Though the proprietors were not yet ready to
abandon the Fundamental Constitutions, the drift was now
clearly away from them and toward a government under the
royal charter, which should retain only the features that
were generally found useful in a proprietary province.   The
policy hitherto followed by the proprietors had made it
impossible for government in South Carolina to reach even
tolerably stable conditions.   Recent experience had shown
that the province at any time might fall a prey to despotism
or anarchy, though its position on a disturbed frontier made
stability and internal peace doubly necessary.   Governors
had followed each other in rapid succession, but without
bringing internal peace.   Though the expulsion of Colleton
was immediately due to the timely appearance of Sothell, it
was an event so unusual as to call for serious attention.   By
heading a faction in the province Sothell had been able to
defy the proprietors for more than a year.   After such
events no one need have been surprised if the rule of the
proprietors had been thrown off at any time.   It was already
more nominal than real.

By a most important communication, which was addressed

[1] N. C. Recs. I. 373.

to Sothell by the leaders of the opposition in the province, much light is thrown on the workings of the proprietary system. "Most of the Gentlemen of this Countrey," say the writers,[1] "are soe unhappy as not to know the Lords Proprietors, or to have any Correspondence with any except one or two of them, and they are discouraged from writeinge to those too, because they have not agreed in opinion with them concerning fundamentall Constitutions, Indentures for land and in matters of orderinge the Indian Trade, but when they have writt freely their minds have been chekt, and some dealt hardly with therefore. And the letters sent to the Lords Proprietors from the Councill, sealed and signed by the Commoners, have not been believed, and others not delivered but misrepresented by construction made according to the Letter of those four or five persons here who must, and we had almost said, dare not write but as shall please those who direct them. For though most of them be Lords Deputyes, yett they are putt in by the Governor here, and their persons and dangerous insufficiencies wholely unknown to the Lords who they represent. And this it is that these men which most of them here are known to be extremely preverse or ignorant men, are the only informers of matters here; which, however, would not bee of soe bad a consequence, if other persons could have an opportunity to speak for themselves. . . ." This statement doubtless has a partisan coloring. But in spite of that it clearly reveals the source of weakness and failure in proprietary rule.

Though in the instructions to Ludwell several features of the Fundamental Constitutions were retained, the document itself was not expressly mentioned. In the private instructions the proprietors state that both Sothell and the people of Carolina had violated the Constitutions, and that Matthews, who claimed to be an agent of the colonists, had told them that the Constitutions were not recognized by the people of the province. Therefore, they add, "Wee have made your Instructions sutable to our Charter from the Crówne." This, however, did not mean the total abandonment of the Constitutions, though it foreshadowed such a result.

[1] Rivers, 426.

Until this time, and even in the instructions to Ludwell, the proprietors clung to the exclusive right of initiative. Though the existence of an elective element in the council had helped to make such a claim endurable, the colonists had repeatedly ignored the pretension. The instructions to Ludwell stated that the governor's council should consist of the proprietors' deputies, thus implying that it should no longer contain an elective element. The inference is confirmed by the first clause of the private instructions, in which the governor was forbidden to call the grand council till the colonists should consent that it initiate legislation — which would be never. This act was the precursor of a concession in the matter of the initiative. On assuming office in 1693, Governor Thomas Smith informed [1] the legislature that the proprietors had consented that the right of initiating laws should be shared between the governor and council on the one hand and the assembly on the other. About this time also the terms "general assembly" and "commons house of assembly" came into general use, showing that the legislature had become permanently divided into two houses. With this naturally went the changes just referred to in the organization of the council and in the right of initiative. Full authority was also given the governor in these instructions to erect county courts and appoint the officials who were necessary for them. Provision was also made for the multiplication of counties as the growth of population should necessitate.

Since Ludwell's authority extended over Albemarle, as well as over the southern counties, he was empowered to summon representatives from them all to a general assembly. But if it should prove impossible for members to attend from Albemarle, — as was actually the case, — he was then authorized to summon seven delegates each from Berkeley and Colleton counties and six delegates from Craven county. By the settlement, since 1685, of Huguenot exiles on the Santee the population of South Carolina had expanded toward the north, and now it was possible to begin the organization of a third county. But as the Huguenots,

[1] Rivers, 171.

owing to the repeal of the act of Sothell's parliament, had
not yet been naturalized, the instruction empowering them
to elect representatives occasioned an outcry against alien
rule. The six Huguenots from Craven county took their
seats, but the assembly proved to be no more subservient
than its predecessors had been. It passed an act giving the
suffrage to every man in the province who was worth £10,
irrespective of the time during which he had been a resident.
Though Ludwell accepted this, it, with an act providing for
the drawing of jurymen, was disallowed by the proprietors.
The assembly demanded an act of oblivion and a confirmation
of the judicial proceedings of the late administration. But
before that resolve reached them the proprietors had issued
a general pardon for all concerned in the late disturbances,
except James Moore and Robert Daniel, two of the leaders
of the opposition in Berkeley county.[1]

During the discussion over indemnity the assembly, in
response to an instruction, presented a statement[2] of grievances which touched all the main points at issue between
them and the proprietors. The most important complaints
were directed against the claim of the proprietors to legislate
for the province by fixing the jurisdiction of courts, putting
in force through the palatine court in Carolina such English
statutes as they saw fit to select, attempting to govern in
general by martial law, prescribing the number of representatives in the assembly. The assembly complained of the
existence of two palatine courts, — one in England and the
other in Carolina, — for one often negatived acts which
the other had approved. Other complaints were directed
against the recent change in the form of land grants, and
against several matters of detail. Though these complaints
brought no specific or immediate acts of redress, yet the
proprietors, both publicly and privately, began to admit that
it would be necessary to govern according to the charter.
But at the same time they yielded only so far as it was
necessary so to do. They retained the agrarian laws intact.
Also in a special instruction to Ludwell, accompanying the

[1] Daniel, however, appears later as an ardent churchman and as deputy
governor.   [2] Rivers, 433.

disallowance of Sothell's acts, they forbade[1] the publication as laws of acts making changes in courts, juries, officials, and elections until they had confirmed them in England. Ludwell made concessions to the popular demand respecting the form of deed which should be used in land grants. He also approved of an *habeas corpus* act, an act relating to juries, as well as the one lowering the qualifications for the suffrage. Because of their dissatisfaction with these acts, and particularly with the one last named, the proprietors removed Ludwell, after he had been in office about a year. But his successor, Thomas Smith, though one of the most prominent men among the proprietary party in the province, because of the revival of the controversy over the payment of quitrents, soon threw up the office in despair.

John Archdale, one of the proprietors, was then sent over for the purpose, if possible, of restoring harmony. The question of quitrents was then uppermost. By the new governor's conciliatory attitude and the concessions which he was empowered to make in reference to land grants, he allayed strife and won considerable personal popularity. His successor, Joseph Blake, also enjoyed a quiet administration, which continued from 1694 till the close of 1700. During that time the final revision of the Fundamental Constitutions was submitted[2] to the commons in assembly for acceptance. The articles concerning manors, leet-men, the system of proprietors' courts, and certain other features of the system had been omitted, though the provisions for a nobility remained. The whole was reduced to forty-two articles, and their acceptance without change was requested. But a committee of the assembly proposed several amendments, which were directed against the right of the nobility to sit in the legislature and the size of their baronies, while they were intended to secure to the people their lands at the existing rents and prices. These proposals caused the proprietors to again lay aside the Constitutions, and thereafter they never appeared as an issue in Carolina politics.[3]

[1] Rivers, 435. [2] *Ibid.* 186.

[3] The proprietors continued to refer to them in later instructions, and occasionally created landgraves and caciques, till as late as 1718. But

The earliest phase of the conflict between the executive
and the colonists in that province thus reached its close.

The civil list in South Carolina, as in the other provinces,
comprised the secretary or register, the surveyor-general, the
receiver and treasurer, sheriffs, and justices.   These offices
were held under appointment from the proprietors or from
their governors.   The officials acted under commissions and
instructions substantially as in other provinces.   As the
bestowment of baronies was not followed by the establishment of manorial courts, and only in a few instances by
settlement, local government long remained undeveloped.

Just after the religious controversy of the years 1704 to
1706 had closed, the lower house secured and held for a
number of years the exclusive right of naming the treasurer
or public receiver, also the comptroller of the duties, the
powder receiver, and all other officials who received fixed
salaries from the public treasury.   Originally the treasurer
or receiver of the province had been appointed by one or
more of the proprietors under the articles in the Fundamental Constitutions which provided for a treasurer's court.[1]
But as early as 1691, and perhaps earlier, this official was
named in the revenue acts.[2]   In the act levying duties for
1703 George Logan was thus appointed, and, as the act was
continued till 1707, he retained the office until that year.
But since in the church controversy Logan had chosen the
side of the dissenters, Governor Johnson resolved that he
should give place to some one else.   But the commons house,
in which the dissenters now had the majority, insisted that
he should be continued in office.   To Johnson's suggestion
of Major Parris for the place, they replied by charging the
governor with trying to abridge their just right of control
over the public moneys.   They also believed that such control would be much safer in their own hands than in those
of governors, many of whom were "needy courtiers come

they never again sought to procure the acceptance of the Constitutions.
See instructions to Governor Johnson in 1702, N. C. Recs. I. 556.   With the
issue of instructions to Tynte and Hyde, references to the Constitutions
wholly disappear.

[1] N. C. Recs. I. 195 ; Shaftesbury Papers, 324, 404.
[2] Statutes, II. 65.

abroad to enrich themselves." In the course of the long dispute which followed the assembly refused to submit the question to the proprietors, but expressed themselves as ready to lay it before the queen and parliament for final decision. To this the governor assented, agreeing also to admit for the time being that the assembly possessed the sole right to appoint the receiver, provided it would not appoint Logan or any one else who during the recent troubles had made himself personally obnoxious to the government. But the house would not abandon Logan, though later he voluntarily withdrew from the contest. Then the house prepared and hastily passed an act declaring its right for the time being to name the public receiver and the other officials to whom reference has been made.[1] This was accepted by the governor. Captain George Smith was then elected receiver, the house not even recognizing a proposal of the governor to approve the selection. The act remained in the hands of the proprietors till 1718, when it was repealed. But the repeal was disregarded, and by a law of 1720 the act was declared to be still in force. But in 1721 another act was passed, vesting again the right of appointing the receiver, comptroller, and other designated officials in the general assembly. This continued to be the law during the period of royal government, though the share borne by the commons in the selection of these officials was far greater than that exercised by the other components of the legislature.[2]

[1] Statutes, II. 299, title only.
[2] Smith, South Carolina as a Royal Province, 15-20.

CHAPTER X

CAROLINA AS A PROPRIETARY PROVINCE. THE ALBE-
MARLE SETTLEMENT, NORTH CAROLINA

PART
III.

WHILE the experiments at Cape Fear and on Ashley river were in progress, another colony was slowly developing on Albemarle sound and Chowan river. Its inhabitants came from Virginia and New England, a few from Bermuda, a few also from various parts of the British Isles. At a later time this colony was strengthened and extended southward to the Pamlico and Neuse rivers by French Protestants, Swiss, and Germans from the Palatinate. But during the period of which we are now speaking its population was English, was chiefly of colonial origin, and numbered only a few hundreds. As occurred elsewhere, especially in the colonies south of the Delaware river, the people of this province established themselves in straggling settlements or detached plantations along the courses of the rivers and sounds. So peaceful was the attitude of the natives during the first generation, that the colonists were not forced to seek protection in compact settlements. They were also kept apart by the deep streams and broad sheets of water which intersected the country from east to west. These streams facilitated travel to and from the coast; but to intercourse and the building of roads along north and south lines, or along east and west lines north of Albemarle sound, they presented almost as serious obstacles as did the forests themselves. The sandy and treacherous coast line proved an hindrance, as in the days of Raleigh, to settlement from Europe.

When the redoubtable James Blair came to the Albemarle country as a missionary, in 1704, he found "mighty incon-

232

veniences in travelling there."[1] He stated that the roads
were not only "deep and difficult to be found," but that
there were seven great rivers in the country, five of which
could not be crossed with the aid of horses alone. Over one
of the other two the Quakers had established a ferry, but
nobody except themselves was permitted to use it. Along
the banks of these streams settlers were then scattered for a
distance in each case of twenty miles or more, while the land
back from the streams was almost wholly unimproved. Blair
declared that he would sooner undertake a journey from
England to Holland, than to go from the Albemarle settlements to those on the Pamlico ; for the only means of transportation across the upper sound which intervened was a
small periagua, while beyond lay a wilderness fifty miles
broad. These statements are confirmed by the accounts of
other missionaries[2] who remained longer in the country than
did Blair.

The proprietors indeed, as we have seen, treated this part
of their province with systematic neglect, and after 1670
their efforts were concentrated on the development of the
southern part of their dominion.   In a letter of theirs written in 1676 we find it stated that the reason of this neglect
was the failure of the inhabitants of Albemarle to settle the
region of the Pamlico and Neuse rivers, so that by this means
intercourse might have been made possible between the
northern and southern parts of the province. The proprietors stated in 1676[3] that, because of their failure to do this,
they looked upon the settlers of Albemarle as a people that
neither understood their own interests nor regarded those of
the proprietors. They admit, however, that they had recently learned their mistake, for they had been told that it
was not the people, but Governor Carteret and the officials,
who were to blame. When attempts had been made to open
communication by land with Ashley river and to settle the
Neuse country, they had been repressed by these officials
with great violence. Some who had settled on the south

[1] N. C. Recs. I. 600.
[2] See letter of Rev. William Gordon, N. C. Recs. I. 708 *et seq.*
[3] N. C. Recs. I. 228.

side of Albemarle sound had been ordered to return, though to their great inconvenience.

These statements reveal a lack of observation and a perversity of reasoning which is unusual, even for this group of proprietors. Had they lived in the country, as Blair did, they would have perceived the reason why the middle region was not filled with settlers. It could be entered successfully only from the coast, and not from the north or the south. The streams and shoals of Cape Hatteras checked communication by sea, and the forests and broad, deep rivers had a similar influence on land. The failure of the experiment at Cape Fear naturally diverted attention for a long time from the coast at that point. All who cared to settle in Carolina were more satisfactorily provided for in other places. Carteret was in office for only a short period; and had the course of settlement tended strongly toward the middle country, we may be sure that the governors would not have had the desire or the power to stay its progress for any long period. At no time did colonists flow into the Carolinas — especially North Carolina — in a vigorous stream, and the current was not strong enough to break through the natural obstacles. Settlements crept slowly back from the coast, and spread out laterally even more slowly. Both colonies existed largely in isolation till late in the colonial period. The backwardness of North Carolina is to be accounted for in part by its isolation.

The extent to which the board of proprietors neglected Albemarle is indicated by a reference to the idea, which prevailed in that region, that Sir William Berkeley was the only proprietor. It was for this reason, as we shall see, that Thomas Miller was sent to Virginia to be tried for treason. A rumor was also abroad, which this letter was intended to discredit, that the proprietors desired to sell Albemarle. They declared that they intended to keep the province intact, and Albemarle, particularly because of its nearness to Virginia, they believed was a material aid in the peopling of the rest of Carolina.

Though the forms of a proprietary government were kept up and the proprietors expressed themselves as pleased with some things that were done, yet there was such lack of system and continuity in their control that a great degree of independence was enjoyed by the colonists. The characteristic features of the proprietary system were to a large extent obscured. Aristocratic elements and tendencies were almost wholly lacking. Such was the weakness of the executive and the lack of developed institutions and traditions, that conditions akin to anarchy sometimes prevailed.

At the outset it was thought that this colony might be organized under two governments, one on the south and the other on the north side of the sound. Sir William Berkeley, governor of Virginia and one of the proprietors, was empowered to appoint a governor and six councillors for each of these settlements. The proprietors reserved to themselves the appointment of a secretary and surveyors, while the governor and councillors were to appoint all other officers. In the granting of land the officials were to be guided in a general way by the "proposals" of 1663. Understanding that the earlier settlers in the Albemarle region had already purchased large tracts from the Indians, the proprietors, fearing that these might be kept out of the market, instructed Berkeley, if possible, to induce those who held by Indian title to take out patents from the proprietors and to be content with the proportions allotted to others. In the fall of 1664 Berkeley appointed William Drummond, a former resident of Virginia, as governor of the entire settlement. For reasons just stated the colony for a considerable time was confined wholly to the northern shore of the sound. An assembly was held, possibly in 1665, but all of its records have perished.[1] From a later source it is inferred that since the time was near for the payment of quitrents to begin, this assembly petitioned the proprietors that the inhabitants of the county of Albemarle might hold their lands on the same terms as those under which land was held in Virginia.

Drummond, after a governorship of three years, is supposed to have been removed by Berkeley. In the autumn of 1667 the proprietors, acting, it is possible, under the advice of Berkeley, and on suggestions from the colonists, appointed

[1] N. C. Recs. I. 48–67; Hawks, History of North Carolina, II. 452.

Samuel Stephens governor of Albemarle.[1] He was given
authority to select a council, and, if the proprietors failed to
act, a secretary and surveyor-general, all to serve during the
pleasure of the board. The instructions issued to Stephens
were the Concessions of 1665, though in 1668 these were
partially superseded by the provisions of the Great Deed of
Grant relating to land.

That an assembly was held in 1669 is made more probable
by the existence of nine acts,[2] which were confirmed by the
proprietors in January, 1670, and which contain references
to landgraves and caciques and to the count palatine as the
head of the proprietary board. None of these provided for
the establishment of offices or courts, or in any way changed
the government of the colony. In one of them the court
of the governor and council is referred to as in existence ;
this was to be expected, and it was probably the only judicial
body in the little group of settlements. Provision was made
in the laws for the collection of thirty pounds of tobacco as a
part of the costs of every suit at law, and that this should go
for the support of the governor and council. The chief object of the laws was the encouraging of settlement by the
temporary exemption of newcomers from the payment of
taxes and from prosecution in suits originating outside the
colony, and by provisions limiting the size of grants to commoners and requiring the speedy improvement of grants.

When the Fundamental Constitutions were sent over, substantially the same instructions were given to the governor
and council of Albemarle as to those of the southern colony.
The ten deputies, five appointed and five elected, now became the grand council, while the governor and the five appointed deputies acted as the palatine's court. The governor
and the council were empowered to establish such courts as
they saw fit, until the " grand modell " could be put into force;
they were also authorized, with the consent of an assembly,
to make necessary laws. Albemarle was divided into four
precincts, from each of which five delegates were elected,
who with the deputies constituted the assembly. We know
that an assembly was held in 1672, and another in 1673.[3]

[1] N. C. Recs. I. 163, 165.   [2] *Ibid.* 183, 238.   [3] *Ibid.* 181, 218, 219.

The former passed at least fifty-four acts, all of which are
lost.   Four acts of no great importance, passed by the assembly of 1673, were received by the proprietors in November
of that year.   The form of enactment was, "by the Pallatine
and the rest of the Lords Proprietors by and with the advice
and consent of the Grand Assembly."   The name "parliament" was not used.

In 1677 we get the first view of the political and social
conditions which existed in the Albemarle settlements.   For
this we are indebted to the representations[1] made to the
proprietors and to the home government by the various parties who were concerned in the so-called Culpepper rebellion.
At the time the number of tithables, or working hands between the ages of sixteen and sixty, was about 1400,[2] of
whom one-third were Indians, negroes, and women.   Estimated upon this basis, it is supposed that the total population was between 2500 and 3000.   About 800,000 pounds
of tobacco were annually raised on the plantations of the
colony, besides an abundance of cattle and Indian corn.
Those were the chief products of a population which was
almost wholly agricultural.   The tobacco was a valuable
article of export, in return for which European goods and
materials were obtained.   As the nature of the coast prevented large craft from entering, small vessels from New
England and Virginia took the tobacco to these colonies,
whence it was shipped, in large part at least, direct to the
continent, and goods were brought back on the return
voyages.   New Englanders and many residents of Albemarle, notably Valentine Bird, the collector, and George
Durant, the first settler, were interested in this illegal
trade.   Governor Peter Carteret, who was a relative of the
proprietor and had been chosen by the grand council to suc-
ceed Stephens, on his return to England was charged by the
proprietors with encouraging the New England trade and
discouraging settlement south of Albemarle sound.   John
Jenkins, when Carteret left, as deputy governor continued the
same policy,[3] and was said to be under the control of Durant.

[1] N. C. Recs. I. 248–333 ; Hawks, II. 467 *et seq.*
[2] N. C. Recs. I. 260.   [3] *Ibid.* 286 *et seq.*

Bacon's rebellion in Virginia had just been suppressed, and with the insurgents in that movement many in Albemarle had sympathized. It may be supposed that some refugees sought protection there against the vindictive measures of Governor Berkeley. But of greater immediate importance was the arrival, about three years before, of John Culpepper, who, because of his "turbulent and factious carriage," had been forced to leave the Ashley river settlement.[1] Evidence is conclusive that the hold of the proprietors over Albemarle was very weak, and that their attempt to establish a nobility was viewed with the utmost aversion. All restraints upon freedom of trade and attempts to draw a revenue from the province in connection with their enforcement were regarded in the same manner. In general the anarchical tendencies of colonial life find perhaps better illustration in the Albemarle settlements at this time than elsewhere in the British-American colonies. We have a vague report of the forcible displacement of Jenkins, and then of a counter movement supported by military force which dissolved the assembly, dispersed the palatine court, and arbitrarily placed and displaced officers. In this Culpepper shared.[2]

In November, 1676, in order if possible to restore quiet and check illicit trade, Thomas Eastchurch, a relative of Lord Treasurer Clifford and formerly speaker of the assembly in Albemarle, was appointed as its governor. He was instructed[3] to divert the trade of the colony from New England to the mother country. As measures contributory to this he was ordered to establish three port towns and to send to the proprietors an exact statement of the depth of the water at low tide in the inlets along the Albemarle coast, that they might know when and where ships from across the ocean could best load and unload. At the same time Thomas Miller was appointed deputy of the Earl of Shaftesbury, secretary, and collector of the royal customs in Albemarle county. Only a year or two before Miller had been indicted for using foul and seditious language concerning the king, and had been taken to Virginia for trial. There he was ac-

---

[1] Shaftesbury Papers, 424; N. C. Recs. I. 259.   [2] N. C. Recs. I. 259.
[3] Ibid. 228–232, 287 et seq.

quitted, and went thence to England to report the proceedings to the proprietors.   Owing to the delay of Eastchurch in the West Indies, Miller was sent on in advance with a commission from the new governor to act as president of the council and commander of the militia.   On the strength of this last appointment Miller, as soon as he arrived in the colony, began to exercise the powers [1] of deputy governor.

Miller, who supplanted Bird and Culpepper as collectors, seems at the outset to have been quietly received, and to have been for a time successful in the administration of the customs.   He and his deputies seized 817 hogsheads of tobacco, and goods illegally imported to the value of £1242.[2]   But, if we are to believe the statements of the proprietors, he rashly undertook to change the law or practice of elections, to lay heavy fines, and to issue warrants commanding some of the chief men of the colony to be brought before him alive or dead.   Reference [3] is also made to the raising of a guard of soldiers, which cost the province twenty thousand pounds of tobacco.

The effect of Miller's conduct was to provoke an uprising, which began on the arrival from Europe, in December, 1677, of Captain Gillam, one of the New England traders, and of George Durant.   Miller tried to arrest both these men on charges connected with illegal trading,[4] but was seized and imprisoned by a body of thirty or forty men in Pasquotank precinct.   With him his deputy, Biggs, and several of the proprietors' officials were also arrested.   Hudson, another deputy, was arrested in the lower precinct.   Their papers and all the tobacco and money which had been collected by the prisoners were also taken.   Culpepper, Bird, Durant, and Crawford were among the leaders of the uprising.   A tumultuous demand was raised by some that the authority of the proprietors should be thrown off ; this, however, the leaders did not expressly favor.

But, assuming powers of government, Culpepper and his followers called an assembly.   Amid tumultuous proceedings at Durant's house a grand jury was impanelled, which under directions from Culpepper found a bill [1] against Miller and his deputies. They were about to proceed to their trial when a proclamation was brought from Governor Eastchurch, who had reached Virginia on his way to Albemarle. The assembly was at once adjourned, and steps were taken to prevent Eastchurch from entering the colony. These were successful, and the governor soon died in Virginia. Miller and his deputies were retained in prison, the insurgents carrying on the government for about one year.

Culpepper during a part or all of that time acted as collector of customs. Biggs, and finally Miller, escaped, and carried their case to England. Culpepper and Gillam were both arrested there, in consequence of charges by Miller and Biggs, and full inquiry was made into the case both by the proprietors and the English government. Culpepper was tried before the king's bench for treason, but through the influence of Shaftesbury he was acquitted. The statement which Shaftesbury made to secure his acquittal was a confession of the failure at the time of proprietary government in Albemarle. He said that Culpepper was guilty only of riot, treason being then impossible in Albemarle, for there was no settled government in that colony. The proprietors, though holding that Miller had acted without lawful authority, finally agreed to see to it that, if possible, his losses and those of his deputies were made good, and that they were protected against vexatious suits. [2] Culpepper was ordered to restore the funds he had seized, but whether or not he obeyed we do not know. Seth Sothell, one of the proprietors, was appointed governor in 1681, but, owing to his capture on the outward voyage by pirates, he did not reach Albemarle till two years later. John Harvey, whom the proprietors had appointed president of the council, and after him Jenkins and Wilkinson, who held appointment for brief terms as governors, were able meanwhile to carry on the government peacefully. An act of oblivion was passed, and neither governors nor collectors were disturbed in the performance of their duties. This all means that the proprietors, such was their weakness and inefficiency, compounded

[1] N. C. Recs. I. 273.   [2] *Ibid.* 329.

with disorder and riot, that they might retain the nominal **CHAP.** hold which they had over the northern half of their province. **X.**

Respecting Sothell's administration, which continued from 1683 to 1688, it is impossible to speak with full assurance. Only brief accounts of his character and doings have reached us, and they proceed from his enemies. If the complaints [1] which were made against him were true, he was one of the most corrupt and arbitrary of governors. He was charged with unlawfully imprisoning parties ; with detention of them on the false charge that they were pirates ; with the unjust seizure of private estates, particularly that of George Durant, which he was said to have converted to his own use without process or color of law; with the refusal to admit a will to probate, and with the acceptance of bribes. It is said that, when Thomas Pollock proposed to go to England to complain of the injustice [2] which was being done, the governor imprisoned him without showing cause for his act. According to these representations, he used both his judicial and executive powers to their fullest extent for the purpose of plundering the inhabitants of the province. The toleration of such conduct by the colonists for a series of years, if not wholly incredible, may perhaps be accounted for by the fact that Sothell was a proprietor and that he did not interfere with illegal trade. But finally he was seized and preparations made to send him to England for trial. He then begged that his case might be heard by the next general assembly. The prayer was granted, and that body banished him from the colony for a year and decreed that he should never again hold the governorship. Of Sothell's career in South Carolina — which immediately followed this — we have already spoken. At its close, ignoring the command of the proprietors to return to England and submit to an investigation, he went back to Albemarle, where he spent· the two remaining years of his life.

[1] N. C. Recs. I. 368, 383.

[2] The detention, or attempted detention, of one who was bent on such an errand, was by no means an unprecedented occurrence in the colonies. Moreover, imprisoning in the colonies, and especially in North Carolina, was very different from incarceration in the Bastile.

The career of Sothell, whether all the charges against him be true or not, illustrates the degree to which, under the Fundamental Constitutions, a governor might be independent of the proprietors. Sothell was both proprietor and governor. Though an appointee and agent of the board, as soon as he arrived in the province he was more than that. By virtue of a place in the proprietary board, which he had reached solely through purchase, he outranked the deputies more than governors ordinarily would do. He might well afford for a period to ignore their commands. The colonists could not with safety oppose him, as they might one who was solely an appointee. As usual, the proprietors did nothing that was effective either to enable him to clear his reputation or to bring him to justice if he was guilty.

During the early period of its existence Albemarle was administered by governors and presidents who were independent of those on Ashley river. Not until the appointment of Philip Ludwell in 1691 was the executive power in all the " counties," or really in the two provinces, united in one. For the preceding two years[1] Ludwell had been governor of Albemarle, but of his administration there nothing is known. Under Ludwell and his successors, until 1712, the northern settlements were administered by deputy governors, who, with one exception, were the immediate appointees of the governors resident at Charlestown. At the beginning of that period the two parts of the province began to be known respectively as North and South Carolina. Alexander Lillington and Thomas Harvey were the two deputy governors under Ludwell and Archdale. On the death of Harvey, in 1699, Henderson Walker was president of the council. By virtue of that office he became acting governor, and continued such till his death[2] in 1704. The appointment of deputies was then resumed, and continued until 1712. Then Colonel Thomas Pollock was elected president, and brought the province to the close of the Tuscarora war. Pollock was again president for a brief time in 1722. But, with that exception, North Carolina had distinct governors of its own ever after 1713.

[1] McCrady, *op. cit.* 235.   [2] N. C. Recs. I. 511, 530 ; Hawks, II. 502.

The governors of South Carolina, even during the years
when they appointed deputies for the northern province,
paid little or no attention to its affairs. The proprietors
also continued toward Albemarle their policy of systematic
neglect, save when internal anarchy compelled brief attention. Occasionally, as in earlier times, they left it without
government. The appointees were nearly all colonists. The
elected presidents, of course, were such. None, except Archdale, were connected with the families of the proprietors.
The proprietors apparently corresponded very little with the
governors, and the governors scarcely ever wrote to the proprietors. None except the usual formal instructions were
given them by the proprietors.

In Albemarle, as on the Ashley river, the council continued to have an elected element until 1691. Ludwell's
instructions brought it to an end in both provinces. After
1718 the deputies were appointed by joint action of the proprietors, and not by the separate act of each proprietor.[1] Of
the council in its legislative capacity we have no distinct
records in the proprietary period. The extant records of
the executive council begin in 1712.[2] In its executive
capacity the council advised the governor concerning appointments, regulated fees, approved the payment of salaries,
ordered the arrest of parties for the non-payment of taxes,
ordered out men and supplies for defence, shared in negotiation with the Indians and with neighboring colonies, laid
embargoes on the exportation of corn in times of scarcity.
The governor and council watched over the interests of the
province in general, so far as they received any attention. The
council was also very largely occupied with territorial administration. Together with the secretary and the receiver-
general, it administered the territorial affairs of the province.
Many references to its activity in this direction appear in
the records. Many petitions were presented to it for the
re-grant of land which had been improved or settled. It
declared good all surveys which did not prejudice the rights
of the proprietors. It ordered rent rolls made out. The

[1] N. C. Recs. II. Introduction, vi.
[2] *Ibid.* I. 841.

question of the form in which quitrents should be paid repeatedly came before it.

In matters of a quasi-judicial nature the council granted letters of administration and guardianship, committed minors as apprentices, ordered the arrest of parties who were committing serious offences against the security or good order of the province. Sometimes punishment was inflicted on such parties at the command of the council.

The council, like the assembly and the general court, met at various places within the province, their sessions being held in private houses. In this respect the contrast between North and South Carolina is very marked. As it was necessary for the members to travel long distances, attendance was burdensome. Prior to 1718 members of the council appear to have paid their own expenses, but an order was then issued that they should be paid out of the proprietary revenue.[1]

Gradually the Albemarle settlements, or Albemarle county in its original sense, expanded into a true province. North of the sound four precincts were formed — Chowan, Perquimans, Pasquotank, and Currituck. After settlement had extended somewhat to the south of Albemarle sound, the proprietors directed that the name Albemarle county should be confined to the region north of that body of water. Governor Archdale was ordered to erect between Albemarle sound and Cape Fear as many counties as the progress of settlement, encouraged by him, would justify. But not until 1705, when Thomas Cary was acting as deputy governor, did he and his council erect the settlements south of the sound into Bath county. This was divided into three precincts, while others were later organized, extending as far south as Cape Fear river. The precincts of North Carolina were, in fact, counties in the ordinary and modern sense of the term, and they came later to be so called.

With the gradual increase of population and its expansion southward, the Quakers assumed an increasing importance among the dissenting sects in North Carolina. Their appearance in the province dates from the missionary journeys of Edmundson and Fox in 1672. They immediately became

[1] N. C. Recs. II. 323.

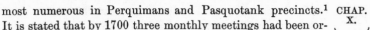

most numerous in Perquimans and Pasquotank precincts.[1] CHAP.
It is stated that by 1700 three monthly meetings had been or-   X.
ganized in those precincts.   The North Carolina yearly meeting began in the same region and about the same time.   But
later, especially in the early eighteenth century, the Quakers
began to settle toward the south and west.   There is no evidence that they took interest in political affairs until John
Archdale,[2] during his term as governor, began introducing
them into the council and courts, after which they became
successful candidates for election to the assembly.   As yet
no religious tests or provisions requiring the oath existed in
the laws of Carolina, which would exclude Quakers from
office.   That they would contribute nothing directly to the
military strength of the province, was certain, while it was
equally certain that they would strengthen the democratic
tendencies which it had been theoretically the purpose of the
proprietors to hold in check.   Especially would they oppose
attempts to secure a church establishment or in any way
to limit religious freedom.   The capacity of the people for
passive resistance to unwelcome measures would also be increased.   Among the dissenters in the province, in addition
to Quakers, were Presbyterians, Lutherans, French Calvin-
ists, and Irish Catholics.

At the time when the political activity of the Quakers was
developing, the English Church began to send missionaries
into the colony and to perform its religious offices where
hitherto they had been totally lacking.   During the presidency of Henderson Walker, after considerable effort, the
Anglicans secured in 1701 an assembly which passed an act
for the establishment of the church in North Carolina.   It
provided for the laying out of parishes, the building of
churches, and the support of ministers by a public levy on
all tithables.[3]   The original act has not been preserved.
Active steps were at once taken for the execution of the
measure, long before it was submitted to the proprietors or

---

[1] N. C. Recs. I. 215–218, 686, 711 *et seq.*, 720 ; Weeks, Southern Quakers
and Slavery, in J. H. U. Studies, Extra Vol. XV. 47.

[2] Letter of Rev. William Gordon, N. C. Recs. I. 708.

[3] N. C. Recs. I. 544, 572 ; Weeks in J. H. U. Studies, X. 274.

received their assent. The dissenters meanwhile were roused to activity by its passage, and prepared to change the majority in the assembly and secure its repeal. But before they had an opportunity to act, the proprietors repealed the measure on the ground that the sum of £30, which was designated in the act as the yearly maintenance of each minister, was too small.[1]

On the death of Henderson Walker, Sir Nathaniel Johnson, who was governor of both the Carolinas, appointed in 1704 as his deputy for the northern province Colonel Robert Daniel. He was already a prominent resident of South Carolina and was an ardent churchman. It is certain that he was personally in favor of the extreme Anglican policy which Johnson, acting under instruction from Lord Granville, forced for a time upon South Carolina. Though the contemporary sources of information are very scanty, it has been maintained with a considerable degree of probability that in 1704[2] the passage of an act by the North Carolina legislature was procured, which not only provided again for the establishment of the church, but also for a religious test.[3] Martin states that the act provided for " a fine on any person holding a place of trust who should neglect to qualify himself by taking the oath required by law." The act itself, like its predecessor of 1701, has been lost, but it has been supposed that it was substantially a copy of the measure which in the same year raised such a storm in South Carolina. In the northern province the commotion which was occasioned by the act was almost as great.

But the Quakers were directly assailed from another quarter. In the same year (1704) the act of parliament of the first of Anne, which imposed a new oath of allegiance, arrived. It made no express exception in the favor of Quaker office-holders, neither did it mention the dominions. The Quakers refused to take the oath and were removed by Daniel from their offices. A province law was also passed, that no

---

[1] N. C. Recs. I. 572, 601.

[2] Weeks, Southern Quakers and Slavery, 161.

[3] Weeks, in J. H. U. Studies, X. 279–289 ; Martin, History of North Carolina, I. 222 ; Hawks, II. 508.

one should hold a position of trust without taking the
required oaths.   The act for the establishment of the
church, with that requiring the oaths, together occasioned
the so-called Cary's rebellion.   While the disturbance
lasted we hear much more of the question of oaths than
of the church question.   But all the dissenters in the province seem to have been profoundly stirred, which would
have scarcely been true if the point at issue had merely
been that of the oaths.

John Ash, who was sent by the South Carolinians to
England to complain of the passage of the act for the establishment of the church, was compelled to find passage from
Virginia, and went thither over land through Albemarle.
Edmund Porter was appointed by the dissenters of Albemarle to accompany Ash.   Porter, with the help of Archdale, secured from the proprietors an order addressed to
Governor Johnson to remove Daniel from the deputy governorship.   This he obeyed, and Thomas Cary, who had
been collector of quitrents for the proprietors, and who is
said to have been concerned in civil troubles in South Carolina, was appointed in his place.   Cary was a churchman.

The new governor not only tendered the oaths, but caused
an act to be passed which provided that any one who should
promote his own election, or sit and act as a member of the
assembly, without duly qualifying himself by taking the
oath, should be fined £5.   So offended were the Quakers
at this that in 1706 they sent John Porter to England, who
again, with the aid of Archdale, induced the proprietors to
suspend Johnson's authority in North Carolina, remove
Cary, and empower the council of the province to choose
a president.   Porter, on his return in 1707, called together
the Quakers, for a number of whom he had procured depu-
tations from the proprietors, and, in the absence of Cary and
the rest of the councillors, chose William Glover president.
Glover was a churchman, and, declining to be used as a tool
by those who placed him in office, insisted as his predecessors
had done that the oath should be taken.   Porter now called
all the members of the council together, both those who had
recently been superseded and those who had not yet been

sworn, declared Glover's election illegal, and chose Cary in his place. Against this Glover and Colonel Pollock protested, and in consequence of it the province at once became divided into hostile factions.

Both Glover and his rival now issued writs of election,[1] and it was agreed that the assembly to be chosen should decide which was the rightful president. Of the seven precincts — four in Albemarle county and three in Bath county — five chose Cary members. All the members from Bath, and those from Pasquotank and Perquimans precincts in Albemarle, were his adherents. Moseley, a supporter of Cary, was chosen speaker. On the strength of representations then made by Porter, the assembly voted that the proprietors had disallowed both of the laws requiring the oaths, though the Quaker members later went through a form of declaration. Cary was chosen president by this body, but was not recognized by Glover and his party. In this divided condition, without recognized and legal government, the province remained for two years, 1708 to 1710, and apparently no effort was made by the proprietors or their representatives in South Carolina to pronounce definitely in favor of either party. Though no hostilities of importance seem to have occurred, some of Glover's leading supporters retired into Virginia rather than live under what they considered an illegal government and amid conditions so unsettled.[2]

In the summer of 1710 Edward Hyde arrived in North Carolina as the deputy of Governor Tynte of the southern[3] province. But the sudden death of the latter had made it impossible for Hyde to procure his commission, and therefore he had to refer for proof of his claims to statements in private letters.[4] But these were convincing; Glover at once retired in his favor; Governor Spotswood of Virginia recognized him, and most of the wealthier inhabitants of

---

[1] Pollock's Letter Book, N. C. Recs. I. 696.

[2] *Ibid.* 727, 731.   [3] *Ibid.* 776, 779.

[4] Baron De Graffenried, who had been made a landgrave and who was then founding the settlement of Palatines at Newbern, confirmed Hyde's statements most fully. He had seen Hyde appointed by the proprietors. *Ibid.* 914.

North Carolina submitted to his government. Cary did
this at first, but later put himself again at the head of a
factious opposition. Hyde called a council, opened the
courts which had been closed during the recent disturbances, and in the summer of 1711 summoned an assembly.
He was thus organizing what proved in the end to be a
legal government, but he was forced to wait nearly a year
and a half for his commission as governor from the proprietors, and did not take the oaths of office till May,[1] 1712.
The assembly, which had been elected under influences
favorable to an establishment, passed acts requiring that
the oaths should be administered and lawful government
maintained. It also provided for the recovery of the rents
and fees which Cary had collected and of the deeds of land
to the Palatines which were in his possession. All of Cary's
acts were declared illegal and void, and he, with Porter, was
ordered to be taken into custody.[2]

But Hyde was unable either to execute the laws or to
bring the prisoners to trial. Cary soon escaped, declared
himself president, and prepared with a brigantine and a force
of men to attack Hyde. In this move, which was essentially
warlike in its character, Cary probably had the assistance of
only a few of the Quakers. The governor and his council
retired to a place of safety and sent an urgent message to
Virginia for aid. Governor Spotswood and his council
resolved at first to try mediation. Therefore they sent John
Clayton[3] with two letters to Cary, the one conciliatory in
tone, and the other — to be delivered only in case he should
persist in his rebellion — declaring the purpose of the Virginia government to support Hyde. At first Cary expressed
his willingness to confer with his opponent and even named
a place. But soon after, whether from fear of foul play
or not, he changed his mind, and advanced again to attack
the governor. Clayton now returned to Virginia bearing a
request for armed assistance. Spotswood ordered out the
militia of the southern counties[4] and sent a body of marines
from a guardship into Carolina. But before they reached

[1] N. C. Recs. I. 785, 799, 842.   [3] *Ibid.* 758 *et seq.*
[2] *Ibid.* 780–794.   [4] *Ibid.* 781.

the Chowan, Cary abandoned forcible resistance and with
a few of his associates retired into the Tuscarora country,
whence they soon passed into Virginia. There they[1] declared their purpose of going to England to justify their
conduct before the proprietors. Spotswood, as soon as he
ascertained by examining them that their only desire was a
fair trial, hastened their departure, with such information as
he could give about the uprising. Sometime later a preliminary complaint was sent over by Hyde and his council, who
in the meantime had resumed the unobstructed administration of government.

In November, 1711,[2] Cary was granted two hearings by the
proprietors, and replied in person and in writing to Governor
Hyde's accusations. But the board of proprietors was
weaker and more indifferent than it had been at the time of
the previous rebellion. The pressure to which it, in connection with all the other colonial proprietors, was being
subjected by crown and parliament, reduced the board to
impotence in the face of internal disorder. It was content
to let disturbances end as they might and with as little
offence as possible. Sorrow was expressed that[3] Hyde had
been compelled to resort to force to uphold his government.
He was instructed to have Cary's accounts with the proprietors audited ; also to make all possible reparation to
those who had suffered injury. A full account of the disturbances should be submitted, so that, if the queen should
require an answer, it might be given in satisfactory form.
Beyond this no action seems to have been taken.

With the outbreak of the Tuscarora war, for which the
divided state of the province furnished an excellent occasion,
civil broils were forgotten in the common effort to save the
province from ruin at the hands of the savages. In 1713,
soon after the close of the Indian war, Charles Eden was
appointed governor, and enjoyed a peaceful and successful administration of eight years. By an assembly in 1715 the laws
of the province were revised and for the first time systematically arranged and printed. By one of the acts of that session[4]

---

[1] N. C. Recs. I. 800 et seq.　　　[3] Ibid. 845, 846.
[2] Ibid. 818, 819.　　　　　　　　[4] Ibid. II. 207.

provision was made for the establishment of the church and for the division of the province into parishes. But, as in the law by which in South Carolina the church secured its permanent establishment, all reference to a religious test was omitted.   The act was allowed to go into effect and, by virtue of it, during the remainder of the colonial period the confession of the minority of the inhabitants of North Carolina became entitled to legal privileges.

During the session of 1715 and for two or three years thereafter Edward Moseley, supported by certain others who had been sympathizers with Cary, led an opposition to the governor. Moseley was in 1715 speaker of the assembly. A series of resolutions [1] was secretly passed by that body, censuring the government for impressing inhabitants under pretence that it was for the public service, for alleged ill treatment of the Core Indians, and for refusing to accept bills of credit in payment of fees and quitrents.   The resolutions were intended for submission to the proprietors, but, if presented, they called forth no action which was favorable to the objects of the petitioners. When, in the following year, their existence became known to the council, it by formal vote condemned them, both on account of their contents and because they had been clandestinely passed.   In 1718 Moseley,[2] because, in conjunction with Maurice Moore, he had seized the journals of the council and other public papers from the house of the deputy secretary, was heavily fined, deprived of his license as an attorney, put under security for good behavior, and declared incapable of holding office for three years. This severe penalty not only closed the career of Moseley as a leader of opposition, but indicated that the province was emerging from its earlier and anarchical conditions, and government within it was assuming a firmer texture. The peace of proprietary North Carolina was not again seriously disturbed.

[1] N. C. Recs. II. 243.   [2] *Ibid.* 321 *et seq.*

CHAPTER XI

PART
III.

THE influence of Quakerism upon the development of ideals and institutions in the Jerseys has already been noticed. The control of that sect over West Jersey was complete, and without attributing too much to a reasoned policy, it may be concluded that the democratic simplicity of that colony was the direct product of Quaker preferences. The share of the sect in the founding of Pennsylvania was equally decisive, though in that case the existence of a single proprietor, who held under a royal grant, necessitated a closer adherence to the traditional forms of the province.

William Penn was not a political theorist, neither was he a systematic thinker on any subject. Scattered[1] through his writings will be found the commonplaces of his time to the effect that government was of divine origin, that its chief objects were to terrify evil-doers and to cherish those who do well. Laying stress on the latter of those two functions, it seemed to him that government was an agency in the moral training of the race. He was fond of dwelling on its ameliorating rather than its compulsive features. To him forms of government signified little, but rather the character of the men to whom the management of its affairs was intrusted. He could not find a model in the world which time, place, and circumstances had not altered. Even ill-designed systems had been made to work well when man-

[1] The most important statement of Penn's views appears in the preface to the first Frame of Government. Pa. Col. Recs. I. 29; Hazard, Annals of Pennsylvania, 558. Penn's observations on the English government are chiefly in England's Present Interest Considered, 1675, Works, III. In his address to the Protestants of all Persuasions, 1679, Works, IV., are his most weighty criticisms of the ecclesiastical policy of England. His writings are largely devoted to the defence of toleration and of the mild and humane spirit.

aged by good men, while bad men would ruin the best institutions.   " That, therefore, which makes a good constitution
must keep it, viz. men of wisdom and virtue, qualities that,
because they descend not with worldly inheritances, must be
carefully propagated by a virtuous education of youth. . . ."

In the history of England, as he read and valued it, the
characteristic which appeared most prominent was the original freedom of the people.   The early existence of representative institutions, the guaranties of property, and the jury
trial, constituted a birthright the value of which he desired
should never be forgotten.   "Here are [1] the three fundamentals comprehended and expressed to have been the rights
and privileges of Englishmen.   I. *Ownership*, consisting of
liberty and property.   In that it supposes *Englishmen* to be
free, there is *liberty ;* next, that they have *freeholds*, there is
property.   II. That they have the *voting of their own laws ;* for
that was an ancient free custom, as I have already proved,
and all such customs are expressly confirmed by the *great
charter*, besides the people helped to make it.   III. An influence
upon, and a real *share in, the judiciary power*, in the execution and application thereof."   These are sentiments which
Penn shared with all Puritans, and they had a decisive influence on the policy which he pursued toward his province.
So desirous was he that the same principles should be known
and valued there, that in 1687 he published,[2] in Philadelphia,
an edition of Magna Carta, of the Confirmation of the Charters, and of the so-called statute De Tallagio non Concedendo.
This was accompanied with an address to the reader in which
the wish was eloquently expressed, that the inhabitants of the
province would resolve " not to give away anything of Liberty
and Property that at present they do . . . enjoy, but take
up the good example of our ancestors, and understand that
it is easy to part with or give away great privileges, but
hard to be gained if once lost."   Sentiments of this nature
were not expressed by any other proprietor concerning the
inhabitants of his province.   Though Penn himself was
thrown much into the society of the great, he felt equally at

[1] Works, III. 218.
[2] Sharpless, A Quaker Experiment in Government, 52.

home among the poorer and middle classes, and it was from their midst that the sect with which he was connected drew most of its recruits.

The significance of the Quakers in American history arises from the fact that their ideas coincided well with the prevailing tendencies of colonial life. The most of the colonists came from the same social classes as did the Quakers. They pursued similar occupations. As they removed into the wilderness and their children grew up under frontier conditions, the traditions of the old world to an extent lost their hold upon them. The aristocrats of Europe were almost totally absent, and society assumed a more democratic form. Local institutions sprang up in which the colonists shared to a greater or less extent. With their preservation the idealized conception of inherited English liberties became interwoven. In judicial administration substantial justice rather than the strict observance of legal forms was sought. The military spirit was weaker than it was even in England, and the occasions for its activity in most of the colonies were less numerous than in any part of the old world. Religious intolerance, except in its minor exhibitions, by the time Pennsylvania was founded had become impossible. With all these tendencies the opinion of the Quakers concerning the oath, war, religious freedom, trial by jury, strict limitation of the power of the executive in the interest of popular liberty, quite fully coincided. Wherever they settled in considerable numbers, religious freedom must necessarily exist, clerical influence would be greatly lessened, the power of the legislature would be fully developed, the tendency toward an elective official system would be strong, the centralizing of power which is often the consequence of war would be difficult. After Quakerism, like other forms of Puritanism, had become somewhat mellowed and broadened, it became favorable to popular education. The equality and individualism of colonial life found their counterpart in Quaker tendencies and beliefs. Quakerism acted as a powerful solvent on the feudal and monarchical elements in the constitution of the province.

Pennsylvania was in the full sense of the word a Quaker

province. Not only was the proprietor a Quaker, but the sect controlled the assembly until the middle of the eighteenth century. In the preparation of his schemes of government, Penn freely consulted his friends, and the result was to an extent the product of their joint wisdom. Penn insisted that government should be "free to the people," that laws should rule, and the people should be " a party to those laws." There was no reference to a nobility in his charter. Penn could never present to livings, or be the head of an ecclesiastical establishment. In the laws agreed upon in England, and afterward enacted in the province, elections were made a prominent feature and provision was made for guarding them against bribery. Courts should be open, and justice neither denied nor delayed. In the courts "all persons may freely appear in their own way and according to their own manner, and there personally plead their own cause themselves, or if unable by their friends." All pleadings, processes, and records should be brief, in English and in ordinary and plain character, so that they might be easily understood. Fees should be moderate and should be fixed by the assembly. Prison reform was sought in the provision that prisons should also be workhouses, that fees should not be required in them, or payment for food and lodging. Persons who were wrongfully prosecuted or imprisoned should have double damages against the informer or prosecutor. No one should hold more than one public office at a time. The provision that these laws should be posted up in all public courts and read annually by the people and accepted by them, together with the formal issue and acceptance of the Frames of Government, is indicative of a regard for the popular will which was rare in those times.

The first recorded utterance of Penn in the provincial council was to this effect: " The Governor answered, they might amend, alter or add for the Public good, and that he was ready to settle such Foundations as might be for their happiness and the good of their Posterities according to ye powers vested in him." When the Frame of Government of 1683 was finally adopted, Penn declared, "that what was inserted in that charter was solely by him intended for the good and benefit of the freemen of the province, and prosecuted with much earnestness in his spirit toward God at the time of its composure." [1] His utterances were in a similar strain in 1701. When taken in connection with the assertions of privilege which he made, these statements afford proof of the benevolent and paternalistic [2] attitude which Penn assumed toward his province. While he was not unmindful of the wealth and power which might accrue from his position, he identified himself with the colonists to an extent which was never attempted or approached by any other proprietor. This result was due to the humane and sympathetic spirit which made him a Quaker, a spirit which in his case, by intercourse with the world, was freed from the extravagances that appeared in the careers of many of the earlier leaders of the sect. Unlike the Carolina proprietors and some of the Calverts, he never sought to play the autocrat or by sharp management to monopolize political power. Unlike the leaders of Massachusetts, though establishing a Quaker province, he expressly renounced the idea of restricting political rights within it to members of his own sect. [3] In him and his sect appeared many of the tendencies which were finally to triumph and to constitute the distinctively American spirit. Fewer obstacles to the ultimate prevalence of that spirit were erected by him than by any other proprietor.

The system of government of Pennsylvania was established under authority transmitted through the Frames of Government of 1682 and 1683, and the Charter of Privileges [4] of 1701. Of these the first was issued by the proprietor after discussion [5] and agreement with the intended purchasers of land in the province; the second was issued by

---

[1] Col. Recs. I. 58, 63 ; Votes, I. 21.

[2] See Charter and Laws, 515. The closing instruction to the commissioners of state in 1688 ran as follows : "Love, forgive, help and serve one another, and let the people learn by your example, as well as by your power, the happy life of concord."

[3] See Penn's letter to Jasper Yeates, Pa. Mag. of Hist. VI. 468.

[4] Col. Recs. of Penn. I. 32, 42, 48 ; II. 56.

[5] Shepherd, Proprietary Government in Pennsylvania, 225.

the proprietor after his arrival in the province; the third
was issued by him just before the close of his second visit to America. A third so-called Frame of Government was issued by Governor Markham in 1696 with the approval of the legislature as an act of settlement. As this instrument was never accepted by the proprietor, it can be said to have been in force only as a temporary act. Furthermore, there is no proof that the Frames of Government and Charter of Privileges were submitted to the crown for its approval, as required by the royal charter. But as the charter did not declare that the acts which were not submitted should be on that account annulled, those which were issued by Penn and approved by the legislature, in spite of the irregularity, must be regarded as in force. Unlike the schemes of government which were issued by Gorges and the Carolina proprietors, the Frames of Penn were submitted to the colonists at the outset for their acceptance, and were put as fully into operation as circumstances permitted.

The existence of a representative system, and one, too, which was unusually developed, was guarantied from the first by the Quaker proprietor. The statement was made in the first Frame that powers of government were vested in the governor and freemen, those of the latter to be exercised in two representative bodies, the council and the assembly. The governor, as executive of the province, was the appointee of the proprietor and the president of the council. In the council he had three votes, but no mention is made of his possessing the right of veto, either over the acts of the council or of the assembly, or of the two combined. The legal position of the governor within the legislature was in some respects like that of the governor of the corporate colony, both being forced to depend largely on the moral influence which they could exert.

The grant of an elective council marks an important departure from the traditional system of the province, one, however, which appears under special and qualified forms in the Carolinas and the Jerseys. It was a concession to the colonists, whether they were rich land-owners and mer-

chants, or men of lower station, which involved serious
consequences for the proprietor, and from which proceeded
many of the complications of the first two decades of Pennsylvania history. It also contributed in an important degree
toward determining the form which the legislature of that
province ultimately assumed. With an abundance of detail
which is a characteristic of all Quaker concessions, as it is
of Locke's Constitutions, provision was made for an elective
council of seventy-two members. A faint attempt was made
to secure for the council the position of an aristocratic body
— one more likely than the assembly to act in harmony with
the proprietor — by the requirement that those of best repute
for wisdom, virtue, and ability should be chosen as its members. For the better performance of its duties as an executive body, the council was empowered to organize itself
into four committees — on plantations, trade and finance,
education and arts, and justice.[1] The combined quorum of
these committees — twenty-four members — constituted the
standing council. This was the form regularly assumed by
the council for the transaction of routine executive business.
It was apparently hoped that over the council, though elective, the proprietor and governor would be able to exert a
controlling influence, for it was given, in addition to the
usual executive powers, the exclusive right of initiating
legislation and of summoning and dissolving the general
assembly. But it could adjourn itself, while over its acts
the governor did not possess the right of veto. He had
only a triple vote in the council. It was also empowered
to present annually to the governor double the number of
persons required as candidates to serve as judges, treasurers,
and masters of the rolls, — the most important subordinate
and local offices, — and from these the governor should make
the selection. The office of secretary, surveyor-general,
receiver-general, and provincial treasurer, the first three of
which were closely connected with the land-office, were filled
by the proprietor or governor.

The assembly of two hundred members, though it was

---

[1] Provision for all except the last-named committee appears in the Constitutions of East Jersey.

also elected by the freemen, was given a decidedly inferior
position.   Its functions were to impeach offenders before
the council, to prepare amendments to the bills laid before
it, and finally to approve or reject those bills.   The position
of inferiority assigned to it is made even clearer by the provision that it should be called and adjourned by the governor
and council.   It thus appears that the characteristic features
of the system of government which was devised by the Quaker
proprietor were the weakness of the governor and the prominence of the elective council.

Penn wrote some time later : " The people have their representatives in Provincial Councell to prepare, and ye Assembly
as it is called has only the power of aye or no, yea or nay.
If they turn debators or Judges or complainers, you overthrow the Charter quite in the very root of ye constitution
of it, for that is to usurp the Provincial councel's part in the
Charter and to forfeit the charter itself ; here would be two
assemblys and two representatives, wheras they are but one
to two works, one prepares and proposes, the other assents
or denys.   The negative voice is by that in them and that is
not a debateing, mending, altering, but an accepting power." [1]

In June, 1681, William Markham, Penn's first deputy, by
virtue of his commission, appointed a council.[2]   The writs
for the calling of the first legislature did not require the
election of a council, and for this reason the legislature of
Pennsylvania, which met at Chester, December 4, 1682, consisted of only one house.   Only seven members were chosen
from each of the six counties into which the province and
" territories " were then divided.   Its organization and procedure were generally in accordance with the forms accepted
in the colonies, it enjoyed all necessary independence, and it
did a large amount of legislative work.[3]   It passed the act
of union with the three Lower Counties, and a naturalization
act.   It passed also the " printed laws," or laws agreed upon
in England.   It carefully considered the " written laws or
constitutions " prepared by the proprietor, consisting of

[1] Hazard, Register of Pa. IV. 103 ; Shepherd, 264.
[2] Charter and Laws of Pa. 471.
[3] Votes and Proceedings, I ; Charter and Laws, 473–482.

ninety chapters. Each chapter was considered separately and many amendments were proposed. Seventy-one chapters were passed, of which the sixty-one which were finally engrossed became the so-called Great Law of Pennsylvania.

The writs which Penn issued for the election of 1683 called for a provincial council of seventy-two members, and declared that the remainder of the freemen might attend in person to constitute the assembly. But the returns from the counties were accompanied by petitions — inspired, it is probable, by Penn himself — that the twelve who had been chosen in each county might together constitute the councillors and assemblymen. It was now so clear that the legislature as planned was far too large for the needs and resources of the province, that the proposal of the petitioners was accepted, though it involved a departure from the Frame of Government.[1] The proprietor expressed his consent to whatever the public weal demanded, while a protest from Nicholas Moore, the president of the Free Society of Traders, led to a hearing before the council and his reprimand.

The chief debate of the session was over the right of initiation. The assembly petitioned for the right, and conferences with the proprietor and council were held. In the debates over the subject in the assembly some of its members used language implying excessive humility, as if it involved ingratitude toward the proprietor even to debate and amend the bills which he submitted. Penn expressed the fear that, if the right of initiation was conceded, an attempt might be made to legislate in violation of the terms of his patent and thus its forfeiture might be occasioned. But in a succession of conferences the clauses of the existing Frame of Government were reviewed. It was amended in several important particulars, and after the revised document had been accepted by both the proprietor and the two houses, it was delivered to them by the proprietor as the Frame of Government of 1683.[2]

The amendments provided that the council should henceforth consist of three members, and the assembly of six members, from each county. The triple vote of the gov-

[1] Charter and Laws, 484; Col. Recs. I. 58. [2] Col. Recs. I. 62, 69, 72.

ernor in the council was abolished; while it is not clear that
the lieutenant-governor — the proprietor's appointee — enjoyed the right of veto. The council was no longer divided
into standing committees. Bills proposed by the council to
the assembly should be published twenty days before the
meeting of the general. assembly. The difference between
the method employed in Pennsylvania for the revision of
concessions of government and that used by the proprietors
of Carolina, is interesting and suggestive.

The proprietor now returned to England, leaving the executive power in the hands of Thomas Lloyd, as president,
and of the council. Quiet prevailed until 1685. Then disputes arose between the council and the assembly over the
form of language used by the council in the promulgation of
bills which were to be considered in the forthcoming session.
The form, " by the authority of the president and council,"
or its equivalent, was thought to violate the Frame of Government and to ignore too much the lower house.[1] The council finally agreed to obey the law, but in 1686 resumed the
use of the form to which objection had been made. This led
to renewed controversy over the privileges of the two houses,
the form in which conferences between them should be held,
the promulgation of bills, and the continuance of temporary
laws. The course of legislation was stopped, and the impotence both of the executive and of the lower house was revealed. Of the eighteen members of the council usually only
five or seven were present at its sessions ; at times less than
the required quorum of one-third. Both parties were fain to
call a truce until the differences could be referred to the proprietor, or until he should return to the province.[2] Attempt
on the part of the assembly to secure the impeachment of
Nicholas Moore for opposition to its will and for arbitrary
proceedings on the bench, and to bring about the removal of

[1] The full form was: "The President and freemen in Provincial
Council mett . . . have prepared to be published according to Charter these
following Bills for the notice and Concurrance of the freemen in Assembly to
meet . . . in the form and Style of Laws, then and there to be Confirmed,
amended, or rejected, as the General Assembly shall in their Wisdome See
meet." Col. Recs. I. 171.

[2] Col. Recs. I. 134, 142, 171–184, 198, 203 ; Votes, I. 31–40.

Patrick Robinson, clerk of the provincial court, for alleged insolence [1] toward the assembly, were incidents of the struggle. In both these efforts the assembly failed.

The reports which came to Penn apparently convinced him that the executive was not properly organized, but the remedy which he prescribed was not calculated to relieve the situation. He associated with Lloyd four other prominent residents of the province, Nicholas Moore, James Claypole, Robert Turner, and John Eckley, the five together to be known as commissioners of state. They were to act in the capacity of deputy governor.[2] Penn instructed them, or any three of them, to compel the members of the provincial council to attend to their duties, "or to take such a council as you think convenient to advise and assist you in the business of the public ; for," he continued, " I will no more endure their most slothful and dishonorable attendance, but dissolve the frame without any more ado ; let them look to it if further occasion be given." He criticised the provincial council as " clogged with a long and slow tale of persons rarely got together, and then with unwillingness, and sometimes reflections, even upon me." The new board of commissioners was instructed to suffer no disorder in the provincial council or assembly, to inquire into their past acts and into the qualifications of members of both houses. They were also to declare the proprietor's abrogation of all that had been done in his absence, preparatory to the reënactment by another assembly of the laws of the province, with such amendments as seemed proper.

But relations with the lower house were no more amicable than they had been before this change, while the sessions of the council were no better attended than they had previously been. The lower house was jealous because it did not possess the right of initiative, while the council irritated it by insisting on its own superiority. In the session of May,

---

[1] Robinson had said that Moore's impeachment by the assembly had been drawn " hob nob at a venture."

[2] Col. Recs. I. 212 ; Charter and Laws, 514 ; Proud, I. 305. Moore and Claypole did not act, and Arthur Cook and John Symcock were substituted. Col. Recs. I. 212.

1688, as had been the practice since the proprietor left the province, the lower house neglected to present its speaker [1] for approval. It also took separately the oaths of allegiance and fidelity, and resolved not to divulge any of its proceedings. At first the provincial council was inclined not to recognize it as a house, and after legislation began bickerings continued throughout the session. As the council refused to confer hereafter with any committee of the house and denied its power to make a committee, the assembly naturally kept insisting on its " privileges." Finally the council had to yield, and a committee from the house was admitted to conference. Though the session ended in a formal reconciliation, the two most important bills, one to prohibit the exportation of deerskins and another the supply bill, failed to pass.

The unsatisfactory relations which still existed caused the proprietor to again interpose, and before the end of 1688 he appointed Captain John Blackwell governor.[2] The commissioners of state were superseded, and a stranger, a man of military training and a Puritan, was introduced as the head of the government. It was not unnatural that the late commissioners should be dissatisfied, and, as they were all men of influence, they could make much trouble for a man who was situated like Blackwell. Alone, unaided, he had to face an elective council and a legislature, the members of which were either indifferent or strongly prejudiced against him. An executive in such a position must needs be helpless, and, if William Penn really desired to maintain the proprietary form of government, it is evidence of his poor judgment that he should have allowed the executive to be thus compromised and weakened.

The new governor first attempted to secure a more regular attendance on the sessions of the provincial council. At its second meeting [3] after his arrival a quorum was not present. By a special effort a quorum, but no more, was brought together at the next session,[4] January 14, 1689. It was then ordered that the sheriffs should acquaint the members of the

---

[1] Votes, I. 43, 44, 46 ; Col. Recs. I. 223.   [3] Ibid. 229.
[2] Col. Recs. I. 229.   [4] Ibid. 230.

council who resided in their respective counties, that one of them should attend each month as required by law and by the charter. But at the session on January 28, a quorum was not present and no business could be done. The same was true on the thirty-first, and, after waiting two hours, those who were present [1] departed. On March 1 all the members from Chester county were present, and the governor asked them to agree among themselves as to the order of their future attendance, and to inform the secretary. Thereupon one of them, John Symcock, who had also been one of the commissioners of state, declared that he would not [2] attend, and left the duty to be performed by the other two. On March 4 no quorum was present; the same was true on the eleventh. On the twelfth, when six were present, the governor stated that the means he had used to secure attendance had failed, and he asked the advice of the council in the matter. At his request the question was put, whether it were not the duty of one of the members elected for each county to " Constantly attend ye Governor in ye affayres of ye Government." Though such a proposition would seem to be fair and moderate, it was debated and its decision postponed till some six weeks later. [3] With this the governor was not satisfied, and later repeated the question of the former session. After much debate and expression of unwillingness to advise the governor in the premises, Arthur Cook, who also had been a commissioner of state, declared that the poverty of the people was so great that they could not bear the charge of constant attendance, as the law required, and that the governor be requested to suspend for the present the execution of the requirement. This resolution passed in the affirmative, the secretary only dissenting. Only occasionally after this did more than a bare quorum of the council attend its sessions. The governor's purpose to secure a full attendance was defeated, and conditions were prepared for a bitter quarrel between him and the council. In this he could not command the support of the assembly and must really face the entire legislature alone.

The obstinacy of the council was probably due in part

[1] Col. Recs. I. 233.   [2] *Ibid.* 234.   [3] *Ibid.* 238.

to dissatisfaction on the part of certain of the commissioners of state at being so summarily removed by the proprietor. Thomas Lloyd was from the first the leader of the faction which opposed the governor, and with him the controversy began. Blackwell, being a stranger and without support, showed poor judgment in venturing upon the conflict.

The governor should have been chancellor, but Lloyd, either when made president or later, had been appointed keeper of the great seal. He had in his possession a blank parchment which the proprietor had sent over in 1684, in order that upon it an instrument should be drawn confirming all valid patents and commissions. Lloyd also had the chief letter of instruction which Penn had sent to the commissioners of state, by which he had ordered Blackwell to be guided. When Blackwell's administration began, the council, at the request of the governor, sent for the instruction, as well as for copies of all letters and other instructions from the proprietor which related to the government. The blank parchment Lloyd delivered at once, and promised a transcript of so much of the letter of instruction as concerned the governor. As to the other letters and documents, he desired time to consult the late commissioners of state and members of the council to whom they were directed. Later, after being reminded again by special order of the council, Lloyd practically refused to deliver certain letters which the governor considered of importance, letters to which Penn is said to have referred him for guidance.[1] Symcock and Cook appear to have sympathized with Lloyd in this attitude, though later Symcock and the keeper were not wholly in agreement.

Shortly after, the governor sent to Lloyd a draft of new commissions for justices of the county court of Philadelphia, with his warrant for passing them under the great seal. This Lloyd refused to obey. The governor then declared that he should issue the commissions under the lesser seal and inform the proprietor. Names of candidates were then propounded to the council and, no record of objections appearing, it is probable that the appointments were[2] made.

[1] Col. Recs. I. 230–239.   [2] Ibid. 231.

Another encounter soon occurred. On March 1, 1689, Lloyd informed the governor that he soon intended to visit New York. The council, on the request of the governor, then advised [1] Lloyd that during his absence the great seal should be deposited with that body. Lloyd therefore submitted a written statement to the council in which he claimed a "fixed estate" in the seal, and complained that he had been used unkindly, causes of accusation being sought against him. But the fact that the quarrel was between Lloyd and the governor rather than between him and the council is proved by the offence which Lloyd's paper gave to Blackwell, while the council treated him with marked consideration.

The state of feeling was speedily shown by a dispute between the governor and Samuel Richardson, a member of the council, over the question whether or not a certain petition should be received. Richardson and Arthur Cook [2] then repudiated the governor's authority, saying that the proprietor only had authority to appoint a deputy. When, because of his insulting language, Richardson was ordered by Blackwell to leave the room, he refused, saying, "I was not brought hither by thee and I will not go out by thy orders; I was sent by ye people, and thou hast no power to put me out." Though the council supported the governor to the extent of ordering Richardson from the room, executive power was challenged in the most direct manner by this event. When Blackwell, apparently in conformity with the Frame of Government and with the laws,[3] sent to the chancellor a list of appointees for provincial judgeships, the latter refused to affix the seal to their commissions, alleging that these documents were "more moulded by fancy than formed by law." The council failed again effectively to support the governor, and he was thwarted in his effort to appoint judges and open the courts.

At the spring election of 1689, Thomas Lloyd and Samuel Richardson were returned as members of the provincial

---

[1] Col. Recs. I. 234–237 ; Charter and Laws, 520.   [2] Col. Recs. I. 244.
[3] *Ibid.* 249 ; see also 45, Art. 16, of the Frame of Government of 1683 ; Charter and Laws, 168, 178.

council.[1] The governor tried to exclude them on the ground
of their offensive conduct, and presented a series of charges
against Lloyd looking toward his prosecution.   This aroused
a hot debate, which soon after was revived by the publication of what was presumably an attack on the governor.
This was traced to Joseph Growdon, another member of
the council.[2] Growdon refused to withdraw at the command
of the governor while this matter was being discussed, and
a general cry was raised that the members who had been
elected, but from whom the governor withheld their seats,
should be admitted.   Thereupon occurred the sharpest debate
among those reported.   But the governor remained firm.
He adjourned the council, and a quorum did not again
appear till several days after the date — May 10 — for the
opening of the session of the general assembly.   Naturally
the lower house, when it met, sympathized with those whom
the governor had excluded from their seats in the council.
As this was an obstacle in the way of securing the attendance of a quorum of the council, and in that way contributed
toward making the organization of the legislature impossible,
the exclusion of the councillors was presented as a grievance[3]
and its redress was demanded.   When the session actually
opened, the governor defended his policy and office in a long
speech, but, owing partly to the disputes, he and the council
had no bills to propose.   Therefore no new laws could be
passed that session.   An irregularity already committed in
not passing laws under the great seal seemed to invalidate
all in existence save the Frame of Government and the Act
of Union with the Lower Counties.   The proprietor had also
ordered the repeal of the existing laws and their reënactment with amendments.   But such was the state of feeling
within the legislature that even this was impossible.   After
wrangling for a week or more over the detention in custody
of one John White, who had been elected a member of the
lower house from Newcastle county, the assembly broke up
without formal adjournment.

It now being evident that the expiration of the laws could
not be prevented by legislation, some action by the governor

[1] Col. Recs. I. 267 *et seq.*   [2] *Ibid.* 278 *et seq.*   [3] Votes, I. 50.

and council became necessary. The question was discussed at length. Growdon and others, who were opponents of the governor, expressed the view, " that ye Laws formerly made were good before ye Governor had confirmed them, and we suppose the Lawes are in force as they are." The governor, supported by Markham, Clarke, and others, insisted on the necessity of a declaration continuing existing laws in force and warning officers to execute them. The governor said that, if that were not issued, he should administer the government according to the Frame and laws which were passed before the proprietor went to England, and should commission the judges under the lesser seal. In spite of interruptions which were caused by appearances of Lloyd and Eckley to demand their seats, all except two members of the council were finally induced to assent to the declaration which the governor desired, and it was issued May 23, 1689. With this the important business of Blackwell's administration came to an end.[1] He had faithfully upheld the cause of the executive, but against an opposition which was too strong for a governor who was not supported by an appointed council. If it was really Penn's intention to centre authority in the council, his system of polity was well adapted for the purpose.

In the arrangement for the continuance of government after the close of Blackwell's brief administration, Penn made another notable surrender to the dominant forces in the province. Finding it impossible for him to return, he sent two commissions between which he permitted a choice.[2] One provided that the provincial council should present three names from which the proprietor should select his governor, and that in the interim an official elected by the provincial council should act in that capacity. The other commission provided that the provincial council itself should act as executive, and to that end should from time to time elect for itself a president. Penn wrote that he threw all into the hands of the provincials, that they might see the confidence he had in them and his desire to give them contentment. Relying, as usual, on moral influence, he ex-

[1] See Blackwell's closing speech, Col. Recs. I. 312.   [2] *Ibid.* 315 *et seq.*

claimed in closing, " Whatever you do, I desire, beseech and charge you all to avoid factions and parties, whisperings and reportings and all animosities, that putting your Common Shoulder to Ye Publick Work, you may have the reward of Good men and patriots." The council at once chose the second alternative that was offered. The provincial council again became the executive, and Thomas Lloyd was chosen president. The opposition against which Blackwell had struggled was again fully installed in power, and that with the consent of the proprietor. Within the province there was now no obstacle to the assertion of the will of the provincials through the legislature. The executive had been subordinated to it. So long as that condition lasted, conflict of course was impossible.

The suspension of Penn's governmental powers in 1692, and the appointment of Benjamin Fletcher, governor of New York, as royal governor of Pennsylvania, came as a rude shock to the dominant party in that province. Fletcher properly considered that the Frame of Government was superseded by his commission. The elective council at once gave place to one appointed [1] by the governor and subject to approval by the king. Among the councillors were Andrew Robeson, Robert Turner, Patrick Robinson, Lawrence Cock, and William Clark. William Markham was appointed lieutenant-governor. The councillors were also placed on the commissions of the peace throughout the province. At the governor's request, they presented a list of names of persons who were qualified to be judges, justices of the peace, sheriffs, and to fill other offices. This was accepted. At the instance of the governor, the representation of the counties in the assembly was reduced to four from Philadelphia county, and three from each of the others. The number of members in the council was also considerably reduced as compared with what it had been under the proprietary régime.

The introduction of the forms and usages of the royal province resulted in one important gain for the lower house :

[1] Col. Recs. I. 364, 366, 369. See Fletcher's statement, on p. 402, of the difference between Penn's system and that of the normal province.

it secured for it the right to initiate legislation. This doubtless, in a measure, reconciled the assembly to the other changes.

As soon as the assembly was organized, it took up in committee of the whole the question which to it and to all friends of Penn's system was of vital importance — to what extent the proprietary laws and constitution were still in force. It unanimously resolved that the laws which were in force on Fletcher's arrival were still in force, and that the governor should be asked to confirm them. Fletcher met these declarations with a prompt denial of the present validity of these laws, and an assertion of the exclusive authority of the royal commission. He declared that he found many of the laws and usages of the province to be repugnant to those of England, and especially cited the elective council, the lodgment of the so-called negative voice in the assembly, the requirement that double the necessary number of candidates for the offices of sheriffs and justices of the peace should be nominated to the governor by the elected council. Though Fletcher would not rank high as legal authority, he certainly attacked the peculiar and distinctive features in Pennsylvania government, those in which it departed most, not only from English precedents, but from those which had been established both in New York and Maryland.

The assembly expressed in reply a willingness to coöperate with the governor under the terms of the royal commission,[1] provided they might be governed according to the laws and constitution of Pennsylvania, so far as these were not inconsistent with the commission and with the king's pleasure. To this the governor replied that he was willing to agree to the passage of suitable laws; but he called the attention of the assembly to several of the existing criminal statutes, to the law relating to the inheritance of land, to marriage, to the person of the proprietor, as examples of acts which he thought repugnant to the laws of England. He also desired that a post-office might be established, that a grant should be made for the defence of New York, and that the New York act against pirates

[1] Col. Recs. I. 405.

might be passed.   The assembly now set about the examination of the laws for the purpose of their revision.   This
was new work for the assembly, as the council had hitherto
prepared all bills.   They found, on consulting the keeper of
the seal, that no laws had been enrolled, because no warrant
for the purpose had been issued ; but he believed that the
council book, which was in the possession of Markham, contained true copies of all the bills that had been passed.
This meant that the acts had never been passed under the
great seal as required by the charter.   The assembly passed
a bill setting forth a part of the provisions of the royal
charter about legislation, and added to it the titles of two
hundred laws which they claimed were already in force, and
asked Fletcher to administer the government in accordance
with them.   This was the so-called " petition of right." [1]

The governor replied that, according to information which
he had received, these acts had never been submitted to the
king or confirmed by him.   Upon this point the members of
the assembly had no definite information.   The most they
could say was, that Penn had carried the larger part of the
acts to England, and that they had never been declared void;
also, as to the rest of the laws, the five years' limit had not
been reached.   The governor and council also insisted with
much force that the bills were all invalidated by the fact that
they had not been passed under the great seal as required
by the royal charter.   They insisted on seeing the original
statute rolls, and refused to be satisfied with a mere list of
titles. [2]   A conference between committees of the two houses
was held, in which the argument of Patrick Robinson in support of the contention of the governor and council [3] carried
the day.   The conferrees from the assembly thereupon agreed
to prepare another revised list of laws which the governor
would accept as valid until further orders could be procured
from England.   The haste of Fletcher to return to New
York caused him to yield on certain points.   The assembly
made an ineffective attempt to coerce him by withholding
the supply bill, but a threat of dissolution brought it to

[1] Col. Recs. I. 410 ; Charter and Laws, 188, 549–551.
[2] Col. Recs. I. 413–415.   [3] Ibid. 418–422.

terms. The supply bill and thirty new bills became law.
The petition of right, containing an amended list of eighty-
six acts, out of the total number of two hundred, was also
accepted by the governor, and an order was appended to it
that all justices, sheriffs, constables, and other officers in
Pennsylvania and the lower counties should cause them to be
executed until their majesties' pleasure should be further
known.[1] No episode illustrates better than does this the contrast between the easy-going methods of government which
were natural in the chartered colonies, and the stricter forms
which the royal governors were bound to see enforced.

Fletcher held but one more assembly in Pennsylvania, and
that was an adjourned session[2] in May, 1694. David Lloyd
was its speaker. The chief point of difference which then
arose between the governor and the lower house concerned
the raising of a supply. Fletcher requested an additional
contribution for the defence of the New York frontier.
With his customary effusiveness he expressed the hope that
they would not "refuse to feed the Hungrie and Cloath the
naked." But when the supply bill was presented it contained a provision for grants of £200 each to Thomas
Lloyd and William Markham, to pay for services which they
had rendered as deputy governors, apparently in part before
the issue of the royal commission. Fletcher reminded the
assembly that appropriations should be made exclusively to
the crown, and that a petition should be presented for special
grants of this character out of the general supply. To the
bill for court levies he also objected, because, contrary to
English usage, it authorized their imposition by the justices
and representatives from the respective counties, without the
coöperation of the grand juries. This assembly also, like its
predecessor, presented an appropriation for the wages of its
own members without any provision for councillors, judges,
or others who held office under the king's commission.
They, moreover, charged the governor with failure to give
them due credit with the Iroquois for the assistance which
they had given the previous year. They attempted, when

[1] Col. Recs. I. 423–433 ; Charter and Laws, 551.
[2] Col. Recs. I. 459 *et seq.*

considering the supply bill, to name a treasurer in the place
of the receiver-general who held under royal appointment.
Recognition of the letter of the queen which required appropriations for the defence of New York, Fletcher was unable
to induce either this assembly or its predecessor to give.
Therefore, after approving of a few measures, he dissolved
the house and returned to New York without the supply on
which he had insisted.[1]

Though in 1694 Penn's powers of government were restored, and Fletcher never again visited Pennsylvania, his
administration there proved not to have been without influence upon the Quaker province. The proprietor again appointed William Markham as his deputy governor, though,
because of his poor health, two assistants, John Goodson and
Samuel Carpenter, were designated to aid him. The elective
council was restored,[2] and many who had been its members
before Fletcher's time were returned. David Lloyd now
appears for the first time as councillor. The election both
for the council and the assembly was held in April, 1695,
and, if the Frame of Government had been obeyed, the legislature would have met on the 10th of May. But the council
decided that it should not be called until September. On
May 20, however, Markham called a full council[3] to prepare bills for promulgation. It was resolved into a grand
committee to inspect and revise the laws. But the first
proposition which it considered was that of laying aside the
Frame of Government and substituting another which should
be "more easie." Though insuperable difficulties appeared
which thwarted this object, the council failed to exercise its
right of initiative. No bills were prepared or promulgated.

When, in September, the legislature met, Markham told
its members that both in reference to the time of holding the
assembly and to the proposing of bills he had tried to obey the
Frame of Government; but, because of the advice and action
of the council, he had not been able so to do. He also submitted to them recent letters both from the queen and Fletcher,
and laid upon them the responsibility for raising money to
meet the queen's demands.[4] The two houses now deliberately

[1] Col. Recs. I. 471.   [2] *Ibid.* 482 *et seq.*   [3] *Ibid.* 484 *et seq.*   [4] *Ibid.* 491.

violated the Frame of Government by resolving that, considering the emergency, they might proceed with legislation without the promulgation of bills. Continuing in this way the practice of the Fletcher régime, it was decided that either house might initiate legislation. An attempt was then made to pass a supply bill. Though it contained no express mention of a grant to the queen, it was intended that a surplus which the levy was expected to yield should go for general purposes of defence. With this was coupled an act of settlement, which was intended to embody the new principle of initiative by the lower house. Though the supply bill contained an appropriation of £300 for Markham, because it made no provision for the relief of New York, and because he thought that the Frame of Government should not be abandoned without[1] further debate, he refused to pass the bill and dissolved the council and assembly. Inasmuch as Penn's government had been restored on the promise that better provision should be made for defence, this result seemed likely again to imperil the proprietor's interests.

At this time and for months thereafter Markham insisted that the Frame of Government had revived after the close of Fletcher's administration, and he waited for some decisive word from the proprietor in support of that opinion. The assembly, however, held that it would require positive legislation to put it again into force. Not only was this a reasonable opinion, if it contemplated express consent on the part of the proprietor, but it tallied well with the desire of the assembly to secure the right of initiative. After waiting a year without receiving decisive instructions from the proprietor, Markham found it necessary, in October, 1696, to call another assembly. Preparatory to this, and in order to strengthen the executive, especially within the legislature, he appointed a council.[2] He selected men of estate and urged on them a diligent regard to the orders of the crown.

[1] A later statement of Markham concerning his attitude was to this effect: " After the proprietor had his Government restored to him, I was of the opinion that his Charter to you was in force, and I then called you together according to it (except in the day), & endeavored to putt the government in that frame it was in before it was taken from him. . . ." Col. Recs. I. 505.
[2] *Ibid.* 497.

An assembly was then called for the special purpose of appropriating the sum required by the queen for the defence of New York. That body, more decisively than its predecessor, coupled supply with a proposed act of settlement as mutually conditioned. After a conference had been held,[1] the governor surprised the assembly by presenting "some heads of a frame of government." The assembly having amended these, and cast them into the form of a bill, brought up with it [2] another bill for the required appropriation, and, on November 7, 1696, the two became law together.

In this way came into existence the act of settlement, which was popularly known as Markham's Frame of Government.[3] Besides the retention of the elective council, its most important feature was the guarantee to the lower house of the right to initiate legislation. This was the first time that the principle was incorporated in an act of the Pennsylvania legislature. But the act itself declared that it should remain in force until the proprietor should signify the contrary, while the evidence is satisfactory that Penn never confirmed it. Thenceforward, however, the lower house, as well as the council, regularly initiated legislation.

When, in 1700, Penn paid his second visit to the province the discussion of the organization of the legislature was resumed. The opinion was then expressed in the council that the Frame of 1683 was still in force [4] "as to its fundamentals." Penn said that Markham's Frame had served until he came, but it could not bind him against his own act, meaning by that the issue of the Frame of 1683. The council then resolved to read both Frames "and keep what's good in either, to lay aside what's inconvenient and burdensome, and to add to both what may best suit the common good," and to present the same before the proprietor. With the discussion of this, which was continued at intervals for several months, was connected the revision of the law of the province and the passage of an act confirming the property rights of freeholders. In the last-named act the assembly was especially interested. The results arrived at on all

[1] Col. Recs. I. 507, 508.

[2] Votes, I. 95 *et seq.* ; Col. Recs. I. 508.

[3] Col. Recs. I. 48.

[4] *Ibid.* 596 *et seq.*

these questions evidently proceeded from the joint action of the proprietor and the legislature, and the two coöperated freely at all stages of the discussion.[1] The final result was embodied in the Charter of Privileges of 1701.[2] In Articles II and III of this document the proprietor fully recognized the independence of the assembly, and by implication also the fact that it should be the only house of the legislature. This inference appears to be justified by the absence from the Charter of Privileges of a provision for the election of any except members of the assembly and by the appearance a few days later of a commission appointing the members of the council and giving them only administrative powers. The council in fact never thereafter exercised legislative powers. It constantly advised the governor concerning proposed legislation, bills were discussed, and law making was influenced by it, but it did not legislate.

The events which have now been outlined present a striking illustration of the difference between Pennsylvania and the other proprietary provinces. Penn, instead of claiming for himself a special right of initiative, committed it wholly to a large executive council. By making his council elective he at once transferred a very large share of the executive power into the hands of the colonists. This, together with a certain carelessness in the transaction of business, soon involved the proprietor and his governor in difficulty. Several devices were resorted to, but none brought permanent relief. By 1700 the necessity of an appointive council had apparently become obvious to those who had the rights of the proprietor and the permanent interests of the government at heart. But in order to secure it Penn tacitly agreed that the council should possess no legislative power. By this process the legislature of Pennsylvania, unlike those of the other provinces, came to consist of the governor and one house, and that house was the assembly.

[1] Votes, I. 119. [2] Col. Recs. II. 56.

CHAPTER XII

THE JUDICIARY IN THE LATER PROPRIETARY PROVINCES

In connection with this subject the first question which calls for an answer is this : What were the courts in the later proprietary provinces ?

In the earlier stages of their history the court of highest rank was that of governor and council. This was literally true in New Netherland. In New York the governor and council retained a certain jurisdiction, while they formed the most important part of the court of assizes, the highest judicial tribunal in the province.

Throughout the early proprietary period in Maryland the governor and council constituted the provincial court. In South Carolina until the beginning of 1683 all judicial business was done by the governor and council.[1] Subsequent to that date they sat as a court of appeal and as a chancery court. In North Carolina, until shortly after 1700, the general court consisted of the deputy governor and the deputies of the proprietors, with occasionally one or two associates.[2]

But in the Jerseys and Pennsylvania the governor and council played a less prominent part in judicial affairs. Owing to the imperfect organization of government in New Jersey prior to the Dutch reoccupation, very slight evidence of the judicial activity of the council appears. Occasionally in the later years of that decade it acted as a court of appeals. In West Jersey, during a few years subsequent to 1693, certain councillors appear as members of the provincial

---

[1] Proof of their activity in this direction appears in the Council Journals, which are printed in Shaftesbury Papers, 346, 356, 384, 385, 412, 425, 430, 451.

[2] N. C. Recs. I. 405, 442 ; Bassett, in J. H. U. Studies, XII. 162.

court of appeals ; but their *ex officio* judicial activity does not seem to have extended beyond this.[1] In Pennsylvania the provincial court became differentiated from the council almost immediately. This course of development in both West Jersey and Pennsylvania was perhaps facilitated, if not made necessary, by the existence of elective councils.

Inasmuch as the councillors were chiefly concerned with executive business, and thus could hardly avoid being in a sense parties to some of the cases which they were called upon to try, their judicial functions were anomalous. The accumulation of duties in their hands was a feature of early colonial government which time and the growth of the colonies tended surely to remove. The same is still more true of the judicial functions of the assemblies, which, for example in Maryland, were exercised for a time, and then disappeared. Before the first century of colonial development had passed, the councils had ceased to regularly perform judicial functions, and supreme or superior courts had been organized. Under the Dutch in New Netherland, however, this stage was never reached. In the English provinces the exercise of the original common law jurisdiction was that which was first separated from the control of the council.

In New York the court of assizes was discontinued at the close of 1683, and by statute provision was made for the exercise of a part of its jurisdiction by a general court of oyer and terminer, which should sit twice a year in each county.[2] By the same act the governor and council, under the title of the supreme court of the province, was given the chancery jurisdiction. The governor was authorized to depute a chancellor to act in his stead, and to appoint other necessary officers. Governor Dongan also, in order better to settle controversies relating to lands and revenues, in February, 1686, erected a court of exchequer.[3] This was known at the time as the court of judicature, and its judges were the governor and council. In New York, then, at the period of transition to royal government, the governor and council

[1] Field, Provincial Courts of New Jersey, 25. Shepherd, Proprietary Government in Pennsylvania, 371.

[2] N. Y. Col. Laws, I. 125, 163.   [3] *Ibid.* III. 390.

heard appeals, and also had jurisdiction over revenue cases and cases in equity. In 1678 Andros had been authorized to erect an admiralty court, but no regular tribunal had been established. In a few instances special commissions had been issued for such trials, but as a rule admiralty cases had been left to the mayor's court of New York City.[1]

In Maryland, until 1661, the governor had acted as chancellor.[2] From that date until 1689 Philip Calvert, an uncle of the governor and a member of the council, held that office. In 1684 the admiralty jurisdiction was also taken from the governor and his associates in the provincial court. One of the judges of the provincial court was appointed judge of admiralty. With the establishment of royal government in 1692, the provincial court was organized apart from the council, though for years thereafter it was common for members of the council to hold seats within it. The one of their original functions which the governor and council now retained was that of high court of appeal. These changes were effected mainly by instruction and ordinance.

In South Carolina the original common law jurisdiction of the governor and council was taken away when, in 1683, the court of Berkeley county was established.[3] As courts were not established in the other counties, this tribunal continued throughout nearly the entire colonial period to try civil and criminal cases for the whole colony. It was really a provincial court, and after 1698 had a chief justice, an appointee of the proprietors, at its head. Before that time a board of assistant justices presided over its sessions, but after the appointment of chief justices began, the assistants disapproved. The organization of this court, with its distinct civil and criminal sessions, left the governor and council with the power of hearing appeals in civil cases involving more than £100. The governor and council also acted as a court of chancery.

At least as early as 1702 the general court of North Caro-

[1] Daly, Historical Sketch of the Judicial Tribunals of New York ; N. Y. Col. Docs. III. 260.

[2] Mereness, op. cit. 232 et seq.

[3] Smith, South Carolina as a Royal Province, 118 et seq.

lina began to act under a commission distinct from that of
the council or of the proprietors' deputies.   A commission
was published in 1702, and the oath of office was taken by
three judges.   In March, 1703, two other judges took the
oath.   We have no further records of the court until March,
1713, and then the bench consisted of a chief justice and
two or more associate justices.   The chief justice was appointed by the proprietors, and at least during and after
Eden's administration the governor appointed the associate
judges.[1]

During the first two decades of New Jersey history we
find a few references to a court — once called the " general
court," and also referred to as the court of assize — whose
jurisdiction extended at least nominally throughout the province.[2]   It was distinct from the council, the latter bearing
toward it and to the other courts of the province the customary relation of court of appeal.   But when, under the
twenty-four proprietors, counties were established in East
Jersey, a provincial court, known as the court of common
right, was permanently organized.   This body was distinct
from the council, consisted of twelve judges, "six at the
least," and met four times a year at Elizabethtown.   Its
members were commissioned by the governor and council,
and, following Scotch usage, the court had, for a time, both
common law and equity jurisdiction.[3]   The supreme court of
appeal, which was constituted in West Jersey in 1693, — the
first of its rank in that colony, — consisted in part of members
of the governor's council and in part of county justices.[4]
The act does not specify how these were to be designated.
In 1697 provision was made that the provincial judges should
be selected annually by the house of representatives and
presented to the governor for his approval.   The county
justices were all elected.   Therefore West Jersey came as near
having an elective judiciary as did the corporate colonies.

Pennsylvania, in this matter, adhered more closely to the

---

[1] N. C. Col. Recs. I. 566, 583 ; II. 80, 148, 217, 264, 299, 535.

[2] Grants and Concessions, 97 ; N. J. Arch. I. 62, 176 ; Field, 8.

[3] Grants and Concessions, 232 ; N. J. Arch. XIII. 24, 42 ; Field, 12, 14.

[4] Grants and Concessions, 517, 563.

provincial ideal.   In 1684 an act was passed which provided
that five judges should be appointed by the governor under
the great seal, any three of whom should constitute the provincial court.   Twice yearly they should sit in Philadelphia,
and in both spring and fall at least two of them should go on
circuit through the counties of the province and territories.[1]

While the central courts of the provinces were in this way
undergoing development, local tribunals were also being organized.   By means of these and of the circuits and appeals
through which they were connected with the central courts,
the judicial system of each province was perfected.

In the seventeenth century the town and the county were
the local judicial centres in the provinces.   Though the name
hundred was sometimes applied, between about 1619 and
1634, to certain of the plantations in Virginia, as an institution it can scarcely be said to have existed there.   So far as
we are aware, no hundred court ever met in that province.
In Maryland, on the other hand, the hundred occupied a permanent place.   It was a unit for purposes of election, and also
a fiscal and military unit.   In some cases at the beginning
the hundred had justices of peace, and in all cases it had constables.   In a few cases where a justice of the peace was appointed, he was empowered to try and punish offenders.   In
early times a few hundred courts probably existed in Maryland, but as the counties were formed their judicial powers
were taken over by the larger unions.   The manorial courts
of Maryland were equally unimportant from the standpoint
of judicial history.[2]   They were curiosities and survivals
rather than vital parts of the provincial organism.

In the case of New Netherland and New York the county
system did not fully develop until late.   When the English
took possession of New Netherland they found a system of
village courts in existence.   Though the court of the patroon
of Rensselaerswyck and that of the vice-director on South
river were slightly suggestive of county courts, in general
it was true that the Dutch had not developed a local sub-

[1] Charter and Laws, 168, 184, 225.

[2] Md. Arch., Council, 1636–1667, 70, 89, 90 ; Howard, Local Constitutional
History, 273–281 ; Wilhelm in J. H. U. Studies, III. 343–367.

division of their province or a tribunal which stood midway between the village court and that of the director and council. The courts of the towns at the eastern end of Long Island were wholly independent of Dutch control and were imitations of the New England model. When the English province was established these towns were brought into due subordination to the central tribunals at New York. This process was accompanied by the first step toward the establishment of counties, for the ridings of Yorkshire virtually were counties. Provision was made in the Duke's Laws for a court of sessions in each riding. This met three times a year and consisted of justices of the peace, though the governor, or any councillor, if present, might preside. Cases went on appeal from these courts before the court of assizes.

Not until after the close of the Dutch reoccupation were the courts of Albany and Esopus fully changed to courts of sessions of the English type.[1] Very gradually did the titles of sheriff and justices of the peace take the place of those of schout and commissaries. As the great majority of the inhabitants in both localities were Dutch, and as no effort was made, so long as they proved obedient subjects, to force either the English language or English institutions upon them, changes were necessarily slow. The commander of the garrison at Albany exercised a general supervision over the administration of justice there, as he did over all other matters. Long intervals passed without any reports at all from the outpost reaching the officials at New York. In January, 1675, we find Andros writing to Lieutenant Knapton, the commander, that early the next summer he intended to visit Albany and regulate its affairs in such manner as seemed to be necessary. Knapton was warned in the meantime to keep on good terms with the magistrates.

The visit was made, though the governor's time was chiefly occupied with Indian affairs. One interesting result of it, however, was the provision that he made, by an instruction of August 30, for a tribunal which was to be known as the "general court." It was to hold one session

[1] See Ms. Calendar of Albany Court Minutes, 1652-1686, in State Library, Albany; General Entries, Ms. 1678-1680; Ms. Recs. of the Court at Kingston.

a year at Albany, and was to act as a subordinate court of CHAP.
appeal for Albany and Schenectady. Its judges were to be ⎯ XII.
five or more commissioners from Albany and two or more
from Schenectady.

No further important change was made until 1683. In
that year the act was passed which divided New York, apart
from its dependencies, into ten counties. This was followed
by the act which provided for the establishment of a court
of sessions, with justices of the peace, in each of the counties.
These acts went into force, and with their execution the
transition from Dutch to English tribunals in Albany and
Ulster counties may be said to have been completed.

A leading characteristic of the English provinces as a
whole, and one which serves to distinguish them not only
from New Netherland as actually organized, but from early
New England as well, is the importance of the county as
an institution of local government. Not only was it the
unit among them for the levy of taxes and the organization
of the militia, but also for the administration of justice.
In Maryland counties began at once to develop and the process steadily continued. At the beginning Saint Mary's
county and Kent county comprised respectively the settled
parts of the Western and Eastern shores. Their bounds
were gradually defined by the formation of outlying counties.
Of the order of 1650 fixing the bounds of Charles county,
and of that of 1654 repealing the above ordinance and erecting and bounding Calvert county, the record has been[1] preserved. The orders for the erection of Somerset county
and for the attempted erection of Worcester county on
Delaware bay are exceptionally detailed.[2] The records of
the origin of the other Maryland counties which were
created by the executive in the seventeenth century do not
appear.

In the Carolinas at the beginning the term "county" was
interpreted to refer to subdivisions of the vast territory
which the proprietors had received, each of which should
have its governor and assembly. In the Concessions of 1665

---

[1] Md. Archives, Council, 1637–1667, 259, 308.
[2] Ibid. 553 ; Council, 1667–1688, 108.

the proprietors spoke of the "County of Clarendon, the County of Albemarle and the County — which latter is to be to the southward or westward of Cape Romania, all within the Province aforesaid." This language suggests subdivisions of a vast domain such as the New England council planned in 1623 and 1635. Going farther back, it suggests such political structures as floated before the imagination of Sir Humphrey Gilbert. Each was intended to be a county palatine, rather than a county in the modern sense of the term.[1] In 1663 these proposed subdivisions were referred to by the proprietors as colonies. In the "proposals" of that year they spoke of the settlement near Cape Fear as "the first colony." We have in this a reminiscence of the language which in 1606 was applied to Virginia. But I have not found the settlement on the Chowan river or that south of Cape Romania referred to as the second colony.

With the issue of the Fundamental Constitutions something more closely resembling a modern county was suggested. The number of these for which provision was made was to be the same as the number of landgraves, and they were to be increased as the settlement progressed. In every county there should be a court consisting of the sheriff and four justices, one for each precinct, and all should be commissioned by the palatine's court.

But, as we are already aware, even these provisions were not carried into execution in either the northern or the southern part of the province. In the Ashley river colony, owing partly to natural causes and partly to political management, the counties did not attain more than a limited and imperfect development until near the close of the colonial period. In the Albemarle colony, though instructions drawn in the spirit of the Fundamental Constitutions were repeatedly issued, nothing resembling counties developed until near the close of the seventeenth century. Then they bore the name of precincts. The extant records of the court of Perquimans precinct, the earliest records of a county court which apparently have been preserved in North Carolina, begin in 1693.[2]

[1] N. C. Recs. I. 44, 79 *et seq.*   [2] N. C. Recs. I. 386.

Reference has already been made to the development of counties in New Jersey. Chester county in Pennsylvania was the outgrowth of the court of Upland on the Delaware. The formation of the three Lower Counties on Delaware bay was completed within four months after Penn received from the Duke of York the deeds which it was supposed transferred to him the Delaware region.[1] Before the close of 1682 the counties of Philadelphia and Bucks were established in Pennsylvania. By that date a system of county courts had been organized in both parts of Penn's dominion.

In the provinces south of New York the town attained very slight prominence, the parish, as the English Church won favor, supplying in many regions the smallest circumscription which was needed for the purposes of local government.

The second inquiry which is suggested by this investigation is, by whom were the provincial and local courts established ? Was it done exclusively under the ordinance power of the executive, or was provision made for them by the legislature ?

By the royal charters the king conveyed to the proprietors the right to establish courts. The Dutch West India company was expressly authorized to appoint and remove officers of justice, as well as other public officers, "for the preservation of the places, keeping good order, police and justice."[2] As a rule, in the provinces the earliest courts were established by the executive, without the coöperation of the assembly. The proprietor exercised his authority in this matter through the officials and by ordinance, rather than through the legislature and by statute. As we have seen, in New Netherland, and in the English provinces as well, the first court to be established was that of the governor and council. It was for a considerable time not only the chief tribunal of the province, but its only tribunal. It, of course, was created as an incident of the appointing of the governor and council.

In New Netherland, until the beginning of Stuyvesant's

---

[1] Hazard, Annals of Pennsylvania, 588, 605, 607 ; Shepherd, *op. cit.* 119, 322 *et seq.*

[2] O'Callaghan, I. 400.

administration, the director presided over trials in person, and constituted, of course, the most important member of the court. When Stuyvesant assumed office he made Van Dincklage, the vice-director, president of the council when it sat as a court of justice. But the director even then insisted that his opinion should be asked in all important cases, while he reserved the right to preside when he chose so to do.[1] Three of the Nine Men were also associated with the tribunal, and civil cases were sometimes referred to them for arbitration.

New Jersey and Pennsylvania, however, afford some exceptions to the rule that the judiciary owed its beginnings wholly to executive action. By the Concessions and Agreement of New Jersey the legislature was given at the outset the authority to establish courts by statute. But the legislature failed for some years to exercise this power in an effective manner, and that left the way open both for local initiative and for the occasional action of the governor and council. West Jersey, because of its peculiar organization, departed even more widely from the proprietary ideal.

William Penn, by his first and second Frames of Government, vested in the governor and the council the right to establish courts.[2] But in this case, as we have seen, the council was elective. It was given the right to present lists of candidates for judges and masters of the rolls, while the assembly was authorized in the same way to nominate sheriffs, justices of the peace, and coroners. From these lists the governor made appointments. But in Pennsylvania, as in the Jerseys, the assembly soon began to legislate concerning the establishment of courts and the appointment of judges. In 1684, as we have seen, it passed an act for the establishment of the provincial court. By that act it provided that the judges of the provincial court should be commissioned by the governor under the great seal. But an act was passed the following year which gave their appointment to the governor and the council without stating whether or not the procedure mentioned in the Frames of Government should be followed. It was this shifty legisla-

[1] Brodhead, I. 467.   [2] Pa. Col. Recs. I. 35, 45; Shepherd, 370 *et seq.*

tion that in part occasioned the controversy with Thomas
Lloyd during the administration of Governor Blackwell.
By a law of 1690 the right of the governor to appoint provincial judges under the great seal was restored.[1] This
provision was continued by the important act of 1701.[2]

It was almost inevitable that in both Pennsylvania and the
Jerseys the legislature should begin at an early date both to
establish and regulate courts. But in this respect they simply anticipated a course of development which was common
to all the provinces. As time passed, the judicial systems in
all of them were greatly extended by statutes, the jurisdiction
of the courts and the relations between them coming in the
end to be regulated by statute more than by ordinance. It
is equally true that the counties within the proprietary
provinces, together with the smaller local subdivisions, were
established by the executive. This applies as well to the
villages in New Netherland, to hundreds and towns, where
they developed, as it does to counties. For the establishment of the county — which because of its universality and
importance may be taken as representative of the whole —
two acts were essential and decisive. These were the fixing
of its bounds and the creation of the county court. In the
early history of the province the fixing of the bounds of
counties was the work of the proprietor, and it was done
through his governor, the council, and the officers who were
connected with the territorial administration. With that
side of proprietary activity it was closely allied.

But the more important act was the creation of the local
courts. In New Netherland the patroon and the city of New
Amsterdam received their judicial authority direct from the
States General and the West India company. That of the
magistrates came ultimately from the same source. The
commissaries on the South river, together with the schouts
and schepens of the villages, received their power immediately from the director and council. The changes which
were early introduced in the courts by the English, were
effected through administrative action. By this means the

[1] Charter and Laws, 168, 178, 184.
[2] Pa. Statutes at Large, II. 134, 148.

courts of sessions in the southern parts of the province and the mayor's court in the city of New York were created ; by it also the changes were made which slowly transformed the courts of the northern parts of the province into English tribunals. But county courts attained their full development in New York under the authority of an act of the legislature. Its share in their creation was much more complete than was the corresponding activity either of the Maryland or the Carolina legislatures. This involved, however, a somewhat radical departure from the early development of New York in other lines.

The history of the establishment of county courts in Maryland is in outline as follows. In January, 1638, John Lewger was appointed conservator or justice of the peace within Saint Mary's county.[1] James Baldridge was about the same time appointed sheriff and coroner. Thus the officials whose presence was necessary to the existence of a county court were in being, but for some years at the outset the governor and council seem to have acted as the court of Saint Mary's county. On December 30, 1637, Captain George Evelyn was appointed by the governor as commander of Kent island with the criminal and police jurisdiction of a justice of the peace, and civil jurisdiction in cases involving £10 or less.[2] Probably on account of the remoteness of Kent island and the difficulties with Claiborne, the commander was authorized to appoint all officers necessary for the preservation of peace and the administration of justice there, and especially a council of six or more with whom to consult respecting all important matters. Notwithstanding this, and though there is no proof of Evelyn's removal, the following February[3] three other justices of peace were appointed by the governor for Kent island and given the authority to hold there a "court leete." A sheriff and coroner were appointed at the same time. Other appointments and orders follow, till in 1642 Giles Brent[4] was made commander and two county commissioners were appointed.

[1] Md. Archives, Council, 1637–1667, 60, 85.   [2] Ibid. 59.
[3] Archives, Council, 1636–1667, 62.
[4] Ibid. 80, 90, 97, 105 ; Assembly, 1637–1664, 55.

It was at that time that Kent island appeared definitely as a
county.[1] When Charles and Calvert counties were erected
we have record of the appointment only of a commander in
one case and of a sheriff in the other. But in June, 1661,
after the disturbed period of the Commonwealth had passed,
an elaborate commission of the peace was issued, appointing
a board of justices[2] for each of the counties then existing in
the province. Such commissions were renewed at intervals
thereafter.[3] But of these counties only one had been erected
by act of assembly. That was Ann Arundel, and it was
created by a law of 1650.[4] No other act for a similar purpose was passed till 1695.[5] Hence, with one exception, the
original counties of Maryland were created — that is, their
bounds were fixed, courts were established, magistrates were
appointed, and to an extent the jurisdiction of the courts
was determined — by prerogative. The institutions thus
founded were developed and perfected by the proprietor in his
legislature. Statutes providing for this appear in the eighteenth century, but they simply elaborate the details of a
system already established by ordinance and custom.

Among the powers of the assembly, as provided in the
Concessions and Agreement which were issued by the Carolina proprietors in 1665, was that of constituting "all Courts
for their respective Countyes, togeather with ye Lymitts,
powers and jurisdiction of ye said Courts; " also the officers,
their number, titles, fees, and perquisites.[6] These Concessions were repeated in instructions to the governor of Albemarle in 1667.[7] But from the records, as preserved, it
cannot be proved that the first courts were established in
Albemarle under acts of assembly. When the Fundamental Constitutions were issued, the liberal intentions which

---

[1] In 1695 Kent island was annexed to Talbot county.

[2] Council, 1636–1667, 422, 425.

[3] *Ibid.* 448, 471, 534, 537 ; Council, 1667–1688, 14, 33, 52, 97. Sheriffs
and coroners were appointed in the same way, save for a few years subsequent to 1662, when a law was in force that sheriffs should be appointed from
lists presented to the governor by the county justices.

[4] Archives, Assembly, 1637–1664, 283, 292.

[5] Bozman, History of Maryland, II. 246 n.

[6] N. C. Recs. I. 82.   [7] *Ibid.* 168.

were indicated in the Concessions of 1665 were abandoned
by the proprietors.   In the Constitutions, as we know, provision was made for an elaborate judicial system to be established by ordinance after the plan had been accepted.
Instructions from that time were drawn in the spirit of the
Constitutions and not of the Concessions.   The acts of the
first assembly of Albemarle, that of January, 1669, so far
as they were ratified by the proprietors, have been preserved, and none of them provide for the establishment of
courts.   In one of them the court of the governor and council is referred to as being in existence.   This was to be
expected, and probably it was the only one in the little
settlement.   The instructions of 1670 to the[1] governor and
council of Albemarle, empowered them to establish such
and so many courts as they should think fit, till "Our Grand
Modell of Government" could be put into execution.   In
the instructions to the governor and council of Albemarle
in 1676, they were commanded not only to administer justice themselves, according to the laws established, but to
propose in the assembly the passage of laws for jury trial
in criminal cases, as provided for in Article 69 of the Fundamental Constitutions, and for bail pending trial.   In the
instructions which were issued to Governor Henry Wilkinson in 1681,[2] he was empowered, with the advice of the
council, to establish such courts as he should think fit, till
the Fundamental Constitutions could be put into operation.
In 1685 the proprietors instructed the governor to appoint justices and hold courts as provided in the Constitutions.[3]   Ludwell, in 1691, was instructed, with the consent
of three of the proprietors' deputies, to appoint a judge and
four justices to try cases in any of the counties which had
fifty freeholders qualified to serve on juries.[4]   In 1733
Governor Burrington had a controversy with two members
of the council, about the right to erect precincts, and was
able to show that, save in the case of one precinct formed in
1722, all had been erected without the coöperation of the
legislature.   By an act of 1715 the legislature recognized

---

[1] N. C. Recs. I. 182, 183.   [3] Ibid. 351.
[2] Ibid. 230, 334.   [4] Ibid. 375.

as legal units of representation the precincts which down to that time had been established by ordinance.[1]

In South Carolina the court of Berkeley county, which, as we have seen, exercised until late in the eighteenth century the common-law jurisdiction for the entire province, was established in 1683 by the governor and deputies under the authority of an instruction from the proprietors.[2] In 1692 the assembly of South Carolina admitted that the power to erect courts belonged to the proprietors, though the claim was made that it should be regulated by law.[3] Almost no statutes, however, were passed relating to courts or their jurisdiction, until the wholesale adoption of English law in 1712.   This, however, in no essential respect affected the basis upon which the judicial system of South Carolina rested.   Until the period when royal government began, the establishment and regulation of courts remained an executive function.

The references which have already been made to the Jerseys indicate that with them the course of procedure was different.   In New Jersey provision was made by statute in 1675 for four county courts, their times and places of meeting were stated, provision was made for the election of their judges, and the conditions under which appeals from these courts should be granted were specified.   At the same session it was also enacted that a court of assize should be held, if there was occasion for it, and that it should meet at Woodbridge or at such place as the governor and council should appoint.   Under the twenty-four proprietors the court of common right was created by statute, while in the same way enlarged provision was made for county courts.   Relying on the Concessions and Agreement of 1665, the legislature in 1682 declared certain recent attempts to establish courts by ordinance to be an infringement of the liberties of the province, and pronounced both the said courts and their proceedings to be illegal.   Town courts were not actually created by the legislature, but their jurisdiction over small causes was early recognized by that body.   In 1698 the

[1] N. C. Recs. III. 439 *et seq.* ; II. 213.
[2] Smith, South Carolina as a Royal Province, 120.   [3] Rivers, 434.

assembly declared that it had the authority to constitute all courts except that of chancery.[1] In West Jersey this principle was recognized from the first, and no court existed in that province save by virtue of an act of assembly.[2] The courts of sessions, as well as the central courts, were created by statute.

The origin of the county courts of Pennsylvania and the Lower Counties is to be found rather in executive action and a process of growth. The administration of justice on the Delaware, which was begun by the Dutch, was continued by officials who held under appointment from the early governors of New York. Resident justices, sheriffs, coroners, and constables were appointed for keeping the peace and administering justice in that region.[3] Courts existed at Upland, Newcastle, and Whorekills, and sessions were held with considerable regularity. In the case of Upland the continuity of the tribunal is unbroken till it became the court of Chester county in Pennsylvania. The region within the jurisdiction of the other courts was annexed to Pennsylvania in 1682 as the three Lower Counties. Upland and Newcastle had been known as counties at least since 1678. The counties of Philadelphia and Bucks in Pennsylvania were established by the proprietor before the first assembly of that province met at Chester. In this way the earliest county courts in Pennsylvania were brought into existence by the exercise of the ordinance power, and in harmony with English custom. But legislation for the purpose of regulating the jurisdiction of these and of the other courts of the province began in 1683 and continued steadily thereafter. The other counties of the province were erected under statutory authority; Lancaster in 1729 and others at later dates.

Though the governments in all the colonies were subordinate, the jurisdiction exercised by their courts was as broad as it would have been in a sovereign state. The authority to establish courts, as given in the royal charters, carried with

---

[1] Grants and Concessions, 96, 97, 99, 227, 229–232, 369.

[2] *Ibid.* 408, 448.

[3] 2 Pa. Arch. V. 585, 597, 598, 607, 615, 618, 619, 649–654, 686, 689, 697, 728; VII. 818; IX. 644 *et seq.*

it no limitation as to the kind of court which might be created. CHAP.
Jurisdictions in all the forms known to English law were   XII.
exercised in the colonies.   The common-law jurisdiction in
its three forms, also the chancery, the admiralty, and even
the ecclesiastical jurisdiction, were exercised there.   Martial
law was also enforced as an incident of the power to wage
defensive war.   The ecclesiastical jurisdiction, however, was
developed far more generally and distinctly in the royal provinces than it was in the chartered colonies.   These forms of
jurisdiction grew up by a process of natural adaptation and
imitation of the English judicial system.   In the development of procedure the process and result were much the
same.   It is through jurisdiction and procedure more truly
than from the names and official personnel of the courts,
that the relationship between the judicial systems of the
colonies and that of the mother country may be perceived.
What is true in these respects of the courts in the English
colonies is true also of those in New Netherland.

As a system of appeals from the colonial to the English
tribunals did not exist till near the close of the seventeenth
century, the judicial institutions in the colonies developed
independently of pressure from the English courts.   Very
great influence, however, was exerted by proprietors and
their higher officials, through instructions and by means of
their activity in the establishment of courts.   Except in
the Quaker provinces, it was they, rather than the colonists,
who took the initiative.   Through their mediation the
transfer of English judicial institutions into the provinces
was effected.   If one desires to see how the colonists spontaneously acted in this, as in other matters, he should look
at New England and at West Jersey.

In New Netherland the jurisdiction of the director and
council was all-embracing.   It was the tribunal before which,
either originally or on appeal, came all cases, civil and criminal, which originated within the province.   No better example than this can be found among the colonies of the
concentration of authority in a single board or tribunal,
almost in the hands of one man.   In the English colonies a
tendency soon appears to restrict the jurisdiction of the

governor and council and to distribute their judicial powers among other tribunals. But as long as the Dutch province existed, the original simplicity of form, as well as the concentration of authority, remained. These were modified only by the establishment of local courts.

All local courts in New Netherland, whether they were those of the villages, of the patroon of Rensselaerswyck, or of the commissary or vice-director on the South river, were empowered to try both civil and criminal cases. The jurisdiction of the patroon and of the court of New Amstel was the broadest, but they, like all the other local courts, were legally subject to appeals before the director and council. This obligation in the case of the patroon was limited to cases involving life and limb and to civil suits which involved more than fifty guilders.[1] By its privileges as finally extended the court of New Amstel was freed from appeals in criminal cases, though the director and council could grant reprieves. In civil suits appeals were allowed in cases involving more than one hundred guilders.[2] Appeals from the village courts were allowed for sums in excess of fifty guilders, and in all except petty criminal cases. In the case of the patroon, however, the obligation of appeals was, as far as possible, disregarded. In his court not only was final judgment given in suits of all kinds which arose within his borders, but he even inflicted the death penalty. On the South river an independent policy like this was not followed. Though appeals from that quarter were rare, no opposition against them appears on record.

In Maryland and the Carolinas, where county courts developed somewhat slowly, the central court for a time transacted all the judicial business of the province, save the few cases which in Maryland came before the assembly. The provincial[3] court of Maryland not only tried civil and criminal cases of all kinds, but did probate business and even held a coroner's inquest. Cases of murder and even of treason[4]

---

[1] O'Callaghan, I. 321.   [2] *Ibid.* II. 330 ; Laws and Ordinances, 388.

[3] Md. Arch., Records of the Provincial Court, Two Vols. 1637–1657.

[4] The charge of treason was urged against Richard Ingle. Recs. of Prov. Court, 1637–1650, 232, 237, 261.

came before it.   Mutinous speeches were frequently inves-
tigated by it.   In 1638 William Lewis, a Catholic, was
tried and found guilty of offensive speech "in calling the
protestant ministers the ministers of the divell."   He was
also found to have exceeded his rights in forbidding his servants to read Protestant[1] books.   The admiralty jurisdiction
was sometimes exercised in the trial of maritime cases and
cases of piracy.   But the court was chiefly occupied with
civil suits and probate business.   As soon as royal government was established in 1692 the governor and council, instead of the upper house, became the court of appeals.   The
governor never again served as chief justice of the provincial
court.   These steps implied the separation of the provincial
court from the council.   This, however, so far as the personnel of the judges was concerned, was never fully effected;
though as the eighteenth century advanced the tendency was
decidedly in that direction.[2]

In Maryland the governor, as we have seen, acted as chancellor until 1661.   Then Philip Calvert, an uncle[3] of the
governor and a member of the council, was appointed to
that office.   With that event the chancery secured an organization distinct from the council.   Until 1673 probate business continued to be done in the provincial court, and was
specially connected with the office of secretary.   At that
date it was transferred to the chancery, with right of appeal
to the proprietor, the governor, or designated commissioners.
Later, the officer who was in general charge of probate business was known as the commissary-general.[4]   He was authorized to appoint a deputy in each county, though it is not
probable that such appointments were often made.   In 1684
the governor ceased to exercise the vice-admiralty power in
person, and one of the justices of the provincial court was
appointed judge of the admiralty court.   By this process of
differentiation a group of central courts developed about the

[1] Recs. of Prov. Court, 1637–1650, 35 et seq.   [2] Mereness, 234.

[3] Md. Arch., Council, 1636–1667, 439.

[4] A very comprehensive act relating to his duties and to the whole subject
of the probate of wills and granting of letters of administration was passed
in 1681.   Archives, Assembly, 1678–1683, 195.

supreme or provincial court, all being the outgrowth of the judicial powers which were conferred by the governor's commission.

Though the accessible records relating to the early activity of the grand council in South Carolina are very imperfect, we find it trying civil suits. A controversy growing out of a marine contract was heard and decided. On one occasion the council held a session of the peace and jail delivery.[1] As jury service proved burdensome to the planters, if the parties agreed the trial might be held before the bench alone and its judgment accepted both as to law and fact.

In South Carolina the governor and council continued to act as a court of chancery and as a high court of appeal. In 1685 and 1686, and probably at other dates, authority was given by statute for the appointment of special commissions to try acts of piracy. In 1697, under authority from the crown, a court of vice admiralty was established at Charlestown, and its activity continued throughout the eighteenth century. In North Carolina the governor and council continued to act as a court of chancery throughout the period; but when the general court was created they lost their authority as a court of appeal. In 1698 the admiralty jurisdiction was transferred to the royal admiralty court, which was then organized for North Carolina as for the other colonies. The general court, from the time of its establishment, exercised the highest common law jurisdiction, both civil and criminal, in the province.[2]

Evidence of the exercise of the admiralty jurisdiction in the Jerseys during the seventeenth century is totally lacking. In 1696 Governor Basse stated in a letter to Secretary Popple, of the board of trade,[3] that he did not know of any courts in those provinces which had power to try cases of piracy. He was not aware that any such cases had ever been tried in either of the provinces. The attorney-general in England had also expressed the opinion that the proprietors of the Jerseys did not have the vice-admiralty power.

[1] Shaftesbury Papers, 346, 356, 384, 385, 425, 430, 451.
[2] N. C. Recs. III. 150 ; Hawks, II. 201 ; Bassett in J. H. U. Studies, XII. 163.　　　　[3] N. J. Arch. II. 156, 160.

The chancery jurisdiction was, however, exercised by the governor and council in East Jersey through the larger part of the proprietary period. For a time after its establishment the court of common right possessed the equity jurisdiction, but in 1698 the assembly took from it that power, and it reverted to the governor and council.[1] The governor and one councillor proved wills. The governor and council also acted as a high court of appeals until 1682, but the court of common right then became the supreme court of the province.

In West Jersey during the proprietary period no jurisdiction except that of the common law seems to have been exercised. No trace appears either of a chancery or an admiralty court. Wills were proved by the governor and specially chosen commissioners; they also administered upon the property of intestates. The supreme court of appeals, which was created in 1693, was strictly an appellate tribunal in civil suits, the court of oyer and terminer, which was established the same year, hearing the criminal cases. The latter was the first court in the province which was expressly empowered to inflict the death penalty. When, in 1699, for the court of appeals was substituted the provincial court,[2] the latter was made a tribunal of original, as well as appellate, jurisdiction. This extended over both criminal and civil cases. Moreover — perhaps an imitation of Pennsylvania usage — its justices were regularly sent on circuit through the counties. Special commissions of oyer and terminer might also be issued to the judges who were about to go on circuit.

In Pennsylvania no provision was made until 1683 for appeals or for the trial of capital offences. In that year appeals from the county courts to the governor and the council were regulated, and exclusive jurisdiction over capital cases was given to that body. The maritime jurisdiction was also exercised by the governor and council in several cases.[3] The impeachment of Judge Nicholas Moore was also tried before the same tribunal.

[1] Grants and Concessions, 369, 370 ; Field, 14.
[2] Grants and Concessions, 430, 517, 520, 564; Field, 25.
[3] Col. Recs. I. 76 *et seq.*, 121, 131, 135, 139.

When, in 1684, the provincial court was established, its justices were required to go twice annually on circuit through the counties. When they were on circuit, as well as at their "fixed" sessions in Philadelphia, they should hear and determine all appeals from county courts, try all controversies over title to land and all causes, civil and criminal, both in law and equity, which were not determinable in the county courts. This is an early and a notable instance in the history of the colonies of the establishment of judicial circuits, an imitation of the time-honored practice in England of carrying the traditions and procedure of the central courts into the localities. In several of the provinces — especially in Maryland and South Carolina, and to an extent also in New York — the people complained of the cost and inconvenience of travelling to the chief centre of government for the transaction of their judicial business. In the Quaker provinces of West Jersey and Pennsylvania an effort was made to remove this difficulty by carrying justice to the people.

But in Pennsylvania the new plan was not in every way a success. The provincial judges found their added task laborious and costly. The county courts were still believed to be best fitted for trying the cases which had originated in their respective localities. For these reasons, in 1685,[1] the system was slightly modified by an act which emphasized the original jurisdiction of the county courts, and provided that heinous crimes and appeals should be tried in the counties by three judges specially commissioned by the governor and council. But dissatisfaction continued, because of inadequate compensation among the judges and among the people because of failure of justice. The proprietor sent over a chiding message. Owing, however, to the controversies of Blackwell's administration, there was no further legislation on the subject until 1690. Then an act was passed restoring the plan which had been tried in 1684, and providing that appeals from the county courts to the provincial courts should be granted in cases involving more than £10, the appellant giving sufficient security to prosecute the appeal and pay the costs.[2] A similar

[1] Charter and Laws, 178; Shepherd, *op. cit.* 371; Col. Recs. I. 199.
[2] Charters and Laws, 184, 225.

act was passed in 1693, while by the law of 1700 circuit courts became a permanent feature of the judicial system of Pennsylvania.[1]

The county courts, except in Pennsylvania, possessed only a common law jurisdiction. Their development tended still further to decentralize the administration of justice in the provinces. In Maryland they attained their full growth soon after 1660.. At that time the terms "justice of peace" or "commissioner" came exclusively into use. Four or more of these officers — due provisions being made for the quorum — were appointed to serve in each county. Their jurisdiction extended to criminal cases which did not involve life or limb, and to civil suits in which the value involved did not exceed three thousand pounds of tobacco. Their duties as orphans' courts is especially emphasized in the act. In reference to criminal cases the limits of their jurisdiction remained unchanged. But in the matter of civil suits a prolonged effort was made by the lower house to extend their authority. This was one feature of the popular reaction against the extreme centralizing system of government which existed in Maryland between 1660 and 1690. It also originated in the very natural desire on the part of the people to avoid, so far as was practicable, the expense of carrying their suits to Saint Mary's for trial.[2] This tendency the proprietary officials opposed. Its triumph would lessen their fees, reduce their power, throw more influence into the hands of the county justices, many of whom were members of the lower house and were identified with the opposition.[3] Previous to the Revolution of 1690 the proprietor and his officials were able to prevent all but one or two slight changes. After royal government was established the jurisdiction of the county courts was considerably extended. But it has required additional and prolonged efforts to secure corresponding restriction of the authority of the provincial court.

[1] Statutes at Large, II. 134 ; III. 302. The latter reference is to the judicial act of 1722, the only one passed for the establishment of courts which was not disallowed by the crown.

[2] The loud and frequent complaints in reference to securing the probate of wills indicates a slightly different phase of the same question.

[3] Mereness, op. cit. 237 et seq.

In South Carolina a series of acts, beginning at least as early as 1683, empowered one or more justices to try petty cases which involved not more than forty shillings.[1] No attempt was made to define the localities within which they should act, but the jurisdiction conferred was essentially that of town courts. The justices could issue warrants, arrest, take recognizances, prove writings, and perform other similar functions. As the courts for the trial of petty cases were the only approach to local courts which existed in the province until near the close of the colonial period, it follows that the administration of justice was extremely centralized. The so-called court of Berkeley county, which very soon separated to form a court of pleas[2] and a court of general sessions, was really a central tribunal. Yet, strangely enough, it had no appellate jurisdiction, unless it were from the courts for the trial of small causes. After 1698 its presiding judge held the title of chief justice. By or before that time the assistant judges, who with the chief judge or sheriff had originally constituted the bench, had disappeared. The chief justice was thus left as the only common law judge, in the full sense of the term, in the province. This was the situation in the days of Nicholas Trott. Besides being chief justice, he was councillor, and after 1716 was judge of the vice-admiralty court. He was also decidedly the ablest among the few trained lawyers in the province. Nearly all the judicial business in South Carolina passed through his hands. It was this concentration of power which contributed strongly toward the revolt of 1719 by which proprietary government was overthrown.

The council and assembly, in a petition to the king in 1720, stated the case as follows : " Neither have they settled any county jurisdiction for the preservation of the peace and regular government according to the laws of England ; neither have they erected one manor for holding court baron

---

[1] S. C. Statutes, II. 27, 34, 47, 74, 331, 337.

[2] A court of pleas is mentioned in 1684. Ms. Council Journal, 65. In 1692 the court of common pleas was ordered by the council to meet four times a year. A court of oyer and terminer was called to meet on July 23 of the same year. One reference appears to the holding of an orphans' court in Charlestown in 1692. Fragment of Ms. Council Journal, 1692.

or views of frank pledge and courts leet for the conservation
of the peace and better government of this colony, but
have abandoned all to an unaccountable disorder and confusion under the adm'n and underhand management of
a single person whom they have commissionated and call
Chief Justice, who solely and by himself holds all courts
of King's Bench, Common Pleas and Exchequer, as also
all assize, county courts and sessions, only in Charles
Towne, the *only* place of judicature in the whole province ;
who makes what lawyers and takes what fees he pleases,
summoning all persons from the remotest parts of the colony to attend his courts.   No appeals from himself but to
himself, nor no method of appeals settled for the ease of
Your Majesty's subjects to Your Majesty and Council, as
is done in the rest of Your Majesty's colonies.   Nor any process suffered to be issued in Your Majesty's name.   He judges
of his own errors.   The marshal and other officers taking
what fees they will, and he upon frivolous pretences adjourning courts and putting off trials, delaying justice in order
to multiply his perquisites, which are according to his own
arbitrary pleasure ; daily exacting and extorting new fees,
to the intolerable burden of the colony ; undertaking himself to draw writings according to his own pleasure; sending
for lawyers and giving secret advice, both to them and the
clients, how to proceed in their cases ; and insists that no
Gen'l Assembly or authority here can either call him to an
account or remove him. . . .   The LPs, notwithstanding
repeated complaints by the public, and by private persons
injured by him, cannot be induced to remove him, he persuading them that he is the only person who can serve their
interests in Carolina."

In North Carolina, and in the Quaker provinces, the
county court underwent a normal development.   In North
Carolina the jurisdiction of the precinct courts, as finally [1]
regulated, extended over criminal offences which were
punishable by fines and forfeitures, and not by the loss of
life or limb.   They could try civil causes which did not
involve more than £100.   The court of the single justice

[1] Hawks, II. 198 ; N. C. Recs. I. 479 *et seq.*

disposed of all claims for less than forty shillings. In the precinct court claims to head rights were proved. The same court also took probate of wills and, when there was no dispute,[1] it granted letters of administration. Acting as an orphans' court, it appointed guardians and bound children out as apprentices. Letters testamentary and letters of administration, however, must be signed by the governor and secretary and sealed with the province seal.

In the Jerseys the monthly court of small causes appears, with its customary jurisdiction[2] and presided over by a single justice of the peace. In East Jersey the jurisdiction of the courts of sessions was in no way restricted. They might try any civil suit. With the exception of the court of Cape May county during the years between 1693 and 1697 the same seems to have been the case in West Jersey.[3] The laws of West Jersey make no reference whatever to the exercise of criminal jurisdiction by county courts.

In Pennsylvania the county courts were from the first given original jurisdiction over cases of debt, slander, and trespass. They also could try all except capital crimes,[4] the latter being tried exclusively by the provincial judges while on circuit in the counties. In 1688 treason, murder, manslaughter, and "other heinous and enormous crimes" were specified as wholly under the jurisdiction[5] of the provincial justices. At the same time Pennsylvania departed from usage elsewhere by making the county tribunals courts of equity for cases which involved less than £10. This power was continued to them by a law of 1693. Twice a year the county justices sat as an orphans' court.[6] In this capacity they administered wholly or in part on the estates of many decedents, though the proving of wills and granting letters of administration in Pennsylvania were the functions of the register-general and his deputies.[7]

---

[1] The governor and the general court also proved wills.
[2] Field, 7, 11, 24 ; Grants and Concessions, 99, 229, 455, 509.
[3] Grants and Concessions, 554.
[4] Charter and Laws, 129, 178.
[5] *Ibid.* 184, 225.
[6] *Ibid.* 131, 205; Statutes at Large, II. 156, 157.
[7] Charter and Laws, 232 ; Statutes at Large, II. 197.

The final subject to be considered in the discussion of the judiciary is that of procedure, though at the present stage of investigation only a few general statements in reference to it can be made.

In all the provinces except New York, where for a time Dutch practice survived, English procedure was spontaneously followed. But in the provinces, as in New England, justice was administered in the seventeenth century chiefly by laymen. Owing to this reason, as well as to the fact of the greater simplicity of colonial life, many of the complexities and technicalities of English procedure were dropped. They exceeded the capacity of the untrained or poorly trained minds of the colonists to understand or apply. Respecting any except the most common English precedents, little knowledge existed. One would infer that those who managed the affairs of North Carolina, New Jersey, and Rhode Island were less concerned about the forms and technicalities of English practice than were the officials of other colonies. Among the officials of Maryland, New York, and South Carolina the legal spirit of England was more strongly felt. It was, of course, in the local courts that the easy-going methods of popular justice most obtained.

Though Dutch [1] procedure in civil suits might be formal and trials be conducted largely in writing, yet in most instances they were not so, and practical conciliation through something approaching arbitration was the object sought. It therefore agreed well with the main tendencies of colonial life. To these tendencies in the administration of justice the Quakers gave peculiarly frank expression. The jury of inquest and trial was universally employed in the common law courts, save in those for the trial of small causes.[2] But wherever Quakers held authority the requirement for its use was expressed in the most sweeping terms. The early declarations of Penn and his associates that judicial pro-

---

[1] Daly, Historical Sketch of the Judicial Tribunals of New York.

[2] For an exception, see Laws of New York, I. 125. For one instance of the burdensomeness of jury service in a new settlement, resulting in an order permitting parties to choose trial by jury or by the court, see Shaftesbury Papers, 430.

ceedings should be simple, plain, and free, stated in more precise form principles which had already been enunciated in the Concessions of East and West Jersey.

Attorneys were freely employed in all the provinces. The evidence of this activity is much more abundant than it is during the same period in the New England colonies. By the Duke's Laws justices of the peace, while in office, were forbidden to act as attorneys. Sheriffs, constables, clerks of courts, were also forbidden to plead as attorneys in their own courts, except at the special request of some poor person, who was unable to plead his own cause.[1] The manuscript records of the court of assizes in New York reveals their activity in connection with all important cases. John Sharpe and John Ryder appear in so many cases that it is clear that they were regular practitioners. The records of the provincial court of Maryland almost from the beginning make frequent reference to attorneys.[2] We hear much of them in connection with the discussion of fees. In 1674 an act[3] was passed to regulate the admission of attorneys to the right to practise in the courts of the province. They were to be admitted and sworn by the governor, and could practice in the county courts only with the permission of the justices of those courts.

In both the Carolinas attorneys were employed in the trial of causes. In the tables of fees which were prescribed by a South Carolina statute of 1694 those of attorneys occupy a prominent place.[4] The general court of North Carolina, in order to prevent men from acting as attorneys who had not been bred in the law, insisted that none should practise before them who had not been licensed by the chief justice and judges of the court.[5] Attorneys who were guilty of unbecoming conduct were debarred by the court from practising before it. No sheriff, under-sheriff, or clerk could act as attorney in the court of which he was an officer unless in

---

[1] Charter and Laws of Pa. 11.
[2] Recs. of Prov. Court, 1637–1650, 147, 191, 205; *ibid.* 1650–1657, 78, 80.
[3] Md. Arch., Assembly, 1666–1676, 409.
[4] Stats. of S. C. II. 88, 92.
[5] Hawks, II. 111, 199.

his own cause or as attorney of some person who resided outside the province.   In New Jersey, in 1676, justices of the
peace were by law forbidden to practise as attorneys or
advocates,[1] or to act in any case as such except in their own
causes, or those of the king or proprietor.   In 1698 Governor
Basse was instructed to consent to the passage of an act
requiring all attorneys who should plead for hire before any
court of the province to be licensed by the governor.   West
Jersey, in its legislation, emphasized the option, which was
doubtless recognized in all the provinces, that no man was
compelled to employ an attorney, but, if he chose, he might
plead his own cause.[2]   An early law of Pennsylvania ran
to much the same effect.[3]

The existence of attorneys, however, and their employment largely in civil suits, by no means implies that the
accused in criminal cases were allowed counsel, or that
colonial usage differed in this respect essentially from that
of the English courts.   Reports of criminal[4] trials, so far as
they have been preserved and are accessible, show that in
general the procedure in the English courts was followed.
The English form of indictment and of pleading was used.
The jury was selected subject to the right of challenge on
the part of the accused.   In the trial of Josias Fendall
Catholics were excluded from the jury as the result of
challenges by the prisoner.   Fendall complained that he
had had no notice of his trial, or opportunity to procure
witnesses or knowledge of the charge against him.   This
was denied by the chancellor and other judges, and the
statement was made that the depositions of the witnesses
for the government had, for the most part, been read to the

[1] In 1694 this prohibition in general terms was extended to sheriffs, under-
sheriffs, clerks, and messengers of courts.   This indicates the class from
which attorneys were likely to appear.

[2] Grants and Concessions, 120, 223, 343, 429 ; N. J. Arch. XIII. 208–210.

[3] Charter and Laws, 128.

[4] A few such cases appear in the Ms. Minutes of the Court of Assizes of
New York, State Library, Albany.   Brief reports of others are in the Pro-
ceedings of the Provincial Court of Maryland.   In Md. Arch., Proceedings of
Council, 1667–1688, are full reports of the trials of Fendall and Coode in 1681.
In N. J. Arch. I. 236, is the minute of the trial of John Fenwick at New
York.

accused when he was before the council. The attorney-general also told him that every accused man was presumed to know what he had done.

The witnesses for the government were called and examined under oath by the attorney-general, the bench from time to time interposing questions. Fendall's witnesses were not sworn, the court ruling that an oath could not be administered for the purpose of strengthening testimony against the lord proprietor. Fendall called a few witnesses on his own behalf. The witnesses on both sides were allowed to tell their stories, and practically no effort was made to test the quality of their evidence. The testimony of two witnesses to the same overt act of treason or sedition was not required, but, in accordance with English rulings at the time, it was deemed sufficient if more than one witness testified to a succession of acts in the same series. The chancellor, during the trial and in his summing up, made no concealment of his prejudice in favor of the government and against the prisoner. The jury was told to pass only on matters of fact. The evidence is clear that, in comparison with modern trials, procedure in the seventeenth century was crude and summary. In cases which had a political coloring, or in which the government was interested, there were no adequate guaranties against gross partiality on the bench.

In proprietary New York, justice was administered in the name of the king. His title was introduced into the style of the courts.[1] Its judges were denominated the king's justices. In Maryland, on the other hand, except when the province was administered under the authority of parliament, the courts were the proprietors' courts; processes were issued and justice was administered in his name.[2] "Att a Provinciall Court," the entry ran, "Held at the Citty of St. Maryes In the Province of Maryland . . . in the Sixth yeare of the Dominion of the Right honorable Charles

[1] Duke's Laws, Charter and Laws of Pa. 21. See also the form of summons to the court of assizes, beginning in 1666; Ms. Journal of Court of Assizes, 1665–1672.

[2] Md. Arch., Provincial Court, 1650–1657, 183, 184; *Ibid.*, Council, 1667–1688, 328.

Lord Baltimore, Absolute Lord and Proprietary, . . . Before his Lordshipps Justices there unto assigned, . . ." In North Carolina, at least after the closing years of the seventeenth century, the judges of the general court were officially designated as the king's or queen's justices. Grand jurors are referred to as acting on behalf of the crown. Writs of precinct courts were issued in the king's name. A similar practice was probably followed in South Carolina.[1] In East Jersey, after 1682, process and writs were issued in the name of the proprietors to arrest parties in the king's name.[2] The laws of West Jersey contain no requirement for the recognition of the crown at any stage of judicial process. In Pennsylvania, at the beginning, judicial commissions, as well as others, were issued in the name of the proprietor. Sometime after the final return of the proprietor to England, the practice was changed, and judicial commissions were issued in the king's name.[3] Governor Keith, in 1718, insisted strongly upon following this latter course. For a few years subsequent to the death of William Penn, Keith's opinion prevailed, but on the accession of Penn's sons to authority, the original practice was resumed. The ordinances which, in the early eighteenth century, were issued by the governors for the continuance of courts, provided that the writs of the supreme court should be issued in the queen's name, but be sealed with the province seal; the duty of the quarter sessions was stated to be that of keeping the queen's peace.[4] But no references of this nature appear in the acts of assembly for the establishment of courts, all of which, prior to that of 1722, were disallowed by the crown.

In all the proprietary provinces, except West Jersey, the office of attorney-general was created for the protection of the rights of the proprietor and of the king. In 1685 James Graham was appointed to that office in New York. At least as early as 1660 the office was created in Maryland.

[1] N. C. Recs. II. 80, 264, 268 ; Hawks, II. 116, 196.
[2] N. J. Arch. XIII. 39.
[3] Charter and Laws, 298, 385 ; Col. Recs. III. 34 ; Shepherd, 386.
[4] Charter and Laws, 320, 353.

In South Carolina, Nicholas Trott, the first attorney-general, received his appointment in 1698. At a somewhat earlier date the office was filled in North Carolina. In East Jersey the twenty-four proprietors appointed an attorney-general. In Pennsylvania the office was in existence in 1693.[1]

[1] N. Y. Col. Docs. III. 351; Brodhead, II. 428; Md. Arch., Council, 1636–1667, 403; McCrady, South Carolina under Proprietary Government, 259, 298; N. C. Recs. I. 424; N. J. Arch. XIII. 42; Charter and Laws, 235.

CHAPTER XIII

ECCLESIASTICAL RELATIONS IN THE LATER PROPRIETARY PROVINCES

IN New England the uniformity of the population in nationality and culture was reflected in its religion. Nearly all of the communities which occupied that region were organized according to the same religious type. That, in fact, was the distinctive characteristic of the section, from which the other qualities of its people proceeded. Among the colonies it was the home, the citadel, of English Independency. That can be affirmed of it with even greater truth than it can be said of the eastern counties in England. The settlement of southern New England proceeded from a single impulse; those who participated in and at the same time controlled it were of a similar mental and moral type; their enterprise gave rise to institutions which closely conformed to a single type.

The proprietary provinces, on the other hand, were of varied origin and did not occupy a distinct section. They were peopled, not only by Englishmen, but by men of Scotch, Welsh, Dutch, French, Swedish, German, Swiss, and even Jewish, origin. Interspersed among the Swedes were some Finns and Poles. The Jews came largely from Portugal, and made New York their residence and the centre of their trade. Only a part of the inhabitants of these provinces became colonists from religious motives. Economic motives predominated among them.

The forms of their religious faith were even more varied than their nationalities. The English nationality contributed men of Catholic and Episcopalian faith, Independents, Baptists, and Quakers. The Dutch were mainly of the Reformed communion, as were also the French. The Swedes were Lutherans, while a part of the Dutch were organized somewhat late as a Lutheran church in New Amsterdam. Some Scotch Presbyterians settled in South Carolina and in East Jersey. The Palatines and Swiss of New Berne in North Carolina were of the German Reformed faith, but their strength was seriously weakened by the ravages of the Tuscarora Indians. During the period of which we are now speaking the German migration had just begun, and only faint indications of the volume which it was to attain after 1710 had yet appeared. The Scotch-Irish immigration, greatly strengthening the Presbyterian element in the population, belongs also, in the main, to the later period. The later German immigrants filled up eastern and central Pennsylvania, and somewhat changed the composition of population in New York; while the Scotch-Irish overflowed into the western parts of all the colonies south of Pennsylvania.

During the seventeenth century New York and the settlements along the Delaware exhibited the greatest diversity of nationalities and faiths. For this reason they were in some respects most typical of the nation that was to be. Governor Andros reported[1] in 1678 that there were Presbyterians, — meaning chiefly the Dutch Reformed communion, — Independents, Quakers, and Jews in the province, but the first two were most numerous and substantial. There was one Anglican church, maintained by the duke and located in the fort, at which his chaplain officiated and which was attended by the officials and garrison. Eight years later, when New York had become a royal province, Governor Dongan described[2] the situation in words which convey a clear idea of the variety of sects and at the same time of the widespread religious indifference. "Here bee not many," he said, "of the Church of England; few Roman Catholicks; abundance of Quakers preachers, men and Women especially; Singing Quakers; Ranting Quakers; Sabbatarians; Antisabbatarians; some Anabaptists some Independents; some Jews; in short of all sorts of opinions there are some, and the most part, of none at all." No contrast could be greater than that between the religious condition of a

[1] N. Y. Col. Docs. III. 262.   [2] *Ibid.* 415.

population like the one which Dongan described and that of CHAP.
the Puritan colonies of New England.

Considered from the standpoint of geographical distribu-
tion, the Catholics were to be found in Maryland and in very
limited numbers in New York. Even in Maryland they were
in the minority, though their social position was relatively
high and their influence greater than their numbers would
indicate.[1] Adherents of the English Church appear in small
numbers in all the provinces. In Maryland they gained
slowly on the Catholics, but during the seventeenth century
scarcely exceeded them. In South Carolina[2] the earliest
settlers and those who came from Barbadoes were of that
faith, constituting an important part of the population of
Berkeley county and living along the banks of the Ashley
and Cooper rivers. A few of the early emigrants from
Virginia into North Carolina[3] may have been Anglicans,
but not one local Episcopalian church existed in that part
of the province during the period of which we are speaking.
Anglicans were practically non-existent both in Pennsylvania and West Jersey. In East Jersey the only Anglicans
in early times were those who were immediately connected
with the governor's family, together with other proprietary officials. We hear of no Episcopalian clergyman in
that province until 1698, when one was settled at Perth
Amboy.[4] In New York the Episcopalian element was somewhat stronger, but it was confined almost wholly to the
government circle in New York city and to the region
afterward included in Westchester county. It is stated
that in 1680 Bishop Compton could find only four ministers
of the Church of England in North America, and that of
these only one or two had been regularly sent over.[5]

---

[1] Johnson, Foundation of Maryland, 32 ; Md. Arch., Council, 1667–1688,
133.

[2] McCrady, *op. cit.* 329.

[3] Weeks, in J. H. U. Studies, X. 259.

[4] Whitehead, Contributions to East Jersey History, 209 ; Whitehead, East
Jersey under the Proprietors, 245 ; Hatfield, History of Elizabeth, 113, 280,
289 ; Dally, History of Woodbridge, 121 *et seq.*

[5] Humphreys, History of Society for Propagation of Gospel, 8 ; Hazard,
Annals of Pennsylvania, 469.

The remaining population of all these provinces consisted of Protestant dissenters and those who were indifferent to all religion. The dissenters fall into two main classes, the followers of the tenets of John Calvin and the Quakers. The Lutherans were a comparatively small body, found chiefly in New York city, on the Delaware, and in South Carolina.[1] In Maryland, Anne Arundel county was settled by Puritans who had removed from Virginia, and they proved themselves to be a very aggressive and disturbing element in the population. Nowhere else outside of Massachusetts did the militant quality in Puritanism show itself so clearly. In South Carolina, Huguenots, Presbyterians, Congregationalists, and Baptists could be found in all the settled parts of the province, but they were most numerous on the Santee and the Edisto. In the northern part of the province no more definite trace of them can be discovered at this period than of Episcopalians. In the provinces farther north dissenters of this type were to be found in small numbers in the settlements on the lower Delaware, but chiefly in East Jersey and New York. In the last-named provinces they constituted by far the chief religious element in the population. They comprised, not only the Dutch of New York and the Scotch Presbyterians of East Jersey, but the Puritans or Congregationalists of the Long Island towns and of that fringe of settlements which had been founded by New Englanders in northern New Jersey.

As early as 1660 a certain Quaker element could be found in all these provinces. In Maryland, South Carolina, and New York it was small and unimportant. In East Jersey it became quite strong under the twenty-four proprietors, a majority of the first twelve on that board being Quakers. At Perth Amboy and Woodbridge Quaker meetings were regularly held after 1686.[2] But the strongholds of Quakerism were West Jersey, Pennsylvania, and North Carolina. The preaching of Quakerism, as we have seen, began in North Carolina in 1672, Edmundson and George Fox himself being the missionaries. By 1676 the Society of Friends was organized there. In 1689 a quarterly meeting was begun,

[1] McCrady, 404.   [2] Dally, History of Woodbridge, 59 et seq.

and in 1703 the first meeting-house was built.[1] At the close
of the seventeenth century the Quakers were the only strong
religious body in the province. In West Jersey they constituted practically all the population, while in Pennsylvania [2]
about one-half the population were Quakers.

CHAP.
XIII.

In view of these facts the great preponderance of dissent
in all the later proprietary provinces becomes evident. If,
in addition, we consider the religious faith of the founders
of these provinces and of their officials, a considerable diversity will also appear, as well as a great divergence between
the faith of proprietors and officials and that of the people of
their provinces. It is true that New York was originally
founded and governed by those who in the light of English law were dissenters, but who at the same time were the
disciples of the recognized faith of the Netherlands. Maryland was founded by a family of Catholic recusants. West
Jersey and Pennsylvania were both settled and governed by
dissenters. The same is true of the three Lower Counties,
and of East Jersey while it was under the management of
the twenty-four proprietors. But an Anglican minority
was either present in these provinces from the beginning or
developed in them with the lapse of time. The original proprietors of the Carolinas, with the exception of Shaftesbury,
were Anglicans, and the officials whom they appointed to
reside within their province were for the most part of that
faith. Later, Blake, a dissenter, and Archdale, a Quaker,
became members of the board. In South Carolina the officials had the support of a part of the population which was
socially important. In North Carolina that support, during
the seventeenth century, was totally lacking. In Maryland
adherents of the English Church slowly won their way to
official positions under a Catholic proprietor. Governor
Stone, who received his appointment in 1642, was an Anglican. After that time adherents of the English Church
shared the office with Catholics. Though the proprietor of
New York was a Catholic, his appointees, until the time of

[1] Weeks, in J. H. U. Studies, X. 260, 270.
[2] Penn and Logan Correspondence, I. 102 ; Sharpless, A Quaker Experiment in Government, 74.

Thomas Dongan, were Anglicans, and special recognition
was given to that communion by the English officials in the
province.   A very few Catholics held office under James II
as king.   The first proprietors of New Jersey were Anglicans,
and so were their leading appointees ; but the English Church
lost even official support after the division of the province.
That support its adherents could never expect to have in
West Jersey or Pennsylvania, or in East Jersey after 1682.

With the exception of the Quakers and the Baptists, all
the inhabitants of these provinces retained a belief in a connection of some sort between church and state, in a regulation by law of the relation between sects, in the bestowment
of privileges upon some one sect, in the public maintenance
of the clergy and the exercise by the civil power of a share
in their appointment, in the maintenance of a close connection regulated by law between education and religion.   This
belief was inherited from the systems of the Old World.   The
proprietors of these provinces, however they might differ,
shared it as a common inheritance.   Among both colonists
and proprietors it, however, varied in intensity from the zeal
shown by the Puritans of Maryland, or by Lord Granville
among the Carolina proprietors, to the quietism of the
Palatines, or the indifferentism of Shaftesbury or of some
of the Calverts.   All had been reared under the state-
church system of Europe, and none had reached the broad
doctrine of liberty which Roger Williams was proclaiming.
The conditions, however, as between province and province,
varied to such an extent that the ecclesiastical system of
each must be largely peculiar to itself.   Outside the Quaker
provinces this was formulated wholly or mainly by the proprietors and their officials.   In some cases it was distinctly
the result of an effort on their part to satisfy the needs of
the province, in others it was simply an expression of their
own preferences.   The variety of faiths among the colonists
and the desire to attract immigrants, however, precluded any
successful attempts to establish systems of uniformity, and
thus to uphold one confession to the exclusion of all others.
It was equally impossible to make religion a condition of
active citizenship.   In other words, a broad and tolerant

ecclesiastical policy was the only practicable one, and to this the legislation of the provinces tended. In order to show what their ecclesiastical systems were, brief reference will be made to each of the provinces in turn.

The king in the charter of Maryland gave to the proprietor the patronage and advowson of all the churches within his province, together with the license to found churches and chapels, and to cause the same to be dedicated " according to the ecclesiastical laws of our kingdom of England." This clause, together with the requirement that the provisions of the charter should be interpreted in such a way that God's holy and true Christian religion and the allegiance due to the king and his successors might not be injured and weakened, did not essentially differ from statements which appear in other charters of the time.[1] Had the grantee been a communicant of the Church of England, they would have been at once interpreted as implying the right to establish that church in the province. But a special significance was given to the terms by the fact that the Maryland grantee was a Catholic, and therefore could not intend to establish the English Church. The language, however, admitted of his using discretion, and the second Lord Baltimore, with tact and skill, took full advantage of the opportunity for freedom of action which was thus afforded.

The Calverts were Catholics of the moderate or Gallican type. There is no proof that they were ever disposed to labor actively for a Catholic restoration in England, or for an interpretation of papal supremacy which would seriously menace the independence of the English nation. They were diplomatic by nature and were forced specially to cultivate this quality in the management of their colonial interests, because of their exceptional position as Catholic proprietors.

While, of course, they were ready to profit by a large Catholic migration from England, should such occur, it was from the first their endeavor to secure Protestant as well as Catholic settlers. When they began to seek for colonists,

---

[1] The language used in the charter of Carolina is almost identical with that of the Maryland charter on this point.

they found recruits chiefly among those who were discontented with the ecclesiastical conditions in England.   On
the first ships that came over, the majority of freemen were
Catholics, and the majority of servants were Protestants.
The officials were instructed[1] to cause all rites of the
Roman Catholic religion on shipboard to be celebrated as
privately as might be, to instruct the Catholics to refrain
from all open discussion of religious subjects, and to treat
the Protestants with as much mildness and favor as justice
would permit.

After Maryland was reached this rule was carefully observed, though Catholic services were publicly held, and the
affairs of the province were administered by Catholics.   Any
hopes which Lord Baltimore may have entertained that a
large Catholic emigration from England would follow were
disappointed, and the Protestant component among the population of his province came to exceed more and more the
number of the Catholics.   This fact, even if the proprietor
had not been a Catholic, would have necessitated the toleration of certain varieties of religious faith.   The fact that the
proprietor was a Catholic made this doubly necessary, and
committed the Calverts to toleration as a necessary course
of policy.   They did not adopt it as a theory, like Roger
Williams; they did not carry it to the extent of recognizing
absolute freedom of thought and action.   They followed the
policy up to a certain limit, because it was the only system
under which a Catholic proprietor of an English province in
the seventeenth century could act.   But owing to the relations which existed with Virginia and to the settlement of
Anne Arundel county by Puritans, the maintenance even of
this policy was rendered for a time impossible, and the province was filled with civil broils.

Before, however, these events developed the proprietor
was given an opportunity to define his relations with the
Catholics in the province, and it was done in such a way
as to show most clearly that he did not intend to depart
from the ancient principles of ecclesiastical law as they were
understood by Englishmen.

[1] Calvert Papers, I. 132.

The three Jesuit priests who were sent to the province CHAP.
with the first colonists, — Andrew White, Thomas Copley, XIII.
and John Altham, — as the result of their missionary work
among the natives, had come into a position where, to the
grants of land which had been made in their behalf by
the proprietor, they might add still larger purchases from
the Indians. This raised the question, whether the Society
of Jesus should be allowed to accumulate estates of indefinite extent in the province.   The priests also,[1] in strict
accordance with the principles of the canonists, claimed that
the canon law extended by its own authority to the province,
and hence that the clergy in Maryland were entitled to all
the rights and to all the exemptions from lay jurisdiction
which the church anywhere enjoyed.   This implied[2] that
the clergy should be exempt from lay taxation and from the
jurisdiction of lay courts, should be entitled to the right of
sanctuary, and to jurisdiction over marriage and wills.   On
these questions the burden of English opinion, even during
the middle age, had been unfavorable to the claims of the
canonists, and with those claims it had finally broken in the
reign of Henry VIII.   The proprietor met the question in
thorough English fashion.

He appointed John Lewger his secretary and sent him to
the province in 1637.   Lewger was an Oxford man, who
had once been a Protestant but had later been converted to
Catholicism.   He was an able man of affairs, and was well
acquainted with the law and history of this question.   He
began to prove wills and grant letters of administration.
From the assembly in 1638, though the majority of its
membership was probably Catholic, acts were procured guarantying the supremacy of the common and statute law in
all important relations.   The priests, though summoned
to this body, absented themselves on the plea of sickness.
Father Copley[3] now wrote to the proprietor, complaining
that Mr. Lewger held that the church was not entitled to
any privileges except those which were granted to it by
the commonwealth.   He asked that the privileges which it

[1] Johnson, Foundation of Maryland, 71 *et seq.*
[2] Calvert Papers, I. 166.   [3] *Ibid.* 162, 172.

claimed might be granted, and in particular that the priests might freely live and work among the Indians. With these demands Thomas Cornwallis, councillor and captain and the richest planter in the province, expressed his sympathy.

These representations and others which came to him from Maryland roused the proprietor to take vigorous action in defence of his right as a secular lord. More legislation was procured from the assembly, and an appeal was taken through Father Henry More, the English provincial of the Jesuit order, to the authorities at Rome. While this was pending Baltimore wrote to Governor Calvert [1] that he believed that the Jesuits were planning his destruction, and, if they could not accomplish it through the English, would call in the aid of the Indians. " If the greatest saint upon earth," he continued, " should intrude himself into my howse against my will, and despite of mee with intention to save the souls of my family, but withal give mee just cause to suspect that he likewise designed my temporall destruction, or that being already in my howse doth actuallie practise it, although he perhaps do manie spirituall goods, yet certeinlie I may and ought to preserve myself by the expulsion of such an enemy, and by provideing others to do the spirituall good he did. . . . For the Law of nature teacheth us that it is lawfull for every man in his owne just defence, *vim vi repellere*."

But the fears of Baltimore were not to be realized. The appeal called forth from Rome a renunciation of all the claims which the Jesuits had made, the lands which they had procured from the Indians were released to the proprietor, while it was acknowledged that no valid grants could exist in the province unless they were derived from him. It was also agreed that no Jesuit priest should thereafter be sent to Maryland. Those who had been there were recalled and their places taken by secular priests. In 1641 new conditions of plantation were issued,[2] by which all the provisions of the English statutes of mortmain were put into force in Maryland. Thus an interesting crisis in the history of this province was passed, and it was brought fully into line with the traditions of English development.

[1] Calvert Papers, I. 217.   [2] Johnson, 64.

Only a brief interval elapsed between this event and the outbreak of the civil war in England. It found government in Maryland in the hands of Catholics, and no act of toleration yet passed. A Protestant opposition now speedily developed, and of this Claiborne and Ingle availed themselves for the purpose of overthrowing the government. Their plans were facilitated by the absence from the province of Governor Calvert, who, since Lord Baltimore had been placed under bonds not to leave the kingdom, had found it necessary to consult him in England. While he was away affairs, amid much confusion, drifted toward Protestant control. In England parliament was with difficulty kept from causing the rights of the proprietor over the province to be forfeited. This, however, was prevented, and in 1648 the proprietor appointed William Stone, a Protestant, to be governor, and associated with him a council the majority of whose members were Protestant. A clause was inserted in the governor's oath[1] which declared that he would not molest in the free exercise of his religion any one who believed in Jesus Christ, especially if that person was a Roman Catholic, and moreover if he kept the peace and was faithful to the lord proprietor ; he would also punish any who did so interfere with the exercise of religious liberty. This clause contained the substance of Lord Baltimore's views concerning the ecclesiastical policy which it was necessary at that time to follow in his province. The gist of it was this, that all believers in the doctrine of the Trinity should enjoy freedom of worship, provided they kept the peace and remained faithful to the proprietor. No provision was made for the toleration of Quakers, Jews, or Unitarians, or in fact for any type of opinion other than that to which Catholics, Anglicans, Presbyterians, and Independents could subscribe. A toleration such as this, of certain definite forms of belief, provided their adherents kept the peace, does not differ in principle from the policy which had generally been pursued by European governments, and was far removed from absolute religious freedom.

But the oath simply imposed a condition upon the pro-

[1] Md. Arch., Proceedings of Council, 1636–1667, 210.

vincial executive. So important was the issue that it merited embodiment in statutory form, and for this reason Lord Baltimore now sent over the bill which, when passed, became the famous act of toleration of 1649.[1] This act simply elaborates the principle set forth in the governor's oath, and the oft-quoted passage near the close of the law reproduces with much exactness the phraseology of the oath itself. The text of the act is mainly occupied with denunciations of heavy punishment against those who should deny the doctrine of the Trinity, or utter reproachful words against any one of the persons composing it, against the Virgin Mary, or the Evangelists, or Apostles.

The profanation of Sunday was also forbidden. The application by way of reproach to any inhabitants of the province, or to any who should visit it for trade or any other purpose, of the terms "heretic," "schismatic," "idolater," "popish priest," "roundhead," "separatist," or the name of any sect used in contempt, was forbidden on penalty of fine or whipping and imprisonment. The evident purpose of these enactments was to check the use of intemperate language, which otherwise might provoke breaches of the peace. It was essentially a police law, broadened somewhat in its bearings by the declaration, "whereas the enforcing of the conscience in matters of Religion hath frequently fallen out to be of dangerous Consequences in those commonwealthes where it hath been practiced . . ." It is clear that this statute originated from motives of political expediency, and that it was intended to meet specific conditions as they then existed in Maryland, with slight regard to freedom of thought as a universal principle.

While Lord Baltimore was perfecting the plan which he hoped would effectually prevent outbreaks of religious animosity in his province, an element was added to its population which was destined soon to defeat his purposes. This was the Puritans who, in order to escape from interference with their worship in Virginia, removed to Maryland and there settled Providence, later called Annapolis. The fact that the proprietor was willing to admit these settlers indi-

[1] Md. Arch., Proceedings of Assembly, 1638–1664, 244.

cates the extent to which he subordinated religious preferences to a desire for the improvement of his province.   But
the Puritans presently objected to the oath of fidelity because
it contained the words, " true and absolute proprietor," and
other similar expressions.   A still more fundamental objection in their eyes to a permanent recognition of the government which had sheltered them was the fact that its authority
was exercised by a Catholic, an adherent of the power of
antichrist.

Therefore, upon the triumph of the cause of the Independents in England and the renewal by Claiborne of his attacks
on the rights of Lord Baltimore, the Puritans joined in an
effort to overthrow the power of the proprietor.   On this
occasion Claiborne acted as one of the commissioners who
were appointed by the commonwealth government in England for the reduction of the plantations within the Chesapeake to submission.   Before this show of authority Governor
Stone and his council were forced to yield, and in 1654 a *de
facto* government was established under the supervision of
the Puritan commissioners.   One of the acts of the first
assembly over which the Puritans had control was the passage of the law withdrawing protection from the Roman
Catholics, though the worship of other sects who accepted
the doctrine of the Trinity was to be tolerated.   Under this
law, for a period of about four years, the Puritans were able
to exclude those who had admitted them to the province
from the protection of the laws.

But at the end of that time the government in England
from which the commissioners had originally derived their
authority began to collapse, and the proprietor was able to
regain his rights.   As the act of 1649 had never been repealed, its authority was held immediately to revive.   Lord
Baltimore also issued a solemn declaration that he would
never assent to its repeal.[1]   On this basis, from and after
1660, the system of religious toleration in Maryland was
continued.   Quakers, as early as 1658, were permitted to
subscribe instead of taking the oath of fidelity.   The subsequent refusal of some of them to bear arms in time of danger,

[1] Scharf, History of Maryland, I. 228.

to take the jurors' oath or give testimony in court, and their insistence that they were governed by the inner light rather than by man's law, led in 1659 to the issue of a severe order [1] against them. But it was not necessary to enforce it, at least on any considerable scale.

As the period of the Restoration advanced, the number of sects within the province somewhat increased, and all enjoyed a full degree of practical toleration. Of the mildness of the proprietary rule in this regard there can be no doubt. But the proportion borne by Catholics among the total population steadily diminished, till they were estimated to constitute not more than one-twelfth. The adherents of the Church of England were about twice as numerous as the Catholics, while the remaining three-fourths of the inhabitants were claimed by the other sects. At the same time, however, the Anglicans were asserting more exclusive claims at home, and the feeling which this induced was reflected within the small body of its clergy in the colonies.[2] In 1676 the first demand for "some established support for a Protestant ministry" was sent to the Archbishop of Canterbury by a resident Anglican clergyman in Maryland, accompanied with a complaint of the godlessness of the colony. That led to a hearing before the privy council, at which Lord Baltimore was able to show that a sufficient number of churches for the accommodation of the people had been provided by voluntary contributions, and that four Anglican clergymen were then laboring in the province. He had, however, to admit that the adherents of his own faith were few, though of wide toleration and generally peaceful relations among the sects there could be no doubt. But with the revival of Protestant zeal which preceded the English revolution; the position of a Catholic proprietor appeared more anomalous. The outcry against "popish plots" which was heard in England was reëchoed in Maryland, and indications multiplied that even Lord Baltimore's policy of toleration could not bring permanent quiet to his province.

[1] Md. Arch., Proceedings of Assembly, 1637–1664, 370; Proceedings of the Council, 1636–1667, 362.

[2] *Ibid.* Council, 1667–1688, 130–133.

The policy of the Carolina proprietors looked steadily toward the establishment of the English Church within their province, though with large liberty for dissenters. By royal charter they, like Baltimore, received the patronage of all churches and chapels within the province, the same to be consecrated according to the ecclesiastical laws of England. This they interpreted as authority for the establishment of the English Church. But the charter also granted to the proprietors right to issue indulgences and dispensations to dissenters and their worship, provided the recipients of these favors were peaceable and loyal. This, because of the remoteness of the province, was thought to be " no breach of the unity and conformity established in this nation."

The sentiment of the charter on the point referred to was repeated by the proprietors in the Declarations and Proposals of 1663, and in the Concessions and Agreement of 1665.[1] In the former they promised as ample freedom in religious matters as would-be colonists should desire. In the latter they declared, almost in the words of the royal charter itself, that no one should be molested or punished for differences of opinion or practice in matters of religion, provided they did not disturb the civil peace. It is true that a Massachusetts Puritan might have approved this declaration, but he would have interpreted the clause about disturbing the civil peace much more strictly than did the Carolina authorities, or the magistrates of any of the later proprietary provinces. The view of the proprietors respecting the charter and the limits of the proposed establishment in Carolina was expressed in the next clause. This was intended to empower the assemblies to provide for the appointment of as many ministers as they saw fit, and also for their maintenance, " Giving Liberty besides to any person or persons to keepe and maintayne what preachers or Ministers they please."

Essentially the same ideas appear in the Fundamental Constitutions,[2] where they are elaborated and receive certain peculiar additions. It was imposed as a duty upon the parliament to care for the building of churches and the mainte-

[1] N. C. Recs. I. 45, 80.   [2] *Ibid.* 202 ; Articles 95–109.

nance of clergymen of the Church of England, "which being the only true and orthodox, and the national religion of all the King's dominions, is so also of Carolina, and therefore it alone should be allowed to receive public maintenance by grant of parliament." This well expresses the natural thought of all adherents of the English Church concerning the ecclesiastical policy which it was proper to exercise toward the dominions. The establishment of the church within the colonies, however, might or might not be accompanied by acts of uniformity. In this case, as in all others which arose subsequent to the Restoration, the maintenance of uniformity was expressly disclaimed. It was provided that any seven or more persons, agreeing in religion, might constitute a church or profession to which they should give some distinguishing name. The names of the persons so uniting, together with the terms of admission and communion, should be inscribed in a book, and this should be kept by the register of the precinct where they resided. By signing such a book a person became a member, and by striking out his name he would cease to be a member of said communion. Under these conditions any religionists who acknowledged a God and the obligation of public worship could enjoy full liberty of conscience. The kissing of the book, or the holding up of the right hand, or any other proper form, might accompany the administration of oaths. But atheists were to be wholly excluded from the estate of freeholders or active citizens within the province. One provision of the Constitutions even went so far as to exclude from the protection of the law all persons above seventeen years of age who had not become members of some church or profession. The framers of this document seem therefore to have intended to create an externally religious community in which many forms of worship might coexist, but within which those who denied the existence of a God or the obligation of public worship should not be tolerated.

It was the intention of the proprietors that the Fundamental Constitutions should be enforced in the northern as well as the southern part of the province. But it is only necessary to refer to the almost total lack of religious worship in the Albemarle region, save that of the Quakers, during the first thirty years of the colony's existence in order to show that the provisions of this document concerning religion were never executed. Even in the southern part of the province no effort was ever made to outlaw the godless. But at the same time the Constitutions set forth the ideal which was cherished by the proprietors, and which at last was measurably realized within the province.

Provision was not made for a church or a resident clergyman in the Ashley river settlement until after 1680,[1] when the town at Oyster Point was laid out. Then the site of the present St. Michael's church, Charleston, was reserved. On this the church then called St. Philip's was built, but how soon thereafter a minister began regularly to officiate there it is impossible to state. It is known that a clergyman of the establishment was in the colony in 1689, for he was fined and imprisoned by Governor Colleton for preaching what the latter considered to be a seditious sermon. In 1696 the Rev. Samuel Marshall became rector of St. Philip's, but died of yellow fever three years later. He was succeeded by the Rev. Edward Marston. By that time another Episcopal clergyman was officiating at Goose Creek, a settlement on a branch of the Cooper river, and which was later organized as St. James' parish. Those were the only Episcopal churches in South Carolina at the beginning of the eighteenth century. But the Anglican population was steadily increasing, and in point of wealth and social position it may be considered the equal of its rivals. According to the best estimates it comprised at the beginning of the eighteenth century nearly one-half of the total population of the southern part of the province.

By 1690, or earlier, a church consisting of Presbyterians and Congregationalists, with some French Protestants, had been organized in Charlestown. In the same town a French Protestant church had been founded by 1693. A Baptist church was organized at the same place in 1699, or 1700, while a Quaker meeting was begun there about 1696.[2] An-

---

[1] Dalcho, History of the Protestant Episcopal Church in South Carolina, 26 et seq.; McCrady, op. cit. 183, 331–334.   [2] Dalcho; McCrady, 329 et seq.

other French Protestant church had been founded on the Santee, and a group of settlers of the same faith had gathered at Goose Creek.[1] Recognition was specially given to the growing body of French Protestants by the statute of 1697. This, though immediately referring to aliens, provided that all Christians, papists excepted, should enjoy full and undisturbed exercise of their consciences, so long as they kept within the professed rules of their religion.

In South Carolina, in 1704, occurred the notable attempt of the period, in a colony outside of New England, to limit the suffrage by a religious test. It was at a time of strong Tory reaction in England, when the High Churchmen there were making their first attempts to pass the bill against occasional conformity. Lord Granville, who at this time was lord palatine in the board of Carolina proprietors, was a High Churchman and strongly favored the policy of his party. Sir Nathaniel Johnson, who was then governor of South Carolina, sympathized with his views, and was ready to coöperate in a plan to exclude dissenters from the legislature of South Carolina. His influence, with that of Nicholas Trott, the chief justice and most astute politician in the province, sufficed to carry the council for the measure. Colonel William Rhett, who as commander of the armed vessels of the province had recently helped to protect Charlestown against an attack of a combined French and Spanish force, supported the same cause. Job Howes, the surveyor-general, was also a member of the official clique. This body of men was resolved to get control of the lower house, a majority of whose members had hitherto been dissenters, and secure its coöperation in the passage of laws which should strongly favor the Anglicans.

Though until a few years previous to the time of which we are speaking a clear majority of the inhabitants of South Carolina had been dissenters and opponents of church establishment, that situation had now somewhat changed. The change had been caused by the immigration of French Huguenots and their practical identification with the Anglicans. The German Lutherans maintained a similar attitude toward

[1] McCrady, 337.

the adherents of the English Church. Though in name dissenters,[1] they were not really such, and the persistent opposition of the Presbyterians and Independents to the extension
of the suffrage to all who were not native-born Englishmen
shows that they realized the fact. The delay of public
business which was caused by this struggle, and that at a
time when the province was menaced by foreign invasion,
furnished to the governor and his Church of England friends
additional excuse for the measure of proscription to which
they now committed themselves.

The assembly which was elected in 1703, with the help, as
it was charged, of every Frenchman in Craven and Berkeley
counties, was still in existence. Job Howes was chosen as
its speaker. In the spring session of 1704 a bill was introduced providing that thereafter all who were chosen members
and took their seats in the commons house of assembly must
within one year have publicly received the sacrament according to the rites of the English Church or have generally
conformed to its worship. If the sacrament had been received, proof of the fact must be submitted in the form of a
certificate signed by the minister who administered it and
supported by the oath of two credible witnesses. Those who
had not received the sacrament within the time prescribed
must by oath or solemn profession declare that they usually
attended the services of the Church of England, and for a
year had not communed with any other church or congregation. The latter provision was probably intended to meet
the case of some of the supporters of the bill who, it was
said, never received the sacrament anywhere. If any person
failed to qualify as the sacrament prescribed, it was further
provided that the candidate who had received the next highest number of votes should be entitled to the seat.

In the laws prescribing the qualifications of members of
the English House of Commons there was no precedent for
a measure of this kind, for, as has been correctly said, the
corporation act of Charles II only affected the borough
members,[2] and that remotely. No serious attempt was ever
made in England to exclude nonconformists from parlia-

---

[1] McCrady, 391, 404, 440.   [2] *Ibid.* 408.

ment. It was natural then that the bill, because of its extreme character, should arouse strong opposition in the commons house. It was attacked on the ground that it violated the chartered rights of the colonists, though really the charter had nothing to say about the organization or membership of the legislature. But the effective argument was urged against the measure, that it was "not proper for the inhabitants of the colony at this time." It was opposed by some of the Churchmen of the province, and notably by the Rev. Edward Marston, the incumbent of St. Philip's, Charlestown. In sermons he violently opposed the measure and abused its supporters.

The bill finally passed,[1] though by a majority of only one in the lower house. The struggle over it was then transferred to England. But before its fate there was decided, the violence of Marston's attack on the government party, coupled with his persistence, caused the passage of an act which, in addition to establishing the Church of England and organizing a parish system in South Carolina, provided for a lay commission for the trial of ecclesiastical causes.[2] The leading members of the government clique were designated in the act as members of the commission. This measure struck at the very foundations of ecclesiastical jurisdiction, and its passage was therefore indefensible. But a certain excuse for it was furnished by the fact that a clergyman who held the principal living in the province, by his violent conduct had made his presence there intolerable, and yet no one had power to remove him. The most that could be done was to deprive him of his salary, and that the legislature was not slow in accomplishing. Viewed from this standpoint, the act embodied the desire of many of the colonists that, in the absence of the proper ecclesiastical authority within the colonies, laymen should have the right of removing, but not degrading, incumbents whose character or work was unsatisfactory. By less direct means the same thing was often attempted, and sometimes accomplished, by parishioners in the colonies where during the

---

[1] Statutes of South Carolina, II. 232, Rivers, 217 *et seq.*
[2] Statutes of South Carolina, II. 236.

colonial period Episcopalian ministers were settled. In
Jamaica and in other royal provinces such powers were both
claimed and exercised by the governors. In South Carolina the same object was sought through a lay commission.

At the time when the two acts in question were passed,
John Ash had been sent to England by the dissenters of
South Carolina as their agent. He was instructed to lay
their grievances before the proprietors and, if possible,
secure redress. But, before he had progressed far with his
mission, Ash died. Joseph Boone was then sent as his
successor, being specially instructed also to protest against
the church act. When he arrived in England excitement
over the occasional conformity bill was at its height, and the
supporters of the Established Church were strongly insisting
both upon its perils and its claims. Before the board of
proprietors Boone met with no success at all. Lord Granville would scarcely listen to arguments against the acts.
He cast his own vote and that of the minor, Lord John
Carteret, in their favor. Craven and Colleton supported him.
Archdale, the Quaker, opposed them. The other proprietors appear to have taken no action. But a majority of the
votes cast were in favor of the acts, and they were thus approved.

Boone now turned to the House of Lords. He was himself a merchant, and had the support of several London
merchants who were interested in trade to the Carolinas.
The Whig majority among the Lords was in sympathy with
the general purposes of the merchants. It had, moreover,
been strengthened by the Whig victory at the recent election, and was further encouraged by the continued successes
of Marlborough on the continent. Boone and his associates
now submitted a memorial [1] to the House of Lords, in which,
though they were supporting the cause of dissenters in
South Carolina, they championed the ecclesiastical jurisdiction of the Bishop of London. The Lords, owing to the
press of business at the end of the session, were unable to
deal thoroughly with the question. But they took up the
cause of the petitioners and addressed the queen, asking

[1] N. C. Recs. I. 637 *et seq*

her to relieve the province of the oppression under which
it lay. The acts were now referred by the privy council
to Northey and Harcourt, the law officers of the crown.
They reported that the acts in question were inconsistent
with that very elastic clause which found a place in all the
royal charters, requiring that laws in the colonies should be
consonant to reason, and not repugnant to the laws of England.[1] The crown, in their opinion, should require the proprietors and assembly to declare them null and void. They
were ready, also, to use the affair as a pretext on which to
institute judicial proceedings for the recall of the Carolina
charter.

But to this step two objections presented themselves. One
arose from the fact that not all the proprietors had approved
the acts, and the justice of punishing the entire board for
an offence committed by a part of its members was doubtful. In addition to this, certain members of the board of
Carolina proprietors were peers, and the query arose whether
the filing of an information against them might not be
thought a breach of the privileges of the peerage. These
considerations furnished a sufficient excuse for dropping
the plan of judicial proceedings, though the informations
were already in course of preparation. But, taking advantage of the weakness of the board, its lack of unanimity on
the question at issue, its desire to avoid *quo warranto* proceedings, the queen ordered it to have the measure repealed.
Instructions in accord with this command were duly for-
warded by the proprietors to the governor.

Governor Johnson, accordingly, in his speech before the
general assembly at the opening of the first session of 1706,
recommended that the acts be repealed, though he urged
that a clause be introduced disenabling Marston from being
a minister in Charlestown. The small majority by which
the laws had been passed had already been changed into a
minority, and no difficulty was found in passing the act of
repeal during the session of November, 1706.[2] That was
immediately followed by the enactment of a law establishing
the Church of England within the province. Under this

[1] N. C. Recs. I. 642.   [2] Statutes of South Carolina, II. 281, 282.

law South Carolina was divided into ten parishes, of which CHAP.
Charlestown formed one, Berkeley county contained six, XIII.
Colleton county, two, while the French on the Santee in
Craven county formed the tenth parish. The act also provided for the building, at the public expense, of six churches
and six houses for the rectors, for the laying out of glebes
and churchyards, and for the payment of salaries to the
rectors. Rectors, as provided in the act of 1704, were to be
chosen by the inhabitants of the several parishes who were
of the Church of England. The introduction of the parish
system was completed by provisions for the annual election
of vestrymen and church wardens by the freeholders of the
parishes who were of the Church of England. Under this
system, and supplied with clergymen by the Bishop of London and the Society for the Propagation of the Gospel,
South Carolina continued to exist until the Revolution.

In explaining the origin of the so-called Cary's rebellion
it has been necessary, in an earlier chapter, to refer at some
length to the ecclesiastical affairs of North Carolina. In
this connection the briefest possible reference to the changes
which took place there in the early years of the eighteenth
century will suffice. The northern, as well as the southern,
part of the province was influenced by the contemporary
religious movement in England. In 1701 the adherents of
the English Church in North Carolina, though greatly in the
minority, secured the passage of an act which provided for
the organization of parishes, laying out of glebes, building
of churches, and the support of ministers by a public levy
on all tithables. This expenditure was to be met by a poll
tax. In Chowan precinct a vestry was at once formed, and
the first house of worship in North Carolina was built. Two
other churches were also built. Though this project had
been started within the province itself, the opposition to it
was strong, and the Quakers had prepared to repeal the law
in the assembly of 1703. But this was not necessary, as the
proprietors disallowed the act on the ground that £30 per
year — the sum provided by the law — was insufficient for
the support of the clergy.

The Society for the Propagation of the Gospel had now

begun to send missionaries into North Carolina. Blair, Gordon, Adams, and later the worthless Urmston, were sent. The first three labored hard, but amid great obstacles, natural and social, for the spread of their system of faith. But the work outside of Pasquotank precinct proceeded very slowly; in most regions it made scarcely any progress. The general ignorance and indifference of the people, the strength of the Quakers, and the activity of certain irregular itinerant preachers presented hindrances which it was wholly beyond the power of a handful of Anglican missionaries to overcome. This was the situation when Lord Granville, Governor Johnson, and their supporters sought to establish the church in South Carolina.

It was the desire of these men to extend a similar policy to North Carolina. Daniel, who was appointed by Johnson in 1704 as deputy governor of North Carolina, was an important agent in this work. Soon after his appointment, under the title of the " vestry act," the law of 1701 was in substance reënacted. But again the act was passed with great difficulty and by a majority of only one or two votes. When, as we have seen, Edmund Porter as the agent of the Quakers of North Carolina accompanied John Ash to England, it is probable that one of his errands was to file a protest against the approval of the " vestry act." His effort to secure the removal of Governor Daniel — which was successful — may well have been undertaken with a view to prevent the enactment, in the northern province, of other measures like those which the South Carolina clique were attempting to embody in law. Whether the " vestry act " was disallowed we are not informed. But it is not probable that it was enforced, for the province was soon after thrown into confusion, partly at least by the dispute concerning the administration of oaths to Quakers. This developed into Cary's rebellion as it was in its early stage.

The second stage of this conflict, in which arms were actually resorted to, was reached in 1711, soon after the arrival of Governor Hyde. The outbreak at that time was doubtless occasioned by the passage of a severe sedition law and also of another act for the establishment of the English

Church in the province. This, like all the earlier acts on the subject, has been ·lost. But in a letter of the missionary Urmston[1] the statement is made that it provided for a vestry of twelve men in every precinct, and required them to choose church wardens. To the church wardens was given power to purchase glebes, build churches and ministers' houses, provide maintenance for them, and see that parishes were supplied with clergymen who should be approved by the Bishop of London. This law apparently remained in force after the restoration of quiet in the province, and under it the church maintained a somewhat feeble existence till the close of the proprietary period.

The ecclesiastical system to which the Dutch in New Netherland had been accustomed provided for the establishment of the Dutch Reformed Church. The secular head of the establishment, occupying the position which was held by the government in the Netherlands, was the West India company. The Amsterdam chamber appointed clergymen, schoolmasters, comforters of the sick, and sent them to the province. The full procedure can be traced in the case of the Rev. Hermanus Bloem, who was settled at Esopus.[2] The Rev. Everardus Bogardus resigned after a violent quarrel with Director Kieft and the council. Had he reached home alive, charges against him might have been heard.[3] The company prescribed, rather than paid, the salaries of clergymen, depending on the people of their charge to furnish mainly or wholly their support. But the company looked to the Classis of Amsterdam to recommend candidates, and from its nominees appointments were made. Correspondence was regularly maintained between the Classis and the clergymen who labored in the province, and they were subject to its ecclesiastical control.[4] As the number of

[1] N. C. Recs. I. 769.

[2] N. Y. Col. Docs. XIII. 102, 103, 130, 155.   The procedure in the case of the dismissal of the Rev. Henricus Selyns, of Brooklyn, appears in N. Y. Col. Docs. XIV. 550.

[3] N. Ý. Col. Docs. XIV. 69, 84 ; O'Callaghan, I. 266, 362 ; II. 34.

[4] Corwin, History of the Dutch Reformed Church in the United States, American Church History Series, 32, 33. The correspondence still exists in manuscript.

clergymen sent to the province was few, the right of choice of the local churches was restricted. They, however, exercised it within limits, and were facilitated in doing so by the fact that they provided most of the support.[1]

The company at first proposed that freedom of worship should be granted to dissenters, and this position it never expressly abandoned. But in the Freedoms and Exemptions of 1640 it declared that " No other Religion should be publicly admitted in New Netherland except the Reformed," [2] and during Stuyvesant's administration the lines were drawn with considerable strictness against some forms of dissent. So extensive were the powers of the director and council that this might be done, notwithstanding the expression of liberal principles on the part of the company. During the middle period of the history of the province the desire to conciliate English colonists doubtless contributed quite as strongly toward a liberal policy as did any views or traditions concerning toleration. But as the year 1660 was approached and passed, fear of English encroachment, as well as the irritable nature of Stuyvesant, occasioned his severity.

In the course of the entire period of Dutch rule the company sent thirteen ministers to New Netherland. The right to consent to the establishment of churches, as well as to present to livings when provided, was claimed by the company. The right of presentation it sought to exercise in the patroonships, as well as elsewhere, though the patroons and heads of colonies were expected to provide for the support of their ministers and schoolmasters.[3] This resulted in a controversy between the company and Van Rensselaer, when in 1642 the latter appointed the Rev. Megapolensis as the minister at Rensselaerswyck. The company [4] insisted on the right of appointment, and this was denied by the patroon. Finally the company had to be content with approving the

---

[1] In Col. Docs. XIV, Index, under Bogardus, Megapolensis, Bloem, Selyns, Polhemus, Drisius, will be found statements sufficient to illustrate the working of the system.

[2] N. Y. Col. Docs. I. 110, 123.

[3] Freedoms and Exemptions of 1629 and 1640; O'Callaghan, I. 119; N. Y. Col. Docs. I. 405.

[4] O'Callaghan, I. 328.

appointment under protest, the patroon reserving his rights in the case. The question never came up again, and the same clergyman, after dismissal from service in the patroonship, long held a living in New Amsterdam.

When New Netherland became New York the control of the West India company over the church in the province ceased. The relationship of that church, however, with the Classis of Amsterdam continued and was not appreciably modified by English rule. In the articles of surrender provision was made that the Dutch should enjoy liberty of conscience and retain their church discipline. This was especially guarantied to the people at Albany and on the Delaware. In the "Conditions for New Planters," which Governor Nicolls published immediately after occupation, the statement was made that liberty of conscience should be allowed, provided such liberty was not converted to licentiousness, or the disturbance of others in the exercise of the Protestant religion.[1] In the presence of a conquered population, the English component of which consisted wholly of Protestant dissenters, no other course was possible.

Though the province had never been formally divided into parishes, that system was assumed by the English to be virtually existing. In the Duke's Laws provision was made for the building of churches in all parishes where they did not already exist, and for the appointment of two of the town overseers to act as church wardens. All ministers who desired to officiate within the province must submit to the governor proof that they had received ordination from some Protestant bishop or minister within the British dominions or within the dominions of some foreign prince of the Reformed religion. This statement, of course, included ministers of the Dutch Reformed Church, of the Lutheran Church, and those who had received ordination in New England. They were to be supported, and the cost of building and repairing churches met, by public levies, to which levies all inhabitants should contribute, as they did toward the maintenance of the state. The ministers should preach every Sunday, pray for the

[1] State Library Bulletin, General Entries, 95, 127 ; N. Y. Col. Docs. XIV. 559 ; Smith, History of New York, I. 35.

king, queen, and members of the royal family, administer the sacrament of the Lord's Supper at least once a year, baptize the children of all Christian parents who should present the same, and ·celebrate marriages after due publication of the banns. It was the duty of the church wardens to prevent the disturbance of religious meetings, and to present for punishment persons who were guilty of profaneness, Sabbath-breaking, drunkenness, and gross immorality. The method of filling pastorates or livings was to be election and presentation by the inhabitants who were freeholders, and induction by the governor.

It is evident that the provisions of the Duke's Laws were wisely adapted to the conditions of the province. They guarantied toleration to the large Protestant sects which existed within it, placing them all on an equality, while the government retained a certain control over the appointment and maintenance of the entire body of the clergy. The officials were required to see to it that there was a church in every town, but the law did not specify the Protestant sect to which it should belong. The provisions concerning the sacraments involved a considerable deviation from New England usage, and went much farther than the broadest of halfway-covenant men would have been willing to go. The power which was given to the governor to instruct ministers and to pass on their credentials, if the Anglicans should become sufficiently numerous in the province or in any section of it, might conceivably be used to further the interests of that communion. Under a Catholic proprietor, however, that was scarcely to be thought of.

In the so-called Charter of Liberties,[1] which was enacted by the legislature in 1683, the ecclesiastical system of New York under the proprietary régime was correctly described as one whereby all the churches of the great Protestant sects within the province were "privileged Churches, and have been so established and confirmed by the former authority of this Government." The civil government was the head of every church within the province, and the time had not come when it was possible for it to show a decided prefer-

[1] Colonial Laws of New York, I. 115, 116 ; Brodhead, II. 660.

ence toward any one of them. In the act just referred to the inhabitants of Long Island were really guarding themselves against such possibility, as well as against the action of ministers, by the provision that contracts with ministers which had been made by two-thirds of the inhabitants of any town should stand.

But though the natural tendency of the great majority of the English officials would have been to favor the Established Church of England, conditions both at home and in the province made that impossible during the proprietary period, or indeed until after the English revolution. The number of Anglicans in the province, though slowly increasing, was still too small to justify steps intended to secure special privileges for them. For more than thirty years after the English conquest the only place where the English Episcopal service was celebrated within the province of New York was the church in the fort, and the officiating clergyman was the chaplain of the garrison. The building was the first Dutch church, and its congregation permitted the English to use it, after their own morning service was ended.[1] This being the case, the government was called upon to deal almost exclusively with dissenters.

The position of the Lutherans was at once improved by the advent of the English. The persecution which they had suffered under Stuyvesant, ending in the banishment of their minister, came to an end. Governor Nicolls, in December, 1664, granted liberty to the Lutherans of the province to send for a minister.[2] The Rev. Jacobus Fabricius was sent over, and received from Governor Lovelace permission to officiate. He was first settled at Albany. But in that town reckless speech apparently brought him into conflict with the Dutch Church and magistrates,[3] and the governor was forced to suspend him, though he was allowed to preach in New York city. He soon became involved in a quarrel there, and was sent to the Delaware. While in that region he fell twice

---

[1] N. Y. Col. Docs. IV. 526 ; Brodhead, II. 44.

[2] State Library Bulletin, General Entries, 136.

[3] Albany Court Minutes Ms., 1668 et seq. ; N. Y. Col. Docs. XII. 512, 521, 529, 531, 537 ; Brodhead, II. 159, 174, 255, 301.

into the clutches of the law, the last time under a charge of riot.   This was after the beginning of Andros's administration, and Pastor Fabricius was again suspended from his functions.   Meantime the Lutherans had built a church in New York city, and with another pastor peacefully enjoyed their worship both under the English government and during the period of the Dutch restoration.

Throughout the administrations of Nicolls and Lovelace the most friendly relations were maintained between the government and the Dutch Church.   In New York city the church wardens were annually reëlected.   The assistance of the government was also regularly given toward raising the support for the ministry there.   In 1671 the Dutch Church in New York city was authorized by an order in council to lay taxes on the congregation for the support of the ministers and the poor.[1]   In 1670 the governor, in response to a request from the officers of the church and the city, declared that to such acceptable minister as they should call from Holland he would guaranty the payment of a salary of a thousand guilders, a house rent free, and a supply of firewood.[2]   At its sessions in 1672 and 1675 the court of assizes by special order reimposed the obligation on all inhabitants of towns to contribute by special rates for the support of the ministry.[3]

When Andros became governor of the restored English province in 1674, the Duke of York had proclaimed his adherence to the Catholic faith.   It was natural that his instructions to the new governor should not have the Protestant ring which sounded in earlier utterances, and particularly in the Duke's Laws.   " You shall permit," he declared, " all persons of what Religion soever, quietly to inhabitt within ye precincts of your jurisdiccon, without giveing them any disturbance or disquiet whatsoever, for or by reason of their differring opinions in matters of Religion," provided they keep the peace.[4]   This statement was broad enough to embrace

[1] Brodhead, II. 176.

[2] Records of New Amsterdam, VI. 18, 79, 240, 300, 310.   N. Y. Col. Docs. III. 189.

[3] Charter and Laws of Pa. 73, 76.   [4] N. Y. Col. Docs. III. 218.

Catholics, Quakers, and other sects then considered dangerous and extreme. It was the duke's declaration of indulgence
to his province, and was less restricted in words than was
the famous law of the other Catholic proprietor, Lord Baltimore.

But the duke appointed a rigid Anglican to govern his
province, and some tendency on his part to favor his own
communion presently became apparent. The first case
which came up, in which religion was to an extent involved,
illustrates rather the imperious methods of Andros than his
attitude toward dissenting sects. When, in the spring of
1675, a proclamation was issued requiring that the Dutch
who intended permanently to reside in the province should
take the oath of allegiance, some appeared before the mayor
of New York city and asked that the governor would confirm to them their freedom of religion and assure them that
in time of war they should not be pressed into service. The
latter request was the same in intent as that which nearly
a century later to such an extent determined the fate of the
so-called neutral French in Acadia. The former request
was suggested by the fact that, when the oath of allegiance
was administered in 1664, Governor Nicolls issued a declaration assuring the Dutch that the liberties guarantied to
them in the articles of capitulation would in no way be
imperilled by it. But Andros ordered the oath to be taken
without qualification or explanation. Eight prominent
burghers of New York, among whom were Steenwyck, Van
Brugh, De Peyster, and Bayard, then petitioned Andros that
they might be allowed, either to take the oath as it had been
administered by Nicolls, or be permitted to sell their estates
and remove elsewhere. This petition was not only rejected,
but its signers were imprisoned as factious men who were
trying to raise a disturbance against the government. After
a hearing before the council they were laid under heavy
bonds to appear for trial before the court of assizes. Bayard
was actually tried,[1] found guilty, and all his lands and goods

[1] Orders and Warrants, Ms. III. 65 et seq., 142 ; Calendar of Council
Minutes, 21 ; Report of State Historian, 1897, II. 283 et seq. ; N. Y. Col. Docs.
II. 738–740 ; III. 237 ; Brodhead, II. 277.

were adjudged to be forfeited to the king. A record exists
of the issue of an order to a constable to seize them, but of
its execution no entry has been found. The accused petitioned the States General for relief, and the matter was
brought to the attention of the Duke of York by the Dutch
ambassador. Andros was reminded of the desire of the proprietor that the Dutch should be treated with all the gentle-
ness which was consistent with honor and safety. There
apparently the matter rested, and the case was not further
pressed against the accused.

But another event soon occurred which had a bearing
more distinctly ecclesiastical. That was an attempt of the
governor to exercise the right of induction to a living in the
Dutch church. Nicholas Van Rensselaer, a younger son of
the first patroon, and one who had been attached to the
Stuarts and their cause since the time of their exile, came
over with Andros. He had been ordained in the English
Church, and is said to have received ordination also in the
Netherlands. He was recommended by the Duke of York
to be made minister of one of the Dutch churches of New
York or Albany, when there should be a vacancy. The
governor in 1675 inducted [1] Van Rensselaer into a living at
Albany, as assistant of Dominie Schaats. This was done
without recognition by the Classis of Amsterdam. Because
of this irregularity in the procedure, Dominie Niewenhuysen
forbade Van Rensselaer to baptize children in his church in
New York city, and denied the legality of his induction.
Niewenhuysen was summoned before the council, and there,
while admitting the validity of ordination by an English
bishop, claimed that no one could legally officiate as pastor of
a Dutch Reformed congregation until he had sworn fidelity
to the church of the Netherlands. This was accepted, and
after Van Rensselaer had solemnly promised to conduct his
ministry in accordance with the Reformed Church of Holland, the case was dismissed and the induction allowed to
stand.

About a year after Van Rensselaer began his ministrations at Albany he was arrested on complaint of Jacob

[1] Doc. History of New York, III. 872 *et seq.*; Brodhead, II. 272, 288, 300.

Leisler and Jacob Milborne, afterward to be so famous, for using certain " dubious words " in a sermon. The share taken by Dominie Schaats in this prosecution would indicate that the expressions were regarded as false and heterodox. On appeal the case was heard before the governor, council, mayor and aldermen, and ministers of the city of New York. It was by them determined to refer the case back to the magistrates and church officers at Albany, by whom, after another hearing, a reconciliation was effected between the two ministers. But only a year later Andros was forced to suspend his protégé [1] because of his evil and scandalous life. The first attempt of an English governor to induct a pastor in the Dutch Church thus resulted in conflict and ultimately in failure.

In 1679 Andros, through the complaisance of the Dutch clergy, was able to procure the ordination of a minister by a classis of the province, and the confirmation of this act by the Classis of Amsterdam. [1]   The minister who was thus ordained was Peter Teschenmaker, and the scene of his labors was to be the settlements along the Delaware river. This act was exceptional, and was not repeated while New York remained a colony. In no other colony does anything like it seem to have occurred. Since no attempt was made to use it as a precedent, it cannot be regarded as indicating in any special way a tendency of the civil power under Andros to encroach on the liberties of the church.

Of interference on the part of the magistrates with the officers of churches on Long Island, whether Dutch or English, very little evidence appears. Occasionally the aid of the government was invoked to enforce the payment of rates for the support of a minister or to settle a dispute about the location or erection of a church. [2]   As each community readily supplied itself with a church building and settled a minister, the governor was given little or no opportunity to exercise the authority in such matters to which he might have considered himself entitled under the Duke's Laws.

By the proprietors of New Jersey the same degree of religious freedom was guarantied at the outset as was contem-

[1] Corwin, 74.   [2] N. Y. Col. Docs. XIV. 734.

plated in the Carolina Concessions and Agreement of 1665.
The assembly might provide for the appointment and support of ministers, but others had the same right as well, and
no one was to be molested because of his religious faith so
long as he kept the peace.[1] The varied origin and belief of
the settlers within that province insured a faithful observance of the rule. The influence of Quakers in the southern
and eastern parts of the province, with the declaration of
principles contained in their concessions, confirmed the
tendency beyond the possibility of change. The language
of the West Jersey Concessions on this point was : "That
no Men, nor number of Men upon Earth, hath power or
Authority to rule over Men's Consciences in religious Matters, therefore it is consented, . . . that no Person or Persons whatsoever within the said province, . . . shall be any
ways upon any pretence whatsoever, called in question, or in
the least punished or hurt, either in Person, Estate, or
Priviledge, for the sake of his Opinion, Judgement, Faith
or Worship towards God in Matters of Religion. But that
all and every such Person and Persons, may from Time to
Time, and at all times, freely and fully have, and enjoy his
and their Judgments, and the exercise of their Consciences
in Matters of Religious Worship throughout all the said
province." [2]

The reference to the same subject in the Fundamental
Constitutions of East Jersey, issued in 1683,[3] reveals the
influence of the Scotch Presbyterian element among its
board of proprietors. In this document the free benefits
of liberty were extended only to those who confessed and
acknowledged one almighty and eternal God ; nor was
liberty to be granted to avow atheism or irreligiousness, or
to indulge in stage plays, masques, revels, or similar abuses.
No one should be admitted to the great council or the common council, or to any place of public trust, who did not
profess faith in Jesus Christ. In the act of 1698 which set
forth the rights and privileges of inhabitants of East Jersey,
the statement was made [4] that those who professed faith in

[1] N. J. Arch. I. 30.
[2] *Ibid.* 253.
[3] *Ibid.* 405.
[4] Leaming and Spicer, 372.

God by Jesus Christ, his only Son, should not be molested
for any difference of opinion on religious subjects. The
qualifications, however, were specified that this liberty should
not be used to licentiousness, and that it should not extend
to Roman Catholics who presumed to worship according to
forms prohibited by the laws of England. When, in the
following year, the proprietors of East Jersey offered certain
conditions on which they would surrender their powers of
government to the crown, they insisted that there should be
no religious qualification whatever for office, and that no one
should be deprived of any civil right on account of religion.
Two years later, however, the proprietors of both East and
West Jersey,[1] speaking jointly on the same subject, expressed
a willingness to restrict office-holding to Protestants. But
there is no evidence in the laws or history of New Jersey, or
of either of its divisions, during the proprietary period that
religious tests in any form were ever enforced. An establishment was never a subject of discussion.

William Penn was undoubtedly one of the most powerful
advocates of religious liberty who appeared in the seventeenth century. The influence in its favor which by his
zeal and manifold activities he exerted on his contempo-
raries was far greater than that of Roger Williams. But
Penn was less a pioneer in the cause than was Williams,
and the temper of the age in which Penn lived was slightly
more favorable to the message of freedom than was that of
the generation which was contemporary with the great civil
war. The utterances of Penn himself respecting the project
of founding a province in America — "his holy experiment" — clearly reveal his purpose. "I went thither," he
wrote to Roger Mompesson, "to lay the foundation of a free
colony for all mankind, more especially those of my own
profession, not that I would lessen the civil liberties of
others because of their persuasion, but screen and defend
our own from any infringement on that account."[2] This
implied that, while his immediate object was to provide a
refuge for members of his own sect, people of other types of
faith would be freely admitted. An example of his method

---

[1] N. J. Arch. II. 296, 407.   [2] Penn and Logan Correspondence, I. 373.

of procedure, as applied to Anglicans, appears in the charter which Penn procured from the king. The only clause in that document which referred to matters ecclesiastical provided that when as many as twenty inhabitants of the province should apply in writing or through an agent to the Bishop of London for the appointment of one or more clergymen to minister to them in Pennsylvania, the appointees should be allowed to settle in the province without hindrance or opposition. The liberty which was enjoyed by the communicants of the English Church in organizing themselves and procuring ministers it was Penn's intention that all other distinctively Christian sects should enjoy.

But Quakers everywhere insisted that the society on which the political structure rests should be Christian in type. Penn himself was not indifferent to the religious belief of those who were to hold office in his province. In the first Frame of Government and in the so-called "Great Law," both of which set forth Penn's ideas, believers in one God were designated as the class who should not be molested because of their faith or worship. The Frame of Government contained the requirement that all officials within the province and members of the general assembly should be persons who professed faith in Jesus Christ. This was confirmed by act of assembly in 1682; and had Romanists appeared to demand the benefit of the law, it must have been extended to them in common with Protestants. Provision was made that Sunday should be observed, while looseness, irreligion, and atheism were not to be allowed, under pretence of conscience, to creep into the province.[1] These principles, however, suited well the conditions of the province, and, during the time when they were in force, the Lower Counties on the Delaware were annexed, and provision was made by law for naturalizing the Dutch and Swedish inhabitants of the region who had already become subjects of England.

It thus appears that, though Penn laid no restriction on the right of public or private worship, he did impose upon office-holders a religious test. The Quaker province was never free from a restriction of this kind. When, in 1693–1694,

[1] Charter and Laws, 102, 107, 108.

Penn's rights of government were suspended and Governor Fletcher of New York was appointed to administer the affairs of Pennsylvania, another important step was taken in the same direction. Fletcher was required [1] by his commission to administer to all who should be chosen members of the general assembly the oaths and tests prescribed by acts of parliament. The act here referred to was the famous toleration act of William and Mary, and the oaths and tests which it prescribed were directed against the claims of the pope to temporal supremacy, against the doctrine of transubstantiation, the mass, the worship of saints, and the Virgin Mary, and involved also a profession of belief in the Trinity and in the inspiration of the Scriptures. In England they were intended to secure to certain dissenters the privilege of public worship. But in Pennsylvania they were made to serve a most important political object. They, or the equivalent declaration, were imposed not only on all members of the legislature, but Fletcher interpreted the powers which were bestowed upon him as governor of New York and its dependencies as authority for administering the same tests to all officials. Pennsylvania he was ready to consider as a dependency of New York. Thus vanished all possibility of Roman Catholics holding office, or in fact enjoying political rights, in Pennsylvania.

It is true that, because Romanists formed no appreciable component of the population, the practical effect of those requirements was slight. Still, they are important as indicating tendencies which, under the influence of the home government, were operative even in a Quaker province. In this connection it should also be borne in mind that by his charter Penn was required to submit all the acts of his legislature to the crown for its approval.

The system of tests which had been introduced by Fletcher did not disappear with his retirement. Provision was made for their continuance in the so-called Markham's Frame of Government of 1696. But this, as we believe, never received the approval of the proprietor, and we are certain that its

[1] Col. Recs. I. 353; Stillé, Religious Tests in Pennsylvania, Pa. Mag. of Hist. IX. 365–406.

provision concerning tests was not in harmony with his views.   When Penn returned to the province he caused an act to be passed in the Lower Counties in which belief in Jesus Christ·was the only religious qualification which was prescribed either for voters or office-holders.   In 1700 an act was passed by the legislature of Pennsylvania which reaffirmed the provisions of the act of 1682 concerning freedom of worship, but contained nothing on the subject of official tests.[1]   This, however, was disapproved by the queen in council.[2]   Penn in the Charter of Liberties of 1702 re-affirmed to the full extent his doctrine of religious liberty, but again extended full political rights only to those who professed belief in Jesus Christ.   We have no proof that this charter was ever submitted to the privy council.   At any rate, its provisions on the subject in question were ignored by the home government and by later governors of Pennsylvania. In 1702 the queen issued an order that all who held public offices in the colonies should take the oaths and subscribe the declaration required by the act of toleration.   After some objections these conditions were accepted, not only for officials but for members of the legislature, and the law of the province was brought into harmony with them. The system of religious tests which was thus established in Pennsylvania continued until the Revolution.

[1] Statutes at Large, II. 3.   [2] Pa. Col. Recs. II. 57.

CHAPTER XIV

THE FINANCIAL SYSTEM OF THE LATER PROPRIETARY
PROVINCES

IN no department of public activity are tendencies toward self-government clearer than in this. Conflicts between legislatures and executives arose more from fiscal questions than from those of any other character. The attitude of more or less passive resistance which the colonists maintained toward the plans of the home government and its officials relating to defence originated largely in a consciousness of fiscal weakness. Not only were the resources of the colonists inadequate for purposes of large and continuous expenditure, but loose methods of administration prevented their governments from fully utilizing the resources which actually existed.

In the provinces the territorial revenue was a private resource of the proprietor, and as such has been described in the chapter which treats of the land system. The revenue which was derived from fines and forfeitures appeared in similar forms in all the colonies, and was an incident rather than an essential feature of their fiscal systems. Taxes, duties, and fees were the characteristic sources of income in the provinces, as well as in the corporate colonies. A consideration of provincial, as distinguished from local, revenue in the seventeenth century may be limited to these ; and they will be treated more from the administrative than from the economic standpoint.

Under the head of direct taxes in the provinces appear the poll or personal tax, the property tax, and, in a few instances, a land tax. The poll tax, by itself or combined with a property tax, was levied in all the provinces which are now being considered, with the exception of New Netherland. The nearest approach to it in that province was the levy, after 1655, upon the Jews who were resident in New Amsterdam of a monthly payment *per capita* in lieu of service in the burgher guard and in the watch.[1] In the proprietary provinces generally the poll tax, either alone or in conjunction with the property tax, was the earliest form of levy. It was so in Maryland, where by an act of 1642 a subsidy of twenty pounds of tobacco per poll was granted to the proprietor. Often thereafter a similar form of tax was resorted to in that province.[2] In South Carolina the same form of tax was employed in 1690. Occasionally in New Jersey an annual poll tax was levied to pay the salary of the governor.[3] In Pennsylvania the poll tax appears, though from the first in combination with a land or property tax.[4] In most cases, except in the province of Maryland, the poll tax and property tax were combined. In Maryland even, because the poll tax was assessed upon servants and slaves but paid by their masters, it approximated to a property tax.

Wherever the poll tax was resorted to, it necessitated a definition of tithables. Under the act of 1642 in Maryland they included all free persons, apprentices, servants, and slaves who were twelve years of age or over. The act of 1654 excepted white women servants from the list. By the act of 1674 priests and ministers were excepted from the list of taxable freemen, while sixteen was designated as the age limit in the case of freemen.[5] The act of 1690 in South Carolina defined taxables as freemen and white servants who were sixteen years of age. In the New Jersey acts males who were fourteen years old and upward were made liable ; while in Pennsylvania, in 1683, males between sixteen and sixty were designated. The tendency to make the lower age limit for freemen correspond to that fixed for military service is noticeable.

[1] Laws and Ordinances, 192.

[2] Md. Arch., Proceedings of Assembly, 1638–1664, 123, 359 ; Statutes of South Carolina, II. 40.

[3] Leaming and Spicer, Grants and Concessions, 125, 130, 136.

[4] Charter and Laws, 147, 233 ; Shepherd, Proprietary Government in Pennsylvania, 436.

[5] Md. Arch., Assembly, 1666–1676, 399 ; Mereness, Maryland as a Proprietary Province, 341.

In Maryland, until 1670, the lists of tithables were prepared by the sheriffs.   But in that year it was found that the
lists were imperfect and an order was issued intrusting this
duty to the constables of the hundreds.   It, however, did
not remain long in their hands, for in 1675 the duty was
again being performed by sheriffs.   In 1677, owing to the
remissness of the sheriffs, as shown in their omission of
names, the justices of the peace were ordered to review and
correct[1] the lists.   In South Carolina, in 1690, the constables
were utilized, while again, in 1703, the lists of the militia
companies were used[2] as the basis of levy.   In New Jersey
and Pennsylvania[3] the town constables kept the lists of
taxables.

But in the provinces generally the levy on polls early disappeared, or played its chief part as a feature of the property
tax.   The property tax was the leading form of direct levy
in all the proprietary provinces.   In most cases it took the
form of a percentage of the value of property, — as a penny
on the pound, — while in others the common forms of property were taxed at fixed rates, as land at a penny an acre
and cattle at eight pence per head.[4]   In cases where the tax
was laid in the form of a percentage, it became necessary to
appraise the value of the property.   After a comparison had
been made between the total valuation and the sum which
it was necessary to raise, the rate of levy was found.   Provisions,[5] more or less detailed, for the assessment of the
property tax in either case became necessary.   The statutes
in all the provinces except Maryland designated how this
should be done.   In that province control over the details
of assessment was left to the governor and council.

In Maryland, in 1654, when the province was being administered by commissioners of parliament, a law was passed

[1] Md. Arch., Council, 1636–1667, 456, 515, 527 ; *ibid.* 1667–1688, 76 ; *ibid.*
1671–1681, 156.

[2] Statutes of South Carolina, II. 41, 208.

[3] Many references in tax laws.   See Grants and Concessions ; also Charter and Laws of Pa. 222, 254.

[4] New York and Pennsylvania furnish good examples of the former
method, and West Jersey of the latter.

[5] Md. Arch., Assembly, 1638–1664, 342.

providing that for the coming year the public charges should
be met, not only by a levy on taxable persons, but by a tax
on visible estates as well.   Land and cattle, the principal
forms of taxable property in all the colonies, were then subjected to a tax.   In 1657 a return was temporarily made to
the poll tax.   But after 1660 the levy came regularly to be
imposed each year [1] on persons and estates.   The county was
the unit of levy.   The annual charges which were to be met
by the tax were estimated, and a levy was ordered which
should yield the lump sum that was needed.   When the levy
of a property tax was resorted to, an assessment became necessary.   In Maryland the levy was assessed by commissioners
from the different counties, who were summoned by the
sheriff to meet the governor and council for the purpose.
In 1650 [2] and 1651 acts were passed requiring the election
of commissioners for this purpose by the counties.   This
feature of the system, however, was soon abandoned.   The
taxes were collected by the sheriffs, and the treasurers —
one for each shore — were the custodians of the revenue.
These officers were appointees of the governor. [3]

In South Carolina the property tax first appeared in 1682.
In 1685, on the occasion of the destruction by the Spanish of
Lord Cardross's colony at Port Royal, an act was passed
for the levy of £500 on the inhabitants of the province
according to their estates and profits. [4]   The taxables in this
instance were all the inhabitants — servants excepted — who
were in the province when the act was passed, or who should
come in before the assessment was made.   Provision was
made in the act for the assessment of the tax by a board of
thirteen freeholders appointed by the grand council and sit-
ting at Charlestown.   On the completion of their work a
return of the same should be made to the grand council,
which should order the two receivers to collect.   Provision
was made for a special commission of appeal to hear complaints and remedy inequalities in assessment.   The receivers

[1] Md. Arch., Assembly, 1666–1676, 235, 338, 415, 554.
[2] *Ibid.* Assembly, 1638–1664, 298, 313.
[3] *Ibid.* Council, 1671–1681, 50, 99, 120.
[4] Statutes of South Carolina, II. 16.

were named in the act, and were allowed as their reward ten per cent of all they should collect. They were required to give security and to keep and submit accounts of their transactions. As was usually the case in the colonies, the tax was paid in commodities at specified rates, and authority was given to levy by distress on failure of payment. This is one of the most carefully drawn statutes which appears on the subject of taxation among the early laws of any colony.

The system which the act of 1685 prescribed in South Carolina was followed,[1] with slight variations, throughout the proprietary period. The poll tax of 1690 was collected by the constables in each division of Berkeley county, and was paid by them to the designated receivers. The act of 1702, under which a general tax on estates was levied, provided for a large board of special assessors. The tax was to be collected under the immediate authority of the public receiver, an officer already in existence, who was designated in the act. The law of 1703 provided for " inquirers," who should make inventories of estates. They reported to several local boards of assessment, which were required in turn to report to a general board which sat at Charlestown. This acted as a board of equalization, and submitted the results of its work to the clerk of the commons house and to the public receiver. Notice of the amount of each individual's assessment was given through the captains of the militia companies. The tax was to be paid at Charlestown, and the assistance of the constable was required only when it was necessary to collect arrears through distress. Provision was also made in this act for special commissioners of appeal. It thus appears that the provisions of the law in South Carolina for the assessment of taxes were unusually specific.

Wherever the Duke's Laws were in force in New York the New England poll tax and country rate were regularly collected. The elected officers of the localities were made use of for the purpose. Annually in June the high sheriff sent forth his warrants to the constables to call together the overseers of the towns. Their duty was to prepare the lists of taxables, who in this case were the males from sixteen years

[1] Statutes of South Carolina, II. 23, 40, 182, 189, 206, 229, 263.

upward, identical with those who were liable to military service. The varieties of real and personal estate, which the
overseers should also list, were designated with care. The
assessment lists, when completed, were delivered to the constables and by them to the high sheriff. He examined and
equalized them, and ultimately delivered them to the governor.
But as soon as the sheriff had completed the equalization,
orders might be issued to the constables for the collection of
the tax. The general list was arranged, as in early years in
New England, in the form of quotas by towns. With the
sheriff and the courts rested the authority to compel both
rate payers and constables to perform their duty. As yet
the office of treasurer had not been created, and the revenue
was to be paid over to the governor and council.[1] The
country rate, as we have seen, was approximately a tax of a
penny in the pound on real and personal estate. Its adoption in New York was later perpetuated by legislative grants.
From New York as a centre the same form of tax was introduced into other provinces farther south. In 1683 the first
grant of a penny in the pound of the value of all real
and personal estate in New York was made. By this time
counties were in existence, and for the assessment of this tax
a board of commissioners for each county was designated in
the act.[2] Local assessors chosen by the towns were required
to report the assessment lists of their towns to the county
boards. These boards, after examining the lists, should designate two or more collectors in each county and order them
to collect the tax and pay it over to the receiver-general of
the province or his deputies. Threepence in the pound was
paid for collecting, and twopence in the pound for the services of the receiver-general. Punishment for default,
whether of officials or of taxables, was inflicted at the instance of the county assessors.

[1] N. Y. Col. Laws, I. 59, 124 ; N. Y. Col. Docs. XIV. 626, 704, 707, 758.
The last entry contains a full account of the receipt and disbursement of
public money by High Sheriff Young for the year 1680.

[2] N. Y. Col. Laws, 137. As early as 1676 this rate was known as the penny
in a pound. Andros, in August of that year, ordered its levy. Orders and
Warrants, Ms. 1674–1685, 108.

In New Jersey resort was had from the outset to the country rate, and it was levied by quotas on the towns.[1] A country treasurer was designated in the earliest act for a tax levy, and the custom was apparently continued after that time. Collectors were also sometimes named in the acts. This was consistent with the Concessions and Agreement of 1665, which gave to the assembly the right to regulate very fully the collection and expenditure of revenue. The town apparently assessed its quota, as was the custom in New England.

The twenty-four proprietors abandoned the town quotas, and levied by counties a general rate " on lands and stocks." [2] County boards of assessors were named in the act, as was also a province treasurer. The rate was collected by the constables of the towns, and both they and the treasurer were paid by a percentage out of the levy. In 1688 the New York practice was imitated, and a tax of a penny in the pound was imposed on estates. In West Jersey, beginning with 1684, in addition to a land tax, provision was made in the acts for levies on the personal property of merchants, artisans, tavernkeepers, and others who possessed little or no land. The inhabitants of the tenths — which were to become counties — were required to choose in each case a board of assessors and two collectors. The latter were to pay the revenue which they collected to the treasurers of the province. For all purposes of levy and collection, Salem tenth was treated separately until 1701. Then the system of assessment and collection by counties was fully instituted, and Salem county was incorporated with the rest of the province.

In Pennsylvania, during the administration of Governor Fletcher and thereafter, a tax of a penny in the pound on real and personal estates was levied throughout the province. This was clearly an imitation of New York usage, and it continued to be the form under which the property tax was levied in Pennsylvania during the remainder of the colonial period.   The proprietor and his deputy were exempt, and by the act of 1693 those also whose real and

[1] Leaming and Spicer, 81, 89, 104, 122, 128.   [2] *Ibid.* 274, 306.

personal estate was less than £30. By later acts — those of 1696 and 1699 — adult males who were worth less than £72 were required to pay only a poll tax of six shillings.[1]

The method of assessing the tax differed in Pennsylvania from that employed in New York. No special board of commissioners was named in the act, neither were the towns ordered to elect persons to coöperate in the assessment. The county was the unit of levy, and its officials were almost exclusively utilized for the purpose. The members of the assembly from the counties were authorized to appoint three justices of the peace or other freeholders of their county to serve with them as a board of assessors. This board ordered the constables to bring in lists of names and valuations. From these the assessments were made. Collectors were appointed by the county boards of assessors, and the assessors acted as boards of equalization. Provision was made for the payment of the funds collected to the receiver or treasurer. By the first act — that passed during Fletcher's administration — the right to name this officer was reserved to the governor, but he was designated by name in the other laws. The first two of the Pennsylvania acts which are here referred to were accompanied by laws for the levy of a penny in the pound to meet county charges. The method of assessing and collecting these levies was the same as that prescribed for the province tax, though county officers performed all the duties.

The forms of levy to which reference has been made occupied a more prominent place in the revenue system of the English colonies than they did in that of New Netherland. In the Dutch parts of that province the chief form of the direct tax was the tithe, or the tax on land. It was an annual tender to the government of one-tenth of the produce of land. Provision was made as early as 1638 that its payment should begin on any plantation ten years after its settlement. The requirement extended to the English, as well as to the Dutch, planters, and provision for it was introduced into the patents of some of the Dutch towns. But it presently appeared that, because of sparse settlements and unimproved

[1] Charter and Laws, 221, 233, 253, 256, 280.

lands, the tithe, in Manhattan and the country outside, was difficult to collect. It fell into arrears. So inadequate was the revenue that, when in 1654 it again became necessary to improve the defences, a small loan had to be raised. Stuyvesant's property was mortgaged for its payment.[1]

In order to pay this loan the land tax was further utilized and extended. An annual tax of twenty stivers was imposed on every morgen of land — about two acres — which was held by patent. A tax of the same amount was levied on every head of horned cattle, goats and sheep excepted, which was above three years old, and twelve stivers on those which were two years old. During the following years the rate on land was lowered to ten stivers, and the twentieth penny, or five per cent per year, was imposed on the rentals of houses. In 1658, in order to lessen the number of vacant lots in New Amsterdam, a special annual tax of the fifteenth penny was laid on the value of unimproved land within the city. The revenue was to be applied to the building and repair of the defences of the city.[2] At New Amstel a tax was levied on sales of land and also on transfers which resulted from executions.[3]

When resort was had to the land tax, the tenth was not abandoned. In 1658, and probably in other years as well, two commissioners were appointed to collect the tenth among the towns which were subject to Dutch control on Long Island. Those who were liable to the tax were forbidden to remove from the fields crops of grain, maize, or tobacco before they had been visited by the commissioners and the tenth had been taken out. Tenths were sometimes farmed out, the farmers receiving the same powers as the commissioners. The revenue obtained from this source was distributed among

---

[1] Laws and Ordinances, 16, 180, 197, 413; N. Y. Col. Docs. XIV. 270, 287, 325. The statements concerning the rates of this tax, as given in the Ordinances and the Documents, differ. I have followed the former. Entries in Albany Records, Court Minutes, 1652–1656, refer to Stuyvesant's call for contributions to a loan for the repair of the fort at Manhattan, and state that 2225 florins had been obtained from subscribers at Albany. About the same time contributions were made at Albany for presents to the Indians, and for the ransom of Esopus people from the Indians.

[2] Laws and Ordinances, 326.   [3] N. Y. Col. Docs. II. 61.

the towns, and was used by them to meet the deficits arising from the inadequacy of other taxes.[1]

Among the English colonies in the seventeenth century, the only instances of resort to a land tax, as distinct from the property tax, appeared in the Jerseys. In 1675 and 1676 a land tax was levied in East Jersey, though the rate is not specified in the laws. The tax was imposed on land which had been patented, whether by residents or non-residents, and on land for which patents had been solicited in accordance with the rules prescribed in the Concessions. Between 1684 and 1688 the proprietors also repeatedly levied on the land of their respective proprieties to meet the expenses of the board.[2] In West Jersey, beginning in 1684, land was assessed at specified rates, a distinction being made between divided estates and those which were parts[3] of undivided shares. In 1693 this tax was merged with the general property tax.

The forms of indirect taxation to which resort was had in the provinces, as well as in the corporate colonies, were export and import duties and a tonnage duty. In New Netherland, however, the excise on liquors played an important part, and this feature of the Dutch revenue system was inherited by the English of New York. In that province the excise continued to be levied throughout the colonial period. In Pennsylvania it was first resorted to in 1700, and was continued thereafter. In East Jersey an excise was laid in 1692, but the following year it was discontinued.[4] In no other English province during the early colonial period did the excise play any part as a fiscal measure.

As has previously been stated, the excise was first levied in New Netherland, in June, 1644. It was imposed on beer, wine, brandy, and beaver, the excise on beer being divided between the brewer and the tapster. Recourse to it was occasioned by the necessities of an Indian war. The need of

---

[1] Laws and Ordinances, 232, 356, 402 ; N. Y. Col. Docs. XIV. 287, 360.

[2] Grants and Concessions, 98, 120 ; N. J. Arch. I. 481, 497 ; II. 38–40.

[3] Grants and Concessions, 494, 506, 522.

[4] N. Y. Col. Docs. III. 400 ; N. Y. Col. Laws, I–III ; General Entries, Ms., January 29, 1676, June 3, 1679 ; Statutes at Large of Pa. II. 107 ; Grants and Concessions, 319, 332.

revenue with which to clothe and feed a body of soldiers who CHAP.
had arrived from Curaçoa for the relief of the province fur- XIV.
nished the reason for its continuance by an order of August
of the same year. It then [1] became a permanent feature of
the system of taxation, and was extended to all parts of the
province. Orders were issued from time to time to regulate
the manufacture and sale of beer so as best to prevent smuggling. In 1656 the regulations in force for this purpose in
the fatherland were ordered to be executed in the province.
When, in 1653, the revenue from the excise in New Amsterdam was resigned to the city to be spent for local purposes,
the rates levied on wine, brandy, and spirits throughout the
province were increased.[2] An extensive system of tavern
licenses and regulations resulted from the efforts to enforce
the excise. Its collection was farmed out annually in each
of the principal sections of the province to the highest bidder,
and local collectors were appointed, with the approval of the
director and council, to assist the farmer in his work.[3]

In 1656, in order to prevent the unlicensed killing of
domestic animals throughout the country districts, an
order was issued requiring that in those regions no cattle
should thenceforth be slaughtered without permit. For the
issue of such permits fees were collected[4] which were the
equivalent of an excise. The revenue from this tax was
reserved for expenditure in the localities where it was raised.
It was collected at the Esopus and on Long Island.

Unlike the English colonies, New Netherland had its
staple port. Provision was made in the Freedoms and
Exemptions of 1629 that all peltries should be brought to
Manhattan for shipment. Until 1645 both the export and
the import trade of the province was carried on exclusively
in the vessels of the company and in those of the privileged
patroons. Entrances and clearances were all at Manhattan.
When, in the last-mentioned year, trade was thrown open to
private merchants, strict orders were issued that commodi-

[1] Laws and Ordinances, 38, 40, 184, 204 ; O'Callaghan, II. 304.
[2] Laws and Ordinances, 142, 263.
[3] Ibid. 184, 265, 297, 419 ; O'Callaghan, II. 298.
[4] Laws and Ordinances, 208 ; N. Y. Col. Docs. XIII. 76.

ties, both inward and outward, should pass through New Amsterdam. This rule was applied to coastwise trade, as well as to trade with Europe. This regulation of the course of trade was soon followed by the levy of export and import duties. In 1629 fur traders who trafficked in regions where the company had no factories were required to pay an export duty on their goods. Not until 1647 was an ordinance issued on this subject within the province, and then specific rates were prescribed for beaver, otter, and elk hides.[1] The duty on peltry was afterward changed by the company into an eight per cent ad valorem rate. This occasioned a diminution of revenue, and for this reason, in 1652, Stuyvesant and his council added a duty of four stivers on each skin. As early as 1638 a duty was levied on the export of tobacco; this, though of slight consequence, was not abolished until 1652. Peltry was the only article of export in Dutch times from which a revenue of importance was derived.

Prior to 1642 import duties were not collected in New Netherland. But beginning on that date, under instructions from the company, a duty of ten per cent was levied on all imported merchandise which had paid nothing in Holland, Brazil, Guinea, or the Dutch West Indies. In 1654, because of the low state of the treasury, specific duties were imposed on a list of commodities which were imported especially for the Indian trade, together with liquors and salt. The revenue on imports from Europe suffered from the fact that merchants were accustomed to land commodities in Virginia or in the New England colonies and introduce them thence into New Netherland. To meet this difficulty, in 1652, a duty of sixteen per cent was imposed on all merchandise which was imported from the English colonies. In 1658 a general ten per cent duty was levied on imports, with a free list consisting of provisions, malt, tobacco, and sugar.[2] The accumulation of duties[3] in the Netherlands and in New Netherland was a burden to commerce and a cause of the high prices of European commodities which prevailed in the province. For this reason it occasioned loud complaint

---

[1] Laws and Ordinances, 6, 73, 125, 136.   [2] *Ibid.* 31, 88, 126, 154, 348.
[3] N. Y. Col. Docs. I. 372.

during the agitation which filled the early years of Stuyvesant's administration.   But there is no proof that the duties
which the Dutch were forced to pay were higher than those
to which consumers in the English colonies were subjected
after the financial systems of the latter had been fully
developed.

As soon as New Netherland was conquered by the English
the customs duties which at the time were prescribed in the
English book of rates were put into force.   In February,
1665, a special tariff was proclaimed, to be in force until the
following September.   It provided for a ten per cent import
duty on liquors and goods for the Indian trade, and eight
per cent on other merchandise which was not of the growth
and manufacture of England.   English products were subject only to a five per cent duty.   An export duty of ten and
a half per cent was levied on peltries, and one of $2d.$ per
pound on tobacco.   These duties were required to be paid
partly in beaver and partly in wampum.[1]

Among the instructions which were given to Andros in
1674[2] was a provision for new rates of customs duties.   The
low ad valorem rate of two per cent should be levied on the
importation of all merchandise which was shipped in England, or in the English colonies.   Ten per cent was required
on foreign goods, even though they had come by the way of
England and had paid duties there.   A special duty of three
per cent was levied on all goods which were sent up the
Hudson, except axes, ploughshares, shovels, and some other
articles which were needed in the working and improvement of farms.   Specific rates of duty were levied on the
importation of wine, brandy, and rum, and these were doubled
when the liquors were sent up the Hudson.

An export duty of $1s.$ $7d.$ per skin on beaver was also
required, and proportionately on other peltry.   Two shillings per hogshead were levied on tobacco, provided bond
was given, as required by the act of 25 Charles II, to land
it in England.   If bond were not given, the owner must
pay $1d.$ per pound.   These were the only export duties.

[1] General Entries, Bulletin N. Y. State Library, 133, 166.
[2] N. Y. Col. Docs. III. 217.

Regulations and rates on the Delaware were the same as those on the Hudson. There is no evidence that during the proprietary period a tonnage duty was collected in New York.

By an act of the first legislature [1] of New York new rates of duty were imposed, and those largely specific. The rates were increased, and the distinction between the imposition on foreign goods and on goods brought direct from England and the English colonies was dropped. These rates continued in force until after New York became a royal province. There is, in fact, no evidence that they were legally changed until 1692, when the first revenue act of Fletcher's administration was passed.

Indirect taxes figured much less prominently among the English colonies in general in the seventeenth century than they did among the Dutch, or in New York under English rule. In Maryland no indirect tax of importance was levied until 1671. Then the duty of 2s. per hogshead, to which reference has elsewhere been made, was levied on tobacco exported from the province. This grant was made in return for an agreement on the part of the proprietor that he should receive tobacco in payment of his territorial revenue [2] at the rate of 2d. per pound. Of the revenue from the duty one half went for the support of the government in Maryland and the other half went directly to the proprietor. The law was reënacted in 1674 and continued through the lives of Charles and Cecilius Calvert. No import duties whatever and no additional export duties were levied until after the establishment of royal government.

In South Carolina the first export duty was levied in 1691,[3] to meet the cost of defence. The duty was imposed wholly on peltry, and the rates were specific. The receiver was entitled to one-tenth of the duty which he collected and paid into the treasury. In 1700 an import duty was levied on liquors and merchandise. The act imposing this duty has been lost, but we know from another which was passed

---

[1] N. Y. Col. Laws, I. 116 ; N. Y. Col. Docs. III. 400.
[2] Proceedings of Assembly, 1666–1676, 284, 386.
[3] Statutes of South Carolina, II. 64.

later in the same year that its administrative regulations had
been inadequate to prevent smuggling in the export trade,
and therefore had to be strengthened.   In 1703 a much
more elaborate act was passed, which provided for export
and import duties at specific rates on a considerable list of
commodities.   Liquors and furs, however, occupied the
most prominent places.   The system was continued by
later enactments.[1]

No record remains of the levy of customs duties in either
East or West Jersey prior to 1702.   A port was established
by the East Jersey proprietors at Perth Amboy, but no
attempt was made to collect duties there.[2]   This indeed
furnished one of the arguments which were urged by the
authorities of New York against permitting vessels to load
or unload there at all.   They declared that, if this policy
were tolerated, inasmuch as no duties were collected in New
Jersey, the trade of New York would be drawn away and
lost.   The royal customs would thus suffer serious diminution.   In 1682 an act[3] was passed by the assembly of Pennsylvania laying specific rates of duties on imported liquors
and an ad valorem rate on all other merchandise, molasses
excepted.   An export duty was also levied on hides and
peltry.   This law remained in force until 1690, when it was
repealed.   No other act for the levy of a customs duty was
passed until 1705.

Maryland and South Carolina[4] were the only provinces
which, prior to 1690, resorted to a tonnage duty.   This was
regularly paid in powder, or in powder and shot, and furnished a most important source of their supply for the province.   The duty was first instituted in Maryland by a law of
1650, followed by an act of 1661.   In South Carolina the first
law on the subject was passed in 1686.   A second act on the
subject was not passed in Maryland until 1692, but in South
Carolina no less than five acts requiring the payment of this
duty were passed between 1690 and 1703.   These made pro-

[1] Statutes of South Carolina, 162, 200, 247, 295.

[2] N. J. Arch. II. 233, and many other entries.

[3] Charter and Laws, 138, 182.

[4] Proceedings of Assembly, 1638–1664, 293, 418 ; Statutes of South Carolina,
II. 20, 42, 73, 82, 125, 150, 213.

vision for a controller, and afterward for a powder receiver, who was designated in the act, for the surveying of vessels to ascertain their tonnage, the keeping of accounts and entries and clearances. In the law of 1698 the same person was designated as master gunner and powder receiver. Under the stress of the colonial wars nearly all the colonies resorted to this form of duty, and made use of the regulations necessary for its collection as an aid in the administration of their customs service in general.

In all the colonies, before the development of the salary system, officials derived their support to a large extent from fees. Especially in the provinces was it true that payment was made in this form for all varieties of official service. In the absence of any provision to the contrary, the limiting of the amount of fees was properly regarded as an incident of the power of the executive to constitute offices and appoint officers. But in most of the proprietary provinces the legislature early undertook to some extent to regulate the discretion of the executive in this matter. So directly did the question of fees affect the pockets of the colonists, that action of this kind was scarcely avoidable. In New Netherland the director and council, as a matter of course, determined the rates of notarial and judicial fees, both for localities and for the province at large. When they were left undefined and became so exorbitant that popular complaint was aroused, tables of fees were prescribed by ordinance and enforced under its authority.[1] In the Duke's Laws fees connected with judicial procedure were prescribed, as those of the sheriff, constables, justices of the peace, clerks of the courts, at least for a part of their services. Justices of the peace were paid a small salary in addition. When, in 1683, the first legislature of the province met,[2] it by a general enactment confirmed the fees of sheriffs, clerks of courts, and other officers, and jurymen, at the rates which had customarily been taken. Beyond this, in New York, legislative interference with the right of the executive to limit fees did not proceed until after 1690.

[1] Laws and Ordinances, 187, 190, 249, 329 ; see Index under Fees.
[2] Colonial Laws of New York, I. 32, 80, 136.

In Maryland the legislature early undertook the task of limiting fees. In 1638 a comprehensive bill on the subject was introduced, and ultimately, though not by direct enactment, it became law.[1] In 1642, however, it ceased to be operative, and the rates of fees for the secretary, surveyor-general, sheriff, and clerks of court were determined by the governor and council and published in a proclamation. Not until 1650 did the assembly again attempt to legislate on the subject. It then passed acts limiting the fees of the secretary and sheriffs, and, under the name of a fee, the salary of the muster-master general. The following year the fees of the surveyor-general were also fixed[2] by law, and the provisions of this act were in force as late as 1666. About 1669 there was much complaint of the high rates of fees charged by attorneys, and in 1675 an act[3] limiting them was passed. Incidentally also the fact was revealed that the fees of the governor, when acting as chancellor, had not been limited ; and the same was undoubtedly true of other officers and many other functions. But no controversy over the subject arose, and no further action was taken until after 1690. Taking the period in Maryland as a whole, it may be said that fees were regulated partly by statute and partly by ordinance, but more by the latter than by the former.

The Carolina Concessions of 1665 provided, among other things, that fees should be determined by the legislature. As early as 1671 we find the grand council preparing a table of fees to be submitted to the parliament.[4] In 1683 a comprehensive act on the subject was passed, but it has been lost. In 1685 acts were passed limiting the fees of the governor, the surveyor-general, the clerk of the peace, the clerk of the crown, the coroner, and the clerk of parliament. The part of the governor's activity which came within the scope of the statute was that which concerned the granting of licenses, probate of wills, and admiralty business. Other acts were passed at frequent intervals until 1694, when a

[1] Proceedings of Assembly, 1638–1664, 57, 84, 162.
[2] Ibid. 289, 292, 312, 497.
[3] Ibid. 1666–1676, 167, 169, 176, 467.
[4] Shaftesbury Papers, 346.

general act was passed specifying at great length the fees of all important offices in the province. Another general act was passed in 1698; in 1700 an act especially relating to fees in the admiralty court was passed; in 1706 one was passed specifying again the fees of the coroner.[1] It thus appears that in respect to fees in South Carolina the principle of action laid down in the Concessions and Agreement was carefully followed. From the beginning fees were regulated by statute. Only once during the proprietary period do we hear a complaint concerning fees. During Ludwell's administration, about 1692, in a list of grievances which was laid before the governor appears the charge that public officers were receiving higher fees than were allowed by act of parliament in England for the same services.[2]

Among the laws of New Jersey no extended reference to fees appears until an act which was passed in East Jersey in 1686. That established full lists of fees for the secretary, surveyor-general, sheriffs, and clerks of the county courts. By an act of 1681, in West Jersey, the governor and commissioners were given authority to limit the fees of all officials, and the exacting of any at higher rates than those which were thus prescribed was forbidden. Not until 1695 was a list of fees in that province actually prescribed by statute.[3] The law of Pennsylvania required from the beginning that fees and salaries should be moderate, that they should be limited by the governor and assembly, and that lists showing their amount should be posted in every court. Those who were convicted of taking fees in excess of the legal rates should be fined and dismissed from office. An elaborate table of fees, covering the chief duties of the governor, secretary, treasurer, and other leading officials of the province, was enacted into law. By this and later special acts the precedent was early established in Penn's province that fees were a subject for statutory regulation.[4]

It thus appears that in all the provinces, except Maryland and New York, the rates of fees were early regulated by

[1] Statutes of South Carolina, II. 3, 4, 14, 39, 78, 86, 143, 167, 269.
[2] Rivers, 434.   [3] Leaming and Spicer, 97, 298, 426, 538.
[4] Charter and Laws, 117, 147, 220, 235.

statute; and it is possible that on no subject, even among those connected with finance, was legislation considered more necessary by the people than on this.

Respecting the general objects of expenditure in the proprietary provinces, it is possible to speak with some definiteness. They were defence, the salaries of officials, the salaries of agents, the erection and repair of jails and of the few other public buildings which were needed, the board and lodging of judges and jurors during the sessions of courts, and payment for a variety of miscellaneous services. In South Carolina they included the salaries of ministers of the Established Church and of schoolmasters. In New Netherland also clergymen of the Dutch Church, schoolmasters, and comforters of the sick received public support. The wages of members of the assembly were usually paid by their constituents, though at rates fixed by law. The sums which were devoted to these objects it is impossible, save in a few cases, to specify. The order of relative importance in the various objects of expenditure varied, we may suppose, with every province. Except in Pennsylvania, and possibly in the Jerseys, defence claimed by far the largest part of the public revenue. The appropriation acts, so far as they have been preserved, refer chiefly to provision for expeditions against the Indians or other enemies of the colonists or colonial government, the building and repair of forts, the maintenance of watches, the procuring of a supply of arms and ammunition, the payment of the wages of officers and soldiers. This is as true of New Netherland and New York as it is of the southern provinces. In Maryland, as we have seen, a part of the expenditure took the form of pensions.

In the provinces, as in the corporate colonies, the salary system was a gradual development. Throughout the seventeenth century the lower officers received their support from fees, and that of the higher officers came partly in that form. The governor in all cases received a salary. So did some of the other officers of higher rank, but it is not easy to tell just how far the salary system extended. In New Netherland the director, the members of the council, the schout fiscal, the receiver-general, military commanders, commissaries, and skippers are early referred to as recipients of salaries from the company.[1] By 1644 two clergymen and a schoolmaster had been added, and the total annual expenses for the civil list were 20,040 guilders. Respecting the list in proprietary New York, we have almost no information. The probability, however, is that in the case of both provincial and local officers it did not greatly differ from that of the Dutch period. In Dongan's time the governor received a salary of £600. By an act of 1684, which was never approved by the proprietor, provision was made for the payment[2] of salaries out of the revenue of the counties to the justices of sessions and judges of oyer and terminer within the counties.

In Maryland the governor received a salary, or grants of land, from the outset, though a system of salaries was not established till the period of royal government. Whether the council received support in that form before the levy of the export duty on tobacco, in 1671, it is impossible to state.[3] Previous to 1689 no legislative provision was made for the salary of the judges of the provincial court. No attempt was made to designate what part of the country levy should go as a reward to the justices. The county courts were empowered to levy sums, sometimes limited, but often not specified, to meet general county expenses. But the amount which they reserved for themselves is unknown. In South Carolina we hear almost nothing of salaries until about 1700, when a salary was provided by law for the receiver-general. In 1698 the first chief justice received a salary of £60 per annum. The governor, during the later proprietary period, received £200 per annum. In North Carolina the chief justice received the same salary as did the incumbent of that office in the southern part of the province, and in both cases they were paid by the proprietors.[4] By a law of New Jersey, in 1676, provision was made for the payment of a daily wage to the governor, councillors, and deputies during the sessions of the assembly. According to this enactment, it was to be paid by the prov-

[1] N. Y. Col. Docs. I. 112.   [2] Colonial Laws, I. 168.
[3] Mereness, 171, 181, 248.
[4] Charleston Year Book, 1885; N. C. Recs. III. 197.

ince; but a law of 1682 devolved the support of the deputies
on the towns.   With some regularity a salary was annually
voted to the governor.   In 1697 and 1701 Governor Andrew
Hamilton received the same recognition in West Jersey.[1]
The governor's salary is the only instance of reward in that
form distinct reference to which in proprietary New Jersey
has come down to us.   Receivers and collectors were com-
pensated by percentages of what they held or collected.   The
fee system was predominant in the provinces, and salaries
played but a small part in the fiscal system.

The detailed appropriation acts of Maryland furnish the
best illustrations of the nature of colonial expenditures in
general.   Among the objects for which provision was made
in June, 1674,[2] were expenses of a session of the legislature,
charges of grand juries, cost of keeping prisoners, cost of
removing and caring for the public records, payment for
building stocks and a whipping post, cost of collecting the
public levy, hire of a horse and man.   Whenever a military
expedition was fitted out, the wages of officers and men and
the other expenditures connected therewith appear in detail.
The same is true if envoys or commissioners were sent on
public errands.   Messenger service often appears as an item
in supply bills.   Long lists of names of persons who have
rendered special services also appear, with a statement
of the sum due to each individual.   The appropriation by
South Carolina, in 1712, of £1000 with which to buy land
and build a house for the governor indicates a special object
of expenditure which proved to be of some importance in
several of the provinces as the eighteenth century advanced.[3]
Owing to the lack generally of detailed appropriation acts at
so early a date as 1690, it is not easy to speak at length of
colonial expenditures.   But it is believed that enough has already been said to indicate sufficiently their general character.

In New Netherland, and in proprietary New York until
1683, the finances, like all other public interests, were wholly
under the control of the provincial executive.   In New

[1] Grants and Concessions, 122, 276, 119, 125, 561, 587.
[2] Proceedings of Assembly, 1666-1676, 415.
[3] Statutes of South Carolina, II. 380.

Netherland the officials who were immediately concerned with financial administration were the schout fiscal, the receiver-general, the commissaries, and the farmers of the customs and excise.   The schout fiscal had as a part of his many duties that of enforcing the laws relating to trade,[1] navigation, and the excise, preventing smuggling, inspecting vessels, taking entries and clearances of vessels, issuing passes for trade on the North or South river, at times even of collecting duties.   He was also concerned in prosecuting violations of the laws of trade.   The receiver[2] was more closely connected with the actual work of collecting duties, while he was distinctively the treasurer or keeper of the provincial revenue, so far as it came from customs and the excise. Goods for export and import must be entered at his office. The fees of the weigh-house were paid at the same place. Prior to 1653 the receiver seems to have been concerned with the collection of the excise.   But in that year its collection in New Amsterdam was farmed, and the two following years, under orders of the director and council, the same method was employed for the province at large.   This mode of collection was followed probably during all of the remaining years of Dutch rule.   In the later years of the province the collection of the customs was also farmed out.   The collection of the tenth and of the fees of the weigh-house were also managed in the same way.

The farming of the excise was continued for a considerable period after the beginning of English rule.   It was separately farmed at New York, Kingston, and Albany, the letting of the contracts at New York being a part of the duties of the secretary of the province and the vendue-master.   The custom-house, by Andros's time, was organized on the English model, with a collector and such other officers — controller, surveyor, and searcher — as the business of the office demanded.   The collector held under appointment from the Duke of York.[3]   The other officials appear to have

---

[1] Laws and Ordinances, 92, 111, 136, 143, 210, 238, 350, 382.

[2] *Ibid.* 31, 84, 91, 176.

[3] N. Y. Col. Docs. III. 310, 335.   Andros states that he added the office of controller.

been appointed by the governor. With the office of collector was combined that of receiver of all the forms of revenue which accrued to the duke, even including the quitrents. It was this office, with its varied and responsible duties, which was held by William Dyer and afterwards by Lucas Santen and Matthew Plowman.

In all the provinces, except New Netherland and New York, customs revenue, as well as direct taxes, was levied exclusively under the authority of acts of the legislature. The legislature always determined the rates of duty, but it did not always specify the method of collecting it, or designate the officials who should administer the finances. The degree to which responsibility to the legislature was enforced, by audit of accounts or by other methods of control, also varied greatly in the different colonies and at different times. The tendency was for the legislature to assume, as time passed, more exclusive power of regulation.

In Maryland the port or tonnage duty and the export duty on tobacco were collected by the naval officers. It was paid by them to the treasurers, of whom there was one for each shore. Both the naval officers and treasurers were appointees of the governor. By the act of 1691, in South Carolina, the person who should hold the office of receiver was designated, and his salary was fixed at one-tenth of the duty which he should collect and pay into the treasury. The duty of administering the law was divided between the secretary and the receiver. In the office of the secretary entry was made by the exporter of his peltry, and a certificate was given him, on the presentation of which to the receiver and the payment of the duty, a permit was issued to export. In one or both of these offices a record was made of the merchants who owned the furs, and of the number, size, and marks of the bundles. The receiver was also given the right of search and seizure, and no vessel was permitted to receive despatches until the receiver reported that the master had cleared with him. By the act of 1700 the exporter was required to make a declaration under oath before a justice of the peace, and this was filed with the receiver as the evidence on which he should issue the permit

to export. Since the act of 1703 greatly increased the duti-
able list, the office of controller was added to assist in search
and seizures. The public receiver was still designated in
the act. He was also put under bond to account as often as
required to the assembly, or a committee of the same, for all
the revenue he collected. The system of customs duties was
established by this act in essentially the form which it was
to retain until the close of the proprietary period.

In Maryland and Pennsylvania the regulations contained
in the laws concerning the entry and clearance of vessels and
the collection of duties were very meagre and inadequate.
Indirect taxation played so small a part in the early history
of Pennsylvania that this will scarcely occasion surprise. It
is also in harmony with the summary character of much of
the early legislation in that province. A similar character
attaches to many of the laws of Maryland, and in this, as in
many other things, the legislature left to the proprietor and
his officials discretionary power in what related to the collection of the tobacco duty.

In the English provinces, with the exception of New York,
the proprietors and their officials were dependent from the
first on their legislatures for appropriations. They could
not tax without legislative authority. In the early laws of
New Jersey and Pennsylvania this principle was expressly
stated. In the other provinces it was acted upon. By 1660
that question had been settled in England, and the colonies
began with the full advantage of English precedents in this
matter. It was by withholding appropriations that the
legislatures were chiefly able to bring pressure to bear on
the provincial executives. This, however, became more
distinctly a feature of colonial history in the eighteenth century than it was in the seventeenth. In the proprietary
provinces salaries seem, so far as they existed, in all, or nearly
all, cases to have been from the first subject to legislative
grant. In Maryland, in 1642, the assembly imposed an export
duty on tobacco for the support of the government. In
1650 it gave Governor Stone one-half bushel of corn per
poll. The revenue from a poll tax payable in tobacco was
given to the governor for about a decade after 1660. In

1671 and thereafter, as has already been stated, one-half of the revenue from the export duty of 2*s.* per hogshead on tobacco was set apart for the support of the governor and council and for a supply of arms and ammunition.

After the middle of the century, the appropriation acts in Maryland became very detailed and specific. As early as 1657 an act that was intended to meet charges which had been incurred in finally reëstablishing proprietary government after the close of the administration by the commissioners of parliament, contained such items as the following : [1] payment for the use of a boat, care and victualling of prisoners, supply of shoes and stockings for the soldiers, a pension for a widow whose husband had been slain in the public service, relief for parties who were wounded or who had lost their crops, payment of a captain for a part of the expense which he had incurred in the public service. Provision was also made for paying the cost of negotiating with the Indians, for paying the clerk, doorkeeper, and guard of the assembly. The levy was raised and payments were apportioned by sections, corresponding more or less fully to counties. In the case of Patuxent county provision was made for charges which later find a place exclusively in local levies.

A similar appropriation act was passed in 1658, while orders of council concerning the levy of 1660 reveal a considerable variety of services for which payment was provided.[2] With the year 1669 the form of the annual appropriation act [3] became fixed as it was to continue during the period. A full list of persons to whom sums were due, with the amount due to each, was prepared. Though the services for which the payments were demanded were not generally specified in the bill, yet the list, when completed, formed a very full itemized account. It was arranged by counties. The words of appropriation were then framed so as to cover the sums of the several accounts which made up

[1] Md. Arch., Assembly, 1638–1664, 363.

[2] Proceedings of Council, 1636–1667, 556, 557.

[3] Proceedings of Assembly, 1666–1676, 227, 302, 338, 415, 468, 551; *ibid.* 1678–1683, 87, 208, etc.

the total. " Whereas there are severall sumes of Tobacco dew to severall persons from the Province, as by account hereunto Annexed at Large Appeareth, amounting in the whole to . . . pounds of Tobacco, as also . . . pounds of Tobacco to the Severall delegates from the Severall Counties for their Expenses at St. Maries during the Assembly, besides what they have for their Boates or other necessary Expenses in coming down to this Assembly. Be it enacted etc." As expenditures increased, the list of items became larger and the acts contained an ever growing accumulation of details. Under this system, — and it was one which came to exist in many of the provinces, — though the treasurers were appointed by the proprietor or his governor, and though they paid out money exclusively on the governor's warrant, the discretion of the executive in the matter of expenditures was effectively limited. The control of the assembly in Maryland was confirmed by the requirement that the treasurers should regularly account to it for the management of the revenue. Near the close of the early proprietary period the houses began appointing joint committees to state accounts, while the list of detailed appropriation acts show that accounts had long been stated with care.[1]

The form of appropriation acts in South Carolina was somewhat different from that followed in Maryland, but it shows an equal resolution on the part of the commons to direct the course of expenditure. When providing, in 1685, for the building of watch-houses, it directed that the grand council should by warrants require the public receiver to pay all who should be concerned in doing the work. The wages of those who were to constitute the guard of the watch-houses were designated in the act. By an act of 1690 for maintaining a watch on Sullivan's island, the receiver was required to keep accounts of expenditure and be ready to submit them to the assembly. Any surplus should be expended as the assembly saw fit. Later acts were equally specific, especially one passed in 1702 for maintaining lookouts and purchasing military supplies. In the revenue act of 1703 the receiver, as well as a con-

[1] Proceedings of Assembly, 1678–1683, 336, 474.

troller, was designated in the law, and the former was put
under oath and bond. This act also contained a clause
threatening the receiver with a heavy fine if he diverted
any of the revenue to purposes other than those designated
in the statute. An act of 1706 contained an especially comprehensive appropriation clause. A specific sum was set
aside for the payment of the salaries of ministers, while the
rest was to go toward paying the public debts. Under this
head the assembly undertook to designate those among the
creditors of the province who were most in need of their
money, and to direct the receiver to pay them first of all.
The remaining creditors were to be paid in the order fixed
by lot, the lots being drawn under the direction of a committee named in the act.[1] In 1707, when the fiscal regulations in South Carolina had fully developed, examiners
were designated who should annually inspect the receiver's
books.

In early New Jersey and in East Jersey the acts were
brief, and no special effort was made to specify the objects of
expenditure. In two cases the wages of the assemblymen
were designated and in one case those of the governor and
council as well, while they were in attendance on the legislature.[2] Certain annual votes of salary to the governor also
appear, as we have seen. In 1678 and 1682 province treasurers were designated in acts of supply. Local collectors
and treasurers for special levies were repeatedly named in
the laws.[3] Much the same practice obtained in West Jersey.
Until 1701, just at the close of the proprietary period, no
effort was made to specify in detail the objects of appropriation, though on repeated occasions a definite annual salary
was voted to the governor, and once at least to the speaker
and the clerk of the assembly. In 1681 and 1682 the treasurers were named in the acts.[4] In this province, however,
the question of specific appropriations was no more important than it might have been in any New England colony,

[1] Statutes of South Carolina, II. 10, 41, 184, 210, 275, 305.
[2] Grants and Concessions, 122, 276.
[3] *Ibid.* 275, 306, 350.
[4] *Ibid.* 425, 449, 561, 583, 587.

for ultimate popular control was secured through the election of nearly all officials.

The legislation of Pennsylvania on this subject did not, as a rule, go into details. Though the spirit of the province was favorable to very large legislative control over expenditures, as in the Jerseys, the machinery for exercising it was only imperfectly developed. Not until 1696, when the tax of a penny in the pound was levied for a second time, was an effort made to determine its expenditure. The province treasurer was named in the act. It was also specified that £300 should go for the relief of the friendly Indians on the Albany frontier, and £300 for the salary of the governor. The remainder should be used as the governor and council should order, to pay the debts and defray the expenses of the province. Full accounts should be rendered by the receiver to the governor and council, and by them to the assembly.[1] If, however, we are justified in drawing an inference from the remissness of officials in collecting this tax, one might conclude that the specifications concerning the use of the money may also have been ignored.

[1] Charter and Laws, 255, 263, 274.

CHAPTER XV

THE statements which were made in a previous chapter
concerning the equipment, organization, and general character of the militia of New England hold true also of the proprietary provinces. The same is true of forts and harbor
defences. The general conditions affecting military service
were much the same in all the colonies. Much, then, which
has already been said need not be repeated, but may be
borne in mind along with the additional fact, that in some
of the provinces the crudities of New England military
administration were intensified.

Of the provinces which fall within this group, South
Carolina and New York were situated on the border. Upon
them rested with special weight the obligations of defence.
They were forced to act, not only on their own behalf, but
for the protection of their neighbors. In the history of
South Carolina this was an ever present fact. In her case
not only was protection against the Indians necessary, but
as well against the Spaniards of Florida and European assailants who might approach from the ocean. The development of the slave system, in her case as in that of the other
southern provinces, also necessitated the maintenance of a
semi-military patrol. New York was at first menaced by
the Dutch. Her northern frontier was occasionally disturbed by the wars between the French and the Iroquois,
but was not directly assailed until after the close of the
brief proprietary period of her history. The great Indian
war in New England only remotely affected her interests.
Though at first she was not compelled to act so continuously on the defensive as did the New England colonies or

375

South Carolina, yet conditions were developing which, after 1680, were to thoroughly test her capacity for military activity and Indian negotiation. After that time it became clear that she lay in the strategic centre of the northern frontier.

It is true that North Carolina was forced to contend with the Tuscarora Indians in her own midst, and that this was one of the greatest local conflicts of the period. Moreover her western border, like that of the other southern colonies, was occasionally disturbed by the raids of the Five Nations and their conflicts with the southern Indians. But nature gave her a comparatively inaccessible coast, while on the south as well as on the north she was protected by adjacent provinces. Pennsylvania was exposed to Indian raids on the west and north, but was shielded on other sides by neighboring provinces. From the sea she could be approached through Delaware bay, but this exposure Philadelphia shared with the ports of southern New Jersey and of the Lower Counties. Maryland and New Jersey had a coast line, but one which was relatively destitute of ports or of attractive points of attack. To landward their borders were better protected than those of any other colonies. These were the general natural conditions which helped to determine the attitude of this group of provinces toward measures of defence.

Owing to the peaceful attitude of the natives, the middle and northern provinces of the group were not disturbed by Indian wars. The presence of Quakers in New Jersey and Pennsylvania indisposed those provinces to offensive operations of any kind, and increased their indifference even to ordinary provisions for defence. The necessity of harmonizing a number of somewhat incongruous elements among the population of New York made it difficult to utilize for military or any other purposes even the limited resources which were in existence. North Carolina was too weak in population, resources, and government to provide for the defence of her territory, and when her time of trial came she was forced, as we shall see, to depend on Virginia and South Carolina for rescue and protection. When this occurred, moreover, the intercolonial wars were already well advanced.

These references to special conditions which affected the proprietary provinces indicate the reasons why at least three among them failed to provide adequate means of defence, and also show that as a group they were not so active or so well organized in a military sense as were the Puritan colonies of New England.

In all these provinces the authority to organize a militia, to build forts or fortify towns, was derived from the king through the proprietors. The proprietor of Maryland made his governor commander of forces by land and sea, with the special titles of lieutenant-general, admiral, and chief captain. This, together with the general appointing power which was also bestowed upon the governor, gave him authority, with the advice of the council, to appoint and instruct all subordinate military officers in the province. In the first set of proprietary instructions the governor was ordered to cause the adult males of the province to be trained weekly or monthly.[1] Upon the reorganization of the government in 1658 a full set of instructions was given to the captains of the trained bands. In the commissions issued by the Carolina proprietors the military powers of the governor likewise stood in the forefront, he being authorized to resort to all measures which were necessary for defence.[2] The governors of New York were themselves military officers, and Nicolls and Andros each brought over under his command a small body of English troops. They exercised to the full extent the right of appointment, though they usually made selections of officers lower than the rank of major from the lists of nominees presented by the inhabitants of the localities.[3] Various instances are on record of the exercise of the same power by the first governor of New Jersey,[4] though in the scanty records which have been preserved of East Jersey and West Jersey only slight evidence of such activity ap-

[1] Proceedings of Council, 1636–1667, 49, 108, 345 ; Calvert Papers, I. 139.

[2] N. C. Recs. I. 84, 97, 171, 194, 336, 695, 780; Shaftesbury Papers, 404, 407.

[3] Duke's Laws, in N. Y. Col. Laws, I. 50; N. Y. Col. Docs. XIII. 449, 459 ; XIV. 598, 607, 643, 674, 687. Many instances appear in the Ms. volumes entitled Orders, Letters, and Warrants.

[4] E. J. Recs., Liber III., 1675.

pears. As Pennsylvania developed no military system until she was compelled to do so by the ravages of the enemy during the last intercolonial war, for the period under review she may in this connection be safely left out of account.

In Maryland and New York the system of defence was pretty fully developed before the legislature prescribed rules for its management. In Maryland a militia bill was before the assemblies in 1638 and again in 1639.[1] The one which was considered in the latter year, and which passed the second reading, provided for a monthly assize of arms to be taken by the captain of the band at Saint Mary's and by the commander at Kent island. It also provided that on the giving of an alarm the householders of every hundred should send to the place of rendezvous one man in every three of their families or two men in every five, and that they should be completely armed. But this measure did not become law. In its stead an act was passed giving to the respective captain and commander, under the direction of the governor, full authority for the defence of the province.

Not until 1654, when the authority of the proprietor had been temporarily suspended and government was being administered by an appointee of the Puritan commissioners, was the next militia law passed.[2] This was brief, providing simply that the age limits for service should be sixteen and sixty years, that all who were liable to service should be provided with arms, and that the captain and other officers of the county should view the arms and train the militia. The first detailed act on this subject in Maryland was passed in 1661.[3] Until that time military affairs in Lord Baltimore's province remained under the control of the executive, who acted under a series of commissions from the proprietor, supplemented by the briefest possible legislative enactment. The expeditions which during this period were sent against Ingle and Claiborne, or against the Puritans who later attempted to overthrow the proprietor's authority, were under the command of the governor in person or of some councillor, like Thomas Cornwallis, who was specially

---

[1] Assembly Proceedings, 1638–1664, 20, 36, 39, 77, 84.
[2] *Ibid.* 347.   [3] Assembly Proceedings, 1638–1664, 412.

appointed for the purpose. Similar arrangements were
made when it was necessary to proceed against the Indians.[1]
In 1643 Cornwallis was ordered to take, as a quota from
every county or hundred, every third man who was able to
bear arms, together with all who would volunteer, and proceed against the Indians. The localities from which the men
came were required to provide them with arms and all other
necessaries for the expedition. The subordinate officers
through whom the governor regularly acted in early times
were the captain of the band of Saint Mary's, the captain of
the band of Kent island, a muster-master general, who had
general supervision of the training and mustering of the
militia of the whole province, together with the lower officers
who served under them. The captains must be regarded as
essentially county officers, and they sometimes went by the
title of commander.

In 1658, by order of the governor and council, captains
were appointed to command and train the militia in various
specified sections of the province.[2] They were instructed to
take the assize of arms, to organize trained bands from those
who were of military age, to train them once a month, and to
impose fines for failure to appear. In April, 1661, by act of
assembly,[3] authority was given to draft quotas of militia
from each of four counties for an expedition against the
Indians. The wages of officers and soldiers were prescribed,
and a tax was ordered to be levied to meet the expense. By
another act, passed [4] the same session, full legislative sanction
was given to the organization of the militia and to the system of training which had been developed. A comparison
of this act with the instructions of 1658 will show that the
requirements of the two differ only in details relating to
penalties and to the frequency of trainings.

When, after 1660, raids of the Five Nations against the
southern Indians became frequent, expeditions had several
times to be organized by the Maryland government to restore
quiet in the northern parts of the province. The orders for
these reveal the fact that soon after the date just mentioned

---

[1] Proceedings of Council, 1636–1667, 131.   [2] *Ibid.* 344, 349, 351, 401.
[3] Assembly Proceedings, 1638–1664, 407.   [4] *Ibid.* 412.

the militia had been organized by counties, though the levies were not yet regimented. The soldiers who were needed for service on any expedition were raised by draft from those in the counties who were liable to military service.[1] A magazine of ammunition and arms was kept by the province. Commissioners were appointed and ordered to impress supplies from the various counties, and boats or other means with which to transport them. The authority to impress soldiers was given directly by warrant to the colonels of the counties. Early in 1668 every tenth man was ordered to be held in readiness to march, and from among those a force of 287 was raised and provisioned for actual service. If servants or hired persons were drafted who were unable to provide their own arms, their masters were required to furnish the arms or instead to serve in person. Every soldier was required to bring a gun, a sword, two pounds of powder, six pounds of shot, and four flints. Every sixth man should bring an axe for felling trees.

During the years between 1675 and 1681 the peace of Maryland was much disturbed by Indian raids and by the murder of white settlers in various parts of the province. The causes of disturbance, as we have seen, were to an extent identical with those which at that time occasioned Bacon's rebellion in Virginia. The peace within Maryland was imperilled by the reflex influence of that uprising itself. These events occasioned more military activity in the province than anything else which occurred between the defeat of Governor Stone in 1655 and the revolt in 1689. The efforts of those years helped still further to develop the militia system and to give it the characteristics which it had at the close of the first period of proprietary government. The activity of the Indians in the upper part of Anne Arundel county, as well as an appeal from Virginia, led the governor and council, early in September, 1675, to begin[2] ordering out

[1] Proceedings of Council, 1636–1667, 411, 502 ; 1667–1688, 21.

[2] Council Proceedings, 1671–1681, 47 *et seq.* ; Assembly Proceedings, 1666–1676, 475 *et seq.* Among these entries will be found the proceedings relating to the impeachment of Major Truman. See especially the affidavit on p. 483. Compare with the affidavits of Virginia officers printed in William and Mary College Quarterly, II. 39–43.

the militia.   Troopers and rangers were largely relied on, and to their activity we find many references.   The force which, under the command of Major Truman, was sent to aid the Virginians consisted of mounted men.   The order for the expedition called for a regiment of five troops of fifty men each.

The assembly which met in the following May was much occupied with military affairs.   The upper house impeached Major Truman on the charge of violating orders by consenting to the death of the five Susquehanna chiefs, but owing to disagreement with the lower house over the penalty to be inflicted, he escaped with simply removal from the council. Both houses discussed the advisability of continuing rangers longer in active service.   The mode of raising supplies was also considered, as well as the pay of the soldiers.[1]   An act for the defence of the province was passed[2] at this session, which not only made provision for troopers but also for a system of pensions.   The payments were to be made annually to those who were permanently disabled in service and to the families of the slain.   The governor and council were empowered to fix the amount of the payments, and claimants were required to bring as proof of their claims a certificate from the justices of the county in which they lived.   Authority was also given by this act for the appointment of officers to impress provisions in each hundred and county whenever an expedition was fitted out.

At this juncture, also, an unusually elaborate series of articles of war, fifty-three in number, were put into force throughout the province by the governor and council.[3] From these a much more complete idea can be formed of the discipline which officers were under obligation to maintain than from the penalties which are briefly expressed in the statutes.   Provision was made for a court-martial, before which body all serious offences were to be brought for trial.

[1] Assembly Proceedings, 1666–1676, 497, 501.   [2] *Ibid.* 557.

[3] Council Proceedings, 1671–1681, 80, 98.   I am not aware that a series of articles of war so complete as this appears among the records of any other English colony in the seventeenth century.   Its completeness suggests the possibility that it was sent from England.

Profanity, blasphemy, sacrilege, violations of safe-conduct, giving of false alarms, sleeping at post, disobedience, disrespectful behavior, plundering of non-combatants, desertion, treason, and a long list of other military offences were specified. The list was sufficiently detailed to include all the important violations of good order which might arise in a large army. The penalties, however, were not definitely prescribed, but were left to the discretion of the court-martial. Mention is made of regimental courts-martial, as well as a tribunal for the whole province ; but apparently at this period no force larger than about four hundred men was ever called into service at one time, and they served in detached bodies of a score or two each. There is evidence that additions were sometimes made to the articles by order of the council. But, however detailed it might be, it was necessarily administered by men who possessed little military training. Though the officers in Maryland were appointed and were in no sense dependent on the privates for their rank, those whom they commanded were neighbors and friends. From this it follows that, though military law was formally more systematic in Maryland than in some of the other colonies, conditions did not essentially differ from those which existed in the colonies where the militia was best organized.

In July, 1676, a special council of war met at Saint Mary's.[1] This consisted of the governor and the council, with the addition of the colonels, majors, and captains from a number of the counties. No other instance of such a meeting appears on record. Among the orders to which it apparently gave rise was one providing that within the five counties on the west shore the inhabitants, on report of an Indian invasion, should take refuge within garrison houses or palisades. The houses in each hundred which should be used for this purpose it was made the duty of the county justices, with the aid of the local militia captains, to select. In no house should more than ten men able to bear arms be placed for refuge. Thus an effort was made to develop a system such as grew up in New England towns. But the danger soon passed away. Affairs both in Virginia and Maryland became

[1] Council Proceedings, 1671-1681, 99.

more quiet.   After 1676 Maryland was disturbed only by
occasional murders by the savages, the work either of the
Susquehanna tribe or of the raiders from the remoter north.
In 1678 [1] provision was made by law for a company of horse
in each county, the system of impressment and of pensions
was confirmed, and it was made incumbent on the proprietor
to provide a magazine of arms and ammunition from which
the soldiers could in part be supplied.   Under the head of
small charges, the governor and council were permitted to
levy and expend annually a sum not in excess of fifty thousand pounds of tobacco for purposes of defence.   With this
the militia system of Maryland reached the fullest development which it attained before the revolution of 1689.

Arms, powder, and other ammunition of war, costing
nearly £400, with gunners' stores in addition, were sent to
Carolina with West's expedition, in 1669.   Provisions for the
defence of the colony after its settlement [2] at Albemarle
Point in southern Carolina first clearly appear in connection
with the expedition against the Kussoes, a neighboring tribe
of Indians, in the fall of 1671.   Then the grand council
ordered trainings to be held.   The council itself and the
officers who attended it were the only men who were excused from training. [3]   It appears from this order that the
men of the colony were already armed and were formed into
companies, with proper officers.   The officers were required
to return to the council the names of all who absented themselves from trainings, that they might be severely fined or
otherwise punished.   They were also to impress the labor of
smiths for the purpose of repairing firearms.   Provision had
already been made for a town watch under the charge of the
marshal, but it was made more detailed and stringent by this
ordinance.   The obligation to serve on the watch was as
general as that of militia service, and the ordinance in question is the earliest of a long series of acts which had as their
purpose the protection by night of the inhabitants, first of
Charlestown on Albemarle Point and later of Charlestown
on Oyster Point.   By the beginning of 1671 Governor West

was able to report that the settlement was well enough fortified to withstand attack by Indians.[1]

In June and July, 1672,[2] still more comprehensive orders
were issued, which related to the defence of the entire colony.
They provided for the mounting of two cannon on the palisades at Newtown, a settlement which had recently been
founded on James island.   They also established a system of
alarms which should be followed by the retirement of the
inhabitants of the remote plantations to certain specified
points.   Among the equipments of the men the substitution
of cartouche boxes for bandoleers was ordered.   The entire
militia force of the colony was organized into six companies,
besides a guard for the governor.   Commissions were issued
to the officers from captain to lieutenant-colonel, while the
inferior places were filled by persons who were nominated
by the commissioned officers.   In 1675 the number of companies was reduced to three, the governor commanding one
of them in person.[3]

The evidence is clear that, when the chief settlement of
the province was removed to Oyster Point, the vigorous
system of defence which had already been established was
continued.   Though a number of the early militia laws have
been lost, enough remains to enable us to see that much
attention was paid to training and arming the inhabitants.
It may be said that at no time between 1680 and the close
of the second intercolonial war were Charlestown and the
adjacent coast free from danger of attack.   During that
time conditions in the West Indies were always disturbed.
Spanish pirates might at any time descend on the inhabitants.   In 1685 provision was made for the building and
garrisoning of a watch-house on Sullivan island, of another
on or near James island, and a third at Port Royal, where
Lord Cardross's colony was then being settled.   The language
of this act would indicate that the militia of the province

---

[1] Shaftesbury Papers, 250, 267.   The later laws on the defences of Charlestown and its watch, which were passed after the removal of the colony to
Oyster Point, are in Vol. VII. of the Statutes of South Carolina.

[2] Rivers, 379–382 ; Shaftesbury Papers, 395.

[3] Shaftesbury Papers, 464.

was regimented, though there is no other evidence on that point. Care was being taken to keep the lists full and all companies in good military order. Authority was also given by law to the grand council to impress men, arms, supplies, boats, and all else that was necessary for organizing an expedition.[1] But though special reference was made in these acts to defence against the Spaniards, they did not suffice to prevent the destruction by them of the colony at Port Royal.

During the years subsequent to 1707, in the second inter-colonial war, six or eight lookouts or watch-houses were maintained at as many points along the coast of the prov-ince.[2] One duty of the armed watchmen at these posts was to look out for slaves who were trying to escape by sea. The influence of slavery in developing the military spirit and institutions of the province is further evidenced by the creation of the patrol system. The earliest act on this sub-ject was passed in 1704. It provided that, from such militia companies as the governor should designate, ten men each should be selected, mounted, fully armed, and placed as patrolmen under special officers. The province was divided into precincts, and on alarm or at other times when it was considered necessary, each troop was required to ride through its precinct and seize all slaves who were found off their master's plantation without a pass or permit.[3] At the time of which we are speaking the captain of each militia com-pany was required to enroll one slave for every white man. The negroes were separately trained, and armed with guns or lances.

In 1708, according to a report of Governor Johnson,[4] the main body of the militia of the province consisted of 950 white men who were able to bear arms. These were organ-ized into two regiments of foot, consisting together of six-teen companies having about fifty men each. In addition to this force the governor's guards formed a special company of about forty men; the French Protestants of the Santee had a company of forty-five men; and, in case of a general levy

[1] Statutes of South Carolina, II. 9, 15.
[2] Ibid. 300, 354.
[3] Ibid. 254.
[4] McCrady, 478.

to resist invasion, a reserve of about one hundred men was left to guard the houses and families of the colonists.

In 1708, as a defence against expected attacks by the French, a small fort was built on James island, and the defence of the harbor at large was thus begun. It was named Fort Johnson.

The militia force of New Netherland consisted of the regular troops, the rural militia, and the burgher guard of New Amsterdam. English auxiliaries were occasionally employed against the Indians.[1] Because of the presence of regular troops, the garrison was a more important feature of the system of defence in New Netherland and New York than elsewhere. Small stockades and earthworks of the ordinary colonial type were early built at New Amsterdam, Fort Orange, Esopus, at various points on the South river, and in the Dutch towns as they were settled throughout the province. Several of these posts were garrisoned either permanently or temporarily by soldiers of the company who were under the command of its director and his subordinates. The garrison of Fort Amsterdam consisted of recruits from the Netherlands, of soldiers transferred from Curaçoa, and of recruits from the province itself. Some were sent from Europe for short terms of service, and after their discharge remained in the province as colonists; but the larger part were professional soldiers serving on annual enlistments. They were in the pay of the West India company, from which, wholly or in part, they also received their clothing, equipments, and food. They served as a guard at the fort, as an armed police in the town, and as a body-guard of the director.

The garrison troops first appeared in New Amsterdam in 1633, with the advent of Wouter van Twiller as director. Then and for a number of years thereafter they numbered about fifty. In July, 1644, in the midst of the first Indian war, 130 men arrived from Curaçoa. Fifty men came from the same place the following year. But when the war closed, the decisive victories of which were won chiefly by English

---

[1] See the sources already referred to, and articles by L. D. Scisco in the American Historical Register, 1895, 1896.

auxiliaries under Baxter and Underhill, the garrison was again reduced to about fifty men. Early in Stuyvesant's administration it was still further reduced. In 1655 it served in the expedition against the Swedes on the South river, though the force at that time consisted mainly of 200 soldiers from Europe, and volunteers from New Netherland in number sufficient to bring the total up to 600. An armed vessel of thirty-six guns was also sent from Holland to aid in the enterprise. After the return of this expedition garrisons were established at Esopus and other outlying settlements, and in 1660 the total number in this service at Fort Amsterdam and elsewhere was 250, but, under pressure from the company, which alleged that the expense was too great, the total was considerably reduced.

The militia, as distinguished from the troops of the company, consisted of the levies of the rural towns and the burgher guard of the capital. They did not originate from an institution of such general application as the assize of arms among the English colonies. In 1640[1] an order was issued by the director and council that the inhabitants near Fort Amsterdam should provide themselves with arms and be ready to appear when the signal was given of the approach of danger. The founding of settlements in the outlying districts necessitated some such regulations for their defence, but these were made in orders relating to particular towns or in special injunctions from the director and council. The company also, in the Freedoms and Exemptions, made itself responsible for the protection of outlying settlements. It encouraged the arming of the colonists. At times when attack by the Indians or by some expedition from Europe was threatened, special activity was manifested. In 1654, when attacks by the English were expected, the Dutch towns on Long Island organized a local militia[2] and imposed a general obligation of service. Stuyvesant favored such measures, and in 1659 attempted to supplement these levies by a troop of cavalry. Local militia companies existed at Beverwyck, Esopus, Bergen, Haerlem, and on the South river. Under the pressure of repeated Indian attacks the obligation of self-

[1] Laws and Ordinances, 23.   [2] *Ibid.* 159.

defence was imposed on these and the other villages by repeated orders of the director and council.

The burgher guard was the local militia of New Amsterdam.   It was first mustered under Jochem Pietersen Kuyter
as captain, during the Indian war of 1644.   In the spring of
1648[1] the citizens were ordered by Director Stuyvesant to
appear at muster armed with muskets.   When it was found
that there were not enough muskets in town to arm the citizens, a supply was furnished from the company's magazine.
A guard-house was also built for the use of the company.
But after a second training, probably in consequence of the
development of the controversy over municipal rights, the
guard was not called together again for two years.   Van
Couwenhoven, its captain, was a leader of the opposition,
and with Van der Donck and his associates went to The
Hague to lay the complaints of the colonists before the States
General.   In response came an order for the formation of
militia companies throughout the province,[2] while one hundred muskets, with a stand of colors, were sent over for the
use of the burgher guard.   Stuyvesant confiscated the guns
and ignored orders concerning the inspection of arms and
training of the guard.   Martin Krygier soon took the place
of Van Couwenhoven as its captain.

The suspension of military activity in New Amsterdam
continued until the grant of municipal rights arrived from
Holland, when the guardsmen were placed on duty as a city
watch.   Thenceforth they were a prominent institution of
the city.   When, in 1655, during the absence of the garrison
on the expedition against the Swedes, the Indians raided
Manhattan island and the surrounding country, the defence
of the city fell wholly on the burgher guard.   By 1658 the
guard had increased to three companies, each with its distinct flag, its captain, lieutenant, ensign, and sergeant.   In
1657 one of the companies was taken by the director to the
Esopus for a brief campaign against the Indians.   But on
all occasions they were averse to service outside the city, and

[1] N. Y. Col. Ms. 8 ; Fernow in Wilson, Memorial History of New York
City, I. 250.

[2] N. Y. Col. Docs. I. 389, 397.

could therefore never take the place of the regular soldiers
who were maintained by the company.

When, in August, 1664, the report came that an English
force destined for the occupation of New Netherland had
arrived at Boston, the province was found to be very imperfectly protected.[1] On Staten island, opposite the Narrows,
a small blockhouse had been built, in which a garrison of six
or ten partially disabled soldiers[2] had been placed. In the
hamlet of New Utrecht, back from the opposite shore and
facing the bay to the south, a similar defence existed. Each
of these blockhouses contained one or two small pieces of
ordnance. Even as a protection against Indians these defences would be considered weak. The fort at the southern
end of Manhattan island was a small earthwork, about a
hundred and fifty feet square on the inside. Its wall was
eight or ten feet high and three or four feet thick, and it was
mounted with twenty-four small cannon. It contained no
well or cistern. The rising ground which lay to the north,
near the lower end of " The Heerewegh," the modern Broad-
way, was high enough to enable an enemy from that point to
command every part of the interior of the fort. The houses
of the citizens were built close against the walls, and could
be easily utilized by besiegers at once as a protection and as
a means of approach. Under these conditions a siege of the
fort would involve the ruin of a considerable part of the
town. On the river banks the town was wholly unprotected,
and its only defence, except the fort, was the stockade, supported in the rear by a low embankment of earth, which
extended along the northern side of the city and was known
as " The Wall."

The garrison and its supplies were as inadequate as were
the defences. Misled by reports from Holland that the
action which had been taken by the English government was
directed wholly against New England, Stuyvesant had recently visited the northern part of the province, and had left

[1] The original, from which all later accounts have been drawn, is Director
Stuyvesant's Answer to the Observations of the West India Company, N. Y.
Col. Docs. II. 429.

[2] N. Y. Col. Docs. II. 443 ; XIV. 546.

at Esopus and Fort Orange a few soldiers as an additional protection against the Indians. The available regulars for the garrison were thus not more than a hundred and fifty. They had six hundred pounds of powder which was fit for use. An urgent call for aid was sent to the Dutch towns on Long Island, but they needed all their men for their own protection. A part of the militia of the English towns farther east were already in arms against the Dutch. Aid, whether in men or provisions, from all parts of the province outside of Manhattan was speedily cut off. Being thrown back mainly on their own resources, the burghers of New Amsterdam bestirred themselves for the defence of the city outside the limits of the fort.[1] The magistrates, when they heard that the English force which was sent against them had reached Boston, resolved that one-third of the inhabitants should be put to work with spades and wheelbarrows on the defences of the town. A special guard should be mounted and the militia companies of the city should be paraded. The director and council, at their request, loaned them six small pieces of ordnance, and a supply of powder and lead. The negroes who belonged to the company were also put to work on the defences of the city.

But all was to no purpose. Besides the soldiers of the garrison, there were in the city only 250 men who were capable of bearing arms. The farmers on the island, one-third of whom were called out, refused to serve. The resources and defences were so slight that, when the English appeared, no course was left except to surrender. The city was occupied by the enemy without a blow. The Dutch garrison marched out of the fort with the honors of war, and a part of the soldiers were sent back to the Netherlands. When, a month later, Sir Robert Carr, with two vessels, appeared[2] on the Delaware, he found at New Amstel a garrison of less than fifty men. But the director, Hinoyossa, resolved to defend the fort. A company of English was landed and, while they stormed the works, two broadsides were fired from the men-of-war. The Dutch replied

[1] Records of New Amsterdam, V. 105–116.
[2] N. Y. Col. Docs. III. 73 ; Brodhead, II. 51.

with musketry, but not with cannon. The English forced their way at once into the fort and plundered it. Three of the Dutch garrison were killed and two wounded. The English lost none. This event gave the settlement on the South river into their possession. Fort Orange was surrendered without resistance.

The force with which this result was accomplished consisted of three small war vessels and a transport. They carried, all together, less than one hundred guns, and had on board three companies of veteran troops — about 450 men. They were accompanied by one or more engineers, and were in all respects well equipped. The lesson which Stuyvesant drew from the event was this, "Whosoever, by ship or ships, is master on the river, will in a short time be master of the fort."[1] As more fully expressed by the same official, this meant that the colonists, destitute as they were of a navy, of strong coast defences, and of adequate military force, without aid from Europe could not defend themselves against an attack by Europeans. The much earlier exploit of the Spanish at Port Royal, the descent of the English on Quebec in 1628, the later reoccupation of New Netherland by the Dutch, prove the truth of the assertion. The fate of New Netherland was no worse than that which under similar conditions might have befallen any of the English colonies. The defences of New Netherland and its militia system were superior to those of the settlements of northern New England, of Rhode Island, of the later provinces of North Carolina, New Jersey, and Pennsylvania. Had it been possible for the director to have commanded the services at this crisis of the entire population of New Netherland, he might have made, in proportion to his strength, as good a showing as any English colony. The success of the English in 1664, and its reversal in 1673, derive much of their significance from the light which they throw on the weakness of colonial defence. If left to their own resources, the colonies might fall a prey to any European state which took the trouble to attack them in earnest.

[1] N. Y. Col. Docs. II. 446.

The most important result of the substitution of English for Dutch rule arose from the fact that the English could command to a degree the resources of all the Long Island towns. Their militia, which as a body had already been active under Captain John Scott, now became a part of the defensive system of New York. The Duke's Laws contained systematic provisions concerning military affairs which were specially intended for the section of the province of which they were a part. The provisions, moreover, were borrowed from New England usage. They [1] made general and specific the requirements which the Dutch had enforced through special orders and local regulations. As was customary in the English colonies, the limits of military age were fixed at sixteen and sixty years. Physicians, schoolmasters, ministers, and various public officials were excused from service. The assize of arms was to be enforced, and the captains, or other military officers, were required to report annually to the governor the extent to which the inhabitants were provided with arms, that a proper supply might be ordered. Those who, upon the quarterly view of arms by the captain or lieutenant of the town, were found to be imperfectly furnished, should be reported to the constable and overseers and by them be fined.

Each town was required to hold a training four days in the year ; once a year the companies of each riding should train together, and once every two years there should be a general muster of the militia of the three ridings. Absence from training for an entire day was punishable by a fine of 5s., while fines for other offences should be levied more or less at the discretion of the commanding officers. No fine in excess of 10s. should be imposed by a military officer, but they might inflict the usual military punishments or deliver offenders over to the civil officers for punishment by the courts. Provision was made for troops of horse and for their training with the infantry.

The higher military officers were appointed directly by the governor. The captains, lieutenants, and ensigns were commissioned from lists submitted by the militia companies

[1] N. Y. Col. Laws, I. 49.

through the constables and overseers of the respective towns.
Expeditions were called out by warrants from the governor
and council to the sheriff, whose duty it was to summon both
military and civil officers to appear at the time and place
designated, with the quotas from the respective towns.   It
thus appears that the system of filling the lower militia offices
by election, which the towns of eastern Long Island had inherited from New England, was preserved.   When, in 1667,
because of war in Europe, and of Courcelles' invasion of the
Iroquois country, it became necessary to embody the militia
of those towns, Governor Nicolls ordered the troopers of
each town to elect their captain, lieutenant, ensign, and corporal.   One third of the men in each foot company were
ordered to equip themselves as dragoons, and be ready for
active service.   The rest were to serve as home guards.[1]

While these regulations were prescribed for the English
section of the province, on Manhattan island and among
the settlements in the Hudson valley reliance was placed
for garrison duty on the regular troops which had accompanied Nicolls.   With them, for the general purposes of
defence, the militia of the Dutch settlements coöperated.
Owing to the fact that English rule in New York originated
in conquest, regular troops from England, or, as they were
later called, independent companies, played from the outset a part in its system of defence.   Brief articles of war[2]
forbade them to do violence to any person who was not
under arms, or to plunder his goods.   If any were found
committing the latter offence, or inciting to mutiny, they
should suffer death.

At Albany all the lower officers were retained in their
places, while a small garrison was left there under the command of Captain Manning.   It was agreed[3] that, at the
charge of the town, the barracks in the fort should be fitted
up for the accommodation of the soldiers during the ensuing
winter, and that it should furnish them with blankets,
candles, the value of 120 guilders per month in weapons,

[1] N. Y. Col. Docs. III. 158, 167.
[2] General Entries, State Library Bulletin, 79.
[3] *Ibid.* 112 ; N. Y. Col. Docs. III. 117.

and wagons in which to draw their wood. There is evidence that later soldiers were billeted on the inhabitants.[1] The chief officer at the fort and the magistrates were required on all occasions to coöperate in preserving the peace and good government. Manning was soon appointed schout, but before the close of 1665 was relieved of duty at Albany, and his successor retained only military authority. But occasionally thereafter a respected commander was elected schout.[2] The soldiers at first occasioned some trouble by stealing wampum from the inhabitants, but were promptly punished.

The friendliness which in general characterized the relations between the garrison and the people of Albany did not everywhere exist. Captain Daniel Brodhead, who was appointed commander of the garrison at Esopus, though ordered to pursue the most conciliatory course, was overbearing, and in the spring of 1667 he and his men became involved in an open conflict with the inhabitants.[3] This grew out of arbitrary arrests by the captain and a succession of quarrels between the soldiers and the citizens. In the final disturbance one burgher was killed. Governor Nicolls sent a special commission to the place, which found four of the inhabitants guilty of riot. They were sent to New York for final sentence by Nicolls; by him three of them were condemned to temporary exclusion from Albany, Esopus, and New York, and one to banishment from the province for life. Brodhead, who admitted the truth of the charges which were made concerning his conduct, was suspended from command.

In the city of New York collisions sometimes occurred between soldiers and people in the street, but they never became serious, because the presence of the governor made the exemplary punishment of all offences a certainty.[4] The chief difficulty which the city at this time experienced from

[1] N. Y. Col. Docs. III. 143.

[2] Captain Sylvester Salisbury was so chosen in November, 1670. Calendar of Albany Records, Court Minutes, 1668–1672.

[3] N. Y. Col. Docs. XIII. 406.

[4] Records of New Amsterdam, V. 261 ; Valentine's Manual, 1847, 353, 354.

the presence of an English garrison arose from an attempt of Governor Nicolls, in the spring of 1665, to billet about one hundred soldiers on the citizens. This it was within his right to do under the articles of surrender, but it was attended with obvious difficulties. He stated [1] to the burgomasters and schepens that, as the soldiers had not appliances with which to wash and cook for themselves, this course would be necessary. He offered to furnish weekly, for every soldier, a specified amount of meat and pease, while the city should pay two guilders lodging money for each per week. These payments should be made to the householders who would consent to receive the men. In return for its part of the expense the city should receive, in addition to the great excise, the income from the scales and the ferry. Any damage done by the soldiers should also be made good. But when the proposition was submitted to the citizens, nearly all excused themselves and some stayed away from the conference. One Andries Rees doubtless voiced the sentiments of the others, when he gave as his excuse the fear of being robbed. At a later meeting in the presence of the governor, the citizens adhered to their resolution, and said that they had rather contribute than lodge the soldiers. Nicolls, with the imperiousness of a military officer in the presence of a conquered people, left with the burgomasters and schepens a written order for a list of houses in which one hundred soldiers could be billeted, allowing not more than two to a house. The burghers now came to terms, and arrangements were made, though at an advance of two guilders per week, for the quartering of one hundred soldiers. The measure, however, was not to be put into execution until after the return of the governor from the visit to Massachusetts, in which the negotiations between the royal commissioners and that colony came to an unsuccessful end. In the meantime, the burghers were assessed toward the support of the soldiers. The records would indicate that after the return of the governor no further steps were taken until October, when, with the consent of the householders, the soldiers were quartered in

[1] Records of New Amsterdam, V. 207, 211, 220, 232, 302.

private houses for the winter. Respecting the regular troops during the administrations of Nicolls and Lovelace, we know nothing further. On the reoccupation of New York by the Dutch in 1673 they were all sent back to England.[1] When Edmund Andros was appointed governor in 1674, he was commissioned by the Duke of York to raise a company[2] of one hundred men in England, of which he should be captain. Anthony Brockholls and Christopher Billop were appointed lieutenants, and Cæsar Knapton ensign, of this company. It was brought to America by the governor, and remained thenceforth on garrison duty in New York. In 1678 Andros reported[3] that one company of regular soldiers, with gunners and officers, was stationed in the forts at New York and Albany. The payment, in January, 1680, of £1000 out of the English exchequer, illustrates the method by which these troops were supported.[4] The establishment was not increased while New York remained a proprietary province.

Of the two principal forts which were garrisoned by these troops, Andros reported in 1678 that the one at New York was square, with walls of stone and four regular bastions. It contained fifty-six mounted guns and a supply of military stores. The fort at Albany was a long stockaded affair with four bastions and twelve guns. In 1686 Governor Dongan reported that when he arrived he had found most of the guns at New York dismounted, but he had the wooden platforms on which they stood for the most part repaired. The walls and breastwork of the fort he also found it necessary to repair. Over the officers' quarters and the gate he had placed a new roof. The two acres of ground on which the fort stood he had surrounded with a paling. " I am forc't every day," he writes, " by reason of the rotenness of the Timber & Boards to bee making reparation in the Soldiers

---

[1] In Colonial Papers, 1675–1676, 197, is an account by Captain Dudley Lovelace of his experiences and those of fifty soldiers who were being taken back to Europe as prisoners on Dutch ships of war. The Dutch landed at Ferryland in Newfoundland and destroyed considerable property.

[2] N. Y. Col. Docs. III. 219, 220, 221.

[3] *Ibid.* 260.

[4] Colonial Papers, 1677–1680, 466.

quarters or my own." He recommended that the fort at
Albany, which was wholly of wood and earth, should be
built of stone, since the timber and boards which entered
into the present construction must be renewed every six or
seven years. Though the fort of New York, with its thirty-
nine guns and two small mortars, was " inconsiderable,"
Dongan wished there were more like it in the colonies.

We hear nothing of the burgher guard in New York until
August, 1668, when Governor Nicolls was about to leave the
province. Then, by the mayor's court, a resolution was
passed that the townsmen of New York should be listed and
divided into two military bands, and that they should parade
on the occasion of the departure of the governor. With the
assent of the governor, Martin Krygier and Johannes van
Brugh were chosen as captains, and with them were associated a lieutenant and an ensign for each company. In
January, 1672, a third company was organized. We are
informed that the officers of these companies were appointed
by the governor from a list of double the number nominated
by the burgher corps and transmitted to his Excellency by
the mayor.[1] In 1671 Governor Lovelace proposed that a troop
of horse should be raised on Manhattan island, but the plan
was postponed for the time and was not taken up again.[2]

From the extant records of the time, fragmentary though
they are, we can affirm that the military companies of the
towns in Yorkshire, with their equipment and trainings as
prescribed in the Duke's Laws, were continued in active
existence until New York became a royal province. The
people, as well as the governors, were spurred to action in
this matter, not only by the presence of Indians, but by the
fear of attack from the Dutch during the two European
wars of the period. Philip's war in New England also occasioned some anxiety lest it might provoke an outbreak in
New York.

When, in July, 1668, Governor Nicolls was inspecting the
militia company of Flushing, some seditious words were
uttered by one of the men. These seemed to indicate that a

[1] Records of New Amsterdam, VI. 144, 300, 357.
[2] Minutes of Executive Council, May 18, Sept. 25, 1671.

feeling of discontent was widespread in the locality. Nicolls at once had a town meeting called, and, after administering a sharp rebuke, ordered the company to be disarmed, its colors returned, and none of its members to appear again without special warrant. Certain of the company were also forbidden during the period of three months to visit New York without reporting to the officer of the guard at Fort James. This prompt act of discipline quelled sedition, and before two months had passed, submission had been made and the company was in process of reorganization.[1]

In the autumn of 1668, soon after Governor Lovelace took office, he appointed Captain Sylvester Salisbury commander of a troop of horse which he was authorized to raise by enlistment[2] within the north and west ridings of Yorkshire. Those who could not provide horse and equipment themselves were to be supplied by the governor. In 1670 the inhabitants were urged to coöperate with Captain John Young of Southold in organizing a similar troop in the east riding. In 1672 the troop was in existence, and its members were granted certain privileges by the governor. Towns, like Hempstead, which seem to have been backward in the organization of foot companies, were ordered to provide for such and to present lists of nominees from which the governor might appoint their officers. In July, 1672, in view of the disturbed condition of Europe, the militia officers of Long Island were ordered to make a list of all who were of military age and to view their arms. Companies should be trained and a watch set to give warning of any approaching vessels. But neither horse nor foot were to be called outside the east riding except in emergencies. When Governor Andros took office steps were duly taken for reorganizing the militia. A weakness of the system is illustrated by an order of 1678, the issue of which was occasioned by complaint from the militia officers, especially of the east riding, that constables and overseers of towns should no longer neglect to levy the fines due by law for absences from training or for other defaults connected therewith.[3]

---

[1] N. Y. Col. Docs. XIV. 597–609 ; Waller, History of Flushing, 63.
[2] *Ibid.* 607, 608, 643, 672, 674.   [3] *Ibid.* 687, 735.

We learn that at Esopus discipline among the garrison was not maintained ; that the soldiers were accused from all quarters of immoral and violent conduct, of attempting to right their own wrongs, " and becoming more a nursery of Newgate than persons who have taken on them a settled and resolved life." For this reason, in 1669, the garrison at that fort was disbanded and a militia force was organized for the defence of the three settlements which by that time had been founded in the region. A redoubt had been built at Kingston, and upon the inhabitants of that village its defence was imposed.[1]

In accordance with the Concessions and Agreement[2] of 1665, the militia system of New Jersey rested from the first on statutes. That document provided that laws respecting militia companies, trainings, forts, officers, and defensive war and suppression of mutinies and rebellion should be passed by the assemblies. The governor, with the advice of the council, should appoint militia officers, designate soldiers and officers for militia and garrison service, muster and train the forces, and conduct war as well by sea as land. He should not organize a force in excess of the number designated by law, and, without the consent of the assembly, should not call out any except freeholders. In November, 1668, the first militia act which has been preserved was passed.[3] It prescribed for all males between sixteen and sixty years of age, with the usual exceptions, four days of training annually, two being in the fall. The chief officer of any town who should neglect this should be fined 20s., and privates who, without good reason, neglected to attend should be fined at the rate of 5s. for every day's absence. The fines should be collected by the clerk of the band, and those which came from the privates should be expended for the company, while those collected from the officers should go into the treasury of the province. The act was apparently borrowed from early New England legislation, and implied the assize of arms, though no provision was made for enforcing it. It also gave the clerk of the band the usual power to collect fines by distraint.

[1] N. Y. Col. Docs. XIII. 426, 428, 437. [2] Leaming and Spicer, 17, 19.
[3] *Ibid.* 85.

By the charters which were granted, not far from the time of this act, to Woodbridge and Bergen, and by the agreement with the settlers at Piscataway, the right to nominate their militia officers, subject to the governor's approval, was granted to the localities. The relations in which all the towns stood to the proprietary government naturally left much room for independence of action in this, as in other matters. In 1670 we find the governor urging the appointment of a captain, a lieutenant and ensign in Woodbridge. The earliest entry in the Newark records which relates to training and a view of arms was in May, 1671.

The legislature of East Jersey, in its session of November, 1675, provided[1] by law for the taking of the assize of arms in each town at least once every quarter. It also required every town, at its own expense, to provide a fort with a garrison house therein, where the inhabitants, with a supply of provisions and ammunition, could be protected against Indian attack. Every town was also required to keep a stock of ammunition. Under the impulse given to affairs of this kind through the temporary occupation of the province by the Dutch, the towns seem to have taken some measures for self-defence. In July of the same year Elizabethtown had organized a militia company in accordance with the provisions of the act of 1669. Woodbridge began soon after to discuss the subject of a stockade, and town meetings held early in 1676 called for the powder and shot for the local magazine which were required by the recent act.[2] At Newark the militia officers were ordered " to consider about and contrive for the Fortifications belonging to our Town." Somewhat later an order was issued for a small supply of powder and lead.[3]

In 1679, 1682, and 1693 militia laws were passed, but they were essentially repetitions of those which had been previously enacted. In West Jersey no order whatever was passed on the subject of war or a militia, except one to the effect that military forces should not be raised or war declared without the consent of the assembly.[4]

---

[1] Leaming and Spicer, 94.   [3] Newark Town Records, 38, 61, 63.

[2] Dally, 43, 53.   [4] Leaming and Spicer, 135, 277, 331, 348, 424.

CHAPTER XVI

INDIAN RELATIONS AMONG THE LATER PROPRIETARY
PROVINCES

THE frontier which, before 1690, the colonists of New
England were forced to defend was comparatively limited in
extent. Pemaquid was its northeastern and Stamford its
southwestern extremity; the distance between the two points
was about three hundred miles. In their sectional isolation
the New Englanders, during that period, were brought into
conflict with only a few members of the Algonkin family
of tribes. After 1675 New York assumed responsibility, in
part at least, for the defence of Pemaquid, and for a time had
its share in the conflicts on the extreme eastern frontier.
But, notwithstanding the limited extent of the New England
frontier, the forces there involved were comparatively vigorous, and by far the greatest Indian war of the seventeenth
century was fought in that region.

The frontier in the defence of which the people of the
proprietary provinces were concerned stretched from Albany
and Schenectady on the north to the borders of Florida on
the south. It was nearly one thousand miles in length. As
time passed it was destined to become the genuine American
frontier, which has steadily receded westward with the advance of civilization. But during the early generations,
while settlements were few and sparse and while the proprietary régime was at its height, the attitude of the respective
colonies toward this frontier was in most cases narrow and
sectional. To the Marylander the native tribes who lived
at his doors, or within the borders of his province, and the
forests which he inhabited were his almost exclusive concern.
The same was true of the other provinces, with the exception to an extent of New York and South Carolina. The

relations of the former toward the French in Canada and of the latter toward the Spanish in Florida gave them a feeling of greater responsibility for the security of their neighbors than did defence merely against the savages.

Nothing is more evident than that the narrow and sectional views of the colonists toward the question of defence were the natural outgrowth of their economic and social condition. Their numbers were few and scattered. Their resources were very limited. Indian trails, bridle-paths, and the water-ways were the only means of communication. News travelled very slowly. Long journeys involved great hardship. Communication except by sea between the colonies of the south and even a port as central as New York was beset with the greatest difficulties. Almost the entire energy of the set-tler was required to provide for his own needs and those of his family. To work for distant objects was for him an impossibility. The views of the proprietors and of their officials were only slightly broader than those of the colonists themselves. Even their interests were necessarily bound up with their own provinces. Very rarely, if at all, do the instructions of proprietors or their governors contemplate more than local defence. The limited resources of the proprietors precluded thought of contributions on their own part for defence, save from the revenue which the provinces themselves directly yielded. An exception to this state-ment may, however, be found in occasional small shipments of arms and supplies from England. It is therefore true that the social conditions which existed in the colonies were not favorable to large military enterprises, and that under the system of special chartered jurisdictions little outside official pressure could be brought to bear to change this attitude. But it is also true that no circumstance at that time tended so strongly to draw those small communities out of their isolation and to force them to coöperate as did the necessities of defence which arose along this frontier.

The inhabitants of the proprietary provinces were brought into contact with the three great Indian stocks which occu-pied the country east of the Mississippi river. The Algon-kin family of tribes comprised, in addition to the Indians of

New England, the Mohegans and other lesser tribes on the
Hudson river, the Lenâpe or Delawares of New Jersey and
eastern Pennsylvania, the Minisinks who inhabited the mountains along the upper course of the Delaware river ; the Pascataways, Nanticokes, Powhatans, and other neighboring
tribes of Maryland and Virginia. The territory of the
Iroquois confederacy extended from the upper Hudson to
the Genesee, while the Susquehannas of the lower Susquehanna valley and the Tuscaroras of North Carolina belonged
to the same stock. The testimony of language is to the
effect that the Cherokees were also of Iroquois-Huron descent. The third large group of tribes, the Maskokis,
comprised the Chickasaws, Choctaws, Creeks, Yemassees,
Seminoles of South Carolina, Georgia, and Florida, and
much of the region which extended westward to and beyond
the Mississippi.[1]

From the nature of the case, intercourse with the Indians
was subject to much the same regulations in all the colonies.
As in New England, so in the proprietary provinces, both
north and south, the law required that the Indians should receive some form of compensation for their interest in the land.
In order to insure this and also to secure to the proprietor
his exclusive right to the land and to the revenue which
came from it, this was accompanied by the further requirement that so-called purchases should be made only by the
provincial authorities themselves, or under their license.
Dutch law was especially clear on both these points. It
both enjoined payment for lands and forbade purchase otherwise than under authority of the company. The principle
was set forth in the Freedoms and Exemptions of 1629, and
by special ordinances in 1652 and 1654.[2] In the proposed
Maryland legislation of 1639, the procuring or holding of
and by virtue of an Indian grant was forbidden, and this
very properly formed part of a bill which was intended

---

[1] Brinton, The American Race, The Lenâpe and their Legends ; Rutten-
ber, The Indian Tribes of the Hudson River ; Heckewelder, History of the
Indian Nations; Colden's Five Nations ; Morgan, League of the Iroquois;
Hale, The Iroquois Book of Rites ; Gatschet, A Migration Legend of the
Creek Indians; Fiske, The Discovery of America.

[2] Laws and Ordinances, 9, 130, 173.

to secure to the proprietor his title in the land of the province.[1] By positive legislation, in 1649, the purchasing of lands from any who did not hold of the proprietor, unless it were with his consent, was forbidden. This was expressly directed against unlicensed purchases of land from the Indians. But it does not appear that in Maryland the law required that land should be procured from the natives exclusively under form of purchase. In Section 102 of the Fundamental Constitutions of Carolina, all persons were forbidden to hold or claim land by purchase or grant in any form from the natives, or from any one except the proprietors, on penalty of fine or of the forfeiture of their entire estate. This is understood to have operated,[2] until 1675, as a prohibition of purchases of land from the Indians in the southern part of the province. Then, under the initiative of the Earl of Shaftesbury, the policy of rewarding the natives for their concessions was adopted, and it was followed with much consistency thereafter.

In the Duke's Laws the implication is that the policy of the Dutch in the extinguishment of Indian claims should be followed,[3] while among the towns of eastern Long Island New England traditions prevailed in this as in other matters. The proprietors of New Jersey and of East Jersey enforced the same principles in their instructions.[4] In the Concessions and Agreements of West Jersey, as well as by legislation, commissioners were empowered to procure concessions from the Indians for tracts of land when they were needed for settlement. There is evidence that on the Delaware the practice of buying out Indian claims was regularly followed between the period of the English conquest and that of the settlement of Pennsylvania.[5] William Penn entertained feelings toward the Indians similar to those of Roger Williams, though he did not wholly share Williams's notions concerning their rights to land. He regarded the extin-

[1] Md. Arch., Proceedings of Assembly, 1638-1664, 42, 248.
[2] Rivers, Sketches, 124.
[3] Copies of licenses to purchase land of the Indians are in N. Y. Col. Docs. XIII. 554; XIV. 569, 731.
[4] Leaming and Spicer, 37, 54, 172, 401, 465.
[5] Hazard, Annals of Pennsylvania, 437, 442.

guishment of the Indian claim as an act of justice. By a
series of treaties, beginning with that concluded by Markham
in July, 1682,[1] for a tract of land between Delaware river
and Neshaminy creek, purchases of land were peacefully
made as it was needed for settlement. Individuals were
forbidden to buy land of the natives without the permission
of the governor.[2] The chief cause of conflict with the Indians
was without doubt the jealousy that was occasioned by the
steady encroachment of whites on their hunting grounds.
Though the principle of action set forth in the laws of the
Dutch and Quaker colonies was far from being uniformly
observed, yet its frank recognition, especially in New Jersey
and Pennsylvania, undoubtedly contributed toward the
peaceful relations which very generally existed between
the whites and the natives in those provinces.

The next most prolific source of trouble with the Indians was the sale to them of arms, ammunition, and spirituous
liquors. The principle of action as set forth in the laws on
this subject was even more uniform than that which related
to the purchase of land. In 1639 the director and council
of New Netherland forbade the sale of guns, powder, or lead
to the Indians, under penalty of death. In 1645, and again in
1648, this ordinance was renewed.[3] But in reality no attempt
was ever made to execute these ordinances, except in the
southern part of the province and against the Algonkin
tribes of that region. The inhabitants of Rensselaerswyck,
and afterwards free traders from Holland, acting independently of the director and his officials, supplied the Mohawks
with guns and ammunition at most profitable rates. In the
early days the Mohawks are said to have readily given
twenty beavers for a gun and the equivalent of ten or twelve
guilders for a pound of powder.[4] Traffic on such terms was
too profitable to be ignored, and from the stores which were
imported by the traders the Mohawks were soon furnished
with arms. The other tribes of the confederacy were
gradually supplied through the same channel. It was natu-

---

[1] Hazard, 581.   [2] Charter and Laws of Pa. 143, 209.
[3] Laws and Ordinances, 19, 47, 101.
[4] Doc. Hist. of N. Y. IV. 7.

rally a source of irritation to the river Indians that the sale of arms to them was prohibited.

A long series of ordinances was also issued by the Dutch against the sale of liquors to the Indians, the penalty being increased until it reached a fine of five hundred guilders,[1] corporal punishment, and banishment. Special orders were also passed for the South river and Rensselaerswyck. But the government repeatedly confessed that the sale of liquors went on in spite of its prohibitions.

When the Indian war broke out, in 1643, the natives were well supplied with arms and ammunition, which they were known to have procured from private traders. In 1650 the company admitted that the sale of munitions of war to the Indians went on to a considerable extent, that it was concealed from the officers of the company, and yielded a large profit to the small traders.[2] The year before, the company itself had permitted the director to supply Indians sparingly with powder, lead, and guns. Intoxication also became so common among the natives that ordinances were issued for the protection of communities against the outrages of drunken Indians. The testimony of Indians concerning those who furnished them with liquor was made admissible[3] before the courts.

Some vigorous administrative measures were also occasionally adopted. We have the record of the removal from the province, in 1655, of Sonder Toursen and his wife for selling liquor to an Indian. Soon after a similar decree was issued against Jan Dircksen and wife, but this, for apparently good reasons, was softened into a reprimand. Both the parties then under accusation were residents of New Amsterdam. In a conference between certain Mohawk chiefs and the magistrates at Fort Orange, in 1659, reference was made to the sale of brandy to the Iroquois during all the past years of their intercourse with the Dutch. " Eighteen years

---

[1] Laws and Ordinances, 34, 52, 64, 95, 100, 183, 204, 259, 260, 311, 343, 384 ; N. Y. Col. Docs. I. 162, 373.

[2] A forcible statement of these facts is in Observations on the Duties levied on Goods sent to New Netherland, N. Y. Col. Docs. I. 373.

[3] Laws and Ordinances, 100, 183.

ago," said the Dutch, "you requested us not to sell brandy to your people. . . . Brothers, do not allow your people to come to us for brandy, none shall be sold to them ; but only two days ago we have met 20 or 30 little kegs on the road, all going to obtain brandy ; our chiefs are very angry because the Dutch sell brandy to your people, and always forbid it to our people ; and if you desire us to take away from your people the brandy and the kegs, say so now before all these people.[1] . . ." The only declaration which we have from the natives was that, when they went away this time they would take a great deal of brandy with them ; but after that no more. They would burn their kegs. The kegs were burned and brandy drinking stopped only when the natives were exterminated, or the peltries on which they trafficked and the assistance which they could give in war ceased to be objects of competition on the part of the whites.

Several of the Hackensack Indians complained, in 1662, that selfish people not only sold brandy to savages in New Amsterdam, but carried whole ankers of it into their country and peddled it out there. The director and council, conscious of their inability to cope with the traffic or unwilling to attempt it, authorized two of the chiefs to seize the liquor and any who sold it, and present the offenders for punishment. The repeated Indian outbreaks at Esopus were admittedly due in part to drink. Full accounts of the extent of the evil at that place are extant. In 1663 the local magistrates appealed to the director for assistance in suppressing the traffic.[2] Among the colonists at large the Dutch gained an evil reputation from their indulgence in the traffic ; but the English traders almost everywhere were quite ready on occasion to imitate their example.

In Maryland the law always required that trade with the natives should be carried on exclusively under licenses from the proprietor. In that province the point was emphasized specially for the reason that Claiborne had prior rights to trade within the grant, which it was the desire of the colonists to break down. The insistence upon licenses, viewed in

[1] N. Y. Col. Docs. XIII. 67, 109, 113.
[2] *Ibid.* 218, 228, 237, 277.

one aspect, was an incident of the struggle with Claiborne.[1]
Not until 1654 do we find the sale of arms and ammunition
to the Indians forbidden by the statutes, though at intervals,
beginning more than ten years earlier, instructions were
issued against that traffic.[2] In Maryland, as in the other
colonies, when Indian hostilities had been experienced or
were feared, savages who came within the settlements
were disarmed, or they were ordered to be entirely excluded
except when they came for the purpose of concluding a
treaty.[3] An attitude similar to this had been adopted in
Virginia after the massacre of 1622, and later in that province a system of passports had been instituted.[4] In 1643
by proclamation of the governor of Maryland the sale of
arms and ammunition to the savages was prohibited.[5]

At all times, however, it was difficult, if not impossible, to
exclude Indians from the settlements. Especially was this
true where detached farms existed, or straggling hamlets
grew up which were not properly stockaded. During the
years when a settlement or colony was weak and not yet
self-supporting, the visits of the Indians with supplies of
food were welcome. Their assistance in hunting or fishing,
or when tillage began, was valuable. The early settlers at
Ashley river shared these experiences with colonists at an
earlier date at Jamestown, Plymouth, and elsewhere. In
September, 1670, William Owen wrote to Lord Ashley,
"They [the neighboring Indians] have exprest us unex-
pected kindness, for when the ship went to and dureing her
stay att Virginia, provision was att the scarcest with us,
yet they daylie supplied us, that we were better stored att
her return than when she went, having 25 days provision in
store beside 3 tunn of corne more, which they promised to
procure when we pleased to come for it att Seweh."[6] The

---

[1] Md. Arch., Proceedings of Assembly, 1638–1664, 42, 307, 346 ; Proceedings of Council, 1636–1667, 443, 452.

[2] *Ibid.* 144, 160, 260.

[3] *Ibid.* 103, 126, 147, etc. ; also Proceedings of Assembly, 1638–1664, 291,
348.

[4] Hening, Statutes of Virginia, I. 415.

[5] Md. Arch., Proceedings of Council, 1636–1667, 144.

[6] Shaftesbury Papers, 194, 201, 211, 263.

natives are also credited with supplying deer, fish, and fowl
in abundance to the early South Carolina settlers. But
before the English appeared on that coast the natives had
become acquainted through the Spanish with the existence
of firearms, though they probably possessed but few. At
the time of settlement the Westoes, and other Indians from
the remoter south, acting under Spanish direction, used firearms in their attacks on the English and their Indian allies.
But in 1672 we find the council proposing the passage of an
act to forbid the selling or disposing of arms or ammunition
to the Indians.[1]

Until 1677 trade with the Indians in the southern part of
Carolina had been left by the proprietors mainly in the
hands of the colonists and the local authorities. On that
date the proprietary board[2] resolved that, for a space of
seven years, it would take into its hands the entire trade
with the Westoes, Cussatoes, and the other tribes which lived
somewhat remote from the mouth of Ashley river. To the
settlers was left the trade within approximately one hundred
miles of the plantation. It is not, however, probable that
important changes of system or abatement of abuses which
may already have arisen resulted from this step. How far a
system of licenses was enforced it is impossible to state.
Comprehensive acts on Indian trade which were passed at
intervals between 1691 and the close of the proprietary
period in South Carolina repeated the prohibition of the
sale of spirituous liquors to the remoter tribes. The sale of
arms and ammunition to hostile tribes was also forbidden.
Indians who lived within the three settled counties were
kept strictly under control, while trade with the remoter
tribes was regulated by a system of licenses. But abuses
continued, some of them doubtless proceeding from traders
who came from Virginia and North Carolina. Among the
complaints which preceded the outbreak of the Yemassee
war that of the sale of intoxicants appears. With it went
fraud in the purchase of skins, the seizure of land, various
acts of immorality, and personal offences.

[1] Shaftesbury Papers, 19, 194, 227, 394.
[2] Rivers, 122, 390.

By the Duke's Laws the sale of liquors to Indians, save to the extent of two drams in case of sickness, was forbidden. The sale to them of firearms and ammunition without a license, or the repair of their arms, was prohibited. But there is evidence that license was sometimes granted to sell such liquors to the Indians as they might need. In March, 1667, such a license was granted to William Wells, the high sheriff of Yorkshire.[1] Except in times of unusual danger, the sale of powder and arms to the Indians in New York was permitted. This was everywhere a natural condition of the success of the fur trade. As in Maryland in the time of Governor Stone, Indians were furnished with guns that they might kill deer, so Long Island Indians with firearms were frequently employed in the whaling industry.[2] Even in September, 1675, when Philip's war was threatening to extend itself to Long Island, the council at New York resolved that the sale of powder to the Indians should not be prohibited, but regulated as formerly and according to law. During the same crisis, however, the arms of a part of the Indians on Long Island were repeatedly taken from them, and the peril seemed so great at the beginning of 1676 that a general disarmament in that section was ordered.[3] In October, 1675, the sale at Albany of powder and lead to any except the Five Nations was forbidden.[4] Whenever in time of war Indians were taken into active alliance, they were of course furnished, so far as possible, with guns, powder, and lead. But such coöperation was not common till after the beginning of the war with the French.

In East Jersey, under Berkeley and Carteret, the same acts were prohibited and offenders were threatened with heavy fines. The sale of liquors to the Indians was prohibited by a law of 1677, as well as by one passed in 1682, under the twenty-four proprietors. Fines were to be levied on those who sold liquor, or on the party from whose premises the Indian came in a state of intoxication, unless it could be proven

---

[1] N. Y. Col. Docs. XIV. 596.

[2] Md. Arch., Proceedings of Council, 1636-1667, 260; N. Y. Col. Docs. XIV. 608, etc.

[3] N. Y. Col. Docs. XIV. 696, 709, 712.   [4] *Ibid.* XIII. 491.

that the liquor was not procured there. The only act [1] which respecting this traffic contained the usual prohibition, quali-
expressed the sentiments felt by the West Jersey legislators
fied in substantially the same fashion as it was in the law of
New York. The sale of intoxicants to Indians was forbidden
in the early laws of Pennsylvania under penalty of £5,[2] but
the evil certainly prevailed there, as it did in all the other
colonies. The laws of Pennsylvania naturally make no reference to the sale of munitions of war.

The legislation of New England makes considerable reference to the irritation caused between the two races by the
destruction of their crops and by various forms of trespass.
The cattle of the English broke down the fences of the
Indians and trampled upon their corn-fields. The Indians,
by way of reprisal, levelled the fences and destroyed the
growing crops of the English. In New Netherland, in 1640,
an ordinance was issued forbidding trespasses on the maize
lands of the Indians, and requiring that damages caused in
this way should be made good by the whites. But the evil
did not cease, and it is given as one of the causes of the war
which broke out a few years later.[3] The Duke's Laws, borrowed as they were largely from the New England codes,
required that cattle should everywhere be kept from destroying the Indian's corn, and, if injury was inflicted through
the fault of the English, damages should be paid. The English should also assist the Indians in the building of their
fences. All damages which were due to the Indians should
be assessed and recovered in English courts. An act of
1683 in Pennsylvania provided for the trial of cases of trespass by Indians before a mixed jury of natives and white
men,[4] but it is probable that the law remained a dead letter.
Of this phase of Indian relations we find very little in the
laws or administrative records of the provinces farther south.
Stray cattle roaming the woods were sometimes killed by
the Indians, and in Maryland, in 1662, this occasioned legis-

---

[1] Leaming and Spicer, 125, 258, 512.
[2] Charter and Laws, 111, 169, 183.
[3] Laws and Ordinances, 22 ; N. Y. Col. Docs. I. 182.
[4] Charter and Laws, 130.

lation.[1] In 1686 complaints of trespass, both by the Indians
and English, in settlements on the eastern shore were heard
and adjusted by the council of Maryland.[2] In Virginia, after
1660, colonists were required to assist the Indians in building fences, and damages could be collected by the natives
from trespassers or from those who molested them in their
lawful pursuits.

When irritation between natives and the whites reached
the point where the former began to commit murders and
other outrages, steps were taken to exclude them wholly
from the settlements of the colonists. Strict regulations of
this nature were adopted in Virginia after the massacre of
1622. In New Netherland, after the Indian raid of 1655,
orders were issued forbidding the entertainment of Indians
over night on any part of Manhattan island south of the
"fresh water," and directing that armed Indians should be
excluded from villages and hamlets throughout the province.[3]
Fear of Indian attack caused the governor of Maryland, in
1641, to issue an order forbidding any one to harbor or enter-
tain a savage.[4] The commission of certain murders by the
Indians occasioned the passage of an act by the Maryland
legislature, in 1650, excluding them from Kent and Anne
Arundel counties, unless they came expressly to speak with
the commanders of the counties.[5] Though express legislation of this nature does not appear in any of the proprietary
provinces after the Restoration, the colonists always held
themselves ready to resort to such measures when danger
necessitated it. By treaty, in 1668 and again in 1687, the
Nanticokes of Maryland were forbidden to enter any plantation without warning and until after they had laid down
their arms.

In the later proprietary provinces only slight efforts were
made in the seventeenth century to convert the Indians to
Christianity. The declarations of the charters respecting

[1] Md. Arch., Proceedings of Assembly, 1638–1664, 450 ; Hening, II. 140.

[2] Md. Arch., Proceedings of Council, 1667–1687, 482, 493, 519.

[3] Laws and Ordinances, 228, 234.

[4] Md. Arch., Proceedings of Council, 1636–1667, 98.

[5] *Ibid.* Proceedings of Assembly, 1638–1664, 291.

[6] *Ibid.* Proceedings of Council, 1667–1688, 29, 559.

this matter proved to be empty words. The ambitious plans which had been cherished in the London company for their conversion and education in Virginia did not survive the massacre. In their place for a time appeared the stern resolve to exterminate the savages in the colony, if it were possible. Ever after the Virginians held them, as it were, at arm's length. The Dutch in earlier years lived as familiarly with the natives as did the first settlers of Virginia. Indeed, their great familiarity with them was assigned as an occasion of the war of 1643. But the Dutch never undertook to Christianize them.[1] The company declared, in 1650, that every one who was conversant with the Indians in and about New Netherland would say that it was morally impossible to convert the adults among them to the Christian faith. In 1657 the two clergymen of the Dutch Church in New Amsterdam, in a formal report[2] on the state of the churches of New Netherland, wrote, " Of the conversion of Heathens or Indians here, we can say but little, nor do we see any means thereunto until by the numbers and power of our nation they are subdued and brought under some policy, and our people show them a better example than they have hitherto done."

The enthusiasm of the Jesuit and the devotion of the Puritan were the only forces which in the seventeenth century were equal to the task of missionary work among the native Americans. Andrew White, John Altham, and their associates, under the protection of Cecilius Calvert, after celebrating mass and planting the cross on St. Clement's island, addressed themselves, not only to the conversion of their Protestant fellow-colonists, but to active missionary work among the neighboring Indian tribes.[3] Until the rebellion of Claiborne and Ingle, in 1645, they labored without molestation among the Patuxents, Pascataways, and other smaller tribes, who, to escape the scourgings of the Susquehannas, willingly sought the protection of the colo-

---

[1] N. Y. Col. Docs. I. 334, 340.

[2] Doc. Hist. of New York, III. 108 ; O'Callaghan, II. 319.

[3] White, Relatio Itineris, Fund Publications of Md. Hist. Soc. ; Scharf, History of Maryland, I. 183 *et seq.*

nists who settled in their midst. Employing the same methods as were used by their brethren in Canada, each priest, accompanied if possible by an interpreter and a servant, took up his residence in some Indian village. There, while acquiring the language as rapidly as possible, he ministered to the sick, said mass, preached, taught and catechised young and old who would come to hear him, baptized converts, and performed the last rites over the dying. The superstitions of the natives were appealed to; miraculous cures and other indications of special divine favor toward the missionaries and their work were skilfully utilized. The utmost devotion and self-sacrifice were exhibited. When the Indians suffered from famine, the priests labored for their relief. Much encouragement was felt at the conversion of Chitomachen, a Pascataway chief, who had been restored from illness by the ministration of the father. This chief put away all his wives except one, and with her submitted to the sacraments of Christian baptism and marriage. Christian names were given to these and others. " The governor was present at the ceremony, together with his secretary and many others ; nor was anything wanting in display which our means could supply."

Before the band of Puritans entered to destroy this work, the Catholic missionaries had proclaimed their faith along the shore of the Chesapeake from Saint Mary's to Kent island, and up the Potomac nearly to the site of the modern city of Washington. The number of priests in the mission varied from three to four ; and they had one or more assistants. After the storm which broke up the mission and dispersed the priests had somewhat abated, new laborers appeared, and the work was tentatively resumed on a small scale. But Maryland was no longer a Catholic province, and the hopeful period of its missions had forever passed away. Upon the Indians, except in strengthening their tendency toward submission to English control, the effect was too small to be traced.

The only other exhibition of missionary zeal within the proprietary provinces during this period was at the eastern end of Long Island, and subsequent to 1660. This was simply an extension of the missionary efforts of the Puritan leaders of New England. The Rev. Thomas James of East-hampton, sharing the spirit of Eliot, Mayhew, and Fitch, started a local missionary enterprise. He, in part at least, mastered the language of the Montauks, held meetings among them, and prepared a catechism with select passages of Scripture for their use. Governor Lovelace was interested in the experiment, and promised to have the catechism printed. He also agreed that as soon as possible he would relieve Mr. James from his regular charge, so that he could devote all his time to missionary work.[1]

Though the Indians of New Jersey and Pennsylvania were eminently peaceful and accessible, no serious effort was made to Christianize them till the period of Moravian activity in the eighteenth century. The Rev. Thomas Campanius, the Lutheran pastor in New Sweden from 1642 to 1649, attempted to learn the Lenâpe dialect, and translated a cate-chism into that tongue. But his efforts were followed by no conversions. Among the Quakers Penn himself was almost the only individual who was ready to promote efforts to civilize and Christianize the natives. In 1699 he offered to provide the Friends' Meeting at Philadelphia with interpreters to aid in the work of teaching the natives; but this offer awakened no response. In 1701 Penn and John Richardson attempted through interpreters to address the Indians on religious subjects, but their efforts were not continued and hence were without result. Notwithstanding their strong religious spirit, the Quakers were indifferent on this point.[2]

In all the provinces and over small groups of the natives who lived adjacent to the settlements of the Europeans, the rights of a protectorate, varying in extent and details, were gradually assumed. The tracts of land which were left in the possession of the savages after the whites had occupied, or at least surveyed, all the rest of their former hunting grounds, were treated as reservations. The Indians were secured in the possession of these tracts, nominally forever,

[1] N. Y. Col. Docs. XIV. 611.
[2] Brinton, The Lenâpe and their Legends, 126.

but really until they were needed by the white man. As they were gradually surrounded by the advancing settlements of the whites, the Indians, who were steadily diminishing in numbers, were confined more and more strictly to their reservations. The surrender of his original nomadic freedom was the sacrifice which the Indian was forced to make in order that he might be "protected." The "protection" which he enjoyed consisted in the guaranty of the reserved land, where by hunting, fishing, or by rude agriculture he might still subsist ; the assurance that against trespassers, or those who committed worse offences, he might have, not the blood feud, but European justice, a hearing in the courts of the English; in return for skins or wampum he might receive supplies of arms and ammunition for use in hunting or against savage foes who came against him from the remoter wilderness. In cases of peculiar peril he could rely on the armed intervention of the colonists. In return for the peltries which they had to sell, the Indians received the cloths and other paltry wares — not forgetting liquors — which the whites were ready to bestow. Among the Indians of the coast districts, however, where relations of the nature of a protectorate chiefly developed, resources for trade were very slight.

The existence of the protectorate within the later proprietary provinces appears most clearly in the case of some of the tribes of southern Maryland, and in its development the Jesuit may be considered as having a share. The earliest proofs of the submission and peaceful attitude of the Patuxent and Pascataway Indians are furnished by the *Relation* of Father White. Exposed as they were to the attacks of the Susquehannas from the north, they welcomed the advent of the English. As early as January, 1640, Governor Calvert proclaimed [1] the fact that he had taken the Patuxent Indians under the protection of the province, and all Englishmen were forbidden to offer them any injury whatever. When sending Henry Fleet, in 1644, to avert, if possible, by treaty a threatened attack of the Susquehannas, Calvert instructed him to urge them to open their country to settlement, for

[1] Md. Arch., Proceedings of Council, 1636–1667, 87.

then the English would live among them and aid them against their enemies, " as now we doe the Pascataways etc." [1] Soldiers were sent for the protection of the Pascataways when they were in danger.   In 1625 the Susquehannas surrendered to the English their land south of the head of Chesapeake bay, but no relation beyond that of alliance appears in any of the treaties with them.   In 1659 Governor Fendall concluded a treaty with various tribes on the eastern shore, by which their lands were thrown open for settlement, and provision was made that these Indians should submit any wrongs which they suffered at the hands of the colonists to certain designated English officials. [2]

The Nanticoke tribe on the eastern shore held out against the English, and hostile relations with them prevailed at intervals until after 1660.   By treaty, in 1668, however, the process of their humiliation began.   Their chief was then forbidden to conclude any new treaty of peace with the enemies of the province, or to make war without the consent of the proprietor or his governor.   This agreement was violated during the disturbed period of Bacon's rebellion, and, in 1678, the same obligation was again imposed by treaty. [3]   Shortly after it was required of other tribes who lived further south on the eastern shore.   As an incident of the protection which was extended over the Pascataways, by virtue of an act of assembly in 1666, which was renewed in 1670, they were offered in 1668 a tract of land on the west shore as a place of permanent abode, and further settlement within the tract by whites was prohibited.   In consequence of danger of attack from the Senecas and Susquehannas, in 1680, the governor and council designated the Nanticoke river as the place where the Pascataways might take refuge from their enemies. [4]

In the two border provinces, South Carolina and New York, special commissions were created for the management of Indian affairs.   In the other provinces these concerns

---

[1] Md. Arch., Proceedings of Council, 1636–1667, 150 ; *ibid.* 1671–1681, 98.

[2] *Ibid.* Proceedings of Council, 1636–1667, 363, 421.

[3] *Ibid.* 1667–1688, 29, 173, 214.

[4] *Ibid.* 1671–1681, 284 ; *ibid.* 1667–1688, 34.

received in all cases the immediate attention of the governor and council. In South Carolina the systematic regulation of Indian trade began with the act of 1691,[1] which was passed during the administration of Sothell. Its object was to so regulate intercourse with the Savannahs, Yemassees, and other tribes which lay outside the limits of Berkeley, Craven, and Colleton counties as to prevent the sale of arms, ammunition, and spirits there, and to insure, if possible, the conduct of trade henceforth in these regions by bands of traders sent out at definite periods. Over the Indians who lived within the settled parts of the province the attempt was made to exercise a rather strict control. In 1695[2] the governor and one member of the council were designated to settle all controversies between Indian and Indian, or Indian and white man, within that region. The natives were also required to deliver yearly to receivers appointed for the purpose the skin of at least one animal they had slain. For all skins in excess of this they were paid.

No further important legislation was passed on the subject until 1707, when, in connection with a renewed prohibition of the sale of spirituous liquors to Indians and of arms and ammunition to hostile natives, traders, except those who dealt with the neighboring tribes already referred to, were required to purchase licenses. A commission was created by this act, to which was intrusted the granting of such licenses and the exclusive management of trade with the Indians. A resident and salaried Indian agent was also designated in the act, who was given the powers of a justice of the peace, with authority also to settle disputes among the traders and Indians, subject in the more important cases to appeal to the commissioners. He had the right to employ interpreters, and was bound by oath to obey the instructions of the commissioners and not to engage in Indian trade. Indian traders who committed indictable offences were to be sent to Charlestown for trial and punishment. In 1711 traders from other provinces were also brought under the obligation to procure licenses, and were made subject to the other

---

[1] Statutes of South Carolina, II. 64–68.   [2] Ibid. 109.

regulations under which traffic with the Indians in South Carolina was carried on.[1]   Under this well-devised system Indian trade was conducted as long as proprietary government continued in South Carolina.   In 1716 it was further developed by the bestowment of authority on the commissioners to appoint several agents and factors, and to establish trading posts at three several points in the outlying country.   Special powers were also given them to be used in the detection of illicit trading.   From this time the commissioners were required to keep a journal of their proceedings.

In New York, during the administration of Nicolls and Lovelace, a board of commissioners for Indian affairs at the eastern end of Long Island was in existence.   It was created by Nicolls, but does not reappear after the accession of Andros to the government.   Occasional traces of its activity remain.   From the letters of Governor Lovelace it appears that the board, of which Thomas Mulford and other residents of the locality were members, was created as an expedient " to keep the Indians in some Order and Decorum."   It was concerned in the adjustment of boundary disputes between the Indians' and the English.   The relations between the Long Island Indians and the Niantics of Connecticut came before it.   The commissioners were also instructed to facilitate, as far as possible, the missionary efforts of Rev. Thomas James of Easthampton among the Indians.   In the exercise of their functions they assumed quasi-judicial powers, so that in 1672 some of the inhabitants complained that the commissioners were acting too much like justices of the peace.[2]

But a board, whose work was to be of far greater importance, was established at Albany in 1675.[3]   With the opening of relations between the English and the Five Nations after the

[1] Statutes of South Carolina, 309, 357, 359, 691.

[2] N. Y. Col. Docs. XIV. 627, 650, 651, 663.

[3] Brodhead, II. 287 ; Ms. Council Minutes, III.   The extracts by Wraxall, which are now in the State Library at Albany, are all that is left of the four volumes of minutes that were kept by this board.   The only accessible copy of a commission to the board is the one which was issued by Governor Fletcher in 1696, N. Y. Col. Docs. IV. 177.

close of the Dutch reoccupation, Governor Andros designated certain of the magistrates at Albany to act as a special commission for Indian affairs. Robert Livingston was its first secretary. The activity of this board in all matters which related to the Five Nations, and incidentally to relations with the French along the New York frontier, continued without interruption until near the close of the colonial period. Its location made it the most important body of its kind which existed in any of the colonies.

Having outlined the policy which each province pursued toward the Indians who lived within the borders, attention must now be directed toward Indian policy in its broader relations, to tendencies and movements which affected the western frontier as a whole. These were determined in part by the relations which existed among the Indians themselves, and in part by those which developed between the natives and the whites. Among the natives the chief fact in the situation was the state of permanent hostility between the Five Nations and the tribes which lay to the east and south of them. The Mohegans of the Hudson valley, the Lenâpes and Delawares of New Jersey and Pennsylvania, were their immediate antagonists. Long and bloody wars occurred, particularly between the Senecas and the Minsis of the upper Delaware, who were a tribal division of the Lenâpe nation. During the period when these wars were in progress the Five Nations were also destroying the Hurons, the Eries, the Andastes, and were bringing the Illinois into subjection. Their raids, while extending to the Mississippi on the west, were also frequently directed against the Catawbas and other neighboring tribes of the Carolinas. Against those who would neither form an alliance nor enter the confederacy, especially if they were of Iroquois blood, the arms of the Men of the Long House were almost sure to be directed in an implacable feud. Though the extent of Iroquois domination and their alleged superiority to other Indians have probably been exaggerated,[1] they possessed some elements of decided leadership. Partly by good fortune they had occu-

[1] Heckewelder, History of the Indian Nations, Introduction; Ruttenber, 52.

pied a central position, and one from which unusually liberal
supplies of food were procurable.   Their confederacy, though loose, insured the maintenance of peace and a certain amount of coöperation among the tribes that composed it.   But of decisive importance was the fact already referred to, that by the Dutch they had been supplied with firearms in advance of most of the tribes with which they had come in conflict. These facts, when taken in connection with the considerable mental endowment of the Iroquois, sufficiently explain the triumphs which they won.

The relations between the savages and the whites along the entire stretch of frontier, while in most instances friendly during the early years of settlement, became more hostile as years advanced.   In the provinces which were under Quaker government the term of peaceful relations was greatly prolonged.   But even in them, where Indians existed in large numbers, and when other ideas than those of the Quaker came to prevail, the customary hostile relations developed. As the Europeans came first in contact with the Algonkin people of the coast region, those tribes had to sustain the earliest shock of the conflict.   In New Netherland it came, as has been already related, during the years between 1643 and 1664.   At intervals during those two decades the Mohegans of Long Island and the Hudson valley threw themselves on the Dutch and English settlements of the region.   Repeatedly, though with difficulty, they were beaten back and forced into submission.   The clans of the middle Hudson held out till almost the very close of Dutch rule, when they too became peaceful neighbors.   The peaceful attitude of the Indians of southern New York while Philip's war was in progress in New England furnished decisive proof that the natives of that region felt themselves too weak again to attempt armed resistance against the Europeans.   The peaceful, but no less certain, process of elimination could be left to do the rest.

On the upper Hudson and along the remoter stretches of the frontier between the Mohawk valley and the lower Susquehanna, the relations were somewhat different ; and these relations, as we have noticed, affected also the Indians

who lived on the upper courses of the streams of Virginia
and the Carolinas. The assumption by Champlain of the
cause of the Hurons in their feud with the Five Nations
opened a conflict between the latter and New France which
was to last as long as the French power continued on the
waters of the Saint Lawrence. This conflict made the guns
and ammunition which the Dutch — though they nominally
maintained neutrality — were able to furnish, doubly valuable to the Iroquois. Assistance of this kind helped to
strengthen the friendly relations which now grew up between the two parties. Beginning certainly as early as
1659,[1] and probably some years earlier, Fort Orange became
a centre for negotiation with the Mohawks and the other
tribes of the League. The Mohawks, when first the records
of conferences begin, were begging arms and powder from
the Dutch, were urging that smiths might be sent to repair
their arms and assistance be furnished in building palisades
and fortifying their castles. The guns which were sold to
them by the Dutch, they used not only against the French,
but against the river Indians and their other savage foes as
well. It is not improbable that the apparent superiority of
the Iroquois to the river Indians was largely due to this
cause.

At all events, the fear of the Mohawk and Seneca was
spread far and wide, and was felt almost as strongly along
the borders of Maryland and Virginia as elsewhere. By oft-
repeated raids down the Susquehanna valley they drove the
related people of that name in upon the English settlements
or reached the outlying posts themselves. For a long period
subsequent to 1660 this was the principal cause of Indian
disturbances in the colonies about the Potomac. It contributed greatly, as we know, to the origin of Bacon's rebellion.
It compelled the English, as we have seen, to take native
tribes under their protection and to expend heavily from
their resources on armed expeditions and other defensive
measures. But it led also to the beginning of a comprehensive Indian policy, which was intended through the coöperation of a number of provinces to secure the peace of the

[1] N. Y. Col. Docs. XIII. 109.

entire northern and middle frontier.   As disturbances of the
peace came chiefly from the raids of the Iroquois, appeals
were made to the government of New York to permit agents
or commissioners from Virginia and Maryland to negotiate
with the Five Nations at Albany, and to use its own influence as well for the restoration of captives and the maintenance of peace.   It was these events and causes which made
Albany the chief centre among all the English colonies north
of the Carolinas for negotiation with the Indians.   At the
same point inevitably centred many of the lines of influence
which guided French, English, and Iroquois politics.   This
gave to the Indian commissioners of northern New York
and to the interpreters who were in their service an importance the extent of which has already been indicated.

Maryland took the initiative in the despatch of agents to
negotiate at Albany.   In 1677,[1] as a result of the widely
extended movements among the Indians which had contributed so much to occasion Bacon's rebellion in Virginia,
Henry Coursey, a member of the council of Maryland, and
one who was already conversant with Indian affairs, was
sent to Albany as special commissioner.   He was instructed
to apply to Governor Andros for assistance in his business,
and in return for his courtesies to make him a present of
£100 sterling on behalf of the province of Maryland.   On
the way and after his arrival he was to inform himself as
thoroughly as possible concerning the relations, particularly
between the Senecas and the Susquehannas.   As the custom
had already arisen of making presents to the Indians when
conferences were held, Coursey was to ascertain what presents the governor of New York made on such occasions.   He
was of course compelled to rely upon the authorities at
Albany to summon the Indians to the conference.   When
he met them Coursey was to secure from the Five Nations
and also from the Susquehannas, if there was such a distinct
tribe, a treaty of peace, and this should include, not only the

[1] Md. Arch., Proceedings of Council, 1671–1681, 149, 164.   Colden, in his
History of the Five Nations, gives an outline of this event and of the
negotiations which followed, and prints proceedings of some of the early
conferences.

English in Maryland, but the Indians who were under their protection. If possible, he was also to open trade relations between the Five Nations and Maryland.

The conference was held in August. Chiefs from each of the tribes of the Iroquois confederacy were present. The usual gifts were exchanged, and speeches expressive of friendship and of a resolve to forget past injuries were made on both sides. The Indians expressed the desire — whatever it was worth — that the agreement which they were forming with Maryland might be as firm as the covenant with the governor of New York. Colonel Coursey found no difficulty in securing from the natives such promises, and expressions of fidelity to the same, as were held to constitute an Indian treaty.

But war parties which were out when the conference was held captured some prisoners from the Indian allies of the English, while some reprisals occurred on the Virginia border. These events soon necessitated the direct interposition of Governor Andros to secure a return of prisoners. In 1679 Virginia sent two agents to Albany, who addressed their complaints to the Indians, but without effective results save in the case of the Mohawks. Indian outrages continuing, in 1682 the governor of Maryland, after consulting the assembly, sent Coursey and Lloyd to Albany.[1] By this time the Maryland authorities had become considerably aroused in view of the fact, as it seemed to them, that New York was carefully maintaining peace and alliance with Indians who were murdering the inhabitants of other English colonies. New York was also selling the guns with which, very likely, the Indians were committing these murders. Against these conditions the agents protested rather strongly in their correspondence with Lieutenant-Governor Brockholls. They insisted that New York should prohibit trade with the Five Nations, should assist in forcing them to recall war parties which were still supposed to be out to the southward, and should join, if necessary, in offensive operations in behalf of the other colonies. In this correspondence we first

---

[1] Md. Arch., Proceedings of Assembly, 1678–1683, 269, 314, 320, 334, 386 *et seq.*; Proceedings of Council, 1681–1686, 89, 98, 115, 197–216.

hear it stated that defence against the Indian was a common cause, affecting the interests of all the colonies alike. It was even intimated that it might be necessary to appeal to the crown to enforce these views. To this doctrine New York was not yet ready to assent. Both the governor and the commissioners at Albany refused to break off peaceful relations with the Five Nations or to cease trading with them, even in munitions of war. Since the danger proved to be less than the Marylanders feared, and after they had obtained a renewal of peace on favorable terms, Coursey and Lloyd returned home.[1] The desire was at this time expressed by the Maryland government that Newcastle on the Delaware, or some other town in that region, might be the place where future conferences with the Indians should be held, but it was too remote from the centre of activity to be used for such a purpose.

The following year, in 1684, Lord Howard of Effingham, governor of Virginia, visited New York, and, with Governor Dongan, held a conference with the Five Nations at Albany. He demanded that all the Iroquois should be recalled from Virginia and Maryland, and that the Indians of those provinces should not be molested when they hunted on the mountains to the west and northwest. The Oneidas, Onondagas, and Cayugas, who had been the offending tribes, were induced by the Mohawks to accede to these demands. Each of the three tribes then joined with Lord Howard in the ceremony of burying the hatchet. This was the most notable of the early series of conferences held at Albany in which officials from the southern provinces participated. But since lawless and unrestrained bands of young Iroquois warriors still continued to haunt the southern frontier, in 1685, and again in 1687, envoys from Virginia appeared in New York to secure additional assurances of peace.[2] It proved to be a peace which was ever in the progress of making, but never effectually made.

The Indian conferences, however, which were held at Albany during the early years of Dongan's administration were concerned with objects wider and more important than

[1] Colden, Five Nations, Shea's Edition, 50.   [2] Brodhead, II. 430, 482.

the prevention of hostilities on the Maryland and Virginia frontier. The connections which had been established by the early missionaries, fur traders, and discoverers of New France with the Indians of the Great Lakes were now beginning to bear fruit in the form of vast territorial claims. The religious enthusiasm which had animated the first generation of missionaries had now been tempered by a more calculating spirit. The layman had come to assume his share in the great enterprise. Joliet and Father Marquette, in company and acting under authority from the intendant Talon, had discovered the Mississippi. Particularly after the advent of Frontenac and La Salle, and the building of the fort at Cataraqui on Lake Ontario, had decisive steps been taken to establish the claim of France, not only to all the territory drained by the Saint Lawrence, but to the seemingly limitless expanses of the Mississippi valley beyond. The natural centres for trade with the remote Indian tribes, Niagara, Detroit, and Michilimackinac, were already being preëmpted by the French. Events were rapidly multiplying, which threatened to exclude the English from the interior of the continent.

Although French officials had for some time been aware of the possibilities which lay before them, Thomas Dongan was the first English governor who clearly saw the trend of events. He realized, as fully as did the French, that the Iroquois held the key to the situation. They lay in the path of the westward advance of the French, and by their traditional hostility were one of the greatest hindrances to its progress. They at the same time occupied the one river valley which in the north opened to the English an avenue of approach to the western country. Their territory lay adjacent to the outposts of the French on the north, and to those of the English on the east and southeast. For more than twenty years Jesuit missionaries had been vainly striving to win them over to the Catholic religion and the French alliance. By the Dutch and English similar measures had not been attempted, and they had not been necessary. But it was already becoming the custom for the governor annually to meet representatives of the tribes at

Albany or at New York, for the renewal of pledges of alliance. The commissioners at Albany were gradually increasing their functions. Agents, traders, individually and then
in bands, were sent through the Iroquois country for the
purpose of establishing direct relations with the tribes of
the upper lakes. Dongan pursued a well-defined policy of
this kind, for the purpose of diverting the fur trade of the
northwest from the Saint Lawrence to Albany. It was intended as a counterstroke to offset the founding of Fort
Frontenac.

By the course of action thus outlined, the English were
preparing the way for the westward expansion of the province of New York. In the royal charter no westward limit
beyond the valley of the Hudson had been assigned to it.
When Dongan assumed office settlement had not advanced
beyond the boundary thus indicated. But the idea of a
claim to the entire Iroquois country was implied in the
relations which had so long been maintained on the part of
the Dutch and English with that confederation of tribes.
That idea found definite utterance as soon as Dongan
arrived in the province. The occasion of this was an attempt, which William Penn was just then making, to extin-
guish the claims of the savages to the upper Susquehanna
valley. An inquiry was at once made, through the commissioners at Albany, concerning the location of that country
and its relation to the fur trade in general.[1] They reported
that a settlement on the Susquehanna would be much nearer
to the Indians than Albany itself, and that the purchase of
the country by Penn would be prejudicial to the government
of the Duke of York. The Cayugas and Onondagas, who
claimed the chief interest in the region, now informally
transferred their rights in it to New York. The consequence
was that, when Penn requested permission to send agents to
Albany, or even to write to the Iroquois for the purpose of
continuing negotiations for the purchase of the valley, he
was refused.[2] Dongan afterwards admitted that he had
expressed in private conversation a fear that Penn coveted
his neighbor's lands. The refusal of permission to Penn's

[1] Doc. Hist. of New York, I. 393 *et seq.*   [2] Pa. Arch. I. 74, 84.

agents to treat at Albany suggests the idea of a peculiarly
intimate relation between the government of New York and
the lands of the Five Nations.

In connection with the conference of 1684, when the governor of Virginia was present, that idea for the first time
was fully expressed. The Onondagas and Cayugas declared [1]
not only that they had given the valley of the upper Susquehanna to New York as a pledge of protection against the
French, and desired not that any of Penn's people should
settle there; but they put themselves under the protection of
the English king, and would transfer none of their lands to
any but the Duke of York. This submission, agreed to by
the other tribes of the League, was written down that it
might be sent to the "Great Sachem Charles, that lives
on the other side of the great lake." With the consent of
the Indians the arms of the Duke of York were now affixed
to all the castles of the Iroquois. They were also forbidden
to hold any conference with the French without the permission of the English governor.

The transaction of August, 1684, definitely marks the
beginning of the efforts of the English to change an alliance
with the Five Nations into a protectorate over them, and by
this means ultimately to secure possession of their territory.
But the unsubstantial character of the submission then made
is indicated by the fact that a large French force, under
De la Barre, was about invading the country of the Iroquois,
and the Indians strongly felt the need of assistance. When
Arnold Viele, the agent whom Dongan sent to the council of
the League at Onondaga, spoke to them imperiously, as if
they belonged to the English king and the Duke of York, he
was met by the equally definite assertion from one of the Onondaga chiefs, that the League was independent. Onontio,
said he, — meaning the governor of Canada, — was still, as
he had been, their father; and Corlaer—meaning the governor
of New York—was their brother; this they were because the
Indians had so willed it. This assertion of independence
the Iroquois continued to maintain, when it served their purposes, through the entire colonial period. They sought their

[1] Colden, Five Nations, 64.

interest through two related lines of policy, that of apparent
submission to the English when occasion served, and that of
playing the French and English off against each other, the
League thus attempting to hold the balance between them.
The sudden and disastrous failure of De la Barre's expedition, which was due to disease and famine caused largely
by poor management, strengthened the confidence of the
Iroquois. But it occasioned the recall of the incompetent De
la Barre and the appointment of Denonville as his successor.
This occurred just before New York became a royal province;
and, in competition with Denonville, who was an experienced
and able official, Dongan, as royal governor, vigorously continued his defence of English claims and interests.

The decisive conflicts with the Indians of the Carolinas
and along the southern frontier did not occur until after the
beginning of the eighteenth century. The northern colonies
were by that time in the midst of the struggle with the
French power in North America. From the time of its
settlement, South Carolina had occasionally been engaged in
wars with several tribes of Maskoki origin, which lived
within a radius of one hundred miles of Charlestown. Spanish
influences at times roused the Indians to hostilities, as in
1686, when the colony of Lord Cardross at Port Royal was
destroyed. Indians served in large numbers on both sides in
the encounters between the English and Spanish at the opening of the second intercolonial war. On these occasions the
Creeks were in alliance with the English, and the Apalachi of
Florida, who were the active allies of the Spanish, were severely punished by Colonel Moore on his second expedition.[1]

But the first of the great Indian wars of the South occurred in North Carolina, in the years 1711 to 1713, and
resulted in the destruction of a part of the Tuscarora nation,
the flight of the remainder to New York, and the partial
extinction of a number of small coast tribes.[2] Owing to the

[1] Carroll, Hist. Colls. II. 575 ; Rivers ; McCrady.

[2] The sources of information for this war are Baron De Graffenried's
Journal, together with the Correspondence of Spotswood and Pollock and
other material from the Virginia and North Carolina Records, all of which
is printed in N. C. Recs. I. and II. ; the journal of John Barnwell in Va. Mag.
of Hist. V. and VI. ; Hawks, History of North Carolina, II. 525 et seq.

condition, resembling anarchy, which was well-nigh chronic
in North Carolina, no serious effort had been made to regulate intercourse between the whites and the natives. The
colonists lived carelessly in isolated and ill-defended settlements. Means of communication were so poor that the weak
and crude provisions for a militia could scarcely be utilized
to repel sudden attack. At the time when the outbreak
occurred, such armed bands as the province contained had
for some time been arrayed in civil strife, under Cary and
the supporters of Governor Hyde. Sinister reports have
come down to us to the effect that Cary, or some of his supporters, instigated the savages to attack his opponents ; but
the truth of this it would be impossible to substantiate. At
the same time the growth of white settlements in North
Carolina went steadily on, and with it the encroachment on
the hunting-grounds of the savages. The results of this
process had recently been made specially evident to the
natives by the settlement of the palatine colony at New
Berne. It is probable that all these causes, acting in conjunction, occasioned the plot of September, 1711. The Tuscaroras,
who dwelt in the region of the Pamlico river, planned simultaneous attacks on the chief settlements of the province, to
be made in part by themselves and in part by the neighboring tribes. The plan was executed upon the settlement
south of Albemarle sound with appalling thoroughness. On
the Roanoke, in the settlements about New Berne, and at Bath
probably more than three hundred perished. Parties of savages also traversed the country north of Albemarle sound,
and as far west as Chowan, though the execution wrought
there was not so frightful as it was farther south. The
slaughter lasted for three days, and proved to be the greatest
single disaster of its kind which ever fell upon English settlements east of the Alleghanies.

As the military resources of the province were quite too
weak to meet this crisis, appeals for aid were at once sent to
Virginia and South Carolina.[1] Governor Spotswood con-
tented himself with a strong demonstration on the North
Carolina border, which restrained the Indians who were tribu-

[1] N. C. Recs. I. 819, 837 *et seq.*

tary to Virginia and a few Tuscarora towns. The burgesses
expressed strong sympathy with the people of North Carolina and favored a declaration of war against the savages ;
but they did not make an appropriation in such form that
the governor could use it for the purposes of war.   In South
Carolina a relief force under Colonel John Barnwell was at
once organized, which consisted of a small body of militia
and several hundred Indians.   They marched overland
from Charlestown to the Neuse river.   There they formed
a junction with the few militiamen whom Governor Hyde
had been able to raise, and inflicted a severe defeat on the
Indians near King Hancock's fort, which they had constructed in the present Craven county.   Barnwell was, however, restrained from an attempt to storm the fort [1] by the
fear that the whites who were held within it as captives
would be massacred.   The South Carolina Indians now
returned home.   This led Barnwell, who was himself
wounded, to conclude a truce which provided for the surrender of the fort by the Indians and the release of the
captives who were held there.   Barnwell then returned
with his militiamen to South Carolina.

The Indians immediately renewed the war, and the North
Carolina assembly was forced to vote £4000 for defence and
to order the building of three forts.   A small body of ill-
equipped militia, of whose courage Barnwell at least had
a poor opinion, had already been raised.   Appeals for help
were again sent to Virginia and South Carolina.

At this juncture occurred the death of Governor Hyde
and the accession of President Pollock to the management
of affairs.   Virginia voted about £4000 to be used for the
assistance of the Carolinas, but would send no troops unless
Pollock would temporarily mortgage to her a strip of land
along the northern border of the province.   Pollock replied
that for this he had no authority.   The aid which he sought
was again contributed by South Carolina in the form of a
body of fifty whites and a thousand Indians under Colonel
James Moore.   By skilful negotiations with Tom Blunt, a
Tuscarora chief, Pollock also sought to divide the Indian

[1] Va. Mag. of Hist. VI. 46.

forces. In this he succeeded until, in February, 1713, Moore
was able to capture the Tuscarora fort at Snow Hill. The
Indian loss at this encounter was so great as effectually to
break their power of resistance. Though the province was
in great straits for food, the Indians held out only in
detached bands and for a few months longer.

The Yemassee war, which occurred four years later in
South Carolina, throws no new light on Indian relations, but
contributed powerfully and directly to the revolt against
proprietary government in that province.

CONCLUSION

WE have now reviewed the political and administrative system of the British-American colonies as it was developed during the formative period of their existence. In some of the colonies three generations had passed away during the period, in others two, in still others only one. By 1690 the mass of the people who were living in the colonies were American born, or had been brought to the colonies in early life. Though in their large relations they were subordinate to Europe, yet their personal and local concerns were as distinct from those of contemporary Europeans as time or space could well make them. In their languages and in the type and traditions of their culture they were Europeans ; but they were transplanted upon a new and distant continent, and felt chiefly the pressure of its environment. They had already become colonials in the full sense of the word, but had not yet reached a developed American type.

The population of the colonies had been drawn from the middle and lower classes, chiefly of England, but to an extent also of Scotland and Ireland and of various states of the continent of Europe. The extremes of the Old World, whether of wealth or poverty, rank or degradation, were not reproduced in America. Society, as the result of removal and new growth, at once assumed a greater equality. The class distinctions of Europe were softened, and people were thrown more into a general mass. Industrially the great majority of the colonists became tillers of the soil and artisans. A limited minority followed trade, usually in a small way, and some as a supplement to their agricultural pursuits. Indian trade offered special chances, akin to those of discovery and prospecting for land.

Of the professional classes, that of the clergy was most clearly differentiated and had relatively the largest number

of representatives. In New England it was as prominent
and influential as the same class had been in mediæval
Europe. So far as the profession of teaching was followed,
it was generally in close connection with the church and the
clergy. Lawyers were few and were, as a rule, objects of
suspicion. Though in many cases they found their way
into public offices, they cannot be said to have constituted
a class, and they had no clearly distinguishable political
influence. In the provinces the higher offices were more
often filled by men of military training than by those of
distinct legal attainments. Physicians were no more clearly
differentiated as a class than were teachers. Except among
the clergy of New England, intellectual and literary pursuits
were rarely followed in the colonies.

At the same time that colonial society assumed greater
uniformity and equality than were characteristic of social
relations in Europe, it became more isolated. The colonists
were to a great extent shut off from Europe. Intercourse
between one colony and another was also more difficult and
less common than it was between adjacent counties in England. Their relations resembled those between England and
the lowlands of Scotland or the civilized districts of Ireland,
more than they did intercourse between adjacent parts of
the realm. It is true that colonists of southern New England as a group knew and understood each other better than
this comparison would imply. But they did not understand
New Yorkers or settlers in Pennsylvania, Virginia, or the
Carolinas much better than Englishmen understood Scotchmen or Irishmen of the Pale. The same was true of the
notions which inhabitants of the middle and southern
provinces entertained respecting New England. Between
these sections journeys were more easily made by water than
by land. So laborious and difficult were they, whatever the
element that was chosen, that they were undertaken by few
except seamen, traders, and officials. There were no news-
letters or newspapers, no system of couriers or postal service.
The mass of colonists never travelled beyond their own localities or the bounds of their own provinces. The few schools
and books which they had taught them little or nothing

about their own environment. Only occasionally were intercolonial conferences held, and they were attended by only a few officials who came usually from a neighboring group of colonies. Except in New England, signs of a different order of things were only just beginning to appear as the period of the chartered colonies closes.

Not only was the knowledge possessed by individuals crude and rudimentary, but their sympathies were correspondingly narrow. The instruments of culture on a broad scale were lacking. The humanitarian spirit had not begun to awaken among the people. Their feelings of patriotism were as restricted as were their knowledge and sympathies. They found it difficult or impossible to sacrifice for objects which were distant, either in place or time. In many instances the affairs of their own colony were unknown to them, or awakened little interest. In such cases colony patriotism even was too broad for them to grasp. The interests of the moment, the interests of the town, the neighborhood, the family, the individual himself, absorbed the largest share of the colonist's attention. This is a familiar fact in all communities, even at the present day; but it was intensified by the isolation, hard labor, and privations of frontier life. So fully occupied were the mass of the people who were thus situated with clearing the forest, building rude dwellings, laying out towns, fencing their farms, tilling the soil, caring for their flocks, trading with the Indians or protecting themselves against them, that they had time and strength left for little besides. Local and sectional religious interests furnished an added object of attention in New England.

Within the chartered colonies there was much to remind the people that they were parts of a common political system, and yet the fact was not brought constantly or effectively home to their consciousness. Colonies of that type were emphatically special jurisdictions, and they collectively existed under a highly developed system of self-government. We are accustomed to associate the idea of self-government with England and its institutions. In England the element of self-government appears in the counties and boroughs;

in the degree of control which, under statutes and other guaranties of the central government, these localities, at any period, have enjoyed over their officials and over the raising and expenditure of revenue for local purposes. But in the colonies, especially in the seventeenth century, self-government proceeded very much farther than it did in the realm. In the colonies no acts of parliament regulated its development. Agents of the English executive were not to any extent present to direct or restrain the acts of the colonists. Colonial initiative extended without restraint, not merely to the administration of town and county government, to the collection and expenditure of local rates, and to the control of local officials, but to the affairs of entire provinces and germinal commonwealths. It was due to their remoteness and to the consequent absence of sovereign control, that the claim could with truth be made that the New England colonies ranked as political structures higher than municipalities and that provinces were more than English counties. The pressure of the privy council, of the central courts, of the officials of the central government, scarcely reached them, and in consequence they blossomed out into pseudo-statehood. We have seen that at the outset they were the products of private initiative. This, when followed through a remarkable course of development, culminated in the degree of independence which is thus indicated.

All writers who have discussed the early history of the British-American colonies have dwelt with greater or less emphasis on the degree of self-government which they enjoyed. In the preceding chapters an effort has been made to show in some detail in what that self-government consisted and under what forms it appeared. The degree to which it was actually enjoyed is indicated by the fact that it has been possible to describe thus fully the internal organization of the chartered colonies, and to follow the development of their policy, with only an occasional reference to king or parliament.

We have found that the special jurisdictions known as the chartered colonies had their own distinct executives and legislatures, their officials, courts, militia systems, their systems of revenue and expenditure, their territorial and Indian policies, their ecclesiastical systems, and their institutions of local government. In other words they possessed all the organs of statehood. Had they been legally independent of the home government, they would have needed institutionally little more than they already possessed.

These institutions, furthermore, were developed on American soil and were intended to meet needs which were distinctly local and characteristic of the frontier. Of the corporate colonies this is literally true. In the process of adapting the forms of the trading corporation to the purposes of colonial government, the colonists changed its content and created a new structure, distinct in purpose and character from anything which was previously known in English private or public law. In the Massachusetts charter certain faint outlines of the form which the colony was to assume can be seen, but of many of the features of the colony government it gives no indication ; while of the policy which found expression through the forms one perceives no sign whatever in the royal grant. Four of the New England colonies owed their form and not a little of their policy to imitation of Massachusetts. The institutions of two of these, which had developed wholly on American soil, were afterward legalized, though not changed, by the grant of royal charters. The two other corporate colonies passed through the period of their separate existence without recognition by the English government. The settlements of New Hampshire and Maine also fell early under the government of Massachusetts. The latter remained permanently under its control ; the former received an impress from Massachusetts which it was quite beyond the power of any proprietary or royal executive to efface.

Until after the Restoration the corporate colonies enjoyed to the full their system of *de facto* self-government. Instructions or commissions were not regularly received by them from England. By the leading colonies agents were sent to England only when such action could no longer be avoided. The acts of the colonial legislatures were not submitted to the crown, nor to the council of state, for its approval or disapproval. No appeals were allowed to go from the Puritan colonies to the privy council or council of state. The binding force of English statutes was either totally denied, or they were ignored when they operated as a restraining force upon the colonies. The administration of the oath of allegiance was neglected. Justice was not administered in the name of the king nor in that of the keepers of the liberties of England. The Puritan colonies sought precedents, and to an extent law, from the Hebrew commonwealth. In spirit and ideals New England was *sui generis*. So far did its colonies on the whole carry their tendencies toward independence that their position became to a degree anomalous, even in the early English colonial system.

As we have seen, the position of the proprietary provinces was somewhat different from this. None of the provinces originated without a charter from the crown, or a deed of bargain and sale from a proprietor. Their grantees and colonists were not squatters, as at the outset were the settlers of the four southern colonies of New England. Their charters indicated more clearly than did those of the corporate colonies the nature of the structure which was to result from the grants. Though the provinces were special jurisdictions and possessed rights of government by delegation, when normally developed they were not self-centred like the corporate colonies. This arose from the fact that the proprietor, and not the freemen organized in general court, was the grantee of authority. This gave rise to a mixed system. There was in their constitution an hereditary and a monarchical element, and their officials were for the most part appointive. In the transmission of political power from the proprietors to the colonists commissions and instructions were regularly used. The provinces were to a greater or less degree governed from a centre outside themselves and by officials who were independent of the colonists. By virtue of their structure, and so far as the settlers were concerned, the provinces were not in the full sense self-governing. The degree of self-government which their inhabitants enjoyed was limited by the large executive powers of the proprietor and his officials. It resembled that which was possessed by the localities in England. The province was not self-centred as was the New England colony.

The extent, however, to which this was true varied greatly in the different provinces. In New Netherland, New York, and Maryland the power of the executive reached a maximum, though local institutions in these provinces attained a considerable growth. In South Carolina claims quite as sweeping were urged on behalf of the proprietors, and, owing to natural rather than political causes, local government remained very imperfectly developed. Owing to the neglect of the proprietors, institutions in North Carolina were fashioned chiefly by the colonists themselves. The weakness of the proprietary title of Berkeley and Carteret and the liberal spirit of Penn had much the same result in East Jersey and Pennsylvania ; while the increase in the number of resident proprietors, combined with their employment of election as almost the sole method of filling offices, resulted virtually in a system of popular government in West Jersey.

The meaning of this is, that in the provinces wide departures from the model of the county palatine frequently appear. The claims of the proprietors were not always made good ; their programme of monarchical or even autocratic government they were by no means always able to carry through. Some of them did not attempt so to do, but granted away many of their chartered or territorial rights at the outset. The result was that, in the relations between the proprietary executives and the people of the provinces, as organized in their legislatures or in their institutions of local government, there was much variety. The variety was as great in this respect as it was in any feature of the proprietary policy. It ranged through all the stages from the autocratic system of New York to the practical reproduction in West Jersey of the corporate colony with its dominant legislature. Moreover, as time passed, the colonists, through their legislatures and their county governments, gradually defined and restricted the powers of the executive in all the provinces. In this way the balance between the two chief elements in the provincial systems was slowly but steadily shifted. It was in no way possible, under so many proprietary grants, to secure uniformity of development. Various combinations and adjustments were effected, by which the colonists obtained a large share of power ; and though the proprietor and his body of appointed officials were almost everywhere present, their power was often shadowy.

In their relations with the king, however, the proprietary provinces were nearly as independent as were the corporate colonies. None of them, except Pennsylvania, were under obligation to submit their laws to the crown for its approval. The administration of the oath of allegiance to their inhabitants was by no means universal. Agents were only rarely despatched to England. The obligation to send cases on appeal to the privy council had not yet been imposed upon them. In some of the provinces, but not in all, justice was administered in the name of the king. Their ecclesiastical polities were varied and were by no means in agreement with the pretensions of the Anglicans. But, speaking generally, it may be said that in ideals, as well as in forms of government, the provinces and their people approximated more closely to the England of that time than did the Puritans and Puritan colonies of New England. Separatism in religion, with the moral intensity which accompanied it, erected a barrier between New England and the mother country which did not exist between her and the provinces. In form of government the resemblance between the normally developed province and the English monarchy as it existed in the seventeenth century is clear. In the case of the corporate colonies the analogy fails, and the predominance of their general courts resulted in a system which in its main outlines was more like England in the eighteenth and nineteenth centuries, when the supremacy of parliament had been fully established and acknowledged.

The analogy between the century which we have been studying and the Saxon period in the history of England is in its main outlines striking and true. Both were periods of origins. Under the Saxons the foundations of English institutions—particularly those of the localities—were laid. An ecclesiastical system was developed to which, in its essential spirit, England always remained true. The kingship in its broad outlines, though with much less than its later power, appeared as a feature of the constitution. At the close of the period the conditions out of which a nationality might grow were in existence, but a common experience, much enlarged and prolonged, must follow before the nation could be said to have attained a real existence. When, in later times, the nation was brought into conflict with its executive and had to defend itself against the wide-reaching claims of the kingship, with sure instinct it looked back on the centuries before the Norman Conquest as those when the foundations of its liberties were laid. It even idealized those centuries and fondly spoke of them and their achievements as constituting the inheritance, the treasured liberties, of the English people. It is true that this view of the period was exaggerated, that it failed to take into account a multitude of qualifying circumstances. Development in those times was crude, and the so-called liberties of locality or nation were in most cases inadequately guarantied. But notwithstanding this fact, a trend toward national and local independence was established in this period which was not lost during the entire subsequent course of English history.

The same assertion can upon clearer evidence be made concerning the first century of American history. In that period the foundations of American liberty were laid. In their main outlines American institutions, both local and colonial, were fashioned. They developed under American far more than under European conditions. They bore in a large sense the stamp of independence and self-sufficiency, which was the natural result of the remoteness of the colonies and of their isolation. In New England a type of political theory was developed which was a natural expression of the leading facts in their political existence. It is true that the permanence of colonial institutions, in the form which they had assumed, was not expressly guarantied by the sovereign power to which the colonies stood in the relation of dependencies. But their slow and natural growth, their adaptation to the needs and the spirit of the people for whom they existed, furnished guaranties more effective than any which mere statutes or written constitutions could give. The remoteness of the colonies from Europe operated also as a natural guaranty of fundamental importance. These all told in favor of the practical, though not of the legal, validity of the claims which the colonies early put forth to the exclusive power of self-taxation, in some cases even to the sole right of legislation as well. If at any time the acquired rights of self-government of the colonies at large should be imperilled, that type of political theory which had its home in New England could easily be extended to fit conditions in the provinces. With the predisposition in favor of self-government which resulted from the conditions thus outlined, the colonists faced the home government and any plans of systematic imperial control which it might devise and seek to enforce.

INDEX

Abenakis, a tribe of the Algonkins, i. 527; hostilities, i. 572-573.

Acadia, i. 410.

Admiral, admiral (rear), admiral (vice), in Gilbert's expedition, i. 12; in Roanoke, i. 16; sent to Virginia, i. 61, 68.

Admiralty jurisdiction, in Massachusetts, i. 184; in Plymouth, i. 299; in Rhode Island, i. 364; in Maryland, ii. 61, 73, 279; in New Netherland, ii. 105; in New York, ii. 279; in the Carolinas, ii. 296; in New Jersey, ii. 296, 297; in Pennsylvania, ii. 297.

Adventurers, of Southampton, associated with Gilbert, i. 9-10; Gilbert's proposal to, i. 11; in Gilbert's expedition, i. 12-13; of London, associated with Raleigh, i. 20-21; of London, plant Jamestown, i. 26, 32; of Plymouth, plant Sagadahoc, i. 26, 32, 41; their methods for procuring colonists, i. 34, 81, 82; allotments of land to, in Virginia, i. 87; trade with Virginia, i. 88, 89; relations with Separatists of Leyden, i. 108, 109, 113-115; fail to pay shares to New England council, i. 120, 121; of Dorchester, found fishing station at Cape Ann, i. 129; of Massachusetts, procure patent from New England council, i. 130; allotments of land to in Salem, i. 135; relations with the planters of Massachusetts, i. 147-150; relations with Plymouth, i. 290, 293-294; promises of Lord Baltimore to, ii. 20; relations with the Carolinas, ii. 202-208.

Agents, colonial, functions of first, performed by commanders of vessels, i. 43; sent from corporate colonies only when unavoidable, ii. 437; rarely despatched from proprietary provinces, ii. 440; for Plymouth, i. 113, 293; for Massachusetts, i. 260, 268, 286; for Connecticut, i. 327; for Rhode Island, i. 361, 363, 365, 369; for Pennsylvania, ii. 12; for West Jersey, ii. 197; payment of, i. 485, 488.

Albany, in transition from Dutch to English rule, ii. 120, 125; ministrations of Van Rensselaer at, ii. 340-341; defences of, ii. 393, 396; position on the frontier, ii. 401; board of Indian commissioners established at, ii. 419; centre for negotiating with the Indians, ii. 423.

Albemarle, Duke of, a proprietor of Carolina, ii. 201; death of, ii. 201.

Alden, John, detained by Massachusetts, i. 393; gratuity to, i. 487; treasurer, i. 492.

Aldersey, Samuel, treasurer of the Massachusetts company, i. 149.

Aldridge, Ellen, defended by Gorton, i. 347.

Aldworth, Robert, grantee of land, i. 125.

Alexander, Sir William, as a successor to Gilbert, i. 12; his map, i. 121.

Alexander, sachem of the Wampanoags, death of, i. 540.

Algonkins, tribes of, i. 527, 528, ii. 402, 405.

Alienation fines, forbidden in Massachusetts and Connecticut, i. 428 *note*; payment of, enforced, in Maryland, ii. 34, 43.

Allen, Bozoun, captain, i. 195-196.

Allerton, Isaac, agent for Plymouth, i. 113, 117, 149; agent for the "purchasers," i. 118; one of the Eight Men of New Netherland, ii. 145; litigation on the Delaware, ii. 111.

Alrich, Jacob, vice-director of New Amstel, ii. 113; death of, ii. 114.

Altham, John, Jesuit missionary among the Indians, ii. 317, 413, 414; *versus* Lord Baltimore, ii. 317.

America, British North, origin of its institutions, i. xxvi, xxxii; Gilbert's vision of a dominion in, i. 12; first revelation of its value, i. 24; death-rate of first Europeans in, i. 44; spirit of, ii. 256.

Amidas, Philip, admiral at Roanoke, i. 16.

Manner of voting, in Connecticut, i. 310; in Rhode Island, i. 360; in New Jersey, ii. 193, 194.

Judge of, and influence in, in Massachusetts, 159, 163, 245; in Connecticut, i. 310; in Maryland, ii. 88.

Eliot, Rev. John, belief with respect to Puritan church government, i. 208; attitude toward the Mosaic code, i. 210; missionary among the Indians, i. 536, 537, 538, ii. 415.

Elizabeth, Elizabethan, Gilbert's pledges to, i. 8; activities of soldiers and seamen, i. 5, 15, 17; private enterprise in colonization, i. 23; little governmental support to colonization, i. 26.

Elizabethtown, N. J., ii. 37, 39, 48, 170, 174–178, 181, 182, 188–190, 280, 400.

Emes, Anthony, militia captain, refusal to train under, i. 195–196.

Endicott, John, won for plantation enterprise, i. 130; appointed governor of colony at Salem, i. 132, 136; instructions to, i. 132–135; governor of Massachusetts, i. 168; chosen member of the standing council, i. 179; *versus* the Browns, i. 204–205; relations with Roger Williams, i. 226–228; suspended from office, i. 232; in the Antinomian controversy, i. 244; presides at the trial of the Baptists, i. 267, 268; leader of the opposition to the Quakers, i. 278; commissioner of the New England Confederacy, i. 401; colonel, i. 510; sergeant-major general, i. 512; commands an expedition to Block island, i. 533.

England, English, reproduction of institutions in America, i. xxvi.; motives for colonization, i. 3; unwilling to attack Spain openly, i. 8; arms set up in Newfoundland, i. 13; advantage of colonies to, i. 25; nature of earliest colonies, i. 30–32; war with Spain, i. 129; sovereignty recognized by Plymouth, i. 295; no connection of Connecticut with, i. 301; independence of New Haven toward, i. 322, 323; war with the Netherlands, i. 364; allegiance to, acknowledged by Dover, N. H., i. 375; refuses to recognize Dutch claim to New Netherland, i. 409; characteristic of land law obliterated in New England, ii. 16; Commons held up as an example for the Maryland Assembly, ii. 90; title to

New Netherland, ii. 123, 124; laws of Pennsylvania pronounced repugnant to laws of, ii. 270; judicial procedure in the colonies, ii. 303–307; expedition against New Netherland, ii. 389–391; analogy between Saxon period and American colonies, ii. 440–442.

English law, exclusion of from Rhode Island, i. 357; proposed selection from, for Maryland, ii. 93; not all of, introduced into any colony, ii. 124; complaint with respect to selection from, for South Carolina, ii. 228; wholesale adoption of, for South Carolina, ii. 291; attitude of New England toward, ii. 438.

Eries, destruction of by the Iroquois, ii. 420.

Evelyn, Captain George, commander of Kent island, ii. 76, 288.

Evertsen and Binckes, recover possession of New Netherland, ii. 124, 135.

Excise, in Massachusetts, i. 477; in Plymouth, i. 478; in Connecticut, i. 479; in New Netherland, ii. 109, 356; in New York, ii. 356; in Pennsylvania, ii. 356; in East Jersey, ii. 356.

Executive, at Roanoke, principally a council, i. 21, 22; at Sagadahoc, a council with a weak president, i. 44–45; at Jamestown, a discordant council, i. 46 *et seq.*; a "sole and absolute governor," i. 61, 69 *et seq.*; in the corporate colonies, the agent of the general court, i. 319; in Massachusetts, protest against its levy of taxes, i. 156; aristocratic temper, i. 163, 178, 179; tenure, i. 167–168; alliance with the ecclesiastical power, i. 163, 194, 210, 217, 226, 254; attempt to limit the exercise of its administrative function, i. 180–182, 197–198; close union with the judiciary, i. 185 *et seq.*; attempt to limit its discretion in judicial matters, i. 193–195; Hooker objects to the measure of its discretion, i. 303; in Connecticut, loose and imperfect definition of its powers, i. 311; in Rhode Island, distinct from the legislature, i. 358; in the proprietary provinces *versus* the legislature, ii. 13–15, 47, 347; controls the land system, ii. 46–47; powers definitely bestowed upon by charter, ii. 59; close union with the judiciary, ii. 277, 285; in Maryland, an appointive

407; its trading post on the Penobscot, i. 410, 412; Massachusetts levies duties on goods of, i. 419; character of settlement of, i. 424; land system like that of Massachusetts, i. 434; lands granted in town meeting, i. 462; levying of rates, i. 471, 473; assessment of taxes, i. 475; export duties and excise, i. 478; expenditures for Philip's war, i. 482; pensions, i. 483; salaries, i. 487; fish tax for support of grammar school, i. 490; treasurer, i. 492; audit of accounts, i. 493; law concerning size of muskets, i. 500; military discipline and training, i. 507–508, 515; fort, i. 516; choice of military officers, i. 526; regulation of Indian trade, i. 530; determines bounds of lands between Indians, i. 532; Indian reservations, i. 539; negotiates with Philip, i. 540–541; Philip attacks settlements of, i. 542; in Philip's war, i. 547 *et seq.*

Pocahontas, captured by Argall, i. 72.

Pocasset, R. I., settlement of, i. 342; abandonment of, i. 343; compact, i. 343–344; Gorton arrives at, i. 347.

Pocumtucks, in Philip's war, i. 553.

Point Comfort, Va., fort at, i. 69.

Pollock, Colonel Thomas, *versus* Governor Sothell, ii. 241; president of the council of North Carolina, ii. 242, 431; leader of a faction, ii. 248; in the Tuscarora war, ii. 431–432.

Popham, George, a petitioner for the charter of 1606, i. 25; president of the council of Sagadahoc, i. 44; death, i. 45.

Popham, Sir John, gives aid for making voyages of discovery, i. 24; a moving spirit in colonial enterprise, i. 25; supposed to have prepared draft of charter of 1606, i. 26; patron of colony at Sagadahoc, i. 32.

Popple, Alured, secretary of the board of trade, ii. 296.

Poquanocks, reservation of, i. 536.

Porter, Edmund, agent to England for the Quakers of North Carolina, ii. 247, 332.

Porter, John, leader of the Quaker faction of North Carolina, ii. 247–249.

Portland, Me., i. 371, 384, 385.

Port Royal, N. S., i. 36, 99, 410, 411.

Port Royal, S. C., proprietary reserve at, ii. 26; coast attractive as far south as, ii. 207; colonists expected at, ii. 212; colonists at, ii. 213;

Scotch settlement at, ii. 220; destroyed by Spaniards, ii. 222, 385, 391; provision for a watch-house, ii. 384.

Portsmouth (Strawberry Bank), N. H., beginnings of, i. 371; proprietary and Anglican, i. 372; passes under Puritan control, i. 379; discontented under Massachusetts rule, i. 381.

Portsmouth, R. I., plantation covenant, i. 291, 344; settlement of, i. 332, 344–345; provisions for laying out lands of, i. 345; relations with Newport, i. 356, 363; town lands controlled by town meetings, i. 464; fort, i. 516.

Portugal, Portuguese, i. 5, 29, ii. 309.

Pory, John, speaker of first Virginia assembly, i. 92.

Postal service, ii. 434.

Potter, Robert, a signer of the Pocasset compact, i. 344.

Powhatan, Powhatans, i. 40, 51, ii. 403.

Powlett, Earl of, a devisee of William Penn, ii. 18.

Prentice, Captain Thomas, in Philip's war, i. 547.

Presbyterians, reproduce aristocratic phase of Calvinism, i. 203; less tolerant than the Independents, i. 256; in favor of a religious establishment, i. 256; in Massachusetts, i. 257–264, 269; in South Carolina, ii. 219, 325, 327; in North Carolina, ii. 245; in New York, ii. 310.

Prince, Thomas, active in persecuting heretics, i. 289; a commissioner of the New England confederation, i. 401; a commissioner to determine boundary between New Netherland and Connecticut, i. 408.

Pring, Martin, in command of a voyage of discovery, i. 24.

Proprietor, proprietors, varying practice of, as to retention of power, i. xxix; administration of many inefficient, i. xxix; services of, indispensable to colonization, i. 4; their functions in colonization, i. 27, 30–31; early means of communication with the colony, i. 43; great losses to, i. 44; represent the monarchical idea, i. 426; grant to, often an expression of royal favor, ii. 4; their charters, ii. 5–6; territorial rights, ii. 18–19; reserves of land for, ii. 25–26; the political head of the province, ii. 58–59; concessions as to government, ii. 60; attitude toward initia-